BARRY J CONN and KIPIRO Q DAMAS

Trees of Papua New Guinea

Volume 3: Malvales to Paracryphiales

Cover photograph of Utania racemosa

Copyright © 2019 by Barry J Conn and Kipiro Q Damas. 764715
Library of Congress Control Number: 2019900173

ISBN: Softcover 978-1-9845-0510-1
Hardcover 978-1-9845-0511-8
EBook 978-1-9845-0509-5

All rights reserved. No part of this book may be reproduced or transmitted in any form or by any means, electronic or mechanical, including photocopying, recording, or by any information storage and retrieval system, without permission in writing from the copyright owner.

Print information available on the last page

Rev. date: 04/27/2019

To order additional copies of this book, contact:
Xlibris
1-800-455-039
www.xlibris.com.au
Orders@Xlibris.com.au

Trees of Papua New Guinea

Volume 3

Malvales to Paracryphiales

by

Barry J Conn and Kipiro Q Damas

A collaborative project of the Royal Botanic Gardens, Sydney, Australia and the Papua New Guinea Forest Research Institute, Lae, Papua New Guinea

The Royal
Botanic Gardens
& Domain Trust

FRI
Forest Research Institute
Papua New Guinea

Contents

Malvales

PNG families: Dipterocarpaceae, Malvaceae, Thymeleaceae

1a. Fruits winged (enlarged sepals) .... 62. Dipterocarpaceae

1b. Fruits not winged 2

2a. Stipules absent; leaves opposite; petals and/or sepals not contorted in bud .... 61. Thymeleaceae

2b. Stipules present; leaves alternate; petals and/or sepals contorted in bud 3

3a. Large showy flowers; stamens joined at base; hairs often stellate or branched; epicalyx often present .... 63. Malvaceae

3b. Flower 8–12 mm long; stamens free; hairs absent on mature twigs; complex hairs absent; epicalyx absent .... (*Vatica rassak*) 62. Dipterocarpaceae

61. Thymeleaceae

Trees, usually shrubs, lianas, and herbs. Stipules absent. Leaves well-developed, spiral, opposite, and whorled, simple, not dissected or lobed; margin entire; venation pinnate; bracts present and absent. Flowers bisexual and unisexual, then plant monoecious and dioecious, regular and slightly irregular, with distinct calyx and corolla when corolla present, then scale-like and with tepals (not readily resolvable as calyx and/or corolla), sepaline or with petals absent and then sometimes interpreted as staminodes, with calyx petal-like. Sepals 4 or 5. Petals (3 or)4 or 5(–12), free; tube absent. Stamens 2–35, free or fused or fused to calyx; filaments present or absent; staminodes present (petaloid). Gynoecium with carpels at least partially joined, superior; styles partially or fully joined. Fruit simple, indehiscent, achene, drupe, or berry, dry, at least non-fleshy, or fleshy. Seeds without wings.

PNG genera: ***Aquilaria***, *Enkleia*, ***Gonystylus***, ***Gyrinops***, *Kelleria*, *Phaleria*, *Thecanthes*, *Wikstroemia*

References: Airy Shaw (1972), Bank *et al.* (2002), Bayer *et al.* (1999), Ding Hou (1960), Stevens (1974)

1a. Leaves pellucid-dotted; stamens free; petaloid appendages inserted on receptacle; fruits with 3–5(–8) locules .... *Gonystylus macrophyllus*

1b. Leaves not pellucid-dotted; stamens and petaloid appendages joined to or inserted on floral tube; fruits with 1 or 2 locules 2

2a. Annual herbs; stamens 2; inflorescences with 4 partly united involucral bracts .... *Thecanthes cornucopiae* (M.Vahl) Wikstr.[1] (not treated here)

2b. Woody perennial shrub; stamens at least 4; inflorescences without involucral bracts or if present, then bracts free 3

3a. Stamens the same number as calyx lobes 4

3b. Stamens twice the number of calyx lobes 5

[1] Previously known as *Pimelea cornucopiae* M.Vahl. The genus *Pimelea* occurs in Australia and New Zealand.

4a. Shrubs or trees; leaves broadest below middle or near middle, 1.5–2.4 cm long; ovary densely hairy, with 2 locules; fruits a capsule emerging from top or side of floral tube .... *Gyrinops*

4b. Sub-shrubs; leaves linear, broadest throughout, up to 0.5 cm long; ovary hairy on distal half or at apex, with 1 locule; fruits a drupe developing inside floral tube .... *Kelleria ericoides* (Hook.f.) Domke[2] (not treated here)

5a. Fruits a capsule (loculicidal); petaloid appendages usually distinct and always densely hairy .... *Aquilaria filaria* (Oken.) Merr.

5b. Fruits drupe-like; petaloid appendages absent, or when present, then always without hairs 6

6a. Ovary with 2 locules, rarely with 1 by abortion; fruits usually with 2 seeds rarely with only 1; petaloid appendages absent or minute .... *Phaleria* (not treated here)

6b. Ovary with 1 locule; fruits with 1 seed 7

7a. Usually climbing shrubs; inflorescences with 2 leafy bracts on each branch; petaloid appendages distinct; ovary densely hairy .... *Enkleia paniculata* (Merr.) Hall.f. (not treated here)

7b. Erect shrubs; inflorescences without leafy bracts; petaloid appendages absent; ovary without hairs, or with hairs only at apex .... *Wikstroemia* (not treated here)

Aquilaria filaria (Oken.)Merr. Fig. 311

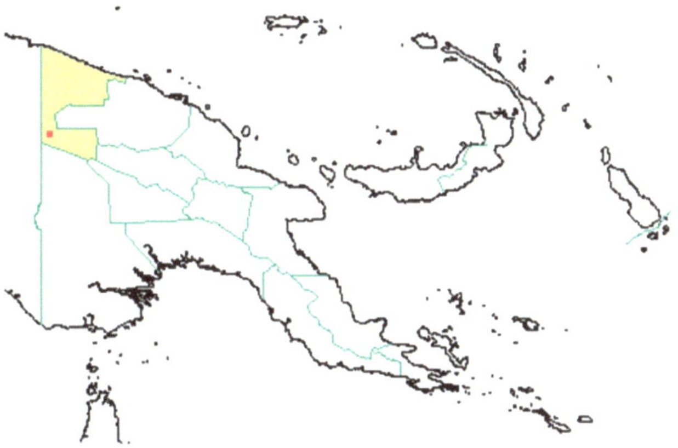

Journal of the Arnold Arboretum Vol. 31: 283 (1950)
Other Literature: Ding Hou, *Flora Malesiana, Series 1* Vol. 6: 11 & 12 (1960)
Timber Group: Non-timber species

Field Characters: Subcanopy trees, up to 20 m high; bole cylindrical, straight; buttresses absent; spines absent; aerial roots absent; stilt roots absent. Bark grey or brown; strongly aromatic; pleasant; blaze consisting of one layer, white or pale yellow, fibrous; exudate absent. Terminal buds not enclosed by leaves.

Indumentum: Complex hairs absent; stinging hairs absent; mature twig hairy (when young) or mature twig soon without hairs; hairs sparse.

Leaves: Spaced along branches, leaves spiral, simple; petiole present, not winged, attached to base of leaf lamina, not swollen; lamina rarely broadest above middle, broadest below middle, or equally broad throughout much of length, 10–20 cm long, 3–5.5 cm wide; base symmetric, margin entire, not dissected or lobed, apex shortly acuminate, venation pinnate, secondary veins open, prominent, intramarginal veins absent; lower surface pale green, green, or grey, upper surface dark glossy green, hairs absent or present (with scattered hairs on lower surface), sparse, oil dots absent, domatia absent; stipules absent.

[2] Previously known as *Drapetes* ericoides Hook.f. The genus *Drapetes* is now regarded as restricted to South America.

Flowers: Inflorescence axillary, flowers arising from a single point; flowers bisexual, with pedicel, with many planes of symmetry (perianth splitting on one side), 5–7 mm long, small, c. 5 mm diam.; perianth present, with distinct sepals and petals (inner perianth minute, usually over-looked, and twice number of sepal lobes) or with all sepals and/or petals (hence tepals) similar (by misinterpretation), white; inner perianth 5, some or partly joined; stamens 10, filaments short, free of each other, joined to perianth; ovary superior, carpels joined, locules 2; styles joined, 1.

Fruits: Arising from a single point, fruit 12–15 mm long, yellow, not spiny, non-fleshy, simple, dehiscent, capsule. Seeds 1 or 2, violet-blue, 60–75 mm long, as wide as long, 60–75 mm long, not winged.

Distribution: West Sepik.

Notes: Previously only known from Indonesian Papua.

Fig. 311. *Aquilaria filaria*. Fruit, seeds, flowers and leaves

Gonystylus macrophyllus (Miq.) Airy Shaw

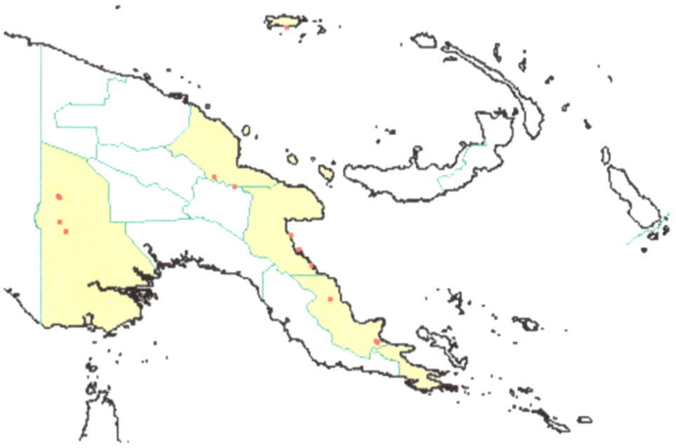

Kew Bulletin Vol. 1947: 9 (1947)
Timber Group: Commercial hardwoods or Occasional timber species

Field Characters: Canopy trees, up to 35 m high; bole cylindrical, 35–70 cm diam., straight, 15–17 m long; buttresses present; spines absent; aerial roots absent; stilt roots absent. Bark grey or brown (greyish brown to dark brown), rough, scaly or flaky, slightly fissured, or slightly pustular; lenticels irregular or rounded/swelling; bark 10 mm thick; under-bark red or brown; strongly aromatic or faintly or non-aromatic; pleasant; blaze consisting of one layer, white, yellow (cream-coloured), pink, or pale brown, with stripes or markings absent, fibrous; exudate present, colourless, not readily flowing, not changing colour on exposure to air, sticky. Terminal buds not enclosed by leaves.

Indumentum: Complex hairs absent; stinging hairs absent; mature twig without hairs.

Leaves: Spaced along branches, leaves spiral, simple; petiole up to 20 mm long, not winged, attached to base of leaf lamina, not swollen; lamina broadest at or near middle or sometimes equally broad throughout much of length, 12–31 cm long, 5.5–12.5 cm wide; base symmetric, margin entire, not dissected or lobed, apex sometimes obtuse or shortly acuminate, venation pinnate, secondary veins open, mostly prominent, intramarginal veins absent; lower surface pale green or dull green, upper surface dull dark green, hairs absent, oil dots present, domatia absent; stipules absent.

Flowers: Inflorescence terminal, flowers on an unbranched axis or flowers on a branched axis; flowers bisexual, with pedicel, with many planes of symmetry perianth present, with distinct sepals and petals, white; inner perianth 20–40; stamens 20–40; ovary superior, carpels joined, locules 5; styles joined, 1.

Fruits: arranged on branched axis, fruit 30–55 mm long, c. 25 mm diam., fruit brown or grey, not spiny, slightly non-fleshy, simple, dehiscent. Seeds 3–5, longer than wide, not winged.

Distribution: Madang, Morobe, Western, Northern, Milne Bay, Manus.

Gyrinops caudata (Gilg) Domke Fig. 312

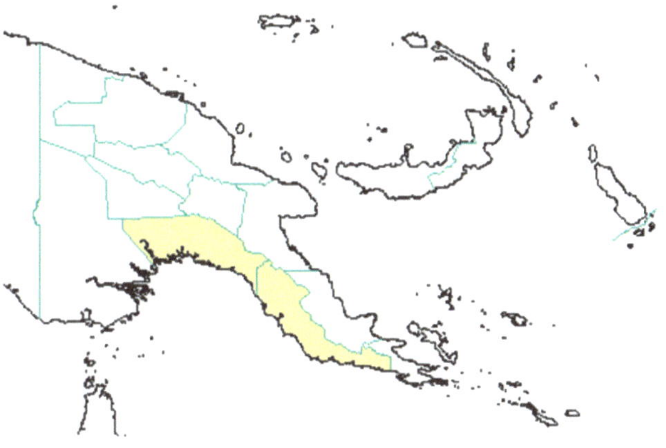

Notizblatt des Botanischen Gartens und Museums zu Berlin-Dahlem Vol. 11: 349 (1932)
Other Literature: Ding Hou, *Flora Malesiana, Series 1* Vol. 6: 42 (1960) Fig. 15 (l–n).
Timber Group: Non-timber species

Field Characters: Subcanopy trees, up to 20 m high, less frequently canopy trees to 27 m high; bole cylindrical, up to 55 cm diam., straight, up to 11 m long (occasionally tree with several trunks); buttresses absent; spines absent; aerial roots absent; stilt roots absent. Bark grey, rough; strongly aromatic; blaze consisting of one layer, fibrous; exudate present, colourless, not readily flowing, not changing colour on exposure to air, not sticky.
Indumentum: Complex hairs absent; stinging hairs absent; mature twig hairy or later mature twig without hairs (becoming glabrescent); hairs dense or sparse (with hairs grey to white).

Leaves: Spaced along branches, leaves spiral, simple; petiole present, not winged, attached to base of leaf lamina, not swollen; lamina broadest at or near middle or slightly equally broad throughout much of length, 6–13 cm long, 1.5–4 cm wide; base symmetric, margin entire, not dissected or lobed, apex acuminate, venation parallel-veined, secondary veins open, not prominent, but visible or almost not visible, intramarginal veins absent; lower surface dull pale green, upper surface dark glossy green, hairs absent, oil dots absent, domatia absent; stipules absent.

Flowers: Inflorescence terminal or axillary, flowers arising from a single point, 3–10-flowered; flowers bisexual, with pedicel c. 5 mm long, with many planes of symmetry, 3–4 mm long, small, c. 2.5 mm diam.; perianth present, with distinct sepals and petals (petals reduced to appendages between calyx lobes) or petals absent (by misinterpretation), yellow or yellowish green; inner perianth 5, free (but joined to throat of floral tube at base of calyx lobes), or some or partly joined (by misinterpretation); stamens 5, filaments almost absent (anthers subsessile), free of each other, joined to perianth (joined to floral tube); ovary superior, carpels joined, locules 2; styles joined (very short), 1.

Fruits: Arising from a single point (each fruit emerging through lateral slit in floral tube of old flower), fruit 10–15 mm long, green when immature, not spiny (sparsely hairy), non-fleshy, simple, dehiscent, capsule. Seeds 1 or 2, about 10 mm long, as wide as long, c. 8 mm diam., not winged.

Distribution: Central, Gulf.

Notes: Previously only known from Indonesian Papua.

Fig. 312. *Gyrinops caudata*. Flowers, leaves and fruit

Gyrinops ledermannii Domke
Fig. 313

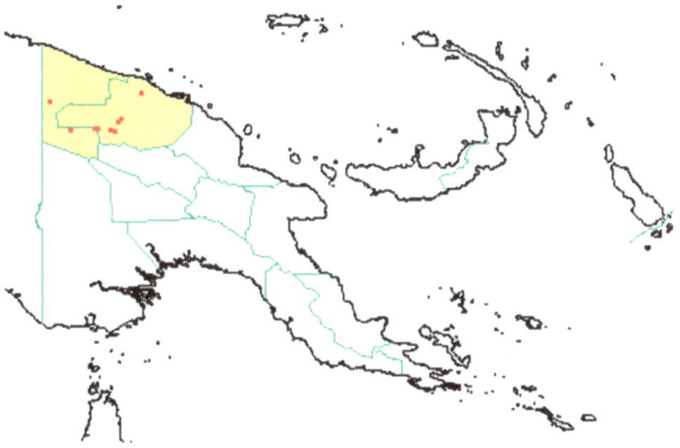

Notizblatt des Botanischen Gartens und Museums zu Berlin-Dahlem Vol. 11: 349 (1932)
Other Literature: Ding Hou, *Flora Malesiana, Series 1* Vol. 6: 41 (1960)
Timber Group: Non-timber species

Field Characters: Subcanopy trees 8–20 m high; bole cylindrical, up to c. 20 cm diam., straight; buttresses absent; spines absent; aerial roots absent; stilt roots absent. Bark slightly white or pale brown, slightly rough, slightly peeling (papery); bark <25 mm thick; strongly aromatic; pleasant; blaze consisting of one layer, pale brown, markings absent, fibrous; exudate present, colourless, not readily flowing, not changing colour on exposure to air, not sticky. Terminal buds not enclosed by leaves.

Indumentum: Complex hairs absent; stinging hairs absent; mature twig hairy; hairs dense or sparse, white.

Leaves: Spaced along branches, leaves spiral, simple; petiole present, not winged, attached to base of leaf lamina, not swollen; lamina sometimes broadest above middle, broadest below middle, or equally broad throughout much of length, 6.5–12 cm long, 2.5–5 cm wide; base symmetric, margin entire, not dissected or lobed, apex sub-acute or acuminate, venation pinnate, secondary veins open, not prominent, but visible, intramarginal veins absent; lower surface green, upper surface dark glossy green, hairs absent or present, sparse (on lower parts of both surfaces), oil dots absent, domatia absent; stipules absent.

Flowers: Inflorescence terminal, flowers arising from a single point, with 2 or 3 flowers; flowers bisexual, not stalked or with pedicel short (flowers subsessile), with many planes of symmetry, 10–15 mm long, small, c. 3 mm diam.; perianth present, with distinct sepals and petals (petals reduced to appendages between calyx lobes) or petals absent (by misinterpretation), yellow or pale green; inner perianth 5, free (but joined to throat of floral tube at base of calyx lobes), or some or partly joined (by misinterpretation); stamens 5, filaments absent, free of each other, joined to perianth (joined to floral tube); ovary superior, carpels joined, locules 2; styles joined, 1.

Fruits: Arising from a single point, fruit 15–18 mm long, green when immature, not spiny, non-fleshy, simple, dehiscent, capsule. Seeds (1 or) usually 2, c. 9 mm long (including appendage), as wide as long, 6–8 mm diam., not winged.

Distribution: West Sepik, East Sepik, Madang, Morobe.

Fig. 313. *Gyrinops ledermannii*. Bark, leaves, flowers and fruit

62. Dipterocarpaceae

Trees. Stipules present. Leaves well-developed, spiral, simple, not dissected or lobed; margin entire; venation pinnate. Inflorescences axillary or terminal. Bracts present. Flowers bisexual, regular, with distinct calyx and corolla. Sepals 5. Petals 5, often joined, at least in part at base or free; tube absent or present. Stamens (5–)15(–many), free; filaments present; staminodes absent. Gynoecium with carpels at least partially joined, superior or partially inferior; styles partially or fully joined. Fruit simple, dehiscent or indehiscent, capsule splitting irregularly, nut, dry, at least non-fleshy. Seeds without wings.

PNG genera: ***Anisoptera, Hopea, Vatica***

References: Ashton (1982)

1a. Leaves with a distinct looping intramarginal veins .... *Anisoptera thurifera*

1b. Leaves without an intramarginal vein 2

2a. Venation between main veins ± reticulate .... *Vatica*

2b. Venation between main veins close and ladder-like .... *Hopea*

Anisoptera thurifera Blume
Fig. 314

Museum Botanicum Lugduno-Batavum sive stirpium Exoticarum, Novarum vel Minus Cognitarum ex Vivis aut Siccis Brevis Expositio et Descriptio Vol. 2: 42 (1852) Fig. 6.
Other Literature: P.S. Ashton, *Flora Malesiana, Series 1* Vol. 9: 333 & 334 (1982) Figs 27 & 31.
Timber Group: Major exportable hardwoods
Trade Name: Anisoptera

Field Characters: Emergent trees or canopy trees, up to 50 m high; bole cylindrical, often slightly spurred, 25–50 cm diam., straight, 15–25 m long; buttresses present or sometimes absent; spines absent; aerial roots absent; stilt roots absent. Bark brown, white, pale green, or grey, rough, scaly or flaky or pustular; lenticels irregular or elongated vertically; bark 10–15(–20) mm thick; under-bark yellow or green; strongly aromatic; pleasant or faintly unpleasant; blaze consisting of one or 2 layers; outer blaze yellow, orange, pale brown, or greenish white, speckled or markings absent, fibrous and granular without splinters; inner blaze yellow and orange or pale brown, speckled or markings absent, fibrous and granular without splinters; exudate absent or present, colourless, not readily flowing, not changing colour on exposure to air, not sticky. Terminal buds not enclosed by leaves.

Indumentum: Complex hairs absent; stinging hairs absent; mature twig without hairs.

Leaves: Spaced along branches, leaves spiral, simple; petiole present, not winged, attached to base of leaf lamina, not swollen; lamina broadest at or near middle and broadest below middle, 9–14 cm long, 4–7 cm wide; base symmetric, margin entire, not dissected or lobed, apex slightly acuminate, venation pinnate, secondary veins open, prominent, intramarginal veins absent; lower surface green or pale brown, upper surface dark glossy green, hairs absent, oil dots absent, domatia absent; stipules absent.

Flowers: Inflorescence terminal and axillary, flowers on a branched axis; flowers bisexual, with pedicel, with many planes of symmetry, 6–10 mm long, small, 4–8 mm diam.; perianth present, with distinct sepals and petals, white; inner perianth 5 (twisted), some or partly joined; stamens c. 50 (with hair-like apices), filaments present, free of each other, free of perianth; ovary superior, carpels joined, locules 1; styles joined, 1.

Fruits: arranged on branched axis, fruit c. 10 mm long (plus wings 90–140 mm long), pale brown, not spiny, non-fleshy, simple, indehiscent, nut with 2 sepal-formed long wings. Seed 1, about 10 mm long, as wide as long, c. 10 mm diam., not winged.

Distribution: East Sepik, Madang, Morobe, Southern Highlands, Western, Gulf, Central, Northern, Milne Bay.

Fig. 314. *Anisoptera thurifera*. Bark, leaves and flowers

Hopea iriana Slooten
Fig. 315

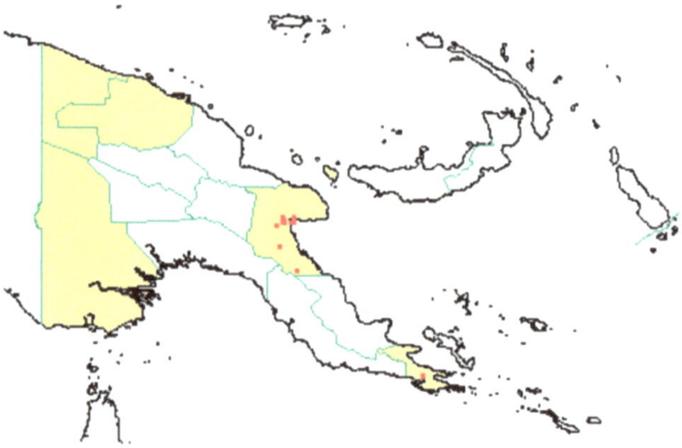

Reinwardtia Vol. 2: 28 (1952)
Other Literature: P.S. Ashton, *Flora Malesiana, Series 1* Vol. 9: 428 (1982)
Timber Group: Major exportable hardwoods

Field Characters: Canopy trees, 30–40 m high; bole cylindrical to slightly spurred, c. 60 cm diam., straight, up to 30 m long; buttresses usually absent, or rarely present, up to 2 m high; spines absent; aerial roots absent; stilt roots absent. Bark dark grey or brown, slightly rough or smooth, tessellated, scaly or flaky, or fissured; bark c. 15 mm thick; under-bark brown; faintly or non-aromatic; pleasant; blaze consisting of one layer, pale yellow, pink, or light brown, markings absent, fibrous; exudate present or absent, colourless, not readily flowing, changing to pale red on exposure to air, not sticky. Terminal buds not enclosed by leaves.

Indumentum: Complex hairs absent; stinging hairs absent; mature twig without hairs (small lenticels present).

Leaves: Spaced along branches, leaves spiral, simple; petiole present, not winged, attached to base of leaf lamina, not swollen; lamina broadest at or near middle or broadest below middle, 8–11 cm long, 3–4 cm wide; base mostly symmetric (slightly asymmetric), margin entire, not dissected or lobed, apex acuminate, venation pinnate, secondary veins open, prominent, intramarginal veins absent; lower surface pale green, upper surface dark green, hairs absent, oil dots absent, domatia absent; stipules absent.

Flowers: Inflorescence terminal or axillary, flowers on a branched axis; flowers bisexual, with pedicel, slightly asymmetric or with one plane of symmetry, 4–5 mm long, small, c. 5 mm diam.; perianth present, with distinct sepals and petals, white or cream-coloured; inner perianth 5, some or partly joined (at base); stamens c. 10, filaments present (broad at base), free of each other, joined to perianth at base and falling with petals; ovary superior, carpels joined, locules 2; styles joined, 1 (thickened to form a stylopodium).

Fruits: arranged on branched axis, fruit c. 10 mm long, c. 8 mm diam., fruit brown, not spiny, non-fleshy, simple, dehiscent, capsule (often referred to as a nut, but splitting at germination into ± 3 regular valves). Seed 1, c. 8 mm long, as wide as long, c. 8 mm diam., not winged.

Distribution: West Sepik, East Sepik, Morobe, Western, Milne Bay.

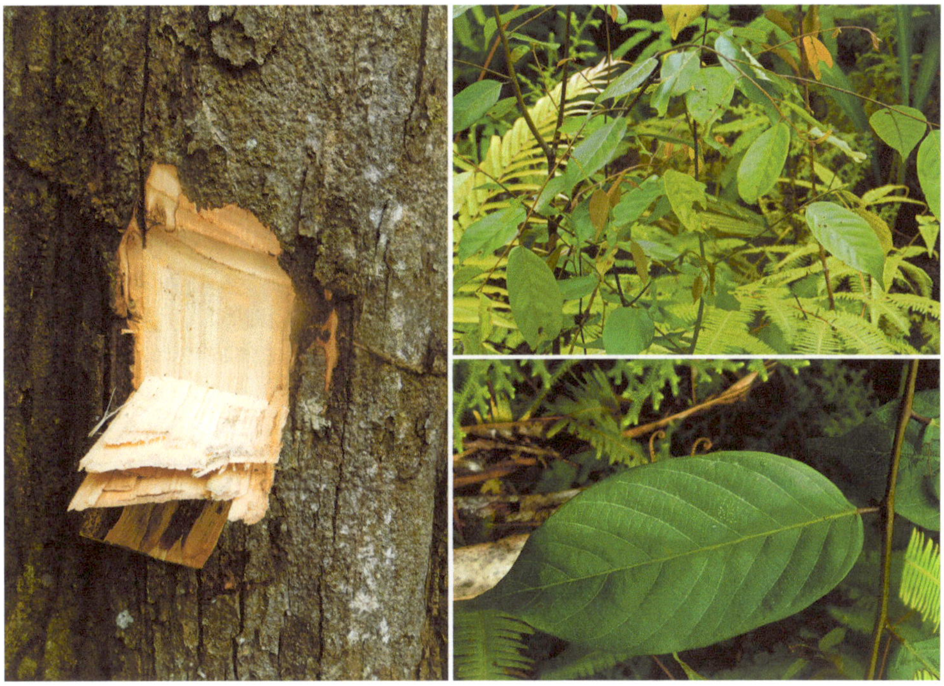

Fig. 315. *Hopea iriana.* Bark and leaves

Hopea papuana Diels

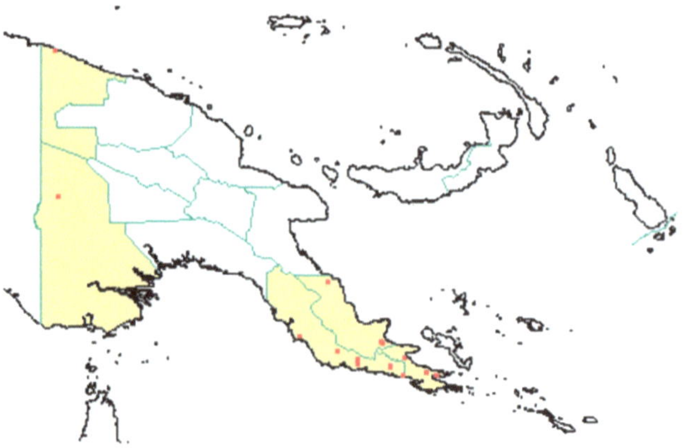

Botanische Jahrbücher für Systematik, Pflanzengeschichte und Pflanzengeographie Vol. 57: 461 (1922)
Other Literature: P.S. Ashton, *Flora Malesiana, Series 1* Vol. 9: 419 & 420 (1982)
Timber Group: Commercial hardwoods

Field Characters: Canopy trees, 30–35 m high; bole cylindrical, c. 35 cm diam., straight, c. 25 m long; buttresses present; spines absent; aerial roots absent; stilt roots absent. Bark dark brown, rough, slightly pustular or scaly or flaky; lenticels irregular; bark 10 mm thick; under-bark yellow or green; strongly aromatic; resinous/liniment-like; blaze consisting of one layer, yellow or orange, markings absent, fibrous; exudate present, colourless, not readily flowing, changing to blue or purple on exposure to air, slightly sticky. Terminal buds not enclosed by leaves.

Indumentum: Complex hairs present; stinging hairs absent; mature twig hairy; hairs sparse.

Leaves: Spaced along branches, leaves spiral, simple; petiole present, not winged, attached to base of leaf lamina, not swollen; lamina broadest at or near middle, (11–)16–24(–28) cm long, (4.2–)7–10.5 cm wide; base symmetric, margin entire, not dissected or lobed, apex acuminate, venation pinnate, secondary veins open, prominent, intramarginal veins absent; lower surface pale green, upper surface dark green, hairs absent, oil dots absent, domatia absent; stipules absent (by misinterpretation) or present not persistent, free, laterally placed, not encircling the twig, hair-like linear, not fringed, large, up to 12 mm long, 5 mm wide, not persistent.

Flowers: Inflorescence axillary, flowers unknown, flowers on a branched axis; flowers presumably bisexual, with pedicel short (in fruit), presumably with many planes of symmetry (based on flowers of other species); perianth present, with distinct sepals and petals; inner perianth presumably 5, some or partly joined because joined at base in other species; filaments present, free of each other, free of perianth; ovary superior, carpels joined, locules 3; styles joined, 1.

Fruits: arranged on branched axis, fruit 10–16 mm long, 7–9 mm diam., fruit brown, not spiny, non-fleshy, simple, indehiscent, nut. Seed 1, about 10 mm long, not winged fruits winged.

Distribution: West Sepik, Western, Central, Northern, Milne Bay.

Vatica rassak (Korth.) Blume Fig. 316

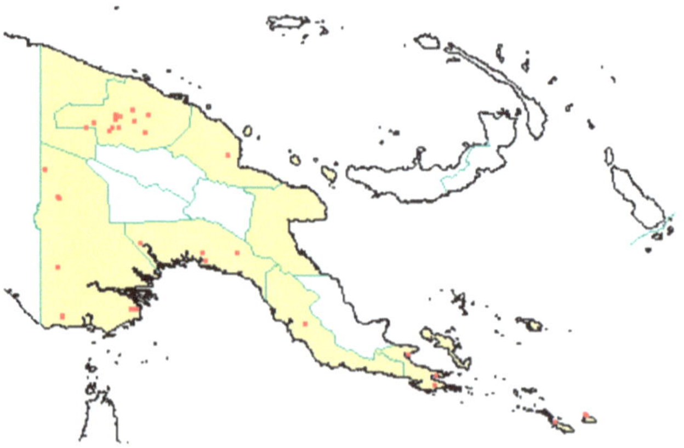

Museum Botanicum Lugduno-Batavum sive stirpium Exoticarum, Novarum vel Minus Cognitarum ex Vivis aut Siccis Brevis Expositio et Descriptio Vol. 2: 31 (1852)
Other Literature: P.S. Ashton, *Tree Flora of Sabah and Sarawak* Vol. 5: 381 & 382 (2004)
Timber Group: Occasional timber species

Field Characters: Canopy trees, 15–30 m high or subcanopy trees; bole cylindrical, 20–80 cm diam., crooked or straight, 5–20 m long; buttresses absent; spines absent; aerial roots absent; stilt roots absent. Bark white, grey, or greyish brown to greenish brown, slight rough, scaly or flaky or slightly pustular, or smooth; lenticels irregular, bark 6–8 mm thick; under-bark brown, white, pale yellow, or with green stripes; faintly or non-aromatic; resinous/ liniment-like; blaze consisting of one layer, pale yellow (straw-coloured) or brown, markings absent, slightly fibrous; exudate present, white or pale yellow, not readily flowing, changing to golden-coloured on exposure to air, sticky. Terminal buds not enclosed by leaves.

Indumentum: Complex hairs absent; stinging hairs absent; mature twig without hairs.

Leaves: Spaced along branches, leaves spiral, simple; petiole present, not winged, attached to base of leaf lamina, not swollen; lamina broadest at or near middle or equally broad throughout much of length, (11–)15–31 cm long, (4–)7–10 cm wide; base symmetric, margin entire, not dissected or lobed, apex occasionally obtuse or shortly acuminate, venation palmate, secondary veins open, prominent, intramarginal veins absent; lower surface pale green or greenish grey, upper surface dark glossy green, hairs present, oil dots absent, domatia absent; stipules present, free, laterally placed, not encircling the twig, leafy, not fringed, large, not persistent.

Flowers: Inflorescence axillary, flowers on a branched axis; flowers bisexual, with pedicel, with many planes of symmetry, flowers (8–)12–20 mm long, large, c. 20 mm diam.; perianth present, with distinct sepals and petals, white or cream-coloured top pale yellow; inner perianth 5, free; stamens 5, filaments present, free of each other, free of perianth; ovary superior, carpels joined, locules 1; styles joined, 1.

Fruits: arranged on branched axis, fruit 40–50(–80) mm long, 25–30(–50) mm diam., fruit brown with persistent green calyx, not spiny, non-fleshy, simple, dehiscent, capsule (fruit often regarded as a nut that splits longitudinally into 3 equal valves at germination). Seed 1, c. 25 mm long, longer than wide, >10 mm diam., winged (a 1-seeded winged fruit) or not winged (by misinterpretation).

Distribution: West Sepik, East Sepik, Madang, Morobe, Western, Gulf, Central, Milne Bay, Papuan Islands.

Notes: Previously known as *Vatica papuana* Dyer.

Fig. 316. *Vatica rassak*. Habit, bark, leaves and flowers

63. Malvaceae

Trees, shrubs, and herbs. Stipules absent or usually present. Leaves well-developed, spiral, simple, dissected or lobed, or not; margin entire; venation pinnate or palmate. Inflorescences axillary or terminal. Bracts absent. Flowers bisexual, regular or slightly irregular, with distinct calyx and corolla. Sepals 5. Petals 5, free; tube absent. Stamens (5–)15–many, fused; filaments present; staminodes absent. Gynoecium with carpels at least partially joined, superior; styles partially or fully joined. Fruit simple, dehiscent or indehiscent, follicle, schizocarp, usually dry, at least non-fleshy, or fleshy. Seeds without wings.

PNG genera: *Abelmoschus, Abroma, Abutilon,* ***Argyrodendron, Bombax, Brachychiton,*** *Camptostemon,* ***Colona, Commersonia, Firmiana,*** *Gossypium, Grewia, Helicteres,* ***Heritiera, Hibiscus, Kleinhovia,*** *Kosteletzkya, Leptonychia, Malachra, Malvastrum, Melhania, Melochia,* ***Microcos,*** *Ochroma,* ***Papuodendron,*** *Pentapetes,* ***Pterocymbium, Pterygota,*** *Scaphium, Seringia, Sida,* ***Sterculia,*** *Theobroma, Thespesia, Urena, Waltheria*

Notes: The families Bombacaceae, Grewiaceae, Sterculiaceae and Tiliaceae, plus several other family groupings, are now included in the family Malvaceae.

References: Bayer and Kubitzki (2003), Borssum Walker (1966), Croft (1981), Fosberg and Sachet (1972), Heel (1972), Kostermans (1950, 1957, 1959, 1960), Royen (1964), Tantra (1976), Wilkie *et al.* (2006)

1a. Leaves usually palmately veined; stamens fused into a long staminal tube and fused to base of petals; anthers with 1 locule, or appearing so 2

1b. Leaves with venation usually pinnate, sometimes palmately veined; stamens free or fused, not fused to petals; anthers with 2 locules 10

2a. Style undivided; stigma ribbed or lobed 3

2b. Style apically divided into 5 spreading branches 9

3a. Spines absent; leaves simple; epicalyx present; evergreen trees 4

3b. Spines often present on trunk; leaves compound; epicalyx absent; trees ± deciduous 8

4a. Androgynophore present 5

4b. Androgynophore absent 6

5a. Inflorescences paniculate, terminal; stigma not lobed .... *Microcos argentata* Burret

5b. Inflorescences cymose, usually axillary; stigma lobed .... *Grewia*

6a. Leaves ± heart-shaped; venation 5–7-palmate at base; petiole swollen distally; calyx with 3 non-persistent bracteoles; staminal tube densely covered on upper half with long wavy sessile anthers; introduced – Balsa .... *Ochroma lagopus* Sw. (not treated here)

6b. Leaves broadest below middle or throughout; venation pinnate or 3-palmate basally; petiole not swollen; staminal tube with anthers on long filaments; calyx subtended by lobed or truncate epicalyx 7

7a. Mangrove trees or shrubs, with pneumatophores often present; epicalyx of 3 basally joined bracteoles .... *Camptostemon schultzii* Mast. (not treated here)

7b. Non-mangrove trees or shrubs, without pneumatophores; epicalyx lobes up to 10 mm long... *Thespesia*

8a. Flowers < 3 cm diam.; petals with woolly hairs on outer surface; flowers in lateral or axillary clusters; pedicels long and slender; stamens 3–15; fruiting calyx persistent; Kapok .... *Ceiba pentandra* (L.) Gaertner (not treated here)

8b. Flowers > 5 cm diam.; petals with stellate hairs on outer surface; flowers solitary or in few-flowered lateral clusters; pedicels short and thick; stamens > 40; calyx not persistent in fruit........ *Bombax ceiba*

9a. Leaves with venation palmate basally, pinnate distally .... *Hibiscus papuodendron* Kosterm.

9b. Leaves with venation pinnate throughout .... *Papuodendron lepidotum* C.T.White

10a. Branches with spines; stamens fused into bundles; fruit spiny; seeds with aril .... *Bombax ceiba*

10b. Branches without spines; stamens usually free or only fused at base; fruit spiny or not spiny; seeds without aril 11

11a. Carpels free; fruit separating 12

11b. Carpels fused; fruit solitary 25

12a. Flowers mostly bisexual, or if unisexual and bisexual flowers present (polygamous), then petals usually present; carpels mostly united, rarely free in fruit 13

12a. Flowers mostly unisexual, or if unisexual and bisexual flowers present (polygamous), then petals rarely present; carpels free in fruit 16

13a. Ovary sessile or subsessile; androgynophore not developed or very short .... *Commersonia bartramia* (L.) Merr.

13b. Ovary stipitate or supported on androgynophore; anthers sessile at top of androgynophore 14

14a. Seeds winged on distally; anther locules parallel, linear .... *Pterospermum* (not treated here)

14b. Seeds not winged; anthers locules diverging 15

15a. Flowers in large terminal panicle; mature carpels membranous, inflated; ovary locules with about 4 ovules .... *Kleinhovia hospita L.*

15b. Flowers axillary; mature carpels not inflated; ovary locules with many ovules .... *Helicteres angustifolia* L. (not treated here)

16a. Petals flat, not hooded at apex, or absent 17

16b. Petals hooded 22

17a. Petals very small, or absent 18

17b. Petals large and conspicuous 19

18a. Fruiting calyx much enlarged and coloured; seeds kidney-shaped, with embryo curved; mature carpels with soft bristle-like hairs .... *Keraudrenia* (not treated here)

18b. Fruiting calyx not enlarged and not coloured; seeds ellipsoid, with embryo straight; mature carpels winged above .... *Seringia corollata* Steeta (not treated here)

19a. Petals mostly persistent and often enlarged after flowering; stamens at least 10, or if 5, then with 5 alternating ligulate staminodes; staminal cup very short 20

19b. Petals deciduous or very inconspicuous after flowering; stamens 5, opposite petals; staminodes absent or minute 21

20a. Anthers 5, alternating with 5 staminodes; bracteoles persistent, often larger than sepals; style branches 5, spreading; shrubs or trees .... *Melhania incana* Heyne (not treated here)

20b. Anthers 10–15, with 2 or 3 between each staminodes; bracteoles caduceus; style entire; herbs of freshwater swamps .... *Pentapetes phoenicea* L. (not treated here)

21a. Ovary with 5 locules; style 5, free or partly joined .... *Melochia* (not treated here)

21b. Ovary with 1 locule; style 1, excentric .... *Waltheria americana* L. (not treated here)

22a. Fertile stamens free; fruits with long soft hairs or tubercles .... *Commersonia bartramia* (L.) Merr.

22b. Fertile stamens joined or in bundles; fruits without hairs or with short hairs 23

23a. Limb of petals not produced into an appendage; capsules leathery ....*Leptonychia glabra* Turcz. (not treated here)

23b. Limb of petals produced into an appendage 24

24a. Fruits a dry capsule, 5-angled, truncate, with 5 horns at apex, with irritant hairs.............................. ....*Abroma augustum* (L.) Murray (not treated here)

24b. Fruits fleshy, indehiscent, with hard core; seeds surrounded by shining pulp; flowers and fruits on short pedicels on trunk (cocoa tree – cultivated)................................. *Theobroma cacao* L. (not treated here)

25a. Fruit indehiscent, winged or keeled, stamens 5, in a single whorl or at least 10 and irregularly crowded.. 26

25b. Fruit mostly dehiscent, not winged; stamens mostly at least 10; anthers irregularly crowded in a cluster at top of androgynophore 27

26a. Stamens 5; anthers mostly in a single whorl...*Heritiera* & *Argyrodendron*

26b. Stamens mostly at least 10; anthers irregularly clustered at top of androgynophore ....*Colona*

27a. Seeds winged and samara-like; anthers sessile, in 5 clusters of c. 5.. ....*Pterogyta horsfieldii* (R.Br.) Kosterm.

27b. Seeds not winged.. 28

28a. Fruits ± woody, dehiscent capsule or a schizocarp separating at maturity with mericarps 29

28b. Fruits membranous and reticulate, ± boat-shaped and 1–few-seeded 40

29a. Fruits a dehiscent capsule 30

29b. Fruits a schizocarp...31

30a. Seeds embedded in placental surface of follicle, irregularly scattered ....*Brachychiton carruthersii*

30b. Seeds arranged in 1 or more rows, not embedded in placental surface of follicle.................... *Sterculia*

31a. Staminal column without teeth, apex split into many filaments 32

31b. Staminal column with 5 teeth at apex; filaments projecting from whole surface of column or from the greater part of it... 38

32a. Style 1, branched, lobed or ribbed apically; branches, lobes or ribs as many as carpels, usually 5..... 33

32b. Styles twice as many as carpels, always 10 37

33a. Style apically divided into 5 spreading branches 34

33b. Style not divided apically.. 36

34a. Calyx splitting on one side during anthesis, minutely 5-toothed at apex, joined to corolla and falling off with it...*Abelmoschus* (not treated here)

34b. Calyx not splitting on one side, 5-lobed to 5-parted, not joined to corolla, persistent after flowering 35

35a. Epicalyx segments 8–10(–20), distinct or basally joined; capsule with 5 locules .... *Hibiscus*

35b. Epicalyx segments 5, joined on basal half; capsule with 10 locules because of false septa.................... .... *Papuodendron lepidotum* C.T.White

36a. Epicalyx segments 3–8, small and narrow, usually not persistent; seeds without hairs or shortly hairy; ovary and fruit 5-merous; black dots absent.. *Thespesia*

36b. Epicalyx segments 3, large and leaf-like, heart-shaped, persistent; seeds densely woolly with long intertwined hairs; ovary and capsule 3–5-merous; nearly all parts with black oil glands..................... .... *Gossypium hirsutum* L. var. *itaitense* (Parl.) Roberty (not treated here)

37a. Epicalyx present; flowers mostly solitary and axillary, sometimes in axillary clusters.......................... .... *Urena lobata* L. (not treated here)

37b. Epicalyx present; flowers arranged in heads with involucral bracts.. .... *Malachra fasciata* Jacq. (not treated here)

38a. Epicalyx present.................................... *Malvastrum coromandelianum* (L.) Garcke (not treated here)

38b. Epicalyx absent.. 39

39a. Seeds 2 or more in each mericarp; mericarps follicle-like, usually dehiscent ....*Abutilon* (not treated here)

39b. Seeds 1 in each mericarp; mericarps closely enveloping seed, releasing seed by withering of mericarp wall or by apical dehiscence...*Sida* (not treated here)

40a. Seeds >1 per follicle, borne on margin of carpels which open long after maturity.............................. .... *Firmiana papuana* Mildbr.

40b. Seeds 1, borne at base of carpel... 41

41a. Calyx large, bell-shaped, persistent in fruit; fruits with double rudder-like keel................................ ....*Pterocymbium beccarii* K.Schum.

41b. Calyx very small and inconspicuous in fruit; fruits with 1 keel.................*Scaphium* (not treated here)

Argyrodendron trifoliolatum F.Muell.

Fragmenta Phytographiae Australiae 1: 2 (1858)
Other Literature: A.J.G.H. Kosterman, *Reinwardtia* Vol. 4: 528 (1959)
Timber Group: Commercial hardwoods
Trade Name: Oak, Brown Tulip

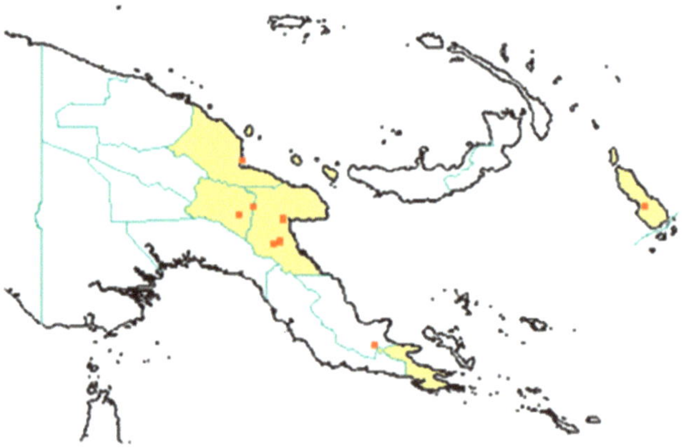

Field Characters: Canopy trees, up to 33 m high, often to 40 m; bole markedly fluted, up to 120 cm diam., straight, up to c. 20 m long; buttresses absent or slightly present; spines absent; aerial roots absent; stilt roots absent. Bark grey or light brown, rough, scaly or flaky and fissured; bark 15–20 mm thick; under-bark mottled, pink, red, and brown; faintly or non-aromatic; blaze consisting of one layer, pale yellow (straw-coloured), pale red, or brown, with stripes (red-brown), granular without splinters; exudate absent. Terminal buds not enclosed by leaves.

Indumentum: Complex hairs present, disk-shaped (scales); stinging hairs absent; mature twig without hairs.

Leaves: Spaced along branches, leaves spiral, compound; petiole present, not winged, attached to base of leaf lamina, not swollen; leaves with three leaflets; petiolule not swollen; leaves with a terminal leaflet, each leaflet broadest at or near middle or broadest below middle, (6.5–)8–14 cm long, (1–)2–3 cm wide, leaflets arranged from one point, symmetric, terminal developing leaflet buds straight; venation pinnate, secondary veins open, not prominent, but visible, intramarginal veins absent; lower surface reddish brown (densely covered with scales), pale green, or greenish grey, upper surface dark glossy green, hairs present (reddish-brown scales on lower surface) or absent (upper surface), dense, oil dots present, domatia absent; stipules absent.

Flowers: Inflorescence axillary, flowers on a branched axis; flowers bisexual, with pedicel, with many planes of symmetry, 3–5 mm long, small, c. 5 mm diam.; perianth present, with all sepals and/or petals (hence tepals) similar, white (inner surface), yellow (inner surface), red (outer surface), or brown (outer surface densely covered with scales); inner perianth 5, some or partly joined, deeply lobed; stamens c. 20, filaments present, joined forming a staminal tube, free of perianth; ovary superior, carpels separate 5, locules 5; styles free, 5.

Fruits: arranged on branched axis, fruit 30–60 mm long (including wing), 5–10 mm diam., fruit brownish red or brown (densely covered with red-brown scales), not spiny, non-fleshy, aggregate, indehiscent, samara. Seeds 2 or 3, about 10 mm long, as wide as long, c. 10 mm diam., not winged (although each fruiting carpel with a single wing 20–50 mm long).

Distribution: Madang, Morobe, Eastern Highlands, Milne Bay.

Notes: The genus *Argyrodendron* was previously classified in the family Sterculiaceae. This species has previously been known as *Heritiera trifoliolata* (F.Muell.) Kosterm.

Bombax ceiba L.
Figs 317, 318

Species Plantarum 511 (1753)
Other Literature: J.R. Croft, *Handbooks of the Flora of Papua New Guinea* Vol. 2: 5 (1981) Fig. 2.
Timber Group: Minor hardwoods

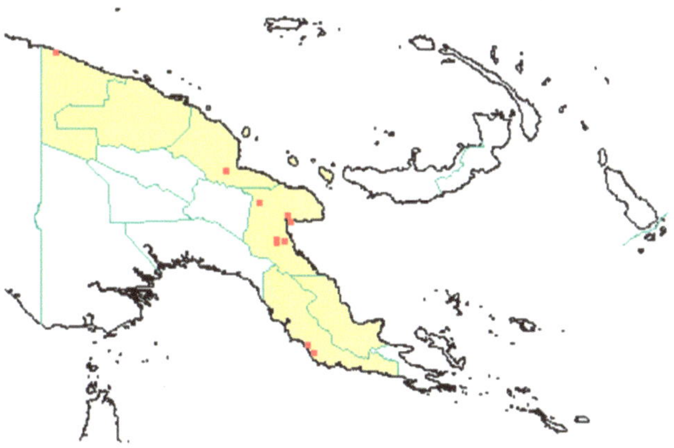

Field Characters: Canopy trees, up to 50 m high; bole cylindrical, up to 1.2 m diam., or slightly markedly fluted, straight, up to 45 m long; buttresses present or absent; spines present (on trunk of young trees) or absent; aerial roots absent; stilt roots absent. Bark green, grey, or brown (greyish brown), rough, fissured irregularly or pustular; lenticels elongated vertically; bark (10–)20–30 mm thick; under-bark green or pale red (with green stripes); faintly or non-aromatic; pleasant; blaze consisting of 2 layers; outer blaze red or brown, with stripes cream-coloured, fibrous; inner blaze pink, red, or brown, with stripes orange, fibrous; exudate present, colourless, not readily flowing, changing to brown on exposure to air, not sticky. Terminal buds not enclosed by leaves.

Fig. 317. *Bombax ceiba*. Bark

Indumentum: Complex hairs present, star-like; stinging hairs absent; mature twig hairy; hairs dense.

Leaves: Spaced along branches, leaves sub-opposite or spiral, compound; petiole present, not winged, attached to base of leaf lamina, not swollen; leaves with three leaflets or palmate; petiolule not swollen; leaves with a terminal leaflet, each leaflet broadest at or near middle or broadest below middle, 11–21 cm long, 5.5–6.5 cm wide, leaflets arranged from one point, symmetric; venation pinnate, secondary veins open, prominent, intramarginal veins absent; lower surface pale green, upper surface green glossy, hairs absent (when old) or present (when young), dense with star-shaped hairs, oil dots absent, domatia absent; stipules absent.

Flowers: Inflorescence on leaf-less branchlets, flowers on an unbranched axis; flowers bisexual, with pedicel, with many planes of symmetry, c. 50 mm long, large, c. 50 mm diam.; perianth present, with distinct sepals and petals, red; inner perianth 50, free; stamens c. 10, filaments present, joined near base, free of perianth; ovary superior, carpels joined, locules 5; styles joined, 1.

Fruits: arranged on unbranched axis, fruit 100–150 mm long, dark brown, not spiny, non-fleshy, simple, dehiscent, capsule. Seeds many (embedded in soft silky hairs), to about 5 mm long, longer than wide, 4–5 mm diam., not winged.

Distribution: West Sepik, East Sepik, Madang, Morobe, Central, Northern.

Notes: This species was previously classified in the family Bombacaceae.

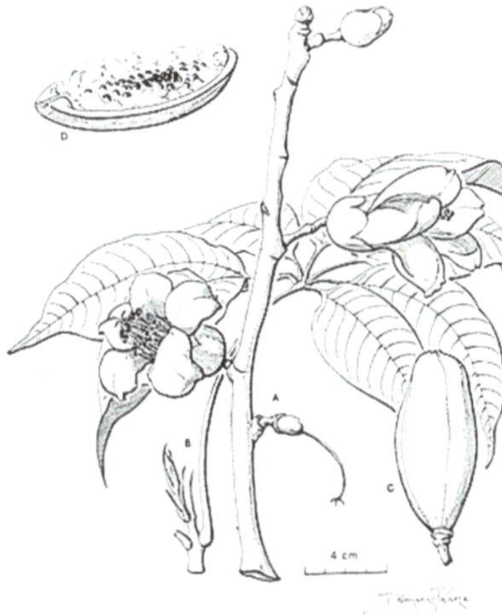

Fig. 318. *Bombax ceiba*. Flower, spines and illustration of branchlet with fruit and flower (illustration © Papua New Guinea National Herbarium, Lae)

Brachychiton carruthersii F.Muell. Fig. 319

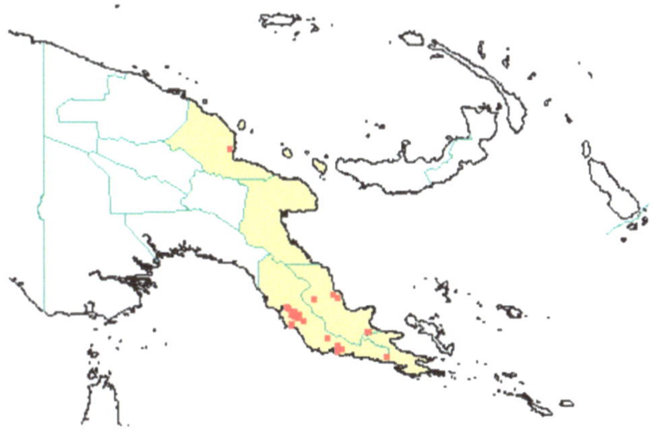

Victorian Naturalist Vol. 3: 50 (1886)
Timber Group: Minor hardwoods

Field Characters: Canopy trees up to 30 m high, or subcanopy trees up to 15 m high; bole cylindrical, up to c. 75 cm diam., straight, up to c. 20 m long; buttresses absent; spines absent; aerial roots absent; stilt roots absent. Bark green, rough or smooth, cracked or pustular; lenticels elongated laterally; bark 10–15 mm thick; under-bark green; faintly or non-aromatic; unpleasant (turnip-like aroma); blaze consisting of one layer, white, markings absent, fibrous; inner blaze white, markings absent, fibrous; exudate absent. Terminal buds not enclosed by leaves.

Indumentum: Complex hairs present, star-like; stinging hairs absent; mature twig hairy; hairs dense (with stellate hairs) or hairs sparse.

Leaves: Spaced along branches, leaves spiral, simple; petiole present, not winged, attached to base of leaf lamina, swollen, lamina broadest below middle, 15–22 cm long, 14–24 cm wide; base symmetric cordate, margin entire, dissected or lobed, palmately lobed, apex sub-acute, venation palmate, secondary veins open, prominent, intramarginal veins absent; lower surface pale green, upper surface pale green, hairs present, dense (with stellate hairs) or sparse, oil dots absent, domatia absent; stipules present, free, laterally placed, not encircling the twig, leafy, fringed, large, not persistent or persistent.

Flowers: Inflorescence axillary, flowers on a branched axis; flowers unisexual, with male and female flowers on the same plant, flowers with pedicel, with many planes of symmetry, 15–25 mm long, large, 10–15 mm diam.; perianth present, with all sepals and/or petals (hence tepals) similar, yellow (petal margin), dull red, or brown; inner perianth 5, some or partly joined; stamens 5, filaments absent, joined, free of perianth; ovary superior, carpels separate, 5, locules 5 (separate); styles free, short, 5.

Fruits: Arising from a single point (by misinterpretation), appearing so because 5 separate fertilised carpels of a single flower, but arranged on branched axis, fruit 180–200(–225) mm long, c. 100 mm diam., fruit brownish orange or light brown fawn-coloured, not spiny slightly rough and hairy, non-fleshy, aggregate, dehiscent, follicle. Seeds many, about 10 mm long, longer than wide, c. 5 mm diam., not winged.

Distribution: Madang, Morobe (cultivated), Central, Northern, Milne Bay.

Notes: The genus *Brachychiton* was previously classified in the family Sterculiaceae.

Fig. 319. *Brachychiton carruthersii.* Bark, leaves and fruit with seeds

Colona aequilateralis (C.T.White) Merr. & L.M.Perry

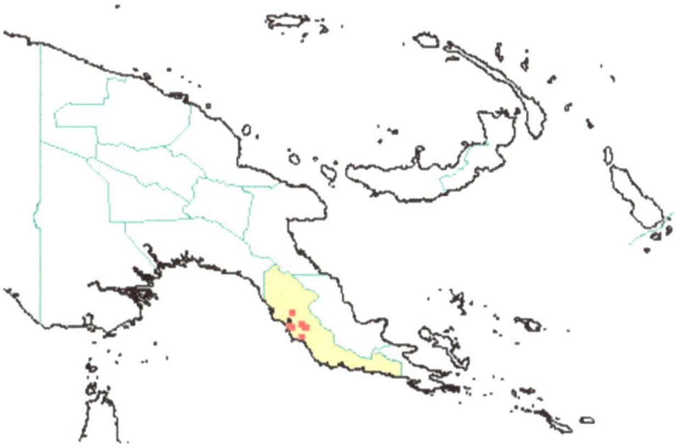

Journal of the Arnold Arboretum Vol. 20: 344 (1939)
Timber Group: Non-timber species

Field Characters: Subcanopy trees, 20 m high; bole cylindrical, 40 cm diam., slightly crooked or straight, 5 m long; buttresses absent; spines absent; aerial roots absent; stilt roots absent. Bark pale brown, rough, pustular; lenticels irregular; bark 10 mm thick; under-bark green with red stripes; strongly aromatic; pleasant (melon-like); blaze consisting of one layer, pink, with white stripes, fibrous; exudate present, colourless, not readily flowing, changing to orange or brown on exposure to air, not sticky. Terminal buds not enclosed by leaves.

Indumentum: Complex hairs present (stellate); stinging hairs absent; mature twigs with stellate hairs.

Leaves: Spaced along branches, leaves simple; petiole 5–12 mm long, not winged, attached to base of leaf lamina, not swollen; lamina broadest at or near middle, 7–15 cm long, (3–)4.5–6.5 cm wide; base symmetric, margin entire, apex shortly acuminate, venation pinnate, secondary veins open, prominent, intramarginal veins absent; lower surface dull green, upper surface dull dark green, hairs present (stellate), dense, oil dots absent, domatia absent; stipules absent.

Flowers: Inflorescence axillary, flowers on a branched axis; flowers bisexual, with pedicel, with many planes of symmetry; perianth present, with all sepals and/or petals (hence tepals) similar, greenish white; inner perianth 5, some or partly joined (deeply lobed); stamens c. 20, filaments present, free, free of perianth, irregular in length; ovary superior, carpels fused, locules 2–4; styles simple, 1.

Fruits: arranged on branched axis, pedicels c. 10 mm long, fruit 15–25 mm long, green or red (wings 4–8 mm wide, dull red with maroon stripes), not spiny, non-fleshy, simple, indehiscent, drupe of usually 2 or 4 drupelets. Seed 1, not winged.

Distribution: Central.

Colona scabra (Sm.) Burret
Fig. 320

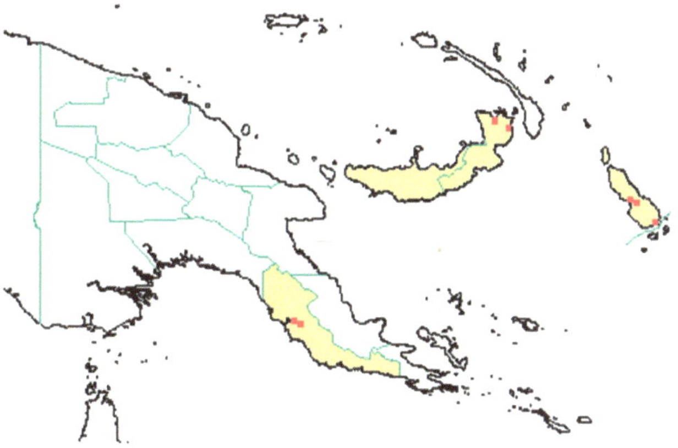

Notizblatt des Botanischen Gartens und Museums zu Berlin-Dahlem Vol. 9: 729, 800 (1926)
Timber Group: Non-timber species

Field Characters: Subcanopy trees, 8–20(–25) m high;

bole cylindrical, 40–50 cm diam., slightly crooked or straight, up to c. 5 m long; buttresses absent; spines absent; aerial roots absent; stilt roots absent. Bark pale brown to grey, rough, pustular; lenticels irregular; bark c. 10 mm thick; under-bark green with red stripes; strongly aromatic; pleasant (melon-like); blaze consisting of one layer, pink, with white stripes, fibrous; exudate present, colourless, not readily flowing, changing to orange-brown on exposure to air, not sticky. Terminal buds not enclosed by leaves.

Indumentum: Complex hairs present (stellate); stinging hairs absent; mature twigs with stellate hairs.

Leaves: Spaced along branches, leaves simple; petiole 5–12 mm long, not winged, attached to base of leaf lamina, not swollen; lamina broadest at or near middle, 7–15 cm long, (3–)4.5–6.5 cm wide; base symmetric, margin entire or slightly toothed, apex shortly acuminate, venation pinnate, secondary veins open, prominent, intramarginal veins absent; lower surface dull, slightly silver-green, upper surface dull dark green, hairs present (stellate), dense, oil dots absent, domatia absent; stipules absent.

Flowers: Inflorescence axillary or terminal, flowers many, on a branched axis; flowers bisexual, with pedicel dusty pink, with many planes of symmetry; perianth present, with all sepals and/or petals (hence tepals) similar (sepals dusty pink to green-brown on outer surface, brownish on inner surface), golden yellow to brown-yellow, mottled red inside lower part of petals; stamens c. 20, yellow, filaments present, free, free of perianth, irregular in length; ovary superior, carpels fused, locules 2–4; styles simple, 1.

Fruits: arranged on branched axis, pediels c. 10 mm long, fruit 15–25 mm long, green, maturing to red or brown (wings 4–8 mm wide, with dull red-maroon stripes), not spiny, non-fleshy, simple, indehiscent, drupe of usually 2 or 4 drupelets. Seed 1, not winged.

Distribution: Central, New Britain, Bougainville.

Notes: Previously known as *Grewia scabra* (Sm.) DC.

Fig. 320. *Colona scabra.* Fruit, leaves and bark

Commersonia bartramia (L.) Merr. Fig. 321

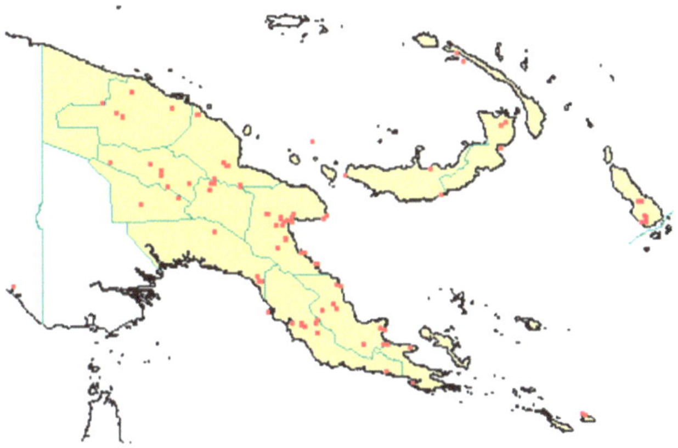

An Interpretation of Rumphius's Herbarium Amboinense 362 (1917)
Timber Group: Non-timber species

Field Characters: Subcanopy trees, up to 25 m high; bole cylindrical, up to 45 cm diam., straight, up to c. 10 m long; buttresses absent; spines absent; aerial roots absent; stilt roots absent. Bark brown (used for making rope), grey, or red, smooth or slightly rough, sometimes pustular (lenticels infrequent or absent); lenticels elongated laterally; bark 12–15 mm thick; under-bark green; faintly or non-aromatic; blaze consisting of one layer, pale red or pale brown, markings absent, fibrous; exudate absent. Terminal buds not enclosed by leaves.

Indumentum: Complex hairs present, star-like; stinging hairs absent; mature twig hairy; hairs dense (with star-like/stellate hairs).

Leaves: Spaced along branches, leaves spiral, simple; petiole present, not winged, attached to base of leaf lamina, not swollen; lamina broadest below middle, 10–19 cm long, 4–14 cm wide; base symmetric, margin shortly serrate to dentate (toothed) or sub-entire, not dissected or lobed (sometimes with a few indistinct, irregular lobes), apex acuminate, venation pinnate, secondary veins open, prominent, intramarginal veins absent; lower surface dull blue-green or dull pale green (often silvery green), upper surface green (subglossy to dull) or pale green, hairs present (with star-like/stellate hairs), dense, oil dots absent, domatia absent; stipules absent.

Flowers: Inflorescence axillary, or leaf-opposed (flowers pleasantly aromatic), flowers on a branched axis; flowers bisexual, with pedicel, with many planes of symmetry, 3–4 mm long, small, 4–5 mm diam.; perianth present, with distinct sepals and petals, white or cream-coloured; inner perianth 5, free; stamens 5 (opposite petals), with 5 staminodes (alternating with stamens; staminodes 3-lobed), each central lobe wider than 2 lateral lobes, but shorter than petals; lateral lobes attached to filaments, filaments present, joined to form a short cup, free of perianth; ovary superior, carpels joined, locules 5; styles joined at base or partly free, 5.

Fruits: arranged on branched axis, fruit 10–20 mm long, 10–20 mm diam., brown, sub-spiny (bristly: bristle up to c. 8 mm long, covered with stellate hairs), non-fleshy, simple, dehiscent, capsule. Seeds 2–6 (per locule), barely visible, 1–1.5 mm long, as wide as long, c. 1 mm diam., not winged.

Distribution: West Sepik, East Sepik, Madang, Morobe, Western Highlands, Eastern Highlands, Southern Highlands, Gulf, Central, Northern, Milne Bay, Papuan Islands, New Ireland, New Britain, Manus, Bougainville.

Notes: The genus *Commersonia* was previously classified in the family Sterculiaceae.

Fig. 321. *Commersonia bartramia.* Illustration of branchlet with flowers ((© Papua New Guinea National Herbarium, Lae)

Firmiana papuana Mildbr.
Fig. 322

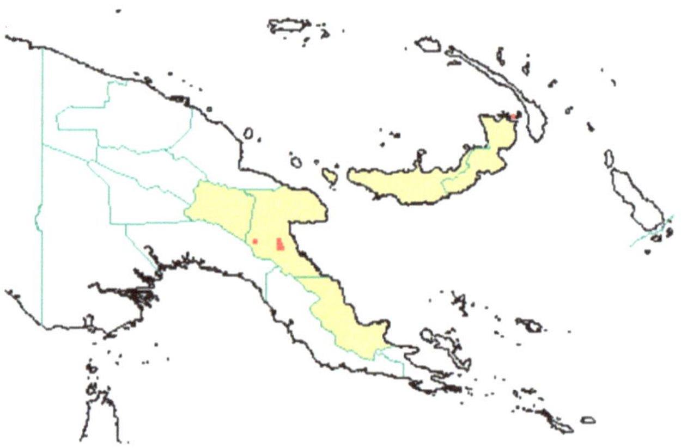

Botanische Jahrbücher für Systematik, Pflanzengeschichte und Pflanzengeographie Vol. 62: 362 (1929)
Other Literature: J. Havel, *Forest Botany, Part 2 Botanical Taxonomy* Vol. 3: 189 (1975) Fig. 51–53.
Timber Group: Occasional timber species (little used because logs split open too easily).
Trade Name: Lacewood

Field Characters: Canopy trees, up to 40 m high; bole cylindrical, up to c. 100 cm diam., straight, up to c. 25 m long; buttresses up to 2 m high; spines absent; aerial roots absent; stilt roots absent. Bark green or grey, slightly rough or smooth, slightly fissured or pustular; lenticels rarely rounded/swelling; bark 15–20 mm thick; under-bark green; strongly aromatic; pleasant; blaze consisting of one layer, pale orange, white, or yellow, with stripes (white streaks), fibrous; exudate present, colourless, not readily flowing, not changing colour on exposure to air, not sticky. Terminal buds not enclosed by leaves.

Indumentum: Complex hairs absent; stinging hairs absent; mature twig hairy; hairs sparse.

Leaves: Spaced along branches, leaves spiral, simple; petiole present, not winged, attached to base of leaf lamina, not swollen; lamina broadest at or near middle, 7–12 cm long, 7–11.5 cm wide; base symmetric, margin entire, slightly dissected or lobed (margin sometimes slightly extended at end of one of the secondary veins that originate from base of lamina) or not dissected or lobed, irregularly palmately lobed (very slightly), apex shortly acuminate or bluntly mucronate, venation palmate, secondary veins open, prominent, intramarginal veins absent; lower surface dull pale green, upper surface dark glossy green, hairs present, dense, oil dots absent, domatia absent; stipules absent.

Flowers: Inflorescence axillary, flowers on a branched axis; flowers unisexual, with male and female flowers on the same plant, flowers with pedicel, with many planes of symmetry, c. 30 mm long, large, 10–15 mm diam.; perianth present, with all sepals and/or petals (hence tepals) similar, yellow or mauve; inner perianth 5, some or partly joined; stamens 5, filaments absent, joined, free of perianth; ovary superior, carpels partially joined, by base, locules 5; styles free, 5.

Fruits: arranged on branched axis, fruit 30–60 mm long, 25–30 mm diam., light brown, not spiny, non-fleshy, simple, dehiscent, follicle. Seeds 1 or 2, to about 5 mm long, as wide as long surface wrinkled, c. 4 mm diam., not winged.

Distribution: Morobe, Northern, Milne Bay.

Notes: The genus *Firmiana* was previously classified in the family Sterculiaceae.

Fig. 322. *Firmiana papuana*. Leaves, fruit and seeds

Heritiera littoralis Aiton
Fig. 323

Hortus Kewensis Vol. 3: 546 (1789)
Timber Group: Commercial hardwoods

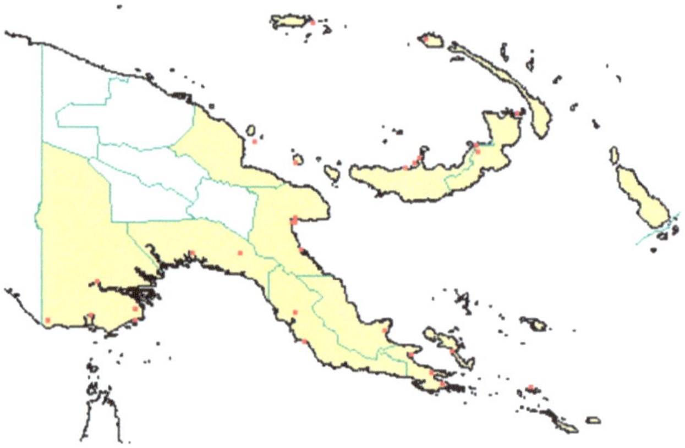

Field Characters: Subcanopy trees or canopy trees, up to 30 m high; bole cylindrical, up to c. 40 cm diam., crooked and leaning or straight, 5–15 m long, or trunk branching from near base; buttresses up to c. 1 m high; spines absent; aerial roots absent; stilt roots absent. Bark grey or brown, rough or smooth, fissured; bark 9–20 mm thick; under-bark green or pale brown; faintly or non-aromatic; blaze consisting of one layer, pale brown, pink, or pale yellow (straw-coloured), with stripes (cream-coloured), fibrous; exudate absent. Terminal buds not enclosed by leaves.

Indumentum: Complex hairs present (dense), disk-shaped (silvery, grey-green scales); stinging hairs absent; mature twig hairy (scales); hairs dense.

Leaves: Spaced along branches, leaves spiral, simple; petiole present, not winged, attached to base of leaf lamina, not swollen; lamina broadest at or near middle, (12–)14–20 cm long, 6–14 cm wide; base symmetric to very slightly asymmetric, margin entire, not dissected or lobed, apex obtuse, venation pinnate, secondary veins open, prominent, intramarginal veins absent; lower surface pale green, grey, or greenish white (dull), upper surface dark green (glossy to subglossy), hairs present (scales), dense (on lower surface), oil dots absent, domatia absent; stipules absent.

Flowers: Inflorescence terminal, flowers on a branched axis; flowers bisexual, with pedicel, with many planes of symmetry, 4–6 mm long, small, c. 5 mm diam.; perianth present, with all sepals and/or petals (hence tepals) similar, greenish white; inner perianth 5, some or partly joined (deeply lobed); stamens c. 20, filaments present, joined (forming a staminal tube), free of perianth; ovary superior, carpels separate, locules 5; styles free, 5.

Fruits: arranged on branched axis, fruit 50–80 mm long, 30–50 mm diam. (per carpel), fruit brown, not spiny, non-fleshy woody, aggregate, dehiscent, follicle. Seeds 1 or 2, about 10 mm long, as wide as long, c. 10 mm diam., not winged (although each fruiting carpel ridged to slightly winged, with ridge/wing up to 10 mm long).

Distribution: Madang, Morobe, Western, Gulf, Central, Northern, Milne Bay, Papuan Islands, New Britain, New Ireland, Manus, Bougainville.

Notes: The genus *Heritiera* was previously classified in the family Sterculiaceae.

Fig. 323. *Heritiera littoralis*. Bark, flowers and fruit (images of flowers and fruits © CSIRO)

Hibiscus papuodendron Kosterm.

Reinwardtia Vol. 5: 325 (1960)
Timber Group: Minor hardwoods
Tradename: Bulolo Ash

Field Characters: Canopy trees, up to 30(–40) m high, or subcanopy trees; bole cylindrical to slightly irregular, up to 1(–1.5) m diam., crooked or straight, 10–20 m long; buttresses present; spines absent; aerial roots absent; stilt roots absent. Bark greenish grey or brown, rough, fissured or slightly pustular; lenticels elongated vertically; bark <25 mm thick; under-bark yellow, green, or mottled; faintly or non-aromatic; blaze slightly consisting of 2 layers; outer blaze white or pale yellow, markings absent, fibrous; inner blaze yellowish white (straw-coloured), markings absent, fibrous; exudate present, colourless, flowing, not changing colour on exposure to air, not sticky. Terminal buds not enclosed by leaves.

Indumentum: Complex hairs present, disk-shaped (dense); stinging hairs absent; mature twig without hairs.

Leaves: Spaced along branches, leaves spiral, simple (smelling like raw cabbage when crushed); petiole present, not winged, attached to base of leaf lamina, not swollen; lamina broadest at or near middle or equally broad throughout much of length, 9–12 cm long, 4–6 cm wide; base symmetric (slightly cordate), margin entire, not dissected or lobed, apex obtuse or sub-acute, venation pinnate or at base palmate, secondary veins open, prominent, intramarginal veins absent; lower surface green or yellow (rough to touch), upper surface dark green (dull, sometimes grey-green), hairs absent but densely covered with peltate scales, oil dots absent, domatia present, scattered along mid-vein; stipules present, free, laterally placed, not encircling the twig, leafy, not fringed, large, not persistent.

Flowers: Inflorescence terminal or axillary, (in distal axils), flowers on a branched axis; flowers bisexual, with pedicel, with many planes of symmetry, 20–30 mm long, large, 20–30 mm diam.; perianth present, with distinct sepals and petals (with sepals 5-lobed), white or at base purple; inner perianth 5, free; stamens many, filaments present (of unequal lengths), joined (forming a staminal tube around style), free of perianth; ovary superior, carpels joined, locules 5; styles joined, 1.

Fruits: arranged on branched axis, fruit c. 15 mm long, pale brown (slightly straw-coloured), not spiny, non-fleshy, simple, dehiscent, capsule. Seeds many.

Distribution: East Sepik, Madang, Morobe, Eastern Highlands.

Notes: This taxon is possibly a synonym of *Papuodendron lepidotum* C.T.White.

Hibiscus pulvinulifer Borss.Waalk.

Reinwardtia Vol. 4: 48 (1956)
Timber Group: Occasional timber species

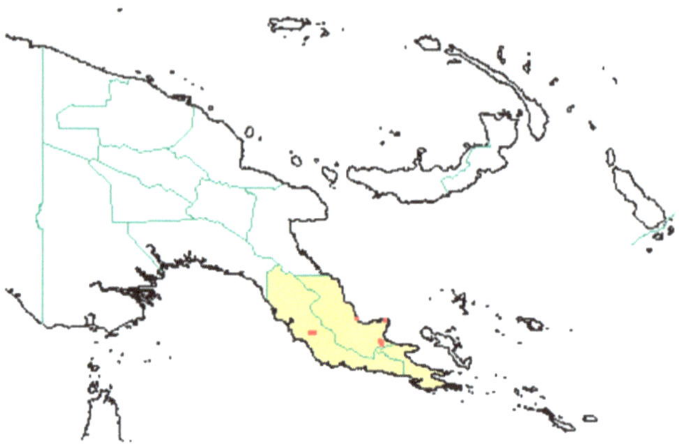

Field Characters: Large canopy tree (up to 35 m high); Bole cylindrical (up to c. 50 cm diam.), straight, up to c. 25 m long; buttresses short or absent; spines absent; aerial roots absent; stilt roots absent; Bark grey or brown, rough, scaly or flaky or slightly fissured; under-bark green; less than 25 mm thick; bark blaze consisting of one layer; faintly to non-aromatic, white or pale yellow (straw-coloured), markings absent or slightly speckled, fibrous;; bark exudate colourless, not readily flowing (spotty), colour not changing on exposure to air, not sticky; terminal buds not enclosed by leaves.

Indumentum: Complex hairs present, disk-shaped (peltate), dense; stinging hairs absent; mature twig indumentum absent.

Leaves: Leaves spaced along branches, spiral, simple; petiole present, not winged, attached to base of leaf blade, not swollen; leaves broadest at or near middle, 9.5–17 cm, (6–)9–13 cm; symmetric, entire, not dissected or lobed, shortly acuminate; venation pinnate or at base palmate, secondary veins open, prominent, intramarginal veins absent; leaves with lower surface pale green, upper surface usually dull dark green, indumentum absent (but densely covered with peltate scales); domatia present, scattered along midrib; stipules present, free, laterally placed, not encircling the twig, leafy, not fringed, large, not persistent.

Flowers: Inflorescence terminal or axillary (in distil axils), flowers on a branched axis; flowers bisexual, stalked, with many planes of symmetry, 12–15 mm long, 12–15 mm diam.; perianth present, with distinct sepals and petals whorls, sepals 5-lobed, inner perianth white, pale yellow (outside), or pink (often finely speckled with red), 5, free; stamens many, with filaments present (of varing lengths), joined (forming a staminal tube around the style), free of the perianth; ovary superior, carpels joined, locules 5; styles solitary, 1.

Fruits: arranged on branched axis, fruit c. 15 mm long, green (probably immature) or brown (presumably pale brown to straw-coloured), not spiny, non-fleshy, simple, dehiscent, capsule; seeds many.

Distribution: Central, Northern, Milne Bay.

Kleinhovia hospita L.

Species Plantarum ed. 2 Vol. 2: 1365 (1763)
Timber Group: Non-timber species

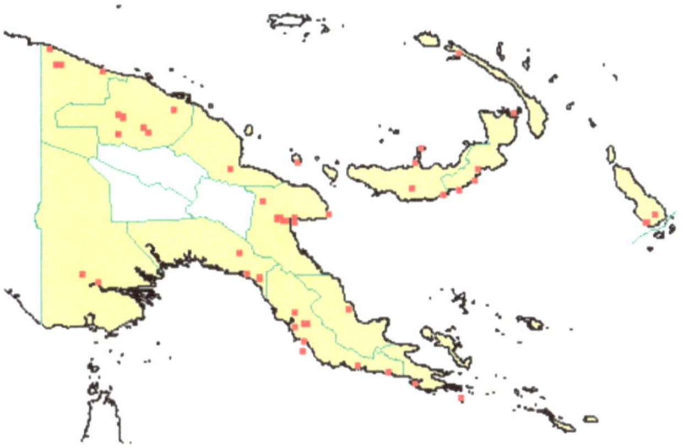

Field Characters: Canopy trees or usually subcanopy trees, 6–25(–30) m high; bole cylindrical, (13–)20–50(–100) cm diam., straight, (2–)3–10 m long; buttresses absent; spines absent; aerial roots absent; stilt roots absent. Bark pale brown or grey, rough, slightly fissured or pustular; lenticels elongated vertically; bark 4 mm thick; under-bark dark brown; faintly or non-aromatic; pleasant; blaze consisting of one layer, pale yellow, with stripes, fibrous; exudate present, colourless, not readily flowing, changing to pale brown on exposure to air, not sticky. Terminal buds not enclosed by leaves.

Indumentum: Complex hairs absent; stinging hairs absent; mature twig without hairs.

Leaves: Spaced along branches, leaves spiral, simple; petiole 7–10(–26) mm long, (juvenile leaves), not winged, attached to base of leaf lamina, not swollen or slightly swollen, lamina broadest below middle, 9–20(–28) cm long (juvenile leaves), 8–12(–24) cm wide (juvenile leaves) ; base symmetric, margin entire or minutely serrate to dentate (toothed) in juvenile leaves, not dissected or lobed, apex acuminate, venation palmate, secondary veins open, prominent, intramarginal veins absent; lower surface pale green, upper surface green, hairs present, dense with minute red-brown hairs, oil dots absent, domatia absent; stipules present, free, laterally placed, not encircling the twig, leafy, not fringed, large, c. 10 mm long, not persistent, or less often persistent.

Flowers: Inflorescence terminal, flowers on a branched axis; flowers bisexual, with pedicel, 2–10 mm long, with many planes of symmetry, 6–8 mm long, small, 5 mm diam.; perianth present, with distinct sepals and petals, pale yellow at apex or pale pink; inner perianth 5, free; stamens 15, filaments present, joined into staminal tube, free of perianth; ovary superior, terminating an androgynophore, carpels joined, locules 5; styles joined, 1.

Fruits: arranged on branched axis, fruit (15–)20–25 mm long, 20–25 mm diam., brown, not spiny, slightly fleshy, simple, dehiscent, capsule. Seeds 1 or 2, 12–14 mm, as long as wide, globose, 10–14 mm, not winged.

Distribution: West Sepik, East Sepik, Madang, Morobe, Western, Gulf, Central, Northern, Milne Bay, Papuan Islands, New Britain, New Ireland, Bougainville.

Microcos argentata Burret
Fig. 324

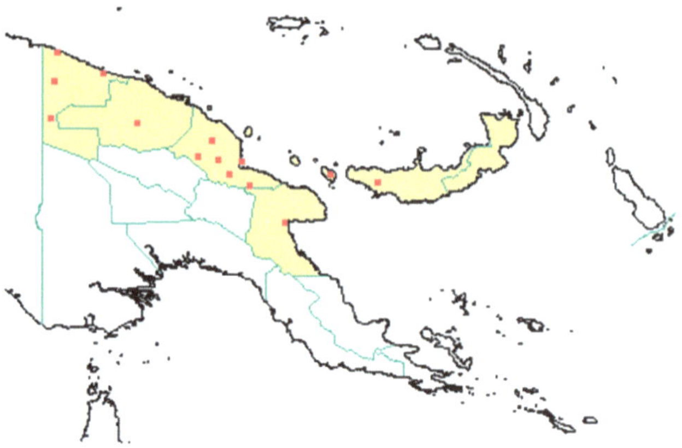

Notizblatt des Botanischen Gartens und Museums zu Berlin-Dahlem Vol. 9: 787 (1926)
Timber Group: Non-timber species

Field Characters: Canopy trees or usually subcanopy trees, 7–22(–33) m high; bole cylindrical or markedly fluted, 25–36(–45) cm diam., slightly crooked or straight, 8–11(–18) m long; buttresses 0.5–1.7 m high; spines absent; aerial roots absent; stilt roots absent. Bark brown or black, rough, pustular; lenticels irregular; bark 10 mm thick; under-bark red or brown; faintly or non-aromatic; blaze consisting of one layer, brown or red, markings absent, fibrous; exudate present, colourless, not readily flowing, changing to orange or brown on exposure to air, not sticky. Terminal buds not enclosed by leaves.

Indumentum: Complex hairs absent; stinging hairs absent; mature twig hairy; hairs dense or sparse.

Leaves: Spaced along branches, leaves spiral, simple; petiole 20 mm long, not winged, attached to base of leaf lamina, swollen; lamina broadest at or near middle, 16–27 cm long, 8–11 cm wide; base symmetric, margin entire, not dissected or lobed, apex acuminate, venation pinnate, secondary veins open, prominent, intramarginal veins absent; lower surface pale green, upper surface dark green, hairs absent, oil dots absent, domatia absent; stipules present, free, laterally placed, not encircling the twig, leafy, not fringed, large, 9–10 mm long; c. 1.5 mm wide, not persistent.

Flowers: Inflorescence axillary, flowers on a branched axis; flowers unisexual, with male and female flowers on same plant, flowers with pedicel, 3–5 mm long, with many planes of symmetry, 8–10 mm long, large, 10–15 mm diam.; perianth present, with all sepals and/or petals (hence tepals) similar, pale yellow or green; inner perianth 5, free; stamens c. 50, filaments present, free of each other, free of perianth; ovary superior, carpels joined, styles joined, 1.

Fruits: arranged on branched axis, fruit 30–38 mm long, 25–28 mm diam., orange, not spiny, fleshy, simple, indehiscent, drupe. Seed 1, 10–34 mm long (including exocarp), as wide as long, 10–24 mm, not winged.

Distribution: West Sepik, East Sepik, Madang, Morobe, New Britain.

Notes: Previously included in the Tiliaceae.

Fig. 324. *Microcos argentata*. Bark and leaves

Papuodendron lepidotum C.T.White

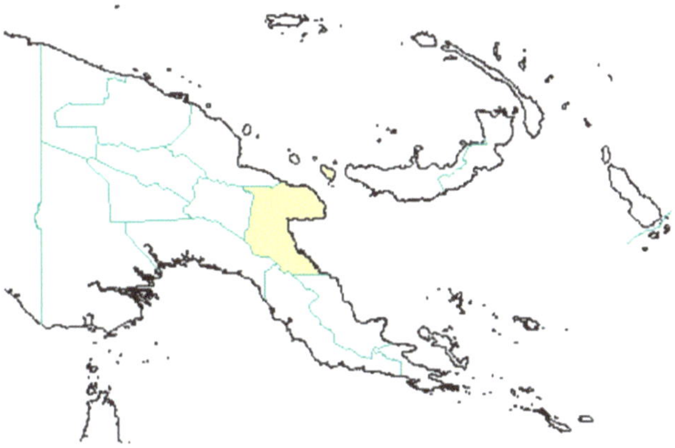

Journal of the Arnold Arboretum Vol. 27: 272 (1946)
Timber Group: Occasional timber species

Field Characters: Canopy trees, up to 30 m high; bole markedly fluted, up to 50 cm diam., crooked, up to c. 20 m long; buttresses present; spines absent; aerial roots absent; stilt roots absent. Bark brown, rough, scaly or flaky, fissured, or slightly pustular; lenticels irregular; bark c. 15 mm thick; under-bark white or pink; strongly aromatic; unpleasant; blaze consisting of one layer, white or pale yellow, markings absent; exudate present, colourless, not readily flowing, changing to pale red (pink) on exposure to air, not sticky. Terminal buds not enclosed by leaves.

Indumentum: Complex hairs present, star-like; stinging hairs absent; mature twig hairy; hairs sparse.

Leaves: Spaced along branches, leaves spiral, simple; petiole present, not winged, attached to base of leaf lamina, not swollen; lamina broadest below middle, 6–21 cm long, 4–10.5 cm wide; base symmetric, margin entire, not dissected or lobed, apex acute, venation pinnate, secondary veins closed, prominent, intramarginal veins absent; hairs present, sparse, oil dots absent, domatia absent; stipules present, free, laterally placed, not encircling the twig, scale-like or collar-like, not fringed, large, persistent.

Flowers: Inflorescence axillary, flowers on a branched axis; flowers bisexual, with pedicel, with many planes of symmetry perianth present, with distinct sepals and petals; inner perianth 5, free; stamens many, filaments present, joined, free of perianth; ovary superior, carpels joined, locules 5, separated by septa so appearing as 10; styles free, 5.

Fruits: arranged on branched axis, not spiny, non-fleshy, simple, dehiscent, capsule. Seeds many, not winged.

Distribution: Morobe.

Pterocymbium beccarii K.Schum. Fig. 325

Botanische Jahrbücher für Systematik, Pflanzengeschichte und Pflanzengeographie Vol. 24, 3 Beible, 58: 21 (1897)
Timber Group: Major exportable hardwoods

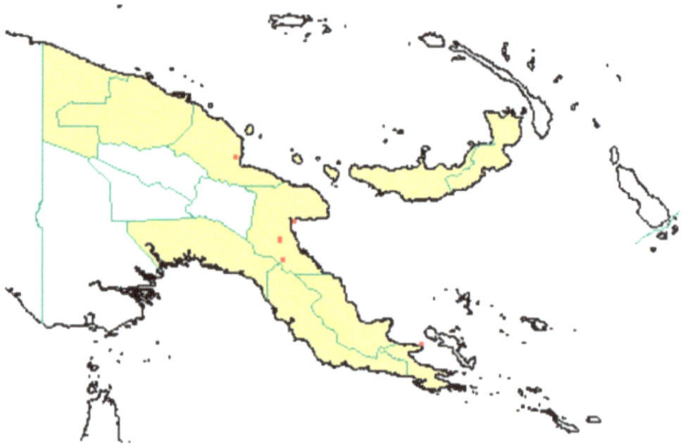

Field Characters: Canopy trees, mostly 40–63 m high; bole cylindrical, up to 30(–60) cm diam., straight, up to 38 m long; buttresses present or occasionally absent; spines absent; aerial roots absent; stilt roots absent. Bark green (stripes), grey, or light brown, slightly rough or smooth, slightly fissured, slightly scaly or flaky (mostly smooth), or scattered pustular; lenticels elongated vertically; bark usually 20–35 mm thick; under-bark white, greenish grey (mottled), pink, or green; strongly aromatic; pleasant; blaze consisting of one layer, pale orange (streaks), white to cream-coloured, or pale pink (streaks), with stripes (pink and orange), fibrous or granular without splinters; exudate absent. Terminal buds not enclosed by leaves.

Indumentum: Complex hairs present, star-like; stinging hairs absent; mature twig hairy (when young) or soon mature twig without hairs; hairs somewhat dense.

Leaves: Clustered at end of branches or slightly spaced along branches, leaves spiral, simple; petiole present, not winged, attached to base of leaf lamina, not swollen; lamina broadest below middle, (65–)70–100 cm long, 60–90 cm wide; base symmetric, margin entire, not dissected or lobed, apex obtuse or slightly acuminate, venation palmate, secondary veins open, prominent, intramarginal veins absent; lower surface pale green or green, upper surface green (glossy), hairs absent (on upper syrface) or present (on lower surface), somewhat dense, oil dots absent, domatia absent; stipules absent.

Flowers: Inflorescence axillary (mostly after leaves have fallen off), flowers on a branched axis; flowers unisexual, with male and female flowers on same plant, flowers with pedicel, with many planes of symmetry, c. 10 mm long, large, 6–8 mm diam.; perianth present, with all sepals and/or petals (hence tepals) similar, white, red (inner surface), or blue; inner perianth 5, some or partly joined (forming a perianth tube and 5 lobes); stamens 15, filaments absent, joined (forming a staminal column), free of perianth; ovary superior, carpels joined, locules 1; styles absent or short, 1.

Fruits: arranged on branched axis, fruit surrounded by a membranous slipper-like wing, 50–60 mm long, 6–8 mm diam., yellowish brown or yellowish green, not spiny, fleshy, simple, dehiscent, follicle. Seeds 1 or 2, c. 8 mm long, as wide as long, 1–10 mm diam., not winged.

Distribution: West Sepik, East Sepik, Madang, Morobe, Gulf, Central, Northern, Milne Bay, New Britain.

Notes: Soon after fertilization, the follicle splits on one side and develops into a large membraneous boat-shaped wing; the exposed seeds develops at or near the base of the open carpel. At maturity the seeds are dispersed, attached to the follicle 'wall' which acts as wings.

The genus *Pterocymbium* was previously classified in the family Sterculiaceae.

Fig. 325. *Pterocymbium beccarii*. Base of trunk, bark and flowers

Pterygota horsfieldii (R.Br.) Kosterm.

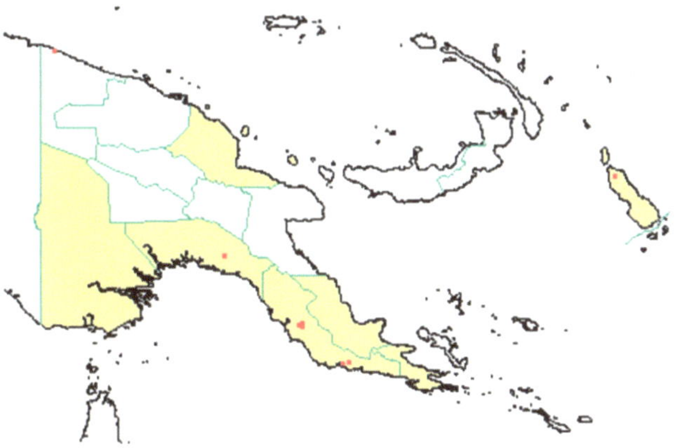

Reinwardtia Vol. 2: 365 (1953)
Timber Group: Non-timber species

Field Characters: Canopy trees, up to c. 30 m high, or subcanopy trees; bole cylindrical, up to c. 100 cm diam., straight, up to 20 m long; buttresses present; spines absent; aerial roots absent; stilt roots absent. Bark brown, pale red, or pale grey (mottled), slightly rough or smooth, slightly cracked; bark <25 mm thick; under-bark white or pale yellow (straw-coloured); faintly or non-aromatic; blaze consisting of one layer, white or pale yellow (straw-coloured), with stripes (pale brown); exudate absent. Terminal buds not enclosed by leaves.

Indumentum: Complex hairs present, star-like; stinging hairs absent; soon mature twig without hairs or mature twig hairy (at least when young); hairs usually sparse.

Leaves: Spaced along branches or clustered at end of branches, leaves spiral, simple; petiole present, not winged, attached to base of leaf lamina, slightly swollen at base, or not swollen; lamina broadest below middle, 14–24 cm long, 9.5–20 cm wide; base symmetric, margin entire, not dissected or lobed, apex obtuse or sub-acuminate, venation pinnate, secondary veins open, prominent, intramarginal veins absent; lower surface green, upper surface dark dull green, hairs usually absent or occasionally present, sparse, oil dots absent, domatia absent; stipules present, free, laterally placed, not encircling the twig, leafy, not fringed, large, c. 3 mm long, not persistent.

Flowers: Inflorescence sub-terminal, on the trunk or branches, or axillary, flowers on a branched axis; flowers unisexual, with male and female flowers on same plant, flowers with pedicel, with many planes of symmetry, 12–15 mm long, small, c. 10 mm diam.; perianth present, with all sepals and/or petals (hence tepals) similar, pale brown (densely covered with reddish brown hairs) or dull red; inner perianth 5, some or partly joined (forming almost subfleshy perianth tube and 5 lobes); stamens c. 25 (in groups of 5 – male flowers; sterile anthers – females flowers), filaments absent, joined to form a staminal column, free of perianth; ovary superior, carpels partially joined, by base, locules 5; styles absent.

Fruits: arranged on branched axis, fruit 70–80 mm long, 60–70 mm diam., red or brown, not spiny, non-fleshy, simple, dehiscent, follicle (opening by one slit). Seeds many, 12–15 mm long (excluding wing) or c. 60 mm long (including wing), as wide as long (slightly flattened), c. 10 mm diam., winged (with a single wing 40–45 mm long).

Distribution: Madang, Western, Gulf, Central, Northern, Milne Bay, Bougainville.

Notes: The genus *Pterygota* was previously classified in the family Sterculiaceae.

Sterculia ampla Baker f.
Fig. 326

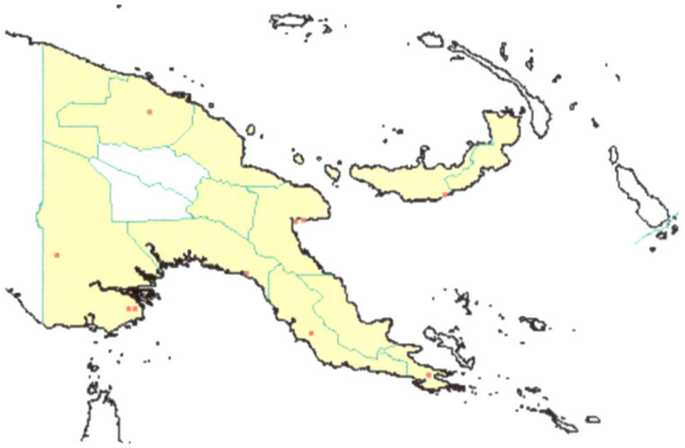

Journal of Botany Vol. 61 (Supplement) 5: (1923)
Other Literature: G.M. Tantra, *Lembaga Penelitian Hutan* Vol. 102: 67 & 68 (1976)
Timber Group: Commercial hardwoods

Field Characters: Subcanopy trees, up to 25 m high, or canopy trees, up to 40 m high; bole cylindrical, 40–70 cm diam., straight, 15–30 m long; buttresses absent or present; spines absent; aerial roots absent; stilt roots absent. Bark grey or dark brown, rough, slightly tessellated, scaly or flaky, or pustular; lenticels elongated vertically; bark 10–14 mm thick; under-bark red or green; strongly aromatic; pleasant; blaze consisting of one layer, white, with stripes, fibrous; exudate present, colourless, not readily flowing, changing to brown on exposure to air, not sticky. Terminal buds not enclosed by leaves.

Indumentum: Complex hairs present, star-like to irregular (hairs reddish brown); stinging hairs absent; mature twig hairy (with complex hairs); hairs dense or sparse.

Leaves: Clustered at end of branches, leaves spiral, simple; petiole present, winged, attached to base of leaf lamina, swollen at tip and base; lamina broadest at or near middle, 17–43 cm long, 12–42 cm wide; base symmetric, margin entire, not dissected or lobed, apex sub-acute or sub-mucronate, venation palmate, secondary veins open, prominent, intramarginal veins absent; lower surface pale green, upper surface pale green, hairs present, somewhat dense or sparse, oil dots absent, domatia present, scattered along mid-vein; stipules present, free, laterally placed, not encircling the twig, scale-like, not fringed, large, not persistent.

Flowers: Inflorescence axillary, flowers on a branched axis; flowers unisexual, with male and female flowers on the same plant, flowers with pedicel, with many planes of symmetry, (0.5–)5–7 mm long, small, c. 3–4 mm diam.; perianth present, with all sepals and/or petals (hence tepals) similar, red; inner perianth 5, some or partly joined forming a perianth tube and 5 perianth lobes; stamens 10–15 (male flowers), filaments absent, joined to form a staminal tube around ovary and style, free of perianth; ovary superior, carpels separate, locules 4; styles free, 4.

Fruits: arranged on branched axis, fruit 70–90 mm long, 60–65 mm diam., green (immature) or bright orange, not spiny (surface hairy), non-fleshy, aggregate, dehiscent, follicle. Seeds c. 4, c. 10 mm long, as wide as long, c. 10 mm diam., not winged.

Distribution: West Sepik, East Sepik, Madang, Morobe, Eastern Highlands, Western, Gulf, Central, Northern, Milne Bay, New Britain.

Notes: The genus *Sterculia* was previously classified in the family Sterculiaceae.

Sterculia ampla is inadequately known and its taxonomic status is unclear.

Fig. 326. *Sterculia ampla*. Habit, buttresses, bark, leaves, seedling and seed

Sterculia edelfeltii F.Muell.

Victorian Naturalist Vol. 3: 47 (1886)
Other Literature: G.M. Tantra, *Lembaga Penelitian Hutan* Vol. 102: 123 & 124 (1976)
Timber Group: Non-timber species

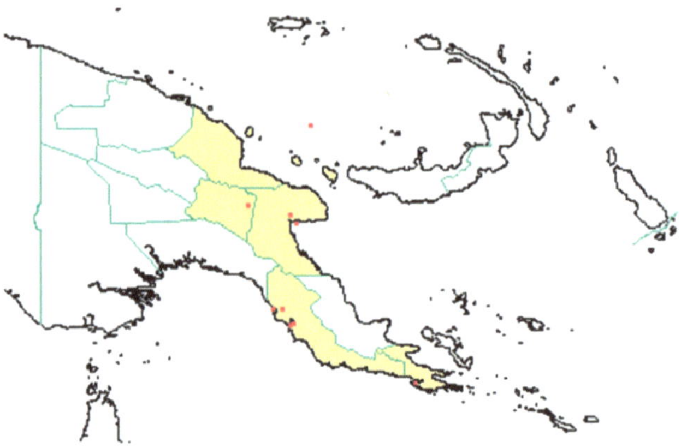

Field Characters: Subcanopy trees, up to 20 m high; bole cylindrical, up to c. 45 cm diam., straight, up to c. 10 m long; buttresses absent; spines absent; aerial roots absent; stilt roots absent. Bark brownish green or brown, rough; bark <25 mm thick; under-bark green; faintly or non-aromatic; blaze consisting of one layer, white or pale yellow (straw-coloured), with stripes, fibrous; exudate absent. Terminal buds not enclosed by leaves.

Indumentum: Complex hairs present (sparse), star-like; stinging hairs absent; mature twig hairy when young or soon mature twig without hairs; hairs dense (stellate hairy) or hairs sparse.

Leaves: Spaced along branches, leaves spiral, simple; petiole present, not winged, attached to base of leaf lamina, not swollen; lamina broadest at or near middle, 9–15 cm long, 5.5–8 cm wide; base symmetric, margin entire, not dissected or lobed, apex shortly acuminate or obtuse, venation pinnate, secondary veins open, prominent, intramarginal veins absent; lower surface green or pale green, upper surface green, hairs present, sparse (scattered stellate hairs, particularly on lower surface), oil dots absent, domatia absent; stipules present, free, laterally placed, not encircling the twig, leafy (triangular), not fringed, large, c. 5 mm long, not persistent (soon dehiscent, only present at growing point of branchlets).

Flowers: Inflorescence axillary, flowers on a branched axis; flowers unisexual, with male and female flowers on same plant, flowers with pedicel, with many planes of symmetry, 7–8 mm long, small, c. 5–7 mm diam.; perianth present, with all sepals and/or petals (hence tepals) similar, greenish red or green; inner perianth 5, some or partly joined forming a perianth tube and 5 perianth lobes; stamens c. 15 (male flowers), filaments absent, joined to form a staminal tube around ovary and style, free of perianth; ovary superior, carpels separate, locules 4; styles free, 4.

Fruits: arranged on branched axis, presumably not spiny, non-fleshy, aggregate, dehiscent, follicle. Seeds c. 10 mm long, c. 10 mm diam., not winged.

Distribution: Madang, Morobe, Eastern Highlands, Central, Milne Bay.

Notes: *Sterculia edelfeltii* is an inadequately known species and its taxonomic status is unclear.

Sterculia lepidotostellata Mildbr.

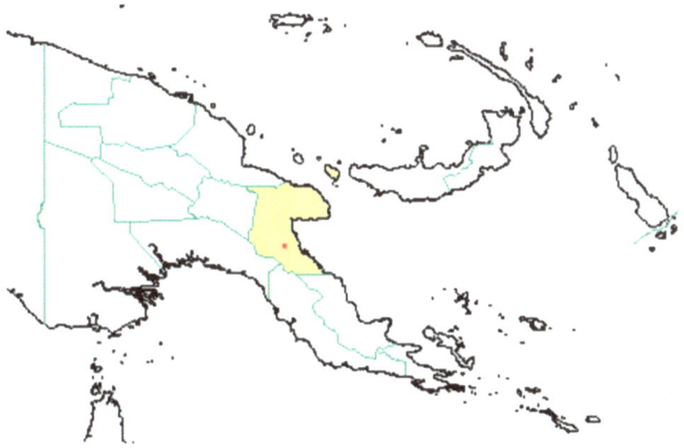

Botanische Jahrbücher für Systematik, Pflanzengeschichte und Pflanzengeographie Vol. 62: 361 (1929)
Other Literature: G.M. Tantra, *Lembaga Penelitian Hutan* Vol. 102: 111 & 112 (1976)
Timber Group: Non-timber species

Field Characters: Subcanopy or canopy trees, up to 30 m high; bole cylindrical, up to c. 40 cm diam., straight, up to c. 18 m long; buttresses absent; spines absent; aerial roots absent; stilt roots absent. Bark brown, slightly rough or smooth, pustular; lenticels irregular (large); bark <25 mm thick; under-bark brown; faintly or non-aromatic; blaze consisting of one layer, pale brown, markings absent, fibrous; exudate absent. Terminal buds not enclosed by leaves.

Indumentum: Complex hairs present (sparse); disk-shaped or star-like (stellate scales); stinging hairs absent; mature twig hairy when young or mature twig without hairs; usually hairs sparse (stellate scales).

Leaves: Clustered at end of branches or spaced along branches, leaves spiral, simple; petiole present, not winged, attached to base of leaf lamina, not swollen or slightly swollen at both base and tip; lamina slightly broadest above middle, 3–4 cm long, 1–1.5 cm wide; base symmetric, margin entire, not dissected or lobed, apex shortly acuminate, venation pinnate, secondary veins open, prominent, intramarginal veins absent; lower surface pale green, upper surface glossy green, hairs present (with stellate scales on lower surface, especially on mid vein), sparse, oil dots absent, domatia absent; stipules present, free, laterally placed, not encircling the twig, leafy (triangular, with a single rib), not fringed, large, c. 5 mm long, not persistent (soon dehiscent, only present at growing point of branchlets).

Flowers: Inflorescence axillary, flowers on a branched axis; flowers unisexual, with male and female flowers on the same plant, flowers with pedicel, with many planes of symmetry perianth present, with all sepals and/or petals (hence tepals) similar; inner perianth 5, some or partly joined forming a perianth tube and 5 perianth lobes; stamens 10–15 (male flowers), filaments absent, joined to form a staminal tube around ovary and style, free of perianth; ovary superior, carpels separate, locules 4; styles free, 4.

Fruits: arranged on branched axis, fruit (50–)60–80 mm long, 25–45 mm diam., glossy brown, not spiny, non-fleshy, aggregate, dehiscent, follicle. Seed c. 10 mm long, c. 10 mm diam., not winged.

Distribution: Morobe.

Notes: *Sterculia lepidotostellata* is a very inadequately known species and its taxonomic status is unclear.

Sterculia macrophylla **Vent.**

Jardin de la Malmison Vol. 2: (1805) Fig. 91.
Timber Group: Minor hardwoods

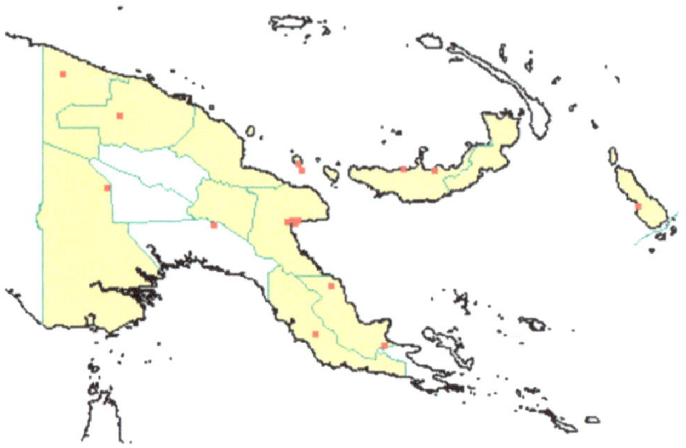

Field Characters: Canopy trees, up to 35 m high; bole cylindrical, 20 cm diam., straight, up to 20 m long; buttresses 0.5–2 m high; spines absent; aerial roots absent; stilt roots absent. Bark brown or pale green, rough, pustular; lenticels irregular; bark 10–12 mm thick; under-bark green; faintly or non-aromatic; blaze consisting of 2 layers; outer blaze red or brown, markings absent, fibrous; inner blaze pale yellow or brown, speckled, with large white dots, fibrous; exudate present, colourless, not readily flowing, changing to brown on exposure to air, not sticky. Terminal buds not enclosed by leaves.

Indumentum: Complex hairs present, especially on abaxial leaf surface, star-like; stinging hairs absent; mature twig hairy; usually hairs sparse.

Leaves: Clustered at end of branches, leaves spiral, simple; petiole (20–)40–200 mm long, not winged, attached to base of leaf lamina, not swollen or slightly swollen at base; lamina broadest below middle, (8–)12–40 cm long, (6–)10–35 cm wide; base symmetric to slightly asymmetric, margin entire, not dissected or lobed, apex rounded, venation pinnate, secondary veins open, prominent, intramarginal veins absent; lower surface pale green, upper surface green, hairs present, dense, oil dots absent, domatia absent; stipules present, free, laterally placed, not encircling the twig, leafy, not fringed, large, c. 30 mm long, 3 mm wide at base, not persistent or persistent distally.

Flowers: Inflorescence axillary, or sub-terminal, flowers on a branched axis; flowers unisexual (male flowers also present) or bisexual, with pedicel 2–3 mm long, with many planes of symmetry, 4–6 mm long; perianth present, with all sepals and/or petals (hence tepals) similar or petals absent; inner perianth 5, some or partly joined; stamens 5–10, filaments absent, joined (forming an androphore), free of perianth; ovary superior, carpels separate, locules 5; styles free, 5.

Fruits: arranged on branched axis, fruit 70–75 mm long, 90–95 mm diam., brown or red, not spiny, non-fleshy, aggregate, dehiscent, follicle (1–)3–5, subsessile, nearly orbicular. Seeds 14 or 15, 17–20 mm, almost as wide as long, 8–12 mm, not winged.

Distribution: West Sepik, East Sepik, Madang, Morobe, Eastern Highlands, Western, Central, Northern, New Britain, Bougainville.

Sterculia morobeensis Tantra
Fig. 327

Lembaga Penelitian Hutan Vol. 102: 54 (1976).
Timber Group: Occasional timber species

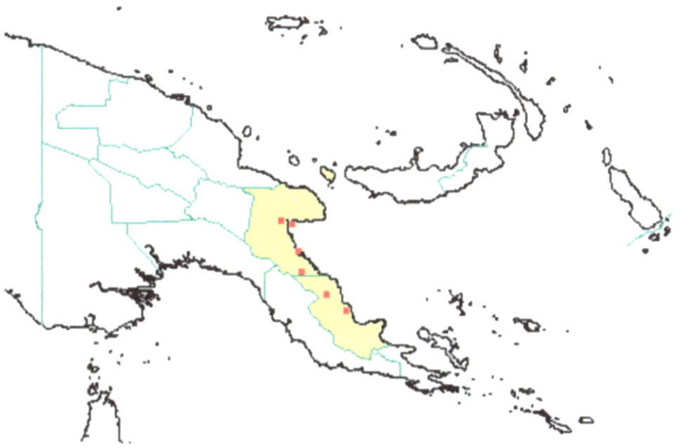

Field Characters: Canopy trees, 25–35 m high; bole cylindrical, 23–45 cm diam., straight, 20 m long; buttresses up to c. 0.7 m high; spines absent; aerial roots absent; stilt roots absent. Bark brown, rough, pustular; lenticels elongated vertically; bark 10 mm thick; under-bark green; strongly aromatic; pleasant; blaze consisting of 2 layers; outer blaze yellow or yellowish brown, with stripes, fibrous; inner blaze brown or red, markings absent, fibrous; exudate present, colourless, not readily flowing, not changing colour on exposure to air, not sticky. Terminal buds not enclosed by leaves.

Indumentum: Complex hairs present, star-like; stinging hairs absent; mature twig without hairs.

Leaves: Clustered at end of branches, leaves spiral, simple; petiole 3–7 cm long, not winged, attached to base of leaf lamina, swollen at both base and tip; stipules present, 8–12 mm long, 1–2 mm wide (not persistent); lamina broadest below middle, 15–33 cm long, 9.5–29 cm wide; base symmetric, margin entire, not dissected or lobed, apex mucronate, venation pinnate (veins yellow), secondary veins open, prominent, intramarginal veins absent; lower surface green or pale green, upper surface green or dark green, hairs absent or with stellate hairs near base and/or on mid-vein, oil dots absent, domatia present, scattered along mid-vein; stipules present, free, laterally placed, not encircling the twig, leafy triangular, brown, not fringed, large, not persistent (soon dehiscent, only present at growing point of branchlets).

Flowers: Inflorescence axillary (or subterminal), c. 80 mm long, 10–20-flowered, flowers on a branched axis, densely hairy (hairs branched – star-shaped); flowers unisexual, with pedicel 3–5 mm long, bracts not persistent, flowers with many planes of symmetry, outer surface densely covered with stellate hairs; perianth present (calyx) 3–4 mm long, with 5 lobes, with inner surface densely covered with woolly hairs; male flowers with 5 anthers, joined together in a ring to form a globose 'head'; female flowers with ovary superior, carpels partly fused, locules 3; styles almost free, 3.

Fruits: arranged on branched axis, fruit 5–8 mm long, (3–)4–6 mm diam., consisting of 2 or 3 follicles green, red, or brown, not spiny, non-fleshy, simple, dehiscent, follicle, outer surface without hairs, inner surface densely woolly. Seeds 7–9, white, as wide as long, c. 10 mm diam., not winged.

Distribution: Morobe, Northern.

Fig. 327. *Sterculia morobeensis*. Bark, buttresses, fruit, seeds and leaves

Sterculia peekelii Mildbr.

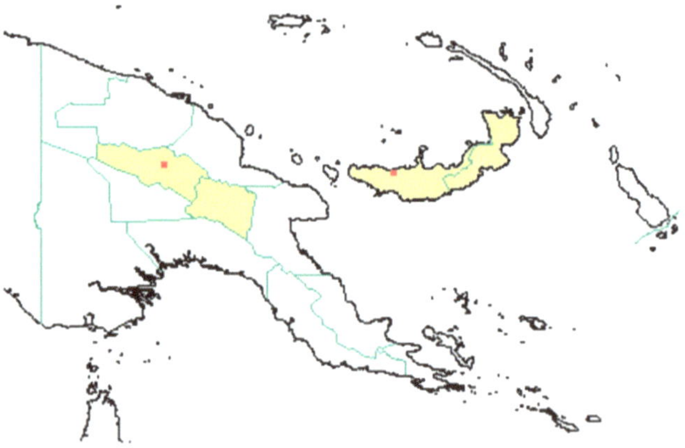

Notizblatt des Botanischen Gartens und Museums zu Berlin-Dahlem Vol. 10: 281 (1928)
Other Literature: G.M. Tantra, *Lembaga Penelitian Hutan* Vol. 102: 124–126 (1976)
Timber Group: Non-timber species

Field Characters: Subcanopy trees, c. 12–20 m high; bole cylindrical, c. 25 cm diam., straight; buttresses absent; spines absent; aerial roots absent; stilt roots absent. Bark grey, usually smooth; bark <25 mm thick; under-bark white; faintly or non-aromatic; blaze consisting of one layer, white or pale yellow (cream-coloured), markings absent, fibrous; exudate absent. Terminal buds not enclosed by leaves.

Indumentum: Complex hairs present, star-like; stinging hairs absent; mature twig hairy or soon mature twig without hairs; hairs sparse.

Leaves: Clustered at end of branches or spaced along branches, leaves spiral, simple; petiole 20–40 mm long, not winged, attached to base of leaf lamina, not swollen or slightly swollen; lamina broadest at or near middle, 16–30 cm long, 9–13 cm wide; base symmetric, margin entire, not dissected or lobed, apex slightly acuminate or obtuse, venation pinnate, secondary veins open, prominent, intramarginal veins absent; lower surface green or pale green, upper surface green, hairs present, sparse (hairs stellate), oil dots absent, domatia absent; stipules present, free, laterally placed, not encircling the twig, leafy, not fringed, large, c. 5 mm long, not persistent (soon dehiscent, only present at growing point of branchlets).

Flowers: Inflorescence axillary, flowers on a branched axis; flowers unisexual, with male and female flowers on same plant, flowers with pedicel, with many planes of symmetry, 10–12 mm long, small, c. 5 mm diam.; perianth present, with all sepals and/or petals (hence tepals) similar, pale brown, red (towards base of inner surface), or green; inner perianth 5, some or partly joined forming a perianth tube and 5 perianth lobes; stamens c. 20 (male flowers), filaments absent, joined to form a staminal tube around ovary and style, free of perianth; ovary superior, carpels separate, locules 3 or 4; styles free, 3 or 4.

Fruits: arranged on branched axis, fruit brown, not spiny, non-fleshy, aggregate, dehiscent, follicle. Seeds c. 10 mm long, c. 10 mm diam., not winged.

Distribution: Western Highlands, Eastern Highlands, New Britain.

Notes: *Sterculia peekelii* is inadequately known and its taxonomic status is unclear.

Sterculia quadrifida R.Br.

Plantae Javanicae Rariores 233 (1844)
Other Literature: A.J.G. Wilson, *Flora of the Kimberley Region* 196 (1992) Fig. 52(G1–G3).
Timber Group: Commercial hardwoods

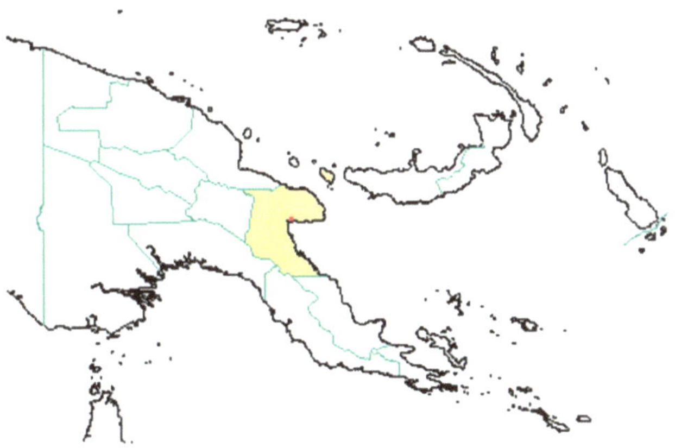

Field Characters: Subcanopy trees, up to c. 20 m high; bole cylindrical, straight; buttresses absent; spines absent; aerial roots absent; stilt roots absent. Bark grey (silvery), usually smooth; bark <25 mm thick; faintly or non-aromatic; blaze consisting of one layer, pale yellow (cream-coloured) or white, fibrous; exudate absent. Terminal buds not enclosed by leaves.

Indumentum: Complex hairs present, star-like; stinging hairs absent; mature twig hairy when young or mature twig without hairs; hairs sparse.

Leaves: Clustered at end of branches or spaced along branches, leaves spiral, simple; petiole present, not winged, not swollen; lamina broadest at or near middle, 8.5–23 cm long, 5–18 cm wide; base symmetric, margin entire, not dissected or lobed, apex shortly acuminate or obtuse, venation pinnate, secondary veins open, prominent, intramarginal veins absent; lower surface pale green or green, upper surface green, hairs present, sparse (with stellate hairs on both surfaces), oil dots absent, domatia absent; stipules present, free, laterally placed, not encircling the twig, leafy, not fringed, large, c. 5 mm long, not persistent (soon dehiscent, only present at growing point of branchlets).

Flowers: Inflorescence terminal or axillary, flowers on a branched axis; flowers unisexual, with male and female flowers on the same plant, flowers with pedicel, with many planes of symmetry, 8–10 mm long, small, c. 5 mm diam.; perianth present, with all sepals and/or petals (hence tepals) similar, yellow or yellowish green; inner perianth 4, some or partly joined to form a perianth tube with 4 lobes; stamens c. 20 (male flowers), filaments absent, joined (forming a staminal tube around ovary and style), free of perianth; ovary superior, carpels separate locules 3 or 4; styles free, 3 or 4.

Fruits: arranged on branched axis, fruit 35–50 mm long, 18–30 mm diam., red or orange (when mature), yellow, green, not spiny, non-fleshy, aggregate, dehiscent, follicle. Seeds 2–4, 12–13 mm long, c. 8 mm diam., black, glossy to subglossy, not winged.

Distribution: Morobe, Western.

Sterculia schumanniana (Lauterb.) Mildbr.

Botanische Jahrbücher für Systematik, Pflanzengeschichte und Pflanzengeographie Vol. 62: 358 (1929)
Other Literature: G.M. Tantra, *Lembaga Penelitian Hutan* Vol. 102: 139 & 140 (1976)
Timber Group: Non-timber species

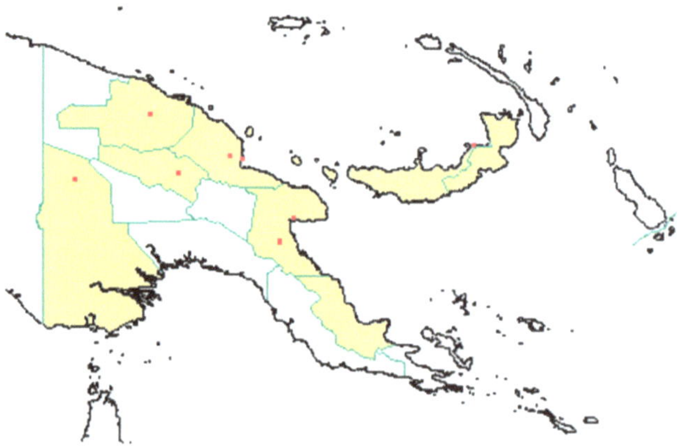

Field Characters: Subcanopy trees, 20–25 m high; bole cylindrical, up to 40 cm diam., straight, up to c. 10 m long; buttresses slightly present; spines absent; aerial roots absent; stilt roots absent. Bark brown or dark grey, rough, scaly or flaky (irregular), fissured, slightly peeling, or pustular; lenticels irregular; bark (10–)16–20 mm thick; under-bark pink; faintly or non-aromatic; pleasant; blaze consisting of one layer, white, pale yellow (straw-coloured), or pink, with stripes (white), fibrous; exudate present or absent, colourless, not readily flowing, not changing colour on exposure to air, not sticky. Terminal buds not enclosed by leaves.

Indumentum: Complex hairs present, star-like; stinging hairs absent; mature twig hairy when young or soon mature twig without hairs; hairs sparse or dense.

Leaves: Slightly spaced along branches or clustered at end of branches, leaves spiral, simple; petiole present, not winged, attached to base of leaf lamina, not swollen or slightly swollen; lamina slightly broadest above middle or broadest at or near middle, (10–)16–30 cm long, (7–)8–14 cm wide; base symmetric, margin entire, not dissected or lobed, apex shortly acuminate, venation pinnate, secondary veins open, prominent, intramarginal veins absent; lower surface pale green or greenish white, upper surface dark green, hairs present, dense, oil dots absent, domatia absent; stipules present, free, laterally placed, not encircling the twig, leafy, not fringed, large, c. 5 mm long, not persistent (soon deciduous, only present at growing point of branchlets).

Flowers: Inflorescence on branchlets below leaves, or axillary, flowers on a branched axis; flowers unisexual (male) or bisexual (unknown), with male and female flowers on same plant, flowers with pedicel, with many planes of symmetry, 10–12 mm long, small, 5–8 mm diam.; perianth present, with all sepals and/or petals (hence tepals) similar, yellow, red (on inner surface near base), or yellowish green; inner perianth 5, some or partly joined forming a perianth tube and 5 perianth lobes; stamens c. 20 (male flowers), filaments present, joined (to form a staminal tube around ovary and style), free of perianth; ovary superior, carpels separate, locules 4 or 5; styles free, 4 or 5.

Fruits: arranged on branched axis, fruit 50–65 mm long, 12–15 mm diam., orange or red, not spiny, non-fleshy, aggregate, dehiscent, follicle. Seeds 5–8, 7–9 mm long, longer than wide, 4–5 mm diam., glossy, black, not winged.

Distribution: West Sepik, East Sepik, Madang, Morobe, Western Highlands, Western, Northern, Milne Bay, Papuan Islands, New Britain.

Notes: *Sterculia schumanniana* is very inadequately known and its taxonomic status is unclear. Several collections from the Kamiali Wildlife Management Area (Morobe) (e.g. *Takeuchi 15181*) were thought to have affinities to *Sterculia shillinglawii*; however, these are now regarded as *S. schumanniana*.

Sterculia shillinglawii F.Muell. subsp. *shillinglawii* Fig. 328

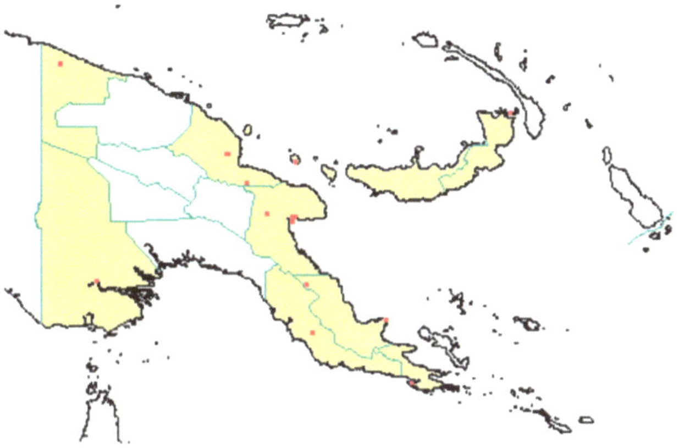

Australasian Journal of Pharmacy Vol. 2: 44 (1887)
Other Literature: G.M. Tantra, *Lembaga Penelitian Hutan* Vol. 102: 59–62 (1976)
Timber Group: Commercial hardwoods

Field Characters: Canopy trees, up to c. 30 m high; bole cylindrical, up to c. 120 cm diam., straight, up to c. 20 m long; buttresses absent; spines absent; aerial roots absent; stilt roots absent. Bark pale grey or pale brown (mottled), slightly rough or smooth, slightly pustular; lenticels elongated vertically or irregular; bark 10 mm thick; under-bark green; faintly or non-aromatic; pleasant; blaze consisting of one layer, white, pale yellow (cream-coloured), orange, or pale brown, speckled, fibrous; exudate present or absent, colourless, not readily flowing, not changing colour on exposure to air, not sticky. Terminal buds not enclosed by leaves.

Indumentum: Complex hairs present, star-like; stinging hairs absent; mature twig hairy when young or soon mature twig without hairs; hairs dense or sparse.

Leaves: Clustered at end of branches or spaced along branches, leaves spiral, simple; petiole present, not winged, attached to base of leaf lamina, slightly swollen at base, or not swollen; lamina slightly broadest above middle or broadest at or near middle, (11–)15–30(–34) cm long, 6–14.5 cm wide; base symmetric, margin entire, not dissected or lobed, apex obtuse or shortly acuminate, venation pinnate, secondary veins open, prominent, intramarginal veins absent; lower surface green or brown (with reddish brown hairs), upper surface green, hairs present (on lower surface), dense, oil dots absent, domatia absent; stipules present, free, laterally placed, not encircling the twig, leafy (triangular), not fringed, large, 3–4 mm long, not persistent (soon dehiscent, only present at growing point of branchlets).

Flowers: Inflorescence axillary, or on branchlets below leaves, flowers on a branched axis; flowers unisexual, with male and female flowers on same plant, flowers with pedicel, with many planes of symmetry, 8–10 mm long, small, 5–7 mm diam.; perianth present, with all sepals and/or petals (hence tepals) similar, cream-coloured, pale yellow, or red (on inner surface near base); inner perianth 5, some or partly joined forming a perianth tube and 5 perianth lobes; stamens c. 20 (male flowers), filaments absent, joined to form a staminal tube around ovary and style, free of perianth; ovary superior, carpels separate, locules 3 or 4; styles free, 3 or 4.

Fruits: arranged on branched axis, fruit 60–70 mm long, c. 15 mm diam., fruit bright orange, bright red, or brown (densely hairy), not spiny, non-fleshy, aggregate, dehiscent, follicle. Seeds 2–4, c. 8–10 mm long, as wide as long, 5–6 mm diam., olive-green to almost black, glossy, not winged.

Distribution: West Sepik, Madang, Morobe, Western, Central, Northern, Milne Bay, New Britain.

Notes: The genus *Sterculia* was previously classified in the family Sterculiaceae. *Sterculia conwentzii* K.Schum. and *S. multinervia* Rech. are both included in this species. An additional subspecies of Sterculia shillinglawii, namely subsp. *malacophylla* (K.Schum.) Tantra, has straight fruits (follicles) that are fissured on the outer surface, whereas subsp. *shillinglawii* has generally curved, relatively smooth fruits.

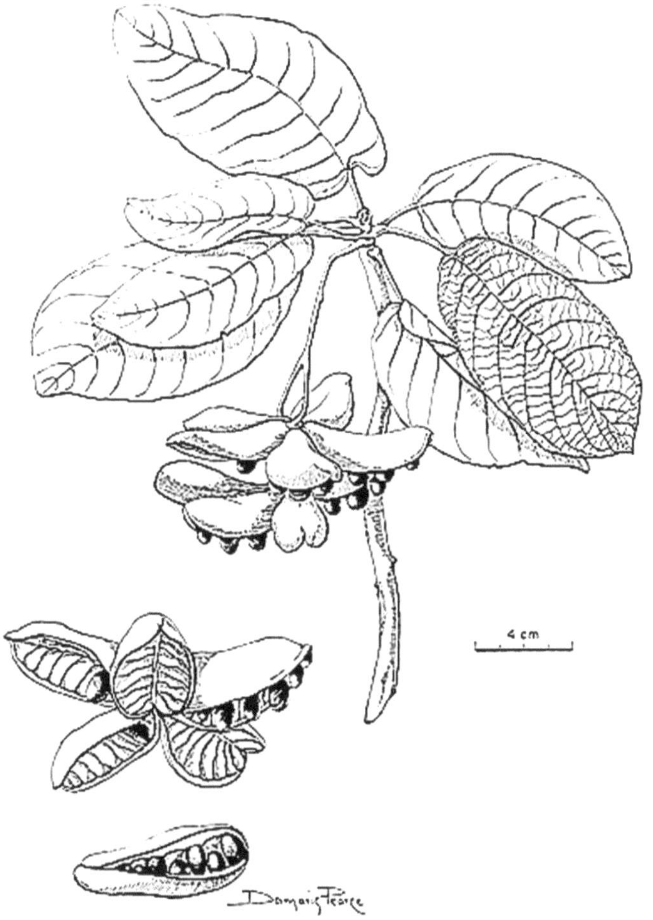

Fig. 328. *Sterculia shillinglawsii* subsp. *shillinglawii*. Bark, buttresses, flowers, leaves and fruit

Thespesia fisscalyx Borss.Waalk.
Fig. 329

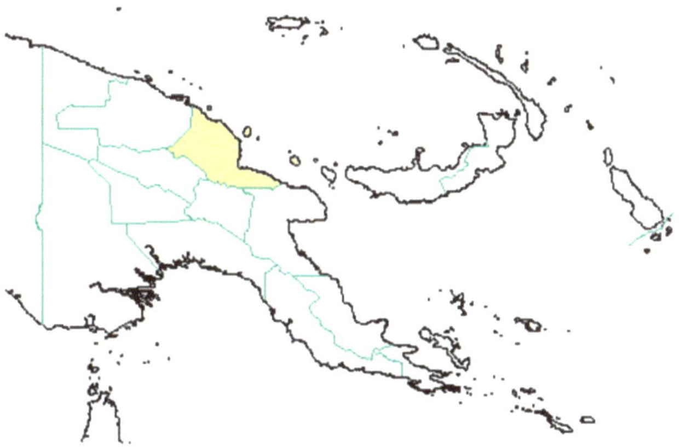

Blumea Vol. 14: 112 (1966)
Timber Group: Occasional timber species

Field Characters: Canopy trees, c. 20 m high; bole cylindrical, straight; buttresses absent; spines absent; aerial roots absent; stilt roots absent. Bark grey, rough, pustular; lenticels elongated vertically; bark 10–15 mm thick; under-bark green with tinge of red; faintly or non-aromatic; onion-like; blaze consisting of one layer, pale red or pale yellow cream-coloured, with stripes, fibrous; inner blaze pale yellow cream-coloured or pale red, with stripes, fibrous; exudate absent. Terminal buds not enclosed by leaves.

Indumentum: Complex hairs absent; stinging hairs absent; mature twig hairy; hairs dense.

Leaves: Spaced along branches, leaves spiral, simple; petiole present, not winged, attached to base of leaf lamina, not swollen; lamina broadest below middle, 8.5–12 cm long, 8.5–12 cm wide; base symmetric, margin entire, not dissected or lobed, apex acuminate, venation pinnate, secondary veins open, prominent, intramarginal veins absent; lower surface green or brown rusty-coloured, upper surface pale green or green, oil dots absent, domatia absent; stipules present, free, laterally placed, not encircling the twig, leafy, not fringed, large, not persistent.

Flowers: Inflorescence axillary, flowers single, bisexual, with pedicel, with many planes of symmetry, 40–45 mm long, large, 30–35 mm diam.; perianth present, with distinct sepals and petals, yellow; inner perianth 5, free; stamens many, filaments present, joined, free of perianth; ovary superior, carpels joined, locules 5; styles joined, 1.

Fruits: single, brown, not spiny, non-fleshy, simple, dehiscent, capsule. Seeds many.

Distribution: Madang.

Fig. 329. *Thespesia fisscalyx*. Bark, old flowers and leaves

Thespesia patellifera Borss.Waalk.

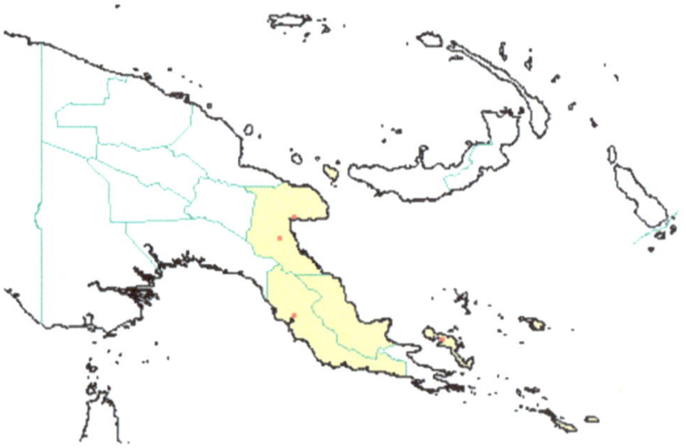

Blumea Vol. Supplement 4: 154 (1958)
Timber Group: Non-timber species

Field Characters: Canopy trees, up to 30(–40) m high, or subcanopy trees; bole cylindrical 25–50 cm diam., straight, up to 25 m long; buttresses absent or sometimes present; spines absent; aerial roots absent; stilt roots absent. Bark red, brownish grey, or pale brown, rough, peeling, fissured, or pustular; lenticels irregular or elongated vertically; bark (5–)10–13 mm thick; under-bark yellow, green, or pink; strongly aromatic or faintly or non-aromatic; pleasant; blaze consisting of one layer, white or pale yellow (straw-coloured), markings absent or with stripes (stripes brownish), fibrous; exudate present, colourless, not readily flowing, changing to dark grey on exposure to air or not changing colour, not sticky. Terminal buds not enclosed by leaves.

Indumentum: Complex hairs present, disk-shaped or star-like; stinging hairs absent; mature twig hairy or mature twig without hairs; hairs sparse.

Leaves: Spaced along branches, leaves spiral, simple; petiole present, not winged, attached to base of leaf lamina, not swollen; lamina equally broad throughout much of length or broadest below middle, (7.5–)10–20 cm long, (5.5–)9–15 cm wide; base symmetric (shallowly cordate), margin entire, not dissected or lobed, apex shortly acuminate, venation pinnate or at base palmate, secondary veins open, prominent, intramarginal veins absent; lower surface pale green or green, upper surface dark green or dull green or glossy, hairs absent or present when young (near base and along midvein of lower surface), sparse, oil dots absent, domatia absent; stipules present, free, laterally placed, not encircling the twig, leafy, not fringed, large, not persistent.

Flowers: Inflorescence axillary, flowers single, bisexual, with pedicel, with many planes of symmetry, 10–12 mm long, large, 10–12 mm diam.; perianth present, with distinct sepals and petals (sepals completely joined together to form a collar, densely hairy, inner surface densely covered with long straight hairs), yellow or dark red at base; inner perianth 5, free or some or partly joined (fused at base to staminal tube); stamens many, filaments present (of different lengths), joined (forming a staminal tube), joined to perianth (to base of corolla); ovary superior, carpels joined, locules 5; styles joined, 1.

Fruits: single, 10–15 mm long, brown, not spiny, non-fleshy, simple, dehiscent, capsule. Seeds many, c. 10 mm long, as wide as long, c. 10 mm diam., not winged.

Distribution: Morobe, Western, Central, Milne Bay, Papuan Islands.

Thespesia populnea (L.) Correa
Fig. 330

Annales du Museum National d'Histoire Naturelle Vol. 9: 290 (1807)
Timber Group: Non-timber species

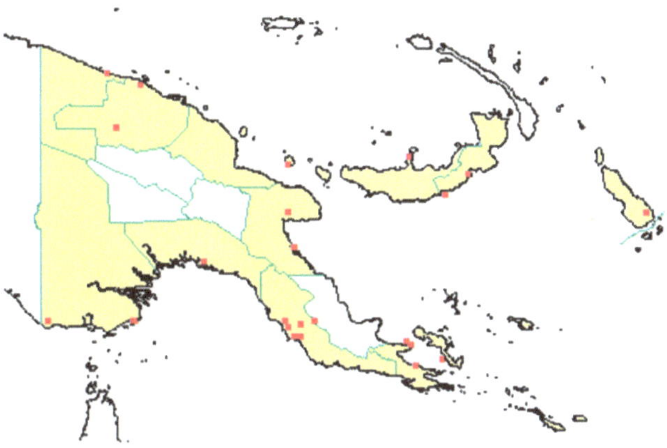

Field Characters: Subcanopy trees, usually 10–15 m high, or shrub, with open to dense spreading crown; bole cylindrical, up to 20 cm diam., straight, up to 5 m long; buttresses absent; spines absent; aerial roots absent; stilt roots absent. Bark pale brownish grey, slightly rough, slightly peeling, pustular; lenticels irregular or elongated vertically; bark thin, < 5 mm thick; under-bark green; blaze consisting of one layer, cream-coloured (straw-coloured) with broad pale pink-brown stripes, fibrous; exudate present, white, not readily flowing, not changing colour on exposure to air, not sticky. Terminal buds not enclosed by leaves.

Indumentum: Complex hairs present, disk-shaped or star-like; stinging hairs absent; mature twig without hairs.

Leaves: Spaced along branches, leaves spiral, simple; petiole present, almost as long as lamina, not winged, attached to base of leaf lamina, not swollen; lamina broadest below middle (triangular heart-shaped), 7–23 cm long, 5–16 cm wide; base symmetric (broadly cordate), margin entire, not dissected or lobed, apex shortly acuminate, venation pinnate or at base palmate, secondary veins open, prominent, 5–7, pale yellow, intramarginal veins absent; lower surface pale green or green, upper surface mid to dark green, hairs absent, oil dots absent, domatia absent; stipules present, free, not persistent.

Flowers: Inflorescence axillary, flowers single, bisexual, with pedicel, with many planes of symmetry, bell-shaped, 60–80 mm long, large, 70–80 mm diam.; perianth present, with distinct sepals and petals inner surface densely covered with long straight hairs), yellow or dark red at base; inner perianth 5, partly joined to form a corolla tube, pale yellow, white or cream-coloured, often with maroon-coloured centre (older flowers becoming dark pink) and 5 red spots at base; stamens many, filaments present, joined; ovary superior, carpels joined, locules 5; styles joined, 1.

Fruits: single, globular or pear-shaped, 20–50 mm long, brown or grey-brown (can be densely hairy with brown hairs), smooth, not spiny, non-fleshy, simple, dehiscent, capsule (5 parts when mature), with abundant yellow sticky exudate. Seeds many, each locule of capsule contains 3 or 4 white seeds, 12–15 mm long, slightly longer than wide, 8–9 mm across, slightly flattened., not winged.

Distribution: West Sepik, East Sepik, Madang, Morobe, Western, Gulf, Central, Milne Bay, Papuan Islands, New Britain, Bougainville.

Fig. 330. *Thespesia populnea*. Bark, leaves, fruit, seeds and flowers

Santalales

PNG families: Aptandraceae, Loranthaceae, Olacaceae, Opiliaceae, **Santalaceae,** Ximeniaceae

1a. Thorns present, with branches usually spiny....*Ximenia americana* L. (Ximeniaceae) (not treated here)

1b. Thorns and spines absent 2

2a. Plants usually attached to host trees by haustoria; ovary inferior or superior, with 1– many locules; fruits berry-like, with many seeds .... Loranthaceae (not treated here)

2b. Root parasites; ovary superior or half-inferior, with 1 locule; fruits a drupe, with 1 seed 3

3a. Leaves with venation ± parallel to palmate; fruits fleshy, drupe; stamens free .... (*Exocarpos latifolius*) 65. Santalaceae

3b. Leaves with venation pinnate; fruits dry, non-fleshy and nut-like or a drupe; stamens joined to form a staminal tube around style 5

5a. Stamens twice as many as petals; petals 3 .... Opiliaceae (not treated here)

5b. Stamens as many as petals; petals 4 or 5, rarely as few as 3 6

6a. Stamens 3–15, as many as or twice number of petals (*Olax* with petals 3) .... Olacaceae (not treated here)

6b. Stamens 4–7; petals 4 or 5 7

7a. Stamens 5–7; petals 5 .... (*Anacolosa papuana*) 64. Aptandraceae

7b. Stamens 4 or 5, as many as number of petals; petals 4 or 5 .... 64. Aptandraceae

64. Aptandraceae

Trees and shrubs, with branches often somewhat zig-zag. Stipules absent. Leaves well-developed, spiral, simple, not dissected or lobed; margin entire; venation one-veined or pinnate. Inflorescences axillary. Bracts absent. Flowers bisexual or unisexual, then plant monoecious or dioecious, regular, with distinct calyx and corolla. Sepals 4 or 5. Petals 4 or 5, free or joined, at least in part; tube absent or present. Stamens 4 or 5, fused, forming a tube around the style; filaments present; staminodes absent. Gynoecium with carpels at least partially joined, partially inferior or usually superior; locules usually 2; styles joined. Fruit simple, indehiscent, nut-like, dry, at least non-fleshy. Seeds without wings.

PNG genus: ***Anacolosa***

Reference: Tipot (1995)

Notes: Previously included in the family Olacaceae. In Papua New Guinea, the Olacaceae now consists of the pantropical genus *Olax* (*O. imbricata* Roxb. – climbing shrubs), with *Ximenia*, a pantropical to warm temperate genus (*X. americana* L. – a thorny, erect shrub on beaches), being transferred to the largely New World family Ximeniaceae

Anacolosa papuana G.Schellenb.
Fig. 331

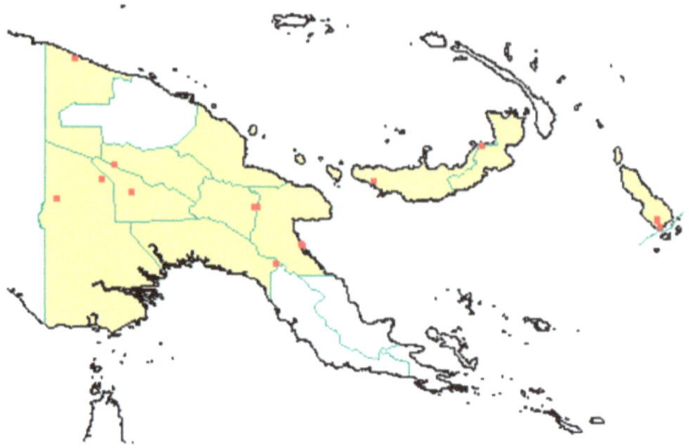

Botanische Jahrbücher für Systematik, Pflanzengeschichte und Pflanzengeographie Vol. 58: 157 (1923)
Timber Group: Non-timber species

Field Characters: Subcanopy trees, up to 15 m high; bole cylindrical, straight, with branches slightly zig-zag; buttresses absent; spines absent; aerial roots absent; stilt roots absent. Bark brown, rough, slightly pustular; lenticels irregular; bark 3–4 mm thick; under-bark red; faintly or non-aromatic; blaze consisting of one layer, red or brown, markings absent, granular without splinters; exudate present, colourless, not readily flowing, changing to brown on exposure to air, slightly sticky. Terminal buds not enclosed by leaves.

Indumentum: Complex hairs absent; stinging hairs absent; mature twigs without hairs.

Leaves: Spaced along branches, leaves spiral, simple; petiole 3–8 mm long, not winged, attached to base of leaf lamina, not swollen; lamina broadest at or near middle, 12–15.5 cm long, 4.5–6.5 cm wide; base symmetric, margin entire, not dissected or lobed, apex obtuse, venation pinnate, secondary veins open, prominent, forming distinct loops inside margin, intramarginal veins absent; lower surface pale green, upper surface green, hairs absent, oil dots absent, domatia absent; stipules absent.

Flowers: Inflorescence axillary, flowers arising from a single point, with 2–8 in each cluster; flowers bisexual, with many planes of symmetry, with pedicel 0.5–2 mm long; perianth present, with distinct sepals and petals; calyx cup-like, c. 3 mm diam.; inner perianth (petals) 5, joined, 2–4 mm long, c. 1 mm wide; stamens 5–7, joined to each other, filaments flat, anthers bearded at apex; carpels joined, with disc cup-like; ovary broadest below middle; styles joined, very short, 1.

Fruits: Arising from a single point, not spiny, simple, glossy red, almost globular to slightly broadest above middle, 15–35 mm long, 13–25 mm diam., not fleshy, indehiscent, nut-like, apex depressed; calyx persistent. Seed 1, not winged.

Distribution: West Sepik, Madang, Morobe, Western Highlands, Eastern Highlands, Western, Southern Highlands, Gulf, New Britain, Bougainville.

Fig. 331. *Anacolosa papuana*. Leaves, immature fruit and bark

65. Santalaceae

Trees, shrubs, and herbs. Stipules absent. Leaves well-developed or much reduced, spiral or usually opposite, simple, not dissected or lobed; margin entire; venation one-veined or pinnate. Inflorescences axillary or terminal. Bracts present. Flowers bisexual or unisexual, then plant monoecious or dioecious, regular, with tepals (not readily resolvable as calyx and/or corolla), usually sepaline or with petals absent. Sepals (3 or)4 or 5(–8). Stamens (3 or)4 or 5(–8), free; filaments present; staminodes absent. Gynoecium with carpels at least partially joined, partially inferior or inferior; styles partially or fully joined or absent. Fruit simple, indehiscent, drupe or nut, dry, at least non-fleshy, or fleshy. Seeds without wings.

PNG genera: *Cladomyza, Dendromyza, Dendrotrophe,* ***Exocarpos****, Santalum, Scleropyrum*

References: Danser (1940, 1955), Der and Nickrent (2008)

1a. Ovary superior; flowers spike-like, mostly unisexual; fruiting stalk (pedicel) enlarged and succulent .. .. *Exocarpos*

1b. Ovary inferior or semi-inferior; flowers in cymes or panicles; fruiting stalk not enlarged.................. 2

2a. Ovary semi-inferior; flowers in cymes or panicles; leaves often opposite; perianth parts with a tuft of hairs behind stamens; trees or shrubs, root parasites .... *Santalum* (not treated here)

2b. Ovary inferior; flowers in umbel-like clusters or in racemes; leaves spiral... 3

3a. Leaves all reduced to triangular scales or up to 1.5 mm long .... *Dendromyza* (not treated here)

3b. Leaves normal, at least 3 mm long, but leaves reduced to scales on climbing branchlets 4

4a. Stem parasites only attacking host plant with primary haustoria (mistletoe-type), with swollen base at point of attachment 5

4b. Stem parasites with secondary haustoria at their axes, or root parasites... 6

5a. Endocarp and seed covered with rounded lobes................................. *Dendrotrophe* (not treated here)

5b. Endocarp surface smooth; seeds only covered at base with lobes............. *Cladomyza* (not treated here)

6a. Terrestrial or root parasites, or rarely stem parasites............................ *Dendrotrophe* (not treated here)

6b. Stem parasites with secondary haustoria at their axes.. 7

7a. Endocarp and seed round in cross-section .... *Dendromyza* (not treated here)

7b. Endocarp and seed star-shaped in cross-section, or base with lobes.......... *Cladomyza* (not treated here)

***Exocarpos latifolius* R.Br.**
Fig. 332

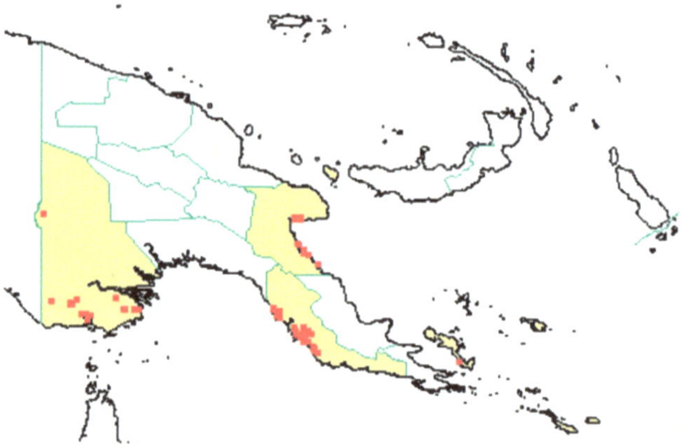

Prodromus Florae Novae Hollandiae 356 (1810)
Timber Group: Non-timber species

Field Characters: Subcanopy trees, (2–)3–15 m high, hemiparasitic; bole markedly fluted, 18–20 cm diam., straight, 2–9 m long; buttresses shortly present; spines absent; aerial roots absent; stilt roots absent. Bark dark brown or black, rough, slightly scaly or flaky or slightly tessellated; bark 1–2 mm thick; under-bark red or brown; faintly or non-aromatic; blaze consisting of one layer, brown, markings absent, fibrous; exudate present, colourless, not readily flowing, not changing colour on exposure to air, not sticky. Terminal buds not enclosed by leaves.

Indumentum: Complex hairs absent; stinging hairs absent; mature twig without hairs.

Leaves: Spaced along branches, leaves simple; petiole present, not winged, attached to base of leaf lamina, not swollen; lamina broadest at or near middle, 6–7.5 cm long, 2.5–3 cm wide; base very asymmetric, margin entire, not dissected or lobed, apex sub-acute, venation parallel-veined, secondary veins open, not prominent, but visible, intramarginal veins absent; lower surface pale green or dull green, upper surface dull green, hairs absent, oil dots absent, domatia absent; stipules absent.

Flowers: Inflorescence axillary or leaf-opposed, with flowers on unbranched or sometimes branched axes; flowers bisexual, with pedicel absent or very short, with many planes of symmetry, 0.5–1 mm long, small, c. 0.5 mm diam., white, cream-coloured, yellow, or yellowish green, with all sepals and/or petals (hence tepals) similar (petals absent), 5, free, ± triangular; stamens 5, filaments present, free, free of perianth; ovary superior, carpels joined, locules 1; styles 1, very short.

Fruits: single, 10–15 mm long, 8–9 mm diam., red, not spiny, fleshy, simple, indehiscent, drupe, fruiting pedicel enlarged. Seed 1, c. 8 mm long, as wide as long, c. 7 mm diam., not winged.

Distribution: Morobe, Western, Central, Papuan Islands.

Fig. 332. *Exocarpos latifolius.* Bark, leaves and fruit

Cornales

PNG families: Cornaceae, Hydrangeaceae, **Nyssaceae**

66. Nyssaceae

Trees and shrubs. Stipules absent. Leaves well-developed, opposite to sub-opposite or spiral, simple, not dissected or lobed; margin toothed or entire; venation pinnate. Inflorescences terminal. Bracts present or absent. Flowers unisexual or bisexual, then plant dioecious, regular, usually with distinct calyx and corolla (calyx small) or sometimes perianth absent. Sepals 4 or 5. Petals 4 or 5, free; tube absent. Stamens 4 or 5(–25), free; filaments present; staminodes absent. Gynoecium with carpels at least partially joined, inferior; styles partially or fully joined. Fruit simple, indehiscent, drupe, fleshy. Seeds without wings.

PNG genera: ***Mastixia***

References: Kostermans (1982), Matthews (1976), Yaoli *et al.* (2002)

Mastixia kaniensis Melch.
Fig. 333

Botanische Jahrbücher für Systematik, Pflanzengeschichte und Pflanzengeographie Vol. 60: 172 (1925)
Timber Group: Non-timber species

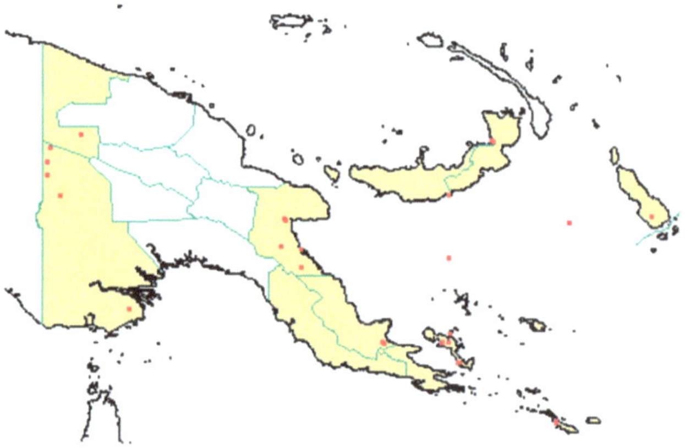

Field Characters: Canopy trees, 25–35 m high; bole cylindrical, up to 60 cm diam., straight, up to 25 m long; buttresses absent; spines absent; aerial roots absent; stilt roots absent. Bark grey or brown, rough, slightly scaly or flaky, fissured, or slightly furrowed cork; bark c. 15 mm thick; under-bark yellow or green; faintly or non-aromatic; pleasant (aroma like sugar-cane); blaze consisting of one layer, pale orange, brown, or grey, markings absent, fibrous; exudate present, pale yellow (slightly golden-coloured) or colourless, not readily flowing, not changing colour on exposure to air, sticky. Terminal buds not enclosed by leaves.

Indumentum: Complex hairs absent; stinging hairs absent; mature twig without hairs.

Leaves: Spaced along branches, leaves opposite to subopposite, simple; petiole present, not winged, attached to base of leaf lamina, not swollen; lamina broadest above middle or sometimes broadest at or near middle, (7–)12–15 cm long, (2.5–)5.5–6.5 cm wide; base symmetric, margin entire, not dissected or lobed, apex shortly acuminate, venation pinnate, secondary veins open, prominent, intramarginal veins absent; lower surface pale green, upper surface dark glossy green, hairs absent, oil dots absent, domatia absent; stipules absent.

Flowers: Inflorescence terminal, flowers on a branched axis; flowers bisexual, with pedicel, with many planes of symmetry, 4–6 mm long, small, 5–8 mm diam.; perianth present, with distinct sepals and petals, white, pale yellow, or pale green; inner perianth 5, free; stamens 5, filaments present, free of each other, free of perianth; ovary inferior, carpels joined, locules 1; styles joined, 1.

Fruits: arranged on branched axis, fruit 20–28 mm long, dark blue or purple (when mature), not spiny, fleshy, simple, indehiscent, drupe. Seed 1, c. 10 mm long, longer than wide, 6–8 mm diam., not winged.

Distribution: West Sepik, East Sepik, Morobe, Western, Central, Northern, Milne Bay, Papuan Islands, New Britain, Bougainville.

Notes: The taxon that occurs in Papua New Guinea is *Mastixia kaniensis* Melch. subsp. *kaniensis*. The genus *Mastixia* was previously classified in the family Cornaceae.

Fig. 333. *Mastixia kaniensis*. Bark, leaves and fruit

Ericales

PNG Families: Actinidiaceae, Balsaminaceae, Clethraceae, **Ebenaceae,** Ericaceae, **Lecythidaceae,** Mitrastemonaceae, **Pentaphylacaceae**, **Primulaceae**, **Sapotaceae**, **Styracaceae**, **Symplocaceae**, **Theaceae**

1a. Small herb 2

1b. Woody shrubs, trees or lianas 3

2a. Small root parasitic herb (often on *Castanopsis*); leaves scale-like; flowers single, terminal, without spur .... (*Mitrastemon*) Mitrastemonaceae (not treated here)

2b. Fleshy her, non-parasitic; leaves normal; flowers held upside-down, with spur .... (*Impatiens*) Balsaminaceae (not treated here)

3a. Ovary inferior or partly inferior........ 4

3b. Ovary superior 6

4a. Flowers small, 4–5 mm diam., on branched axes; style 4–5 mm long, not exserted beyond stamens... .... 72. Symplocaceae

4b. Flowers large and showy, on unbranched axes or solitary; style long, exserted beyond stamens 5

5a. Stamens at least 40, joined together........ 67. Lecythidaceae

5b. Stamens 10, free .... Ericaceae (not treated here)

6a. Flowers unisexual 7

6b. Flowers bisexual........ 13

7a. Male flowers on separate plants to female flowers (plants dioecious) 8

7b. Male and female flowers on the same plant (plants monoecious) 10

8a. Leaves with toothed margin; flowers large 12– to at least 45 mm long; stamens joined to each other; fruit without calyx........ 75. Actinidiaceae

8b. Leaves with entire margin; flowers usually < 10 mm long; stamens free of each other; fruit with calyx persistent 9

9a. Corolla not waxy, distinctly tubular with 4 or 5 lobes; stamens with all whorls attached to corolla; wood hard, black........ 70. Ebenaceae

9b. Corolla thick, waxy, fused at base, with 5 lobes, irregularly splitting to appear like separate petals; stamens with outer whorl attached to base of corolla; wood cream-coloured, pink to orange-brown, not black........ (*Ternstroemia*) 73. Theaceae

10a. Leaves with dark, often black, round to elongate oil dots on lamina; fruits with 1 seed........ 71. Primulaceae (subfamily Maesoideae and subfamily Myrsinoideae)

10b. Leaves without oil dots; fruits with many seeds 11

11a. Stamens mostly 4 or 5(or 6)...... 71. Primulaceae (subfamily Maesoideae and subfamily Myrsinoideae)

11b. Stamens at least 10, usually much more 12

12a. Corolla thick, waxy, fused at base, with 5 lobes, irregularly splitting to appear like separate petals; stamens with outer whorl attached to base of corolla; spines absent .... 73. Theaceae

12b. Corolla not noticeably thickened, not waxy, free, with 5 petals; stamens not joined to corolla; sharp to blunt spines often present .... 75. Actinidiaceae

13a. Flowers without bracteoles 14

13b. Flowers with bracteoles 16

14a. Fruits usually with many seeds; flowers solitary or flowers arranged in heads, umbels or panicles; stamens usually 5 .... 71. Primulaceae (subfamily Primuloideae)

14b. Fruits with 1– few seeds; flowers arranged in racemes, cymes or panicles, sometimes solitary; stamens 4 or at least 8 15

15a. Stamens 4, occasionally 5 or 6; leaves with dark, often black, round to elongate oil dots on lamina; fruits with 1 seed .... 71. Primulaceae (subfamily Maesoideae and subfamily Myrsinoideae)

15a. Stamens 8–10 to at least 20 or more; leaves without dark oil dots; fruits 1– few seeds .... 74. Styracaceae

16a. Stamens <10 17

16b. Stamens 10 or more 18

17a. Stamens 5; anthers dehiscing by pores .... 68. Pentaphylacaceae

17b. Stamens mostly 5–10; anthers dehiscing by longitudinal slits .... 69. Sapotaceae

18a. Fruits with 1–5 seeds .... 69. Sapotaceae

18b. Fruits with many seeds 19

19a. Corolla thick, waxy, fused at base, with 5 lobes, irregularly splitting to appear like separate petals; stamens with outer whorl attached to base of corolla; spines often present .... 73. Theaceae

19b. Corolla not noticeably thickened, not waxy, free, with 5 lobes or with 5 free petals; stamens not joined or joined to corolla; sharp to blunt spines often present or absent 20

20a. Stipules present, minute; stamens usually at least 18, rarely as few as 10; styles 1–many .... 75. Actinidiaceae

20b. Stipules absent; stamens 10; styles 1 21

21a. Leaves spaced along branchlets; anthers not inverted at anthesis, dehiscing by longitudinal slit or apical pores; hairs simple or complex; flowers arranged in spikes, racemes or panicles; ovary with 1–10 locules .... Ericaceae (not treated here)

21b. Leaves clustered at ends of branchlets; anthers inverted at anthesis, usually by apical pores; usually covered with spares to dense stellate hairs; flowers arranged in slender racemes; ovary with 3 locules .... (*Clethra*) Clethraceae (not treated here)

67. Lecythidaceae

Trees. Stipules absent. Leaves well-developed, spiral, simple, not dissected or lobed; margin entire; venation pinnate. Inflorescences terminal, ramiflorous/cauliflorous, or axillary; Flowers bisexual, regular, slightly irregular, zygomorphic, or asymmetric, with distinct calyx and corolla. Sepals 4–6. Petals 4–6, free or joined, at least in part; tube absent or present. Stamens 40–many, fused; filaments present; staminodes absent or present. Gynoecium with carpels at least partially joined, partially inferior or inferior; styles partially or fully joined. Fruit simple, dehiscent or indehiscent, capsule, berry, dry, at least non-fleshy, or fleshy. Seeds without wings.

PNG genera: ***Barringtonia, Planchonia***

References: Payen (1967)

1a. Bracteoles small, not persistent; calyx tube not or hardly extended above ovary; flowers rarely in erect racemes, if so, then pedicels longer than 10 mm, mostly in flaccid, dropping racemes or spikes; flowers usually white or red .... *Barringtonia*

1b. Bracteoles large, not falling off before corolla; calyx tube extended above ovary; flowers in erect racemes; pedicels <10 mm long; petals pale green, often flushed with red; stamens red in lower half, white above .... *Planchonia*

Barringtonia apiculata Lauterb.
Fig. 334

Botanische Jahrbücher für Systematik, Pflanzengeschichte und Pflanzengeographie 57(3): 350 (1922)
Timber Group: Commercial hardwoods

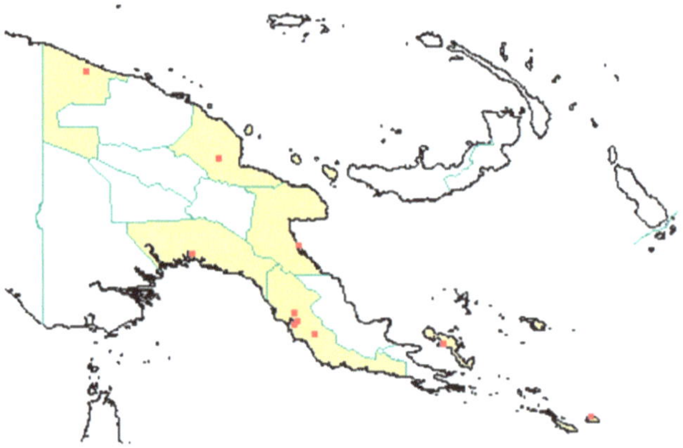

Field Characters: Canopy trees, up to 45 m high; bole cylindrical, up to 55 cm diam., straight, up to 30 m long; buttresses present; spines absent; aerial roots absent; stilt roots absent. Bark brown, rough, tessellated; lenticels elongated vertically; bark 15 mm thick; under-bark brown; faintly or non-aromatic; blaze consisting of one layer, pink or mixed colours, markings absent, fibrous; exudate absent. Terminal buds not enclosed by leaves.

Indumentum: Complex hairs absent; stinging hairs absent; mature twig without hairs.

Leaves: Spaced along branches, leaves sub-opposite or spiral, simple; petiole present, not winged, attached to base of leaf lamina, not swollen or slightly swollen towards base; lamina broadest at or near middle; base symmetric, margin entire, not dissected or lobed, apex obtuse, acuminate, or rounded, venation pinnate, secondary veins open, prominent, intramarginal veins absent; lower surface green, upper surface green, hairs absent, oil dots absent, domatia absent; stipules absent.

Flowers: Inflorescence terminal, flowers on an unbranched axis; flowers bisexual, with pedicel, with many planes of symmetry perianth present, with distinct sepals and petals; stamens many, filaments present, joined, free of perianth; ovary inferior, carpels joined, styles joined, 1.

Fruits: arranged on unbranched axis, not spiny, simple, indehiscent, drupe.

Distribution: West Sepik, East Sepik, Madang, Morobe, Gulf, Central, Milne Bay, Papuan Islands.

Fig. 334. *Barringtonia apiculata*. Leaves, developing fruit and bark

Barringtonia asiatica (L.) Kurz
Figs 335, 336

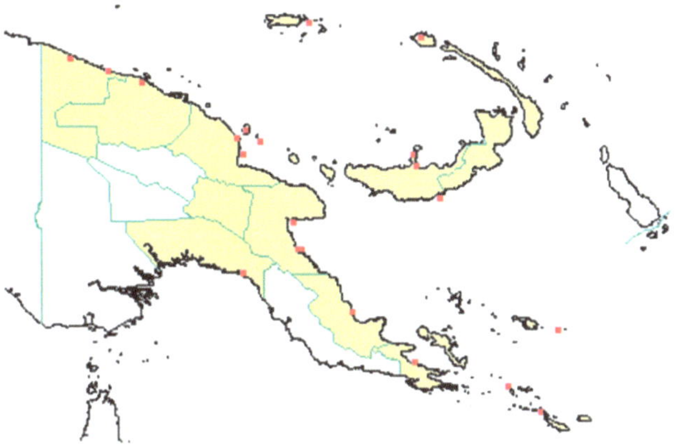

Preliminary Report on the Forest and Other Vegetation of Pegu, Appendix A 65 (1875)
Timber Group: Occasional timber species

Field Characters: Subcanopy trees, 15–20 m high; bole slightly cylindrical irregular, 30 cm diam., crooked often leaning, up to 5 m high; buttresses absent; spines absent; aerial roots absent; stilt roots absent. Bark dark brown, slightly rough, slightly scaly or flaky or slightly pustular; lenticels elongated vertically or irregular; bark 10–15 mm thick; under-bark red or brown; faintly or non-aromatic; pleasant turpentine-like or legume-like; blaze consisting of 2 layers outer very thin; outer blaze white, pale yellow, red patches, or green patches, with stripes straw-coloured, fibrous; inner blaze white or pale yellow, with stripes straw-coloured, fibrous; exudate absent. Terminal buds not enclosed by leaves.

Indumentum: Complex hairs absent; stinging hairs absent; mature twig without hairs.

Leaves: Spaced along branches, leaves sub-opposite or spiral, simple; petiole absent lamina decurrent; lamina broadest above middle, 16(new growth) –38 cm long, 8.5–15 cm wide; base symmetric, margin entire, not dissected or lobed, apex sub-rounded or obtuse, venation pinnate, secondary veins open, prominent, intramarginal veins absent; lower surface dull pale green to subglossy, upper surface dull green to subglossy, hairs absent, oil dots absent, domatia absent; stipules absent.

Flowers: Inflorescence terminal, flowers on an unbranched axis or flowers on a branched axis; flowers bisexual, with pedicel 40–50 mm long, with one plane of symmetry, 90–150 mm long, large, 90–150 mm (including anthers); perianth present, with distinct sepals and petals, white or cream-coloured; inner perianth 5, free; stamens many (white basally, red distally), filaments present, joined, free of perianth; ovary inferior, carpels joined, locules 1; styles joined, 1.

Fruits: arranged on unbranched or branched axis, fruit 100–140 mm long, c. 100 mm diam., fruit green or brown when mature (4- or 5-angled), not spiny, non-fleshy corky tissue surrounding the seed, simple, indehiscent, drupe. Seeds 1 (surrounded by fibrous fruit wall), 60–80 mm long, as wide as long or usually longer than wide, 40–50 mm wide, not winged.

Distribution: West Sepik, East Sepik, Madang, Morobe, Eastern Highlands, Gulf, Northern, Milne Bay, Papuan Islands, New Britain, New Ireland, Manus.

Fig. 335. *Barringtonia asiatica*. Bark, flowers, fruit and seed

Fig. 336. *Barringtonia asiatica*. Developing fruit and flowers

Barringtonia calyptrata (R.Br. ex Meirs) R.Br. ex F.M.Bailey Fig. 337

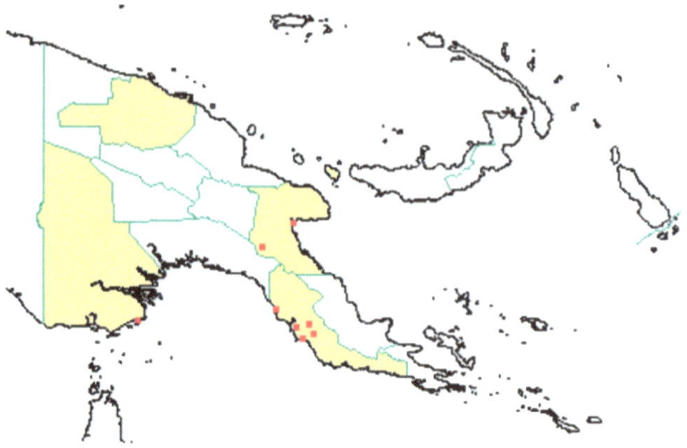

Queensland Agricultural Journal Vol. 18: 125 (1907)
Timber Group: Occasional timber species

Field Characters: Subcanopy trees, up to 20 m high, often heavily branched; bole cylindrical, up to 10 cm diam., straight, up to 5 m long; buttresses absent; spines absent; aerial roots absent; stilt roots absent. Bark pale to medium grey to dark brown, thick, rough, deeply fissured (furrowed), fibrous, with pustules irregular, rounded; bark 20–30 mm thick; strongly aromatic; pine-like slight antiseptic odour; blaze consisting of one layer, pale pink to red-brown, speckled fibrous; exudate absent. Terminal buds not enclosed by leaves.

Indumentum: Complex hairs absent; stinging hairs absent; mature twig without hairs.

Leaves: clustered towards distal end of branches, leaves spiral, simple; petiole present, 5–20(–30) mm long, not winged, attached to base of leaf lamina, not swollen; lamina broadest below middle, or at or near middle, (10–)15–35(–39) cm long, (2–)5–13 cm wide; base symmetric, tapering, margin entire, not dissected or lobed, apex obtuse, sometimes cuspidate or emarginate, venation pinnate, secondary veins open, prominent, intramarginal veins prominent; lower surface pale green or green, upper surface green (old leaves turn red prior to falling), hairs absent, oil dots absent, domatia absent; stipules absent.

Flowers: Inflorescence on the trunk or branches, pendulous, flowers on an unbranched axis up to 25 cm long; flowers bisexual, non-aromatic or fragrant, not stalked, with many planes of symmetry, c. 20 mm long, large, c. 20 mm diam.; perianth present, with distinct sepals and petals sepals reduced to collar, cream-coloured; calyx completely fused in bud, shed as a cap or rupturing as 4 irregular lobes; inner perianth 4(or 5), 1–3 cm long, pale yellow to cream-coloured (once recorded as deep red), free; stamens many, filaments present, joined (staminodes present, joined), free of perianth; ovary inferior, carpels joined, locules (2–)3 or 4; styles joined, 1, yellow-white, thick, terete.

Fruits: arranged on unbranched axis, not spiny, fleshy, simple, ovoid to spindle-shaped, 5–9.5 cm long, 4–6.5 cm wide, indehiscent, berry. Seed 1, subglobular, c. 20 mm long, slightly longer than wide, not winged.

Distribution: East Sepik, Morobe, Western, Central.

Notes: Anonymous (without date-a) regarded *Barringtonia edulis* as a synonym of *B. calyptrata*; however, these are here both regarded as distinct species with several morphological differences discussed by Payen (1967). *Barringtonia calyptrata* is characterised by its thick, rough, furrowed, dark brown to grey bark and coriaceous (leathery) leaves, with margin entire and apex usually obtuse (cf. *B. edulis* has almost smooth grey-brown bark and chartaceous leaves, with margin serrate-crenulate towards the acuminate apex). Although both species are many-flowered, *B. calyptrata* tends to be more floriferous; the flowers of *B. calyptrata* are sessile (cf. *B. edulis* which has a pedicel 5–10 mm long); calyx closed, at anthesis rupturing into a caducous cap 3–8 mm long and a persistent cup-shaped ring c. 2–3 mm high, rarely disrupting into 4 irregular segments c. 5–6 mm long (cf. *B. edulis* calyx also closed in bud, but disrupting into 2 or 3 elliptic, obtuse lobes 8–16 mm long); ovary terete, 3–4 mm long and style rather thick, terete, 30–45 mm. long (cf. *B. edulis* has ovary tetragonous (4-sided), 4–7 mm long, and style 45–70 mm long); fruit ovoid or spindle-shaped, 5–9.5 cm long (cf. *B. edulis* has an ellipsoid fruit, 4.5–5 cm long). *Barringtonia calyptrata* occurs in Aru Island, New Guinea and Northern Australia; whereas *B. edulis* is restricted to Fiji (Payen 1967).

Fig. 337. *Barringtonia calyptrata*. Habit, bark, leaves, flower buds and flowers

Barringtonia calyptrocalyx K.Schum. Fig. 338

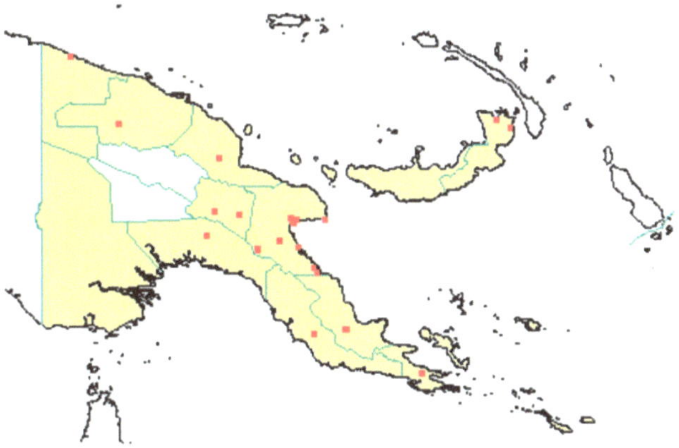

Die Flora von Kaiser Wilhelms Land 91 (1889)
Timber Group: Occasional timber species

Field Characters: Occasional canopy trees, up to 33 m high or subcanopy trees, 10–20 m high; bole cylindrical, straight to 15 m long; buttresses slightly present or absent; spines absent; aerial roots absent; stilt roots absent. Bark light grey to dark, slightly rough or smooth except for folds and fissures, fissured or slightly pustular; bark 18–20 mm thick; strongly aromatic; pine-like slight antiseptic odour; blaze consisting of one layer, pale yellow, speckled yellow and green mottled, smooth; exudate absent. Terminal buds not enclosed by leaves.

Indumentum: Complex hairs absent; stinging hairs absent; mature twig without hairs.

Leaves: clustered towards distal end of branches, leaves spiral, simple; petiole present, 10–15 mm long, not winged, attached to base of leaf lamina, not swollen; lamina broadest above middle, 13–21 cm long, 5–9.5 cm wide; base symmetric tapering, margin entire, not dissected or lobed, apex rounded, venation pinnate, secondary veins open, prominent, intramarginal veins absent; lower surface pale green or green, upper surface pale green or green, hairs absent, oil dots absent, domatia absent; stipules absent.

Fig. 338. *Barringtonia calyptrocalyx*. Habit of juvenile plant and leaves

Flowers: Inflorescence on the trunk or branches, flowers on an unbranched axis; flowers bisexual, not stalked or shortly with pedicel, with many planes of symmetry, c. 20 mm long, large, c. 20 mm diam.; perianth present, with distinct sepals and petals sepals reduced to collar, cream-coloured; inner perianth 5, free; stamens many, filaments present, joined, free of perianth; ovary inferior, carpels joined, locules 2–6; styles joined, 1.

Fruits: arranged on unbranched axis, not spiny, fleshy, simple, indehiscent, berry. Seed 1, longer than wide, not winged.

Distribution: West Sepik, East Sepik, Madang, Morobe, Eastern Highlands, Western, Gulf, Central, Northern, Milne Bay, Papuan Islands, New Britain.

Planchonia papuana R.Knuth Fig. 339

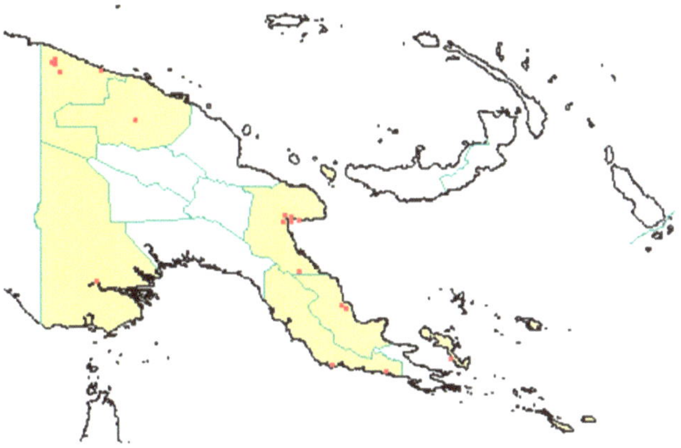

in Engler, H.G.A., Das Pflanzenreich 56 (1939)
Other Literature: J.J. Havel, *Forest Botany, Part 2 Botanical Taxonomy* 226 (1975) Fig. 63.
Timber Group: Occasional timber species
Trade Name: Planchonia

Field Characters: Canopy trees, up to 35 m high; bole cylindrical, 40–100 cm diam., straight, up to 15 m long; buttresses absent or sometimes present; spines absent; aerial roots absent; stilt roots absent. Bark brownish red or light brown, rough or almost smooth, scaly or flaky, fissured, or slightly pustular; lenticels irregular; bark 15–25 mm thick; under-bark pale red (pink); strongly aromatic; pleasant; blaze consisting of one layer, pink, markings absent, very fibrous; exudate absent. Terminal buds not enclosed by leaves.

Indumentum: Complex hairs absent; stinging hairs absent; mature twig without hairs.

Leaves: Spaced along branches, leaves spiral, simple; petiole present, winged (lamina decurrent), attached to base of leaf lamina, not swollen; lamina broadest above middle or occasionally broadest at or near middle when young, (9.5–)11–17 cm long, 6–8 cm wide; base symmetric, margin serrate to dentate (toothed), not dissected or lobed, apex acute, venation pinnate, secondary veins open, prominent, intramarginal veins absent; lower surface pale green or green, upper surface glossy green, hairs absent, oil dots absent, domatia absent; stipules absent.

Fig. 339. *Planchonia papuana*. Bark and leaves

Flowers: Inflorescence terminal, flowers arising from a single point; flowers bisexual, with pedicel, with many planes of symmetry, 75 mm long, large, 60 cm wide; perianth present, with distinct sepals and petals, red or green (with reddish tinge); inner perianth 4 or 5, free; stamens many, filaments present, joined at base to form a staminal ring, free of perianth; ovary inferior, carpels partially joined, by styles, locules 4; styles joined, 1.

Fruits: Arising from a single point, fruit 40–50 mm long, glossy green with sepals and style persistent, not spiny, slightly fleshy, simple, indehiscent, berry. Seeds many (embedded in fleshy pulp), to about 5 mm long, longer than wide, 2–3 mm diam., not winged.

Distribution: West Sepik, East Sepik, Morobe, Western, Central, Northern, Milne Bay, Papuan Islands.

68. Pentaphylacaceae

Trees and shrubs. Stipules absent. Leaves well-developed, spiral, opposite or whorled, simple, not dissected or lobed; margin entire; venation pinnate. Inflorescences axillary or terminal. Bracts present. Flowers bisexual, regular, with distinct calyx and corolla. Sepals 5. Petals 5, free; tube absent. Stamens 5, free; filaments present; staminodes absent. Gynoecium with carpels at least partially joined, superior; styles partially or fully joined. Fruit simple, dehiscent, capsule, dry, at least non-fleshy. Seeds with or without wings.

PNG genera: ***Adinandra***, *Anneslea*, ***Eurya***, ***Ternstroemia***

Notes: *Adinandra, Eurya and Ternstroemia* were previously classified in the family Theaceae. *Archboldiodendron* is included under *Eurya.*

References: Barker (1980, 1982), Royen (1982c)

1a. Branchlets in whorls of (2 or)3–6; leaves in spaced clusters, usually whorled; carpels 1 or 2; fruit irregularly rupturing; seeds 3–30 mm long ..... *Ternstroemia*

1b. Branchlets alternate; leaves ± evenly spaced, alternate; carpels 3–5(or 6); fruit regularly dehiscent capsule or indehiscent berry 2

2a. Leaves opposite; flowers unisexual, 1–25 flowers in axillary clusters; fruits <8 mm long ..... *Eurya*

2b. Leaves alternate; flowers bisexual, 1 or 2 in axils; fruit 15–35 mm long ..... *Adinandra forbesii*

Adinandra forbesii Baker f. Fig. 340

Journal of Botany Vol. 61, Supplement 4: (1923)
Timber Group: Occasional timber species

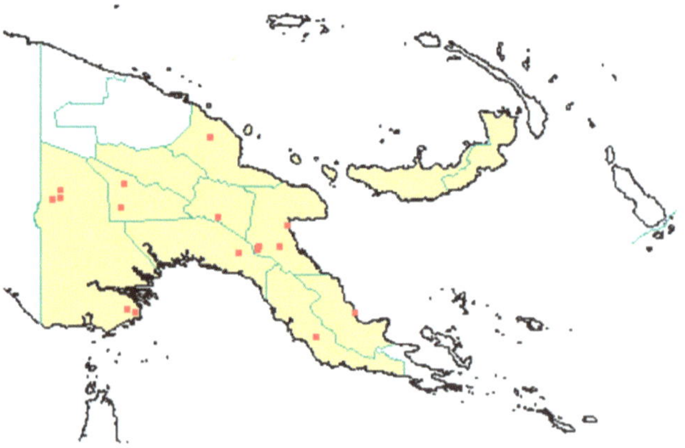

Field Characters: Canopy trees or subcanopy trees, 10–40 m high; bole cylindrical, 20–35(–64) cm diam., straight, 8–25 m long; buttresses absent; spines absent; aerial roots absent; stilt roots absent. Bark brownish grey or dark brown, slightly rough or smooth, scattered pustular; lenticels rounded/swelling; bark 20 mm thick; under-bark red or brown; strongly aromatic; pleasant; blaze consisting of one layer, pale yellow or pink, with stripes orange, fibrous; exudate present, colourless, not readily flowing, slightly changing to light grey on exposure to air, not sticky. Terminal buds not enclosed by leaves.

Indumentum: Complex hairs absent; stinging hairs absent; mature twig without hairs.

Leaves: Spaced along branches, leaves spiral, simple; petiole present, not winged, attached to base of leaf lamina, not swollen; lamina broadest at or near middle, 7–10 cm long, 4–5.5 cm wide; base symmetric, margin entire, not dissected or lobed, apex obtuse or sub-acuminate, venation pinnate, secondary veins open, prominent, intramarginal veins absent; lower surface pale green, upper surface dark glossy green, hairs absent, oil dots absent, domatia absent; stipules absent.

Flowers: Inflorescence axillary, or on branches below leaves, flowers on an unbranched axis; flowers bisexual, with pedicel, with many planes of symmetry, 12–20 mm long, large, 15–25 mm diam.; perianth present, with distinct sepals and petals, white, sometimes dark red, or cream-coloured (with pink-purple to deep red tinge, especially near margin); inner perianth 5, free; stamens many, filaments present, joined, free of perianth; ovary superior, carpels joined, locules 5; styles joined, 1 (base persistent in fruit).

Fruits: arranged on unbranched axis, fruit 20–25 mm long, 15–20 mm diam., dark green (when immature), not spiny, fleshy, simple, indehiscent, drupe. Seeds 5, longer than wide, not winged.

Distribution: Madang, Morobe, Eastern Highlands, Southern Highlands, Western, Gulf, Central, Northern.

Fig. 340 *Adinandra forbesii*. Flowers, leaves and bark

Eurya tigang K.Schum. & Lauterb. Fig. 341

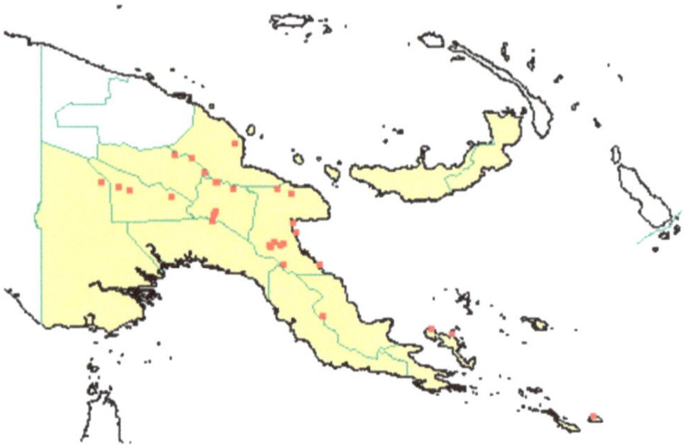

Flora der deutschen Schutzgebiete in der Südsee 447 (1900)
Timber Group: Non-timber species or Occasional timber species

Field Characters: Subcanopy trees, 4 m high; bole cylindrical, 10 cm diam., slightly crooked; buttresses absent; spines absent; aerial roots absent; stilt roots absent. Bark white or grey, rough, slightly fissured or slightly cracked; lenticels elongated vertically; bark 6 mm thick; under-bark green; faintly or non-aromatic; faintly onion-like; blaze consisting of one layer, white or yellow, with stripes, granular without splinters; exudate absent. Terminal buds not enclosed by leaves.

Indumentum: Complex hairs absent; stinging hairs absent.

Leaves: Spaced along branches, leaves spiral, simple; petiole 2–5 mm long, not winged, attached to base of leaf lamina, not swollen; lamina usually broadest at or near middle, sometimes broadest below middle, (3–)6–11 cm long, 2–4.5 cm wide; base symmetric, margin entire or shortly toothed, not dissected or lobed, apex acuminate, venation pinnate, secondary veins open, not prominent, but visible, intramarginal veins absent; lower surface pale green or green, upper surface dark green, hairs absent, oil dots absent, domatia absent; stipules absent.

Flowers: Inflorescence axillary, (often on branchlets below leaves, hence extra-axillary), flowers single, bisexual, with pedicel c. 4 mm long, flowers with many planes of symmetry, 4.5–5.5 mm long, small, 4–5 mm diam.; perianth present, with distinct sepals and petals; inner perianth 5, white, free or some or partly joined at base; stamens 5, filaments present, free of each other, free of perianth; ovary superior, carpels joined, locules 2 or 3; styles joined or free (closely adjacent to each other), 5.

Fruits: single, 5–6 mm long, 5–6 mm diam., red, not spiny, fleshy, simple, indehiscent, berry. Seeds many, c. 0.5 mm long, as wide as long, flattened, not winged.

Distribution: Madang, Morobe, Western Highlands, Eastern Highlands, Southern Highlands, Western, Gulf, Central, Northern, Milne Bay, Papuan Islands, New Britain.

Notes: This species, as currently circumscribed in Papua New Guinea, is morphologically variable and includes many taxa worthy of recognition, few with existing names, that could be applied and none with certainty (W.R. Barker *pers. comm.*, 2019). As described here this species includes plants sometimes named *E. oxysepala* Diels and two varietal manuscript names that have been applied to herbarium specimens at LAE.

Fig. 341 *Eurya tigang.* Bark, leaves and flowers

Ternstroemia britteniana F.Muell.

Journal of Botany Vol. 29: 176 (1891)
Other Literature: W.R. Barker, *Brunonia* Vol. 3: 16–24 (1980) Figs 2–3.
Timber Group: Occasional timber species

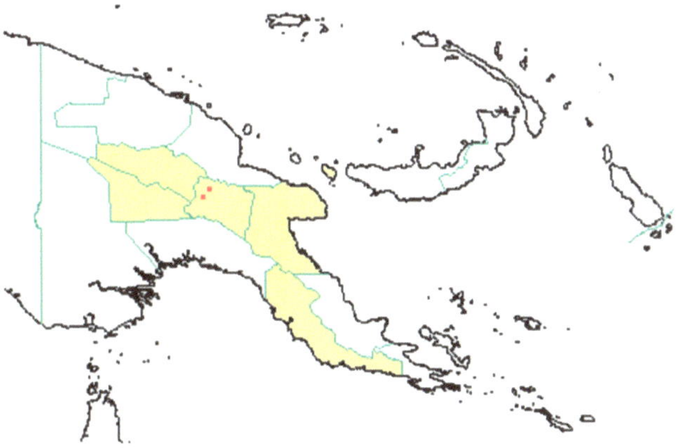

Field Characters: Subcanopy trees, up to 25 m high; bole cylindrical, up to 40 cm diam., straight, up to 10 m long; buttresses absent; spines absent; aerial roots absent; stilt roots absent. Bark brownish red, grey, or brown (sometimes mottled), sometimes rough or smooth, rarely scaly or flaky, slightly fissured, or slightly pustular; lenticels elongated vertically; bark <25 mm thick; under-bark green; faintly or non-aromatic; pleasant (with an aniseed aroma); blaze consisting of one layer, brown, red, or pink, with stripes (yellow and reddish pink streaks); exudate absent. Terminal buds not enclosed by leaves.

Indumentum: Complex hairs absent; stinging hairs absent; mature twig without hairs.

Leaves: Spaced along branches, leaves opposite or usually whorled, 4–7, simple; petiole present, not winged, attached to base of leaf lamina, not swollen; lamina broadest above middle or broadest at or near middle, (1–)2–12 cm long,

(0.5–)1–5(–5.5) cm wide; base symmetric, margin entire, not dissected or lobed, apex acuminate (larger leaves), emarginate or retuse, or rounded, venation pinnate, secondary veins open, occasionally not visible or not prominent, but visible, intramarginal veins absent; lower surface pale green, greenish grey, or yellowish green, upper surface dark green, hairs absent, oil dots absent, domatia absent; stipules absent.

Flowers: Inflorescence axillary, (mostly on branchlets below leaves, hence extra-axillary), flowers single, unisexual (male) or bisexual, with male and female flowers on same plant, flowers with pedicel, with many planes of symmetry, 3.5–8 mm long, small, 5–8 mm diam.; perianth present, with distinct sepals and petals, white, cream-coloured, pale yellow, or slightly pink; inner perianth 5, free or some or partly joined at base; stamens 20–90, filaments present, free of each other, free of perianth; ovary superior, carpels joined, locules 2 or 3; styles joined or free (closely adjacent to each other), 1 or 2(or 3).

Fruits: single, (10–)12–20 mm long, (9–)10–16(–19) mm diam., orange, dark red, or reddish brown, not spiny, non-fleshy, simple, indehiscent (probably rupturing irregularly at maturity), berry. Seeds (absent or)1–14 (in each locule), 5–8(–10) mm long, as wide as long, 3–7 mm diam., not winged.

Distribution: Morobe, Western Highlands, Eastern Highlands, Southern Highlands, Papuan Islands.

Ternstroemia cherryi (F.M.Bailey) Merr. ex F.M.Bailey & C.T.White Fig. 342

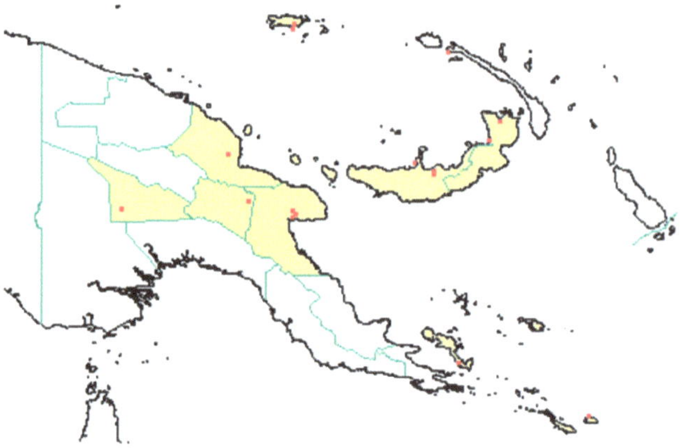

Queensland Department of Agriculture & Stock. Botany Bulletin Vol. 19: 3 (1917)
Other Literature: W.R. Barker, *Brunonia* Vol. 3: 27–32 (1980) Fig. 5.
Timber Group: Non-timber species

Field Characters: Subcanopy trees, up to 20(–25) m high; bole cylindrical, up to 70 cm diam., slightly crooked or straight, up to 10 m long; buttresses absent or sometimes present as low foot buttresses; spines absent; aerial roots absent; stilt roots absent. Bark brown or grey, smooth or rough, fissured, sometimes scaly or flaky, or pustular; lenticels rounded/swelling; bark <25 mm thick; under-bark green, red, or brown; faintly or non-aromatic; blaze consisting of one layer, white, pale yellow (cream-coloured), red, or brown, speckled or with stripes; exudate present, colourless, not readily flowing, changing to pale red or pale brown on exposure to air, not sticky. Terminal buds not enclosed by leaves.

Indumentum: Complex hairs absent; stinging hairs absent; mature twig without hairs.

Leaves: Spaced along branches, leaves whorled or opposite, 3–5, simple; petiole present, not winged, attached to base of leaf lamina, not swollen; lamina broadest above middle or broadest at or near middle, (6–)7–16(–20) cm long, (3–)3.5–8.5 cm wide; base symmetric to slightly asymmetric, margin entire, not dissected or lobed, apex shortly acuminate or obtuse, venation pinnate, secondary veins open, prominent, intramarginal veins absent; lower surface pale green, upper surface green, hairs absent, oil dots present, domatia absent; stipules absent.

Flowers: Inflorescence axillary, (mostly on branchlets below leaves, hence extra-axillary), flowers single, unisexual, with male and female flowers on same plant, with pedicel, with many planes of symmetry, 10–15 mm long, large, 15–20 mm diam.; perianth present, with distinct sepals and petals, white, cream-coloured, or pale yellow; inner perianth 5, some or partly joined at base or free; stamens many, filaments present, free of each other, free of perianth; ovary superior, carpels joined, locules 5; styles joined, 1.

Fruits: single, c. 30 mm long, c. 30 mm diam., yellow or dull orange, not spiny, fleshy, simple, indehiscent, berry. Seeds 4 or 5 (mostly 1 or 2 per locule), 15–20 mm long, longer than wide, c. 10 mm diam., red, not winged.

Distribution: West Sepik, Madang, Morobe, Eastern Highlands, Southern Highlands, Western, Gulf, Central, Northern, Milne Bay, Papuan Islands, New Britain, New Ireland, Manus.

Fig. 342. *Ternstroemia cherryi*. Bark, leaves, fruit and seeds

Ternstroemia merrilliana Kobuski
Fig. 343.

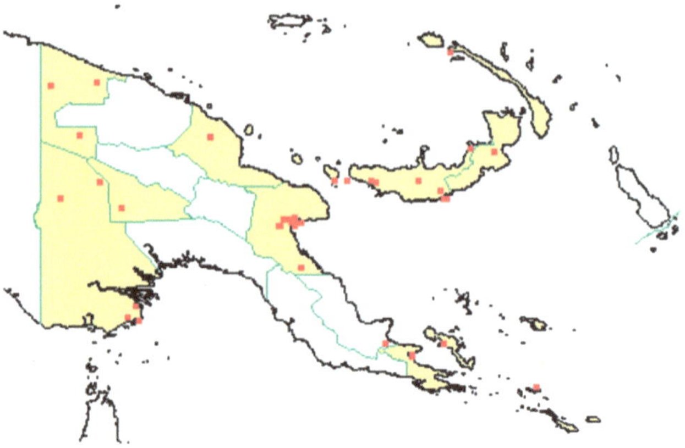

Journal of the Arnold Arboretum Vol. 21: 146 (1940)
Timber Group: Minor hardwoods

Field Characters: Canopy trees, (5–)15–30(–35) m high; bole cylindrical, up to 45 cm diam., straight, up to 20 m long; buttresses absent; spines absent; aerial roots absent; stilt roots absent. Bark brown, rough, pustular; lenticels elongated vertically; bark 10 mm thick; under-bark orange or red; strongly aromatic; pleasant; blaze consisting of one layer or consisting of 2 layers; outer blaze orange or brown, speckled, granular without splinters; inner blaze orange or brown, speckled or with stripes, granular with splinters; exudate present, colourless, not readily flowing, not changing colour on exposure to air, sticky. Terminal buds not enclosed by leaves.

Indumentum: Complex hairs absent; stinging hairs absent; mature twig without hairs.

Leaves: Spaced along branches, leaves spiral, simple; petiole up to 15 mm long, not winged, attached to base of leaf lamina, not swollen; lamina broadest above middle, 14–24 cm long, 6–10 cm wide; base symmetric, margin entire, not dissected or lobed, apex sub-acute, venation pinnate, secondary veins open, not prominent, but visible, intramarginal veins absent; lower surface dark green, upper surface dark green, hairs absent, oil dots absent, domatia absent; stipules absent.

Flowers: Inflorescence axillary, flowers single, unisexual, with male and female flowers on same plant, flowers with pedicel.

Fruits: single, 30–40 mm long, 20–25 mm diam., orange, not spiny, fleshy, simple, indehiscent, drupe. Seeds 3 or 4, about 10 mm long, as wide as long, c. 8 mm diam., not winged.

Distribution: West Sepik, Madang, Morobe, Southern Highlands, Western, Milne Bay, Papuan Islands, New Britain, New Ireland.

Fig. 343. *Ternstroemia merrilliana.* Flowers, leaves and fruits (photograph W.R. Barker)

69. Sapotaceae

Trees and shrubs. Stipules usually present, or sometimes absent. Leaves well-developed, spiral, simple, not dissected or lobed; margin entire; venation pinnate. Inflorescences axillary. Bracts present. Flowers bisexual, usually regular or slightly irregular, with distinct calyx and corolla. Sepals 4–8. Petals 3–10, joined, at least in part; tube present. Stamens 4–15, free; filaments present; staminodes present 2–5. Gynoecium with carpels at least partially joined, superior; styles partially or fully joined. Fruit simple, indehiscent, berry, fleshy. Seeds without wings.

PNG genera: ***Burckella*, *Chrysophyllum*,** *Madhuca, Magodendron,* ***Manilkara*,** *Mimusops, Niemeyera, Northia,* ***Palaquium*, *Planchonella*, *Pouteria*,** *Pycnandra, Sarcosperma, Sideroxylon*

References: Bartish *et al.* (2005), Herrmann-Erlee and Lam (1957), Herrmann-Erlee and Royen (1957), Lam and Royen (1952, 1957), Royen (1952, 1953a, 1953b, 1957, 1960a, 1960b), Vink (1958)

1a. Petals with dorsal appendages 2

1b. Petals without dorsal appendage 3

2a. Flowers 8-merous .... *Mimusops elengi* L. (not treated here)

2b. Flowers 6-merous .... *Manilkara*

3a. Calyx with 2 whorls of 2 or 3 sepals; stamens at least twice as many as petals, in 2 or more whorls; staminodes absent 4

3b. Calyx with sepals spirally arranged, 5–8(–12); stamens as many as petals, sometimes more, in 1 whorl; staminodes often present, rarely absent 7

4a. Sepals 6, in 2 whorls of 3 .... *Palaquium*

4b. Sepals 4, in 2 whorls of 2 5

5a. Tertiary venation of leaves reticulate or transverse to secondary veins .... *Madhuca* (not treated here)

5b. Tertiary venation of leaves ascending 6

6a. Flowers clustered at ends of branchlets; ovary with locules complete; seed scar very large .... *Burckella*

6b. Flowers usually scattered along branchlets; ovary with locules incompletely formed; seed scar small, linear .... *Madhuca* (not treated here)

7a. Stamens 2 or more, opposite each petal .... *Magodendron* (not treated here)

7b. Stamens as many as petals, or at most, less than twice the number of petals 8

8a. Sepals 6, in 2 whorls .... *Manilkara*

8b. Sepals (4 or)5(–12), spirally arranged 9

9a. Flowers with all stamens fertile; staminodes absent .... *Chrysophyllum roxburghii*

9b. Flowers with stamens and staminodes 10

10a. Seeds with plentiful albumen; cotyledons leaf-like .... *Planchonella*[3]

10b. Seeds with albumen absent or only very slightly developed; cotyledons thick .... *Pouteria*

Burckella obovata Pierre
Fig. 343

Notes Botaniques Sapotacèes 4 (1890)
Timber Group: Occasional timber species

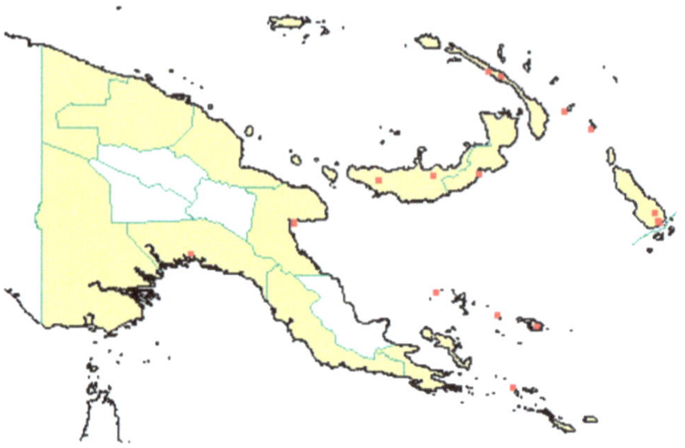

Field Characters: Canopy trees, up to 30 m high, or subcanopy trees, 10–15 m high; bole cylindrical, up to 85 cm diam., straight, up to 12 m long; buttresses present or absent; spines absent; aerial roots absent; stilt roots absent. Bark pale green or grey, rough or almost smooth, scaly or flaky or pustular; lenticels elongated vertically; bark <25 mm thick; faintly or non-aromatic; blaze consisting of one layer, pale pink, with stripes (red to amber-coloured); exudate present, white, flowing, not changing colour on exposure to air, sticky. Terminal buds enclosed by leaves.

Indumentum: Complex hairs absent; stinging hairs absent; mature twig without hairs.

Leaves: Clustered at end of branches, leaves spiral (internodes short so leaves often appearing pseudo-whorled, simple (with milky white exudate when damaged); petiole present, not winged, attached to base of leaf lamina, not swollen; lamina broadest above middle, 8–18 cm long, 4–8 cm wide; base symmetric, margin entire, not dissected or lobed, apex rounded or shortly acuminate, venation pinnate, secondary veins open, prominent, intramarginal veins absent; lower surface pale green, upper surface pale green or green, hairs absent, oil dots absent, domatia absent; stipules absent.

Flowers: Inflorescence axillary, flowers single, bisexual, with pedicel, with many planes of symmetry, 12–15 mm long, small, 6–7 mm diam.; perianth present, with distinct sepals and petals, red (calyx creamy green in colour); inner perianth 5, some or partly joined; stamens 10, filaments present, free of each other, free of perianth; ovary superior, carpels joined, styles joined, 1.

Fruits: single, 11–20 mm long, 8–20 mm diam., brown, not spiny, fleshy, simple, indehiscent, drupe. Seed 1, as wide as long, not winged.

Distribution: West Sepik, Morobe, Gulf, Papuan Islands, New Britain, New Ireland, Manus, Bougainville.

[3] *Planchonella* is here treated as a distinct genus (refer Bartish *et al.* 2005), Although this genus is sometimes regarded as a synonym of *Pouteria*.

Fig. 343. *Burckella obovata*. Leaves, flowers, fruit and seeds

Burckella polymera P.Royen
Fig. 344

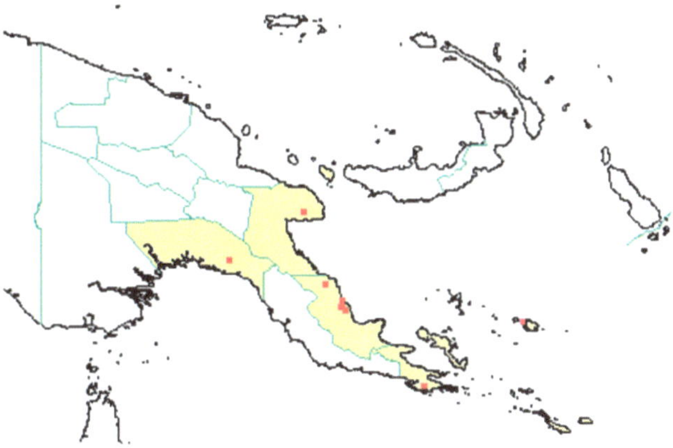

Blumea Vol. 6: 590 (1952)
Timber Group: Non-timber species

Field Characters: Canopy trees; bole cylindrical, straight; buttresses absent; spines absent; aerial roots absent; stilt roots absent. Bark brown, rough, scaly or flaky or slightly pustular; lenticels elongated vertically; bark <25 mm thick; under-bark pink; faintly or non-aromatic; pleasant; blaze consisting of one layer, orange, markings absent, fibrous; inner blaze orange, markings absent, fibrous; exudate present, white, flowing, not changing colour on exposure to air, sticky. Terminal buds not enclosed by leaves.

Indumentum: Complex hairs absent; stinging hairs absent; mature twig hairy; hairs sparse.

Leaves: Clustered at end of branches, leaves whorled, 4 or 5, simple; petiole present, not winged, attached to base of leaf lamina, not swollen; lamina broadest above middle, 25–32 cm long, 9.5–12 cm wide; base symmetric, margin entire, not dissected or lobed, apex emarginate or retuse, venation pinnate, secondary veins open, not prominent, but visible, intramarginal veins absent; lower surface pale green, upper surface green, hairs present, dense, oil dots absent, domatia absent; stipules absent.

Flowers: Inflorescence terminal, flowers arising from a single point; flowers bisexual, with pedicel, with many planes of symmetry, 22–25 mm long, large, 20 mm diam.; perianth present, with distinct sepals and petals, green or yellow; inner perianth 5, some or partly joined; stamens 10, filaments present, free of each other, free of perianth; ovary superior, carpels joined, styles joined, 1.

Fruits: single, not spiny, fleshy, simple, indehiscent, drupe. Seed 1, as wide as long, not winged.

Distribution: Morobe (possibly cultivated), Gulf, Northern, Milne Bay, Papuan Islands.

Fig. 344. *Burckella polymera*. Leaves, flowers, developing fruit and bark

Chrysophyllum roxburghii G.Don

A General History of the Dichlamydeous Plants Vol. 4: 33 (1837)
Timber Group: Minor hardwoods

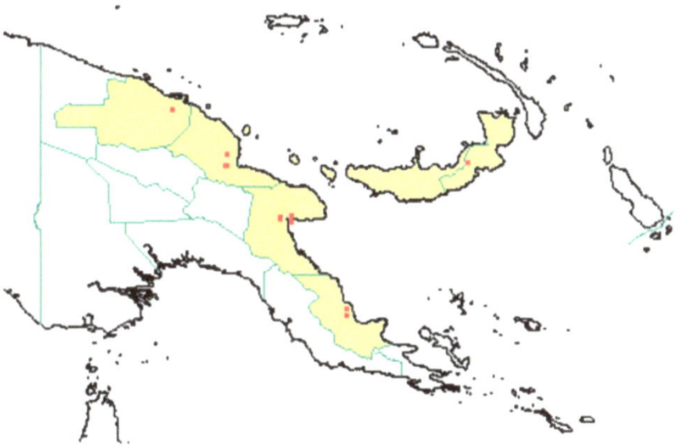

Field Characters: Canopy trees, up to c. 25 m high; bole cylindrical, 30–40 cm diam., straight, c. 15 m long; buttresses up to 1.5 m high, or absent (or slightly spurred at base); spines absent; aerial roots absent; stilt roots absent. Bark grey or brown (occurring in patches), rough, finely fissured; bark 6–10 mm thick; under-bark yellow, dark red, brown, or mottled; faintly or non-aromatic; blaze consisting of one layer, red or rarely brown, markings absent, fibrous; exudate present, white, flowing, not changing colour on exposure to air, sticky. Terminal buds not enclosed by leaves.

Indumentum: Complex hairs absent; stinging hairs absent; mature twig hairy; hairs dense (with short hairs).

Leaves: Spaced along branches, leaves spiral, simple; petiole present, not winged, attached to base of leaf lamina, not swollen; lamina broadest below middle, 8–18 cm long, 2–3 cm wide; base symmetric (to slightly asymmetric), margin entire, not dissected or lobed, apex acuminate or long-tapering, venation pinnate, secondary veins closed, not prominent, but visible, intramarginal veins present; lower surface glossy pale green, upper surface glossy pale green, hairs absent, oil dots absent, domatia absent; stipules absent.

Flowers: Inflorescence axillary, flowers arising from a single point; flowers bisexual, with pedicel, with many planes of symmetry, c. 3 mm long, small, c. 3 mm diam.; perianth present, with distinct sepals and petals, white or pale yellow; inner perianth 5, some or partly joined; stamens 5, filaments present, free of each other, joined to perianth; ovary superior, carpels joined, locules (4 or)5(–12); styles joined, 1.

Fruits: single, 45–60 mm long, dark green (possibly immature), not spiny, fleshy, simple, indehiscent, berry. Seeds 4 or 5, as wide as long, not winged.

Distribution: East Sepik, Madang, Morobe, Northern, New Britain.

Manilkara fasciculata (Warb.) H.J.Lam & Maas Geester.

Blumea Vol. **4, 335 (1941)**
Timber species: Major exportable hardwoods

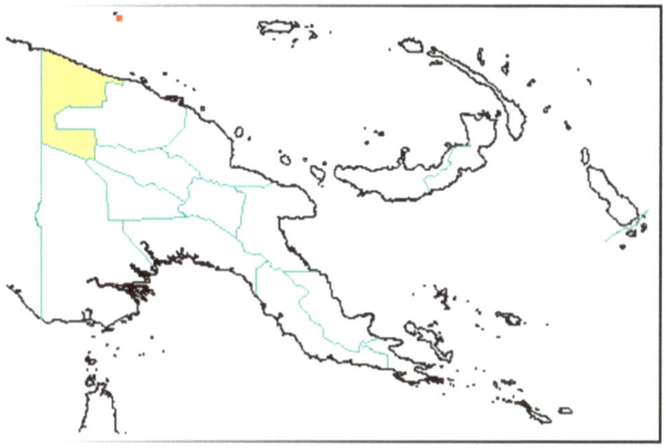

Field Characters: Emergent trees; bole cylindrical; straight; buttresses at least 1 m high; spines absent; aerial roots absent; stilt roots absent. Bark brown, rough, scaly or flaky or fissured; under-bark orange or brown; bark c. 20 mm thick; blaze consisting of one layer, strongly aromatic, pleasant, orange or brown, markings absent, fibrous; exudate white, flowing, not changing colour on exposure to air, sticky. Terminal buds not enclosed by leaves.

Indumentum: Complex hairs absent; stinging hairs absent; mature twig without hairs.

Leaves: Spaced along branches. Leaves spiral, simple; petiole 2–6 cm long, not winged, attached to base of leaf blade, not swollen; lamina broadest above middle, 5–10 cm long, 2–3.5 cm wide; lamina symmetric, margin entire, not dissected or lobed, apex emarginate or retuse, secondary veins closed, not prominent, but visible, intramarginal veins absent; lower surface pale green, upper surface dark green.

Flowers: Inflorescence axillary, flowers in clusters arising from a single point; flowers bisexual, with pedicel 8–20 mm long, with many planes of symmetry, small; perianth present, with distinct hairy sepals (in 2 whorls) and petals, white or pale yellow (to slightly greenish); inner perianth 6 (with appendages 1/2 the length of the central corolla lobe), some or partly joined; stamens 6, glabrous; filaments 1.5–3 mm long, free of each other, joined to perianth; anthers c. 2 mm long; staminodes 6, broadest near middle or sometimes narrow throughout, 0.5–4.5 mm long, 0.3–1 mm wide, apex slightly fringed; ovary superior, carpels joined, locules 6; styles joined, 1, 3–10 mm long.

Fruit: arranged in axillary clusters, broadest towards apex, 1.7–3 3 cm long, 1.5–2 cm diam., simple, fleshy, indehiscent, dark red when mature. Seed 1, broadest towards apex, slightly flattened, 1.6–2 cm long, 1–1.3 cm diam.

Distribution: West Sepik (only known from Wuvulu Island; common to the west, in Indonesian Papua).

Notes: Armstrong (2011) suggested that a new genus should be created for the three Asian species (*M. fasciculata*, *M. dissecta* and *M. udoido*), because of their distinctness to that of *Manilkara sensu stricto* (from Africa/Madagascar). However, this was not done in her subsequent publication (Armstrong 2013).

The leaves of juvenile saplings of this species are much larger (up to 20 cm long and up to 7 cm wide) and are typically broadest at the middle compared to adult plants (eg. *Womersley NGF19398* from Manus).

Palaquium amboinense Burck

Annales du Jardin Botanique de Buitenzorg Vol. 5: 37 (1886)
Other Literature: P. van Royen, *Blumea* Vol. 10: 589 (1960)
Timber Group: Minor hardwoods

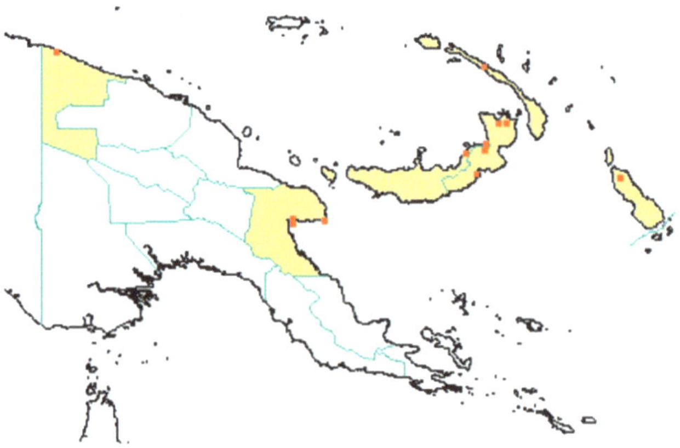

Trade Name: Pencil Cedar

Field Characters: Emergent trees or canopy trees, up to 40 m high; bole cylindrical, up to 60 cm diam., straight, up to 25 m long; buttresses up to 2 m high, or absent; spines absent; aerial roots absent; stilt roots absent. Bark red or brown, rough, pustular; lenticels rounded/swelling (with lenticels orange-brown); bark 20–25 mm thick; faintly or non-aromatic; blaze consisting of one layer, dark red, markings absent; exudate present, white, flowing or not readily flowing, not changing colour on exposure to air, sticky. Terminal buds not enclosed by leaves.

Indumentum: Complex hairs absent; stinging hairs absent; mature twig hairy when young or mature twig without hairs; hairs dense or sparse.

Leaves: Slightly clustered at end of branches or spaced along branches, leaves spiral, simple; petiole 6–14 mm long, not winged or slightly winged (lamina shortly decurrent), attached to base of leaf lamina, not swollen; lamina broadest above middle or broadest at or near middle, (5–)7–16 cm long, 2.5–5.5 cm wide; base symmetric, margin entire, not dissected or lobed, apex acuminate, venation pinnate, secondary veins open, prominent, intramarginal veins absent; lower surface pale green, upper surface green, hairs absent, oil dots absent, domatia absent; stipules present, free, laterally placed, not encircling the twig, hair-like (long and thin – acicular), not fringed, small, 1–2.5 mm long, not persistent (soon falling off without leaving a noticeable scar).

Flowers: Inflorescence axillary, flowers single or flowers arising from a single point (2–6-flowered); flowers bisexual, with pedicel 4–8 mm long, with many planes of symmetry, 4–6 mm long, small, 3–4 mm diam.; perianth present, with distinct sepals and petals, white, pale yellow, pale green, or cream-coloured; inner perianth 6, some or partly joined; stamens 12, filaments present, free of each other, joined to perianth; ovary superior, carpels joined, locules 6 (deeply 6-lobed); styles joined, 1.

Fruits: single or arising from a single point, 36–50 mm long, 35–50 mm diam., red or brown, not spiny, fleshy, simple, indehiscent, berry. Seed 1, 3.5–5 mm, as wide as long (pointed at each end), c. 3 mm diam., not winged.

Distribution: West Sepik, Morobe, New Britain, New Ireland, Bougainville.

Palaquium galactoxylum (F.Muell.) H.J.Lam var. *salomonense* (C.T.White) P.Royen

Blumea Vol. 10: 592 (1960)
Timber Group: Commercial hardwoods
Trade Name: Pencil Cedar

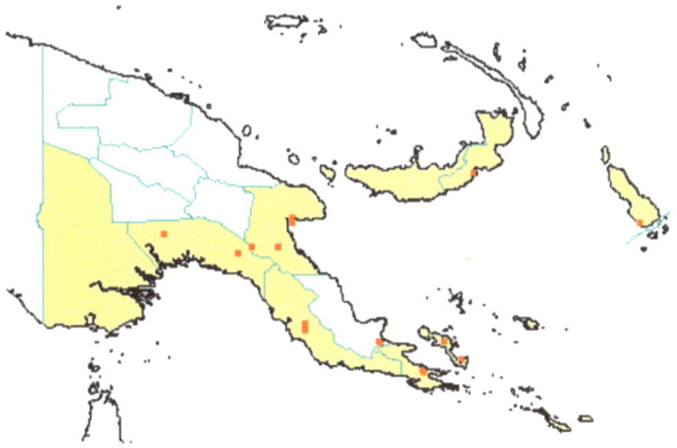

Field Characters: Canopy trees, 25–40 m high; bole cylindrical, up to 100 cm diam., straight, 20–27 m long; buttresses up to 2 m high; spines absent; aerial roots absent; stilt roots absent. Bark white, grey, or brown, rough, fissured; bark 20–25 mm thick; under-bark green, red, or dark brown; faintly or non-aromatic; blaze consisting of one layer, pale yellow or slightly pink, markings absent; exudate present, white, flowing, not changing colour on exposure to air, sticky. Terminal buds not enclosed by leaves.

Indumentum: Complex hairs absent; stinging hairs absent; mature twig hairy or mature twig without hairs; hairs sparse (minute and appressed).

Leaves: Clustered at end of branches, leaves spiral, simple; petiole present, 8–25 mm long, not winged, attached to base of leaf lamina, not swollen; lamina broadest above middle, (7–)9–23 cm long, (2.5–)4–12 cm wide; base symmetric, margin entire, not dissected or lobed, apex rounded, venation pinnate, secondary veins open, not prominent, but visible, intramarginal veins absent; lower surface pale green or pale brown, upper surface green, hairs absent (by misinterpretation) or present, dense or sparse (minute and appressed), oil dots absent, domatia absent; stipules present or absent (by misinterpretation), free, laterally placed, not encircling the twig, hair-like (narrowly ovate to almost linear), not fringed, small, up to 6 mm long, c. 1 mm wide, not persistent (soon falling off without leaving a noticeable scar) or less often persistent.

Flowers: Inflorescence axillary, or usually on branches below leaves, flowers single (appearing clustered because internodes short and occurring below leaves) or flowers usually arising from a single point; flowers bisexual, with pedicel 6–7 mm long, with many planes of symmetry, 9–11 mm long, small, c. 5 mm diam.; perianth present, with distinct sepals and petals, pale green; inner perianth 6, some or partly joined; stamens 12, filaments present, free of each other, joined to perianth; ovary superior, carpels joined, locules 6; styles joined, 1.

Fruits: single, 25–30 mm long, 15–25 mm diam., dark green (possibly immature), not spiny, fleshy, simple, indehiscent, berry. Seeds 1 or 2, 20–25 mm long, longer than wide (laterally compressed), 10–15 mm diam., not winged.

Distribution: Morobe, Western, Gulf, Central, Milne Bay, Papuan Islands, New Britain, Bougainville.

Notes: Two varieties are recognised, namely *Palaquium galactoxylum* var. *galactoxylum* which is restricted to Australia and var. *salomonense* (C.T.White) P.Royen. *Palaquium galactoxylum* var. *galactoxylum* has petioles 3–8 mm long, whereas var. *salomonense* has petioles 8–25 mm long.

Palaquium ridleyi King & Gamble

Journal of the Asiatic Society of Bengal. Part 2. Natural History Vol. 74(1): 196 (1906)
Timber Group: Commercial hardwoods

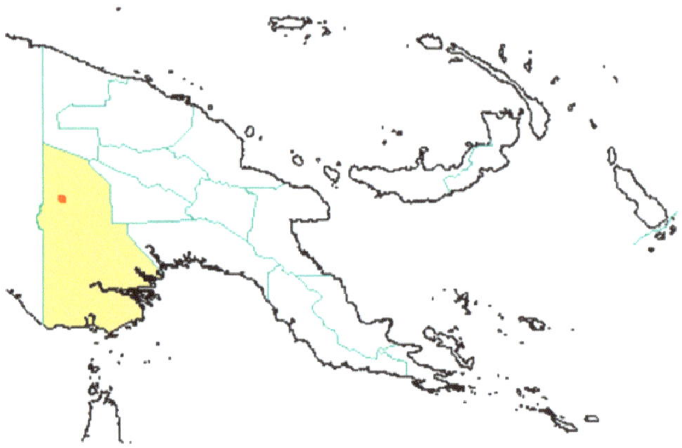

Field Characters: Subcanopy trees, up to 20 m high; bole cylindrical, up to 30 cm diam., straight, 10 m long; buttresses absent; spines absent; aerial roots absent; stilt roots absent. Bark brown, rough, tessellated; lenticels elongated vertically; bark 10 mm thick; under-bark pink or red; strongly aromatic; pleasant; blaze consisting of one layer, grey, pink, or brown, with stripes, fibrous; exudate present, white, not readily flowing, not changing colour on exposure to air, sticky. Terminal buds not enclosed by leaves.

Indumentum: Complex hairs absent; stinging hairs absent; mature twig without hairs.

Leaves: Spaced along branches, leaves spiral, simple; petiole present, not winged, attached to base of leaf lamina, not swollen; lamina broadest above middle, 2–9.5 cm long, 3.5–6 cm wide; base symmetric, margin entire, not dissected or lobed, apex obtuse, venation pinnate, secondary veins open, not prominent, but visible, intramarginal veins absent; lower surface pale green, upper surface dark green, hairs absent, oil dots absent, domatia absent; stipules absent (by misinterpretation) or present, free, laterally placed, not encircling the twig, scale-like, not fringed, small, 1–2 mm long, up to 1 mm wide, not persistent (soon falling off without leaving a noticeable scar).

Flowers: Inflorescence axillary, or on branches, flowers single, bisexual, with pedicel 3–7(–14) mm long, with many planes of symmetry, 3–5 mm long, small, 4–6 mm diam.; perianth present, with distinct sepals and petals, white or pale green; inner perianth 5 or 6, some or partly joined; stamens 10–12, filaments present, free of each other, joined to perianth; ovary superior, carpels joined, locules 5 or 6; styles joined, 1.

Fruits: single, 10–15 mm long, 7–10 mm diam., red, not spiny, fleshy, simple, indehiscent, berry. Seeds 1 or 2, 10–11 mm long, longer than wide, 4–5 mm diam., not winged.

Distribution: Western.

Palaquium warburgianum Schltr. ex K.Krause Fig. 345

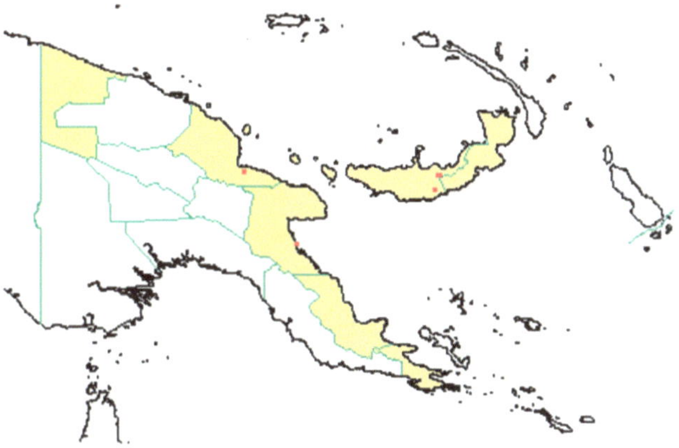

Botanische Jahrbücher für Systematik, Pflanzengeschichte und Pflanzengeographie Vol. 58: 471 (1923)
Other Literature: P. van Royen, *Blumea* Vol. 10: 520–522 (1960) Fig. 12.
Timber Group: Major exportable hardwoods
Trade Name: Pencil Cedar

Field Characters: Emergent trees or canopy trees, up to 44 m high; bole cylindrical, 60–100 cm diam., straight, up to 20 m long; buttresses up to 1.5 m high; spines absent; aerial roots absent; stilt roots absent. Bark grey or pale brown, slightly rough to smooth, scaly or flaky or finely fissured or pustular; lenticels irregular, slightly elongated laterally, or elongated vertically; bark 10–20 mm thick; under-bark pink or red; strongly aromatic or faintly or non-aromatic; pleasant; blaze consisting of one layer, orange, pale yellow, pink, red, brown, or mixed colours, with stripes, fibrous or slightly granular with splinters; exudate present, white, flowing, not changing colour on exposure to air, sticky. Terminal buds not enclosed by leaves.

Indumentum: Complex hairs absent; stinging hairs absent; mature twig hairy (tomentose); hairs dense or sparse.

Leaves: Spaced along branches, leaves sub-opposite (young foliage frequently opposite or sub-opposite) or spiral, simple; petiole 10–22 mm long, not winged, attached to base of leaf lamina, not swollen; lamina broadest at or near middle or broadest above middle, 9–27 cm long, (4.5–)5–15 cm wide; base symmetric, margin entire, not dissected or lobed, apex emarginate or retuse, obtuse, or rounded, venation pinnate, secondary veins open, prominent, intramarginal veins absent; lower surface brown, red, grey, or green, upper surface dark green, hairs absent or present, sparse along petiole and midrib, oil dots absent, domatia absent; stipules present or absent (by misinterpretation), free, laterally placed, not encircling the twig, hair-like (linear), fringed or not fringed, small, up to 3 mm long, c. 0.5 mm wide, not persistent.

Flowers: Inflorescence axillary, flowers arising from a single point or single, bisexual, with pedicel 6–10 mm long, with many planes of symmetry, 5–7 mm long, small, c. 6 mm diam.; perianth present, with distinct sepals and petals, pale yellow or pale brown; inner perianth 5 or 6, some or partly joined; stamens 12, filaments present, free of each other, joined to perianth; ovary superior, carpels joined, locules 5 or 6; styles joined, 1.

Fruits: Arising from a single point or fruits single, fruit (20–)30–45 mm long, 20–30 mm diam., green (probably immature), not spiny, fleshy, simple, indehiscent, berry. Seeds 1–3, c. 2.5 mm, as wide as long (laterally flattened), c. 2 mm diam., not winged.

Distribution: West Sepik, Madang, Morobe, Central, Northern, Milne Bay, New Britain.

Fig. 345. *Palaquium warburgianum*. Bark, leaves and developing fruit

Planchonella chartacea (Benth.) H.J.Lam

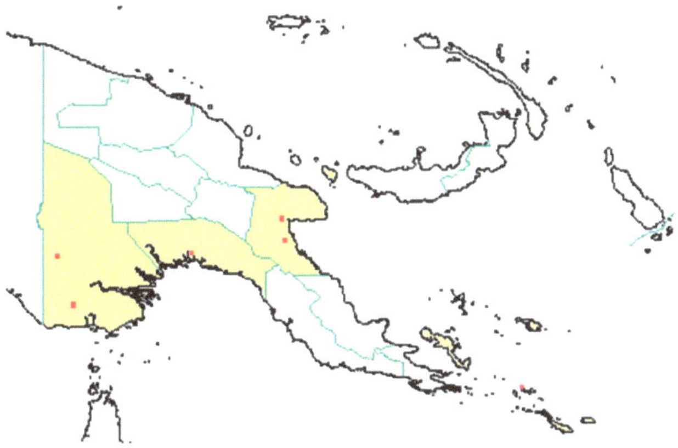

Bulletin du Jardin Botanique de Buitenzorg, Series 3: 7 (1925)
Timber Group: Non-timber species

Field Characters: Canopy trees, 20–42 m high; bole cylindrical, up to c. 90 cm diam., crooked or mostly straight, up to c. 15 m long; buttresses present or absent; spines absent; aerial roots absent; stilt roots absent. Bark yellow or grey, smooth (except for minute cracks); bark 18–20 mm thick; faintly or non-aromatic; blaze consisting of one layer, pale yellow, with stripes (orange), fibrous; exudate present, white, not readily flowing, not changing colour on exposure to air, sticky. Terminal buds not enclosed by leaves.

Indumentum: Complex hairs absent; stinging hairs absent; mature twig without hairs.

Leaves: Spaced along branches, leaves spiral, simple with white exudate when damaged; petiole present, not winged, attached to base of leaf lamina, not swollen; lamina broadest above middle, 6–77 cm long, 2.5–3 cm wide; base symmetric, margin entire, not dissected or lobed, apex acuminate, venation pinnate, secondary veins open, not prominent, but visible, intramarginal veins absent; lower surface pale green, upper surface dark green, hairs absent, oil dots absent, domatia absent; stipules absent.

Flowers: Inflorescence axillary, flowers single, bisexual, with pedicel, with many planes of symmetry, 12–15 mm long, small, c. 10 mm diam.; perianth present, with distinct sepals and petals, white, pale yellow, or cream-coloured; inner perianth 5, some or partly joined; stamens 5, filaments present, free of each other, joined to perianth; ovary superior, carpels joined, locules (4 or)5(or 6); styles joined, 1.

Fruits: single, 12–20 mm long, dark red, not spiny, fleshy, simple, indehiscent, berry. Seeds c. 5, c. 10 mm long, as wide as long (laterally flattened), c. 8 mm diam., not winged.

Distribution: Morobe, Western, Gulf, Papuan Islands.

Notes: Pennington (1991) transferred this species to *Pouteria chartacea* (Benth.) Baehni as part of *Pouteria* section *Oligotheca*. It is here maintained as *Planchonella chartacea* based on molecular data (Bartish *et al.* 2005).

Planchonella firma (Miq.) Dubard

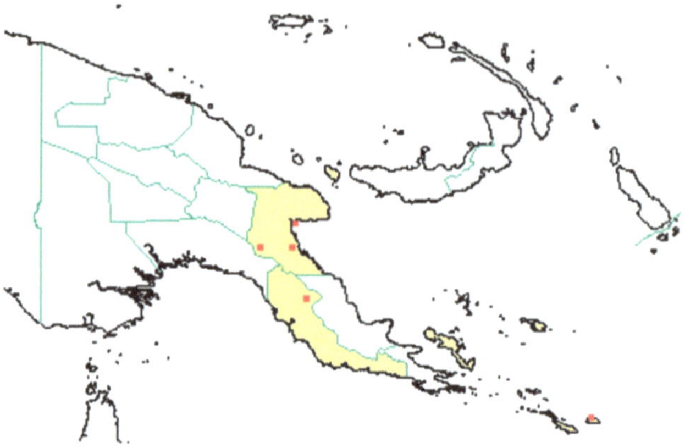

Annales de l'institut botanico-gèologique colonial de Marseille, Sèries 2 Vol. 10: 59 (1912)
Timber Group: Major exportable hardwoods
Trade Name: Pencil Cedar

Field Characters: Canopy trees, 10–35 m high; bole cylindrical, (10–)20–75 cm diam., straight, 15–20 m long; buttresses present; spines absent; aerial roots absent; stilt roots absent. Bark red or brown, rough, pustular; lenticels elongated vertically or irregular; bark 10 mm thick; faintly or non-aromatic; blaze consisting of one layer, pale red, red or brown, granular without splinters; markings absent or with faint stripes; exudate present, white, flowing or not readily flowing, not changing colour on exposure to air, sticky. Terminal buds not enclosed by leaves.

Indumentum: Complex hairs absent; stinging hairs absent; mature twig without hairs.

Leaves: Spaced along branches, leaves spiral, simple; petiole 3–3.5 cm long, winged or not, attached to base of leaf lamina, not swollen; lamina broadest at or near middle, (6.5–)9–14 cm long, (1.5–)4–6 cm wide; base symmetric to very asymmetric, margin entire, not dissected or lobed, apex shortly acuminate, venation pinnate, secondary veins open, prominent, intramarginal veins absent; lower surface pale green or brown (with brown hairs), upper surface green or dark glossy green, hairs absent, oil dots absent, domatia absent; stipules absent.

Flowers: Inflorescence axillary, or on branches (mostly crowded below leaves), flowers arising from a single point or on a branched axis; flowers bisexual, sweetly aromatic like odour of ripe bananas, with pedicel, with many planes of symmetry, 4.5–6 mm long, small, c. 6 mm diam.; perianth present, with distinct sepals and petals, white or cream-coloured (calyx yellow-brown); inner perianth 5, some or partly joined, forming a tube with 5 lobes; stamens 5, filaments present, free of each other, joined to perianth; ovary superior, carpels joined, locules (4 or)5(or 6); styles joined, 1.

Fruits: single or arising from a single point, 15 mm long, dark red, black or brown, not spiny, fleshy, simple, indehiscent, berry. Seeds 1–5, about 10 mm long, as wide as long (laterally flattened), c. 8 mm diam., not winged.

Distribution: Morobe, Central, Papuan Islands.

Notes: Pennington (1991) reduced this species to *Pouteria firma* (Miq.) Baehni as part of *Pouteria* section *Oligotheca*. It is here maintained as *Planchonella firma* (Miq.) Dubard based on molecular data (Bartish *et al.* 2005). However, it is possible that this taxon will eventually be placed in the genus *Beccariella* (L.W. Jessup *pers. comm.*, 2006).

Planchonella keyensis H.J.Lam
Fig. 346

Bulletin du Jardin Botanique de Buitenzorg Ser. III, Vol. 7: 197 (1925)
Timber Group: Hardwood

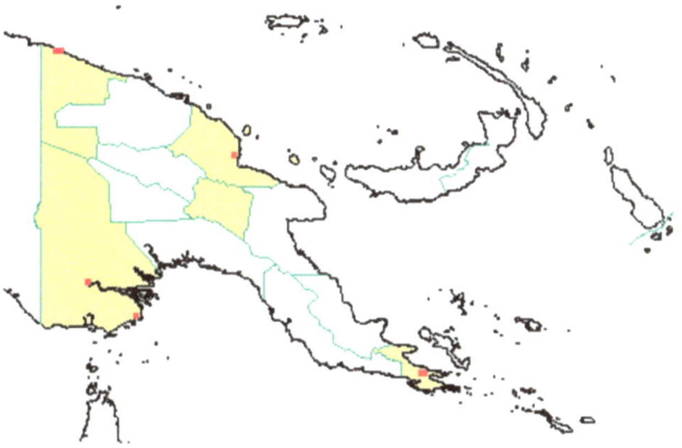

Field Characters: Canopy trees, (9–)13–30 m high; bole cylindrical, sometimes fluted (up to 5 m from base), 25–50(–80) cm diam., straight, 9–20 m long; buttresses absent or up to 2.5 m high; spines absent; aerial roots absent; stilt roots absent. Bark green, green-brown to grey-brown, or pale brown (outer bark dappled and so superficially similar to that of *Eucalyptus deglupta*), almost smooth, pustular with lenticels irregular, not fissured, slightly peeling in thin flakes and leaving shallow depressions, thin, up to 10 mm thick; under-bark green; blaze consisting of one layer, pinkish cream-coloured, flecked, dark green, brown, fawn, reddish brown; exudate present, white (milky), readily flowing, not changing colour on exposure to air, sticky. Terminal buds not enclosed by leaves.

Indumentum: Complex hairs absent; stinging hairs absent; mature twig without hairy.

Leaves: Spaced along branches, leaves spiral, simple; petiole present, not winged, attached to base of leaf lamina, not swollen; lamina broadest at or near middle; base symmetric, margin entire, not dissected or lobed, apex obtuse, shortly acuminate, venation pinnate, secondary veins open, not prominent, but visible, almost at right-angles to midvein, intramarginal veins absent; lower surface pale to mid green, upper surface glossy dark green, hairs absent, oil dots absent, domatia absent; stipules absent.

Flowers: Inflorescence on distal branches below leaves throughout the crown, flowers clustered; flowers bisexual, with pedicel, with many planes of symmetry, small; perianth present, with distinct sepals and petals, pink to pink-red; inner perianth 5; stamens 5, filaments present, free of each other, joined to perianth; ovary superior, carpels joined, locules 1–5; styles joined, 1.

Fruits: arranged in clusters (surrounded at base by persistent pink-red calyx), bright red to purple-black, not spiny, fleshy, simple, indehiscent, berry, broadest above middle. Seeds 1 or 2, c. 8 mm long, as wide as long, not winged.

Distribution: West Sepik, Madang, Eastern Highlands, Western, Milne Bay.

Notes: Also treated as *Pouteria keyensis* (H.J.Lam) Baehni.

Fig. 346. *Planchonella keyensis*. Bark and leaves

Planchonella ledermannii (K.Krause) H.J.Lam

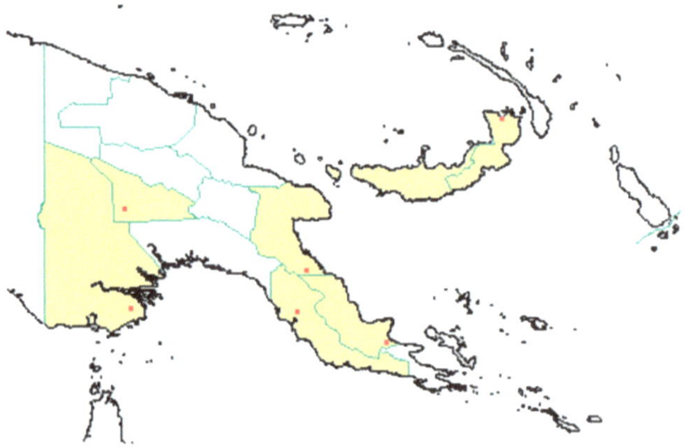

Nova Guinea Vol. 14: 561 (1932)
Timber Group: Major exportable hardwoods

Field Characters: Canopy trees, up to c. 25(–30) m high; bole cylindrical, up to c. 70 cm diam., straight, up to c. 20 m long; buttresses absent or up to 1 m high; spines absent; aerial roots absent; stilt roots absent. Bark pale red or brown, grey, rough, 10 mm thick; faintly or non-aromatic; blaze consisting of one layer, pink, pale red, red or brown, granular without splinters; markings absent; exudate present, white, not readily flowing, not changing colour on exposure to air, sticky. Terminal buds not enclosed by leaves.

Indumentum: Complex hairs absent; stinging hairs absent; mature twig hairy; hairs dense (with brown scurfy hairs).

Leaves: Spaced along branches, leaves spiral, simple; petiole 5–6 mm long, not winged, attached to base of leaf lamina, not swollen; lamina broadest at or near middle, 20–28 cm long, 10–15 cm wide; base symmetric, margin entire, not dissected or lobed, apex rounded, venation pinnate, secondary veins open, prominent, intramarginal veins absent; lower surface pale green to silvery green, upper surface dull dark green, hairs absent, oil dots absent, domatia absent; stipules absent.

Flowers: Inflorescence axillary, or on the trunk or branches, flowers arising from a single point; flowers bisexual, with pedicel, with many planes of symmetry, 6–8 mm long, small, c. 8 mm diam.; perianth present, with distinct sepals and petals, cream-coloured; inner perianth 5, some or partly joined; stamens 5, filaments present, free of each other, joined to perianth; ovary superior, carpels joined, locules 1–5; styles joined, 1.

Fruits: single, c. 15 mm long, c. 15 mm diam., dark green (possibly immature), densely hairy (hairs orange or brown), not spiny, fleshy, simple, indehiscent, berry. Seeds 1 or 2, c. 8 mm long, as wide as long, not winged.

Distribution: Morobe, Southern Highlands, Central, Milne Bay, New Britain.

Notes: Also treated as *Pouteria ledermannii* (Krause) H.J.Lam.

Planchonella macropoda H.J.Lam var. *macropoda*

Nova Guinea Vol. 14: 563 (1932)
Timber Group: Major exportable hardwoods

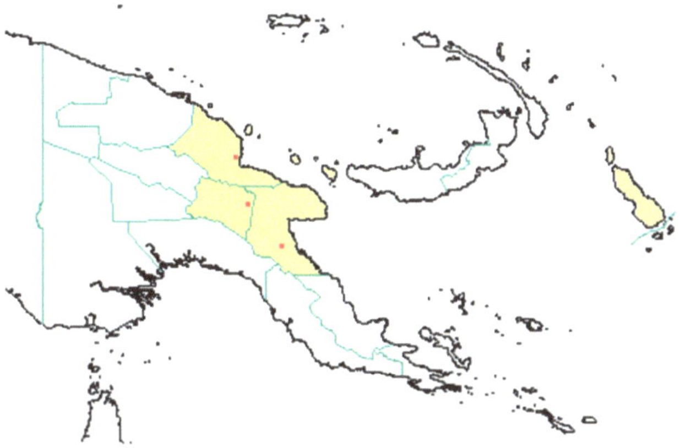

Field Characters: Canopy trees, up to 25 m high, or subcanopy trees; bole cylindrical, straight; buttresses absent; spines absent; aerial roots absent; stilt roots absent. Bark red, brown, rough, 10 mm thick; faintly or non-aromatic; blaze consisting of one layer, red, granular without splinters; markings absent; exudate present, white, not readily flowing, not changing colour on exposure to air, sticky. Terminal buds not enclosed by leaves.

Indumentum: Complex hairs absent; stinging hairs absent; mature twig without hairs.

Leaves: Spaced along branches, leaves spiral, simple; petiole 30–50 mm long, not winged, attached to base of leaf lamina, not swollen; lamina broadest above middle or broadest at or near middle, (6–)15–30 cm long, (3.5–)5–8 cm wide; base symmetric, margin entire, not dissected or lobed, apex rounded or obtuse, venation pinnate, secondary veins open, prominent, intramarginal veins absent; lower surface pale green (silvery) or brown (when young), upper surface green, hairs present, dense or sparse, oil dots absent, domatia absent; stipules absent.

Flowers: Inflorescence axillary, or on branches below leaves, flowers arising from a single point; flowers bisexual, with pedicel, with many planes of symmetry; perianth present, with distinct sepals and petals; inner perianth 5, some or partly joined; stamens 5, filaments present, free of each other, joined to perianth; ovary superior, carpels joined, locules 1–5; styles joined, 1.

Fruits: Arising from a single point, fruit brown or purple, not spiny, fleshy, simple, indehiscent, berry. Seeds 1–5, much more than 10 mm long, as wide as long, c. 10 mm diam., not winged.

Distribution: Madang, Morobe, Eastern Highlands, Bougainville.

Notes: Also treated as "*Pouteria macropoda* (H.J.Lam) Baehni"

Planchonella monticola (K.Krause) H.J.Lam Fig. 347

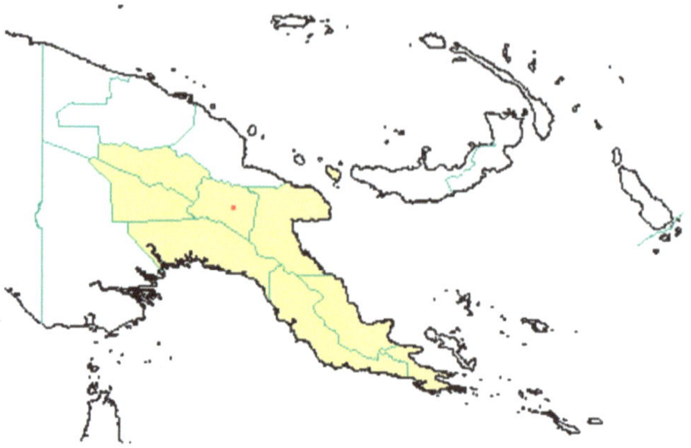

Nova Guinea Vol. 14: 561 (1932)
Timber Group: Occasional timber species

Field Characters: Canopy trees, 20–30 m high, or subcanopy trees; bole cylindrical, usually 80–100 cm diam., crooked, 10–17 m long; buttresses absent; spines absent; aerial roots absent; stilt roots absent. Bark brown, slightly rough or almost smooth, pustular; lenticels irregular; bark 10 mm thick; under-bark green or dark red; faintly or non-aromatic; blaze consisting of one layer, pale yellow, pink, or red, markings absent, slightly granular with splinters; exudate present, white, flowing, not changing colour on exposure to air, sticky. Terminal buds not enclosed by leaves.

Indumentum: Complex hairs absent; stinging hairs absent; mature twig without hairs.

Leaves: Spaced along branches, leaves spiral (internodes very short), simple; petiole 15–20 mm long, not winged, attached to base of leaf lamina, not swollen; lamina broadest at or near middle, (8–)17–20 cm long, (2–)4–5 cm wide; base symmetric, margin entire, not dissected or lobed, apex rarely emarginate or retuse, obtuse, or shortly acuminate, venation pinnate, secondary veins open, prominent, intramarginal veins absent; lower surface pale brown or red, upper surface dark dull green, hairs present, dense or sparse, oil dots absent, domatia absent; stipules absent.

Flowers: Inflorescence axillary, flowers single, bisexual, with pedicel c. 8 mm long, with many planes of symmetry, c. 6 mm long, small, c. 7 mm diam.; perianth present, with distinct sepals and petals, white; inner perianth 5, some or partly joined; stamens 5, filaments present (short), free of each other, joined to perianth; ovary superior, carpels joined, locules 5; styles joined, 1.

Fruits: single, 80–100 mm long, dark red or purple, not spiny, fleshy, simple, indehiscent, berry. Seeds 1–5, as wide as long (broadly ellipsoid), not winged.

Distribution: Morobe, Eastern Highlands.

Notes: This species was tranferred to *Pouteria monticola* (K.Krause) H.J.Lam and this view was accepted by Pennington (1991). However, it is here maintained within the genus *Planchonella* until the relationship between *Pouteria* and *Planchonella* is resolved.

Fig. 347. *Planchonella monticola*. Bark, leaves and flowers

Planchonella myrsinodendron (F.Muell.) Swenson, Bartish & Munzinger

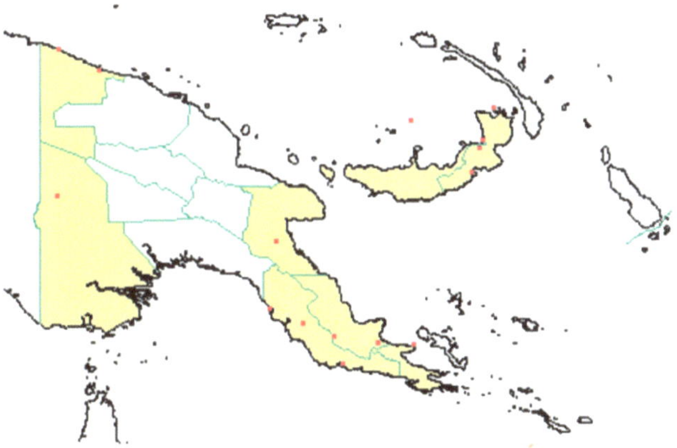

Cladistics Vol. 23: 222 (2007)
Other Literature: *Australian Tropical Rainforest Plants* Vol. http:/keys.trin.org.au:8080/key-server/data/0e0f0504-0103-430d-8004-060d07080d04/media/Html/taxon/Planchonella_myrsinodendron.htm (viewed 24 April 2012):
Timber Group: Major exportable hardwoods

Field Characters: Canopy trees, up to 30 m high; bole cylindrical, c. 30 cm diam., straight; buttresses present (usually not very well developed, often trunk shallowly fluted); spines absent; aerial roots absent; stilt roots absent. Bark grey or brown, slightly rough or smooth, fissured or slightly pustular; lenticels elongated vertically; bark c. 8 mm thick; under-bark green; faintly or non-aromatic; blaze consisting of one layer, reddish white, pale pink, or pale brown, with stripes, granular with splinters; exudate present, white, not readily flowing, not changing colour on exposure to air, sticky. Terminal buds not enclosed by leaves.

Indumentum: Complex hairs absent; stinging hairs absent; mature twig without hairs.

Leaves: Spaced along branches, leaves spiral, simple; petiole (5–)10–15 mm long, not winged, attached to base of leaf lamina, not swollen; lamina broadest above middle or broadest at or near middle, 12–25 cm long, 4.5–10 cm wide; base symmetric, margin entire, not dissected or lobed, apex rounded, venation pinnate, secondary veins open, prominent or not prominent, but visible, intramarginal veins absent; lower surface pale green, upper surface green, hairs absent, oil dots absent, domatia absent; stipules absent.

Flowers: Inflorescence axillary, (pleasantly aromatic), flowers single, bisexual, with pedicel, with many planes of symmetry, 2.5–3 mm long, small, c. 3 mm diam.; perianth present, with distinct sepals and petals, pale green; inner perianth 5, some or partly joined; stamens 5, filaments present (short, with anthers included within corolla), free of each other, joined to perianth; ovary superior, carpels joined, locules 1–5; styles joined, 1.

Fruits: Arising from a single point, fruit 12–20 mm long, red or purple, not spiny, fleshy, simple, indehiscent, berry. Seeds 1 or 2, as wide as long, not winged.

Distribution: East Sepik.

Notes: Previously known as *Planchonella obovoidea* H.J.Lam. Lawrie Jessup (2001) reduced this species to the synonymy of *Pouteria myrsinodendron* (F.Muell.) Jessup, based on *Chrysophyllum myrsinodendron* F.Muell., *Fragmenta* Vol. 6: 178 (1868).

Planchonella sarcospermoides H.J.Lam

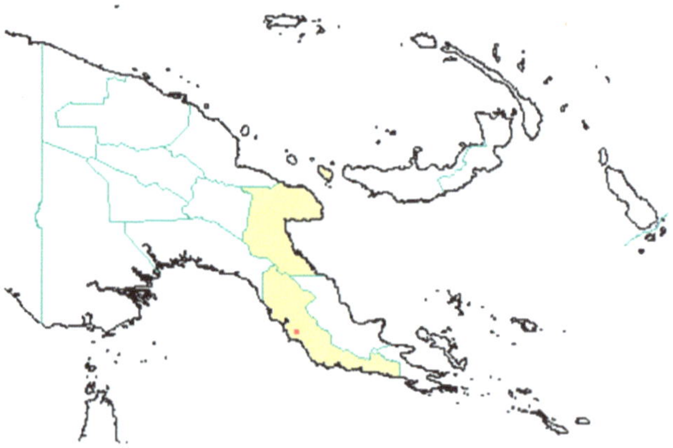

Boissiera Vol. 7: 94 (1943)
Vernacular name: Mangrove.
Timber Group: Non-timber species or an occasional timber species

Field Characters: Canopy or subcanopy trees, (7–)10–30 m high; bole cylindrical, 15–30(–52) cm diam., straight, up to c. 10–16 m long; buttresses present, 0.5–2.5 m high; spines absent; aerial roots absent; stilt roots absent. Bark dark brown, brown or red, rough, slightly scaly or flaky, fissured, peeling, slightly pustular or slightly tessellated; lenticels irregular or elongated vertically; bark 5–10 mm thick; under-bark pale yellow (straw-coloured), orange, pink, or red; strongly or faintly aromatic, or non-aromatic; pleasant; blaze consisting of one layer, pale yellow (straw-coloured), orange, pink, or red, markings absent or with faint stripes, fibrous or granular with splinters; exudate present, white, moderately flowing, not changing colour on exposure to air, slightly sticky. Terminal buds not enclosed by leaves.

Indumentum: Complex hairs absent; stinging hairs absent; mature twig without hairs.

Leaves: Spaced along branches, leaves opposite, simple; petiole 15–30 mm long, not winged, attached to base of leaf lamina, not swollen or slightly swollen; lamina broadest at or near middle, 13–46 cm long, 5.5–12 cm wide; base symmetric, slightly asymmetric, or very asymmetric, margin entire, not dissected or lobed, apex acute or abruptly acuminate, venation pinnate, secondary veins open, prominent, intramarginal veins absent; lower surface pale green, upper surface dark green, hairs absent, oil dots absent, domatia absent; stipules absent.

Flowers: Inflorescence axillary, or terminal, flowers on an unbranched axis or flowers arising from a single point, closely clustered to other flowers; flowers bisexual, not stalked or subsessile, with many planes of symmetry, 8–12 mm long, small, 8–10 mm diam.; perianth present, with distinct sepals and petals, white or pale yellow (calyx brown because covered with brown hairs); inner perianth 5, some or partly joined; stamens 5, filaments present, free of each other, joined to perianth; ovary superior, carpels joined, locules 1; styles joined, 1.

Fruits: Arising from a single point or from an unbranched axis, single (clustered together), c. 15 mm long, 10–20 mm diam., purple (inside red) or yellow to pale yellow, not spiny, fleshy, simple, indehiscent, drupe. Seed 1, 14–15 mm long, as wide as long or longer than wide, 10–15 mm diam., not winged.

Distribution: Morobe, Gulf, Central.

Notes: Previously known as *Pouteria sarcospermoides* (H.J.Lam) H.J.Lam (refer: *Blumea* Vol. 5: 337, 1943).

Planchonella solida P.Royen
Fig. 348

Blumea Vol. 8: 433 (1957)
Timber Group: Occasional timber species

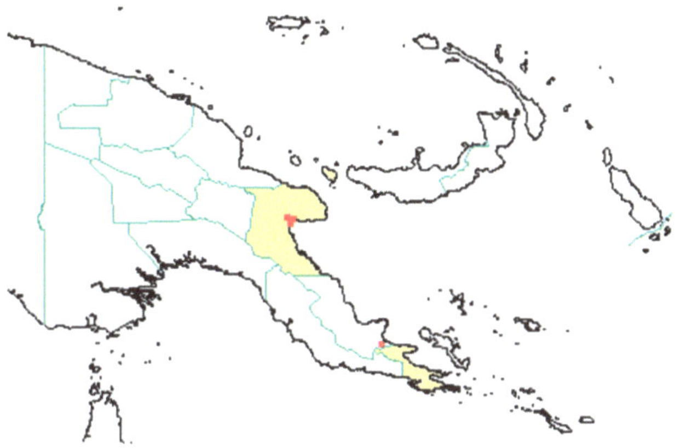

Field Characters: Canopy trees, up to 35 m high; bole usually not cylindrical, up to c. 80 cm diam., straight, up to c. 22 m long; buttresses usually absent; spines absent; aerial roots absent; stilt roots absent. Bark brown, smooth, finely fissured, with occasional transverse ridges; lenticels elongated vertically (within fissures); bark up to c. 20 mm thick; under-bark pale orange; faintly or non-aromatic; blaze consisting of one layer, pink or brown, with stripes, granular with splinters (white to yellow-brown streaks); exudate present, white, not readily flowing, not changing colour on exposure to air, sticky. Terminal buds not enclosed by leaves.

Indumentum: Complex hairs absent; stinging hairs absent; mature twig without hairs.

Leaves: Spaced along branches, leaves spiral, simple; petiole 10–15 mm long, not winged, attached to base of leaf lamina, not swollen; lamina broadest above middle or broadest at or near middle, up to 8 cm long, up to 3.5 cm wide; base symmetric, margin entire, not dissected or lobed, apex obtuse, sub-acute, or acuminate, venation pinnate, secondary veins open, prominent, intramarginal veins absent; lower surface pale green, upper surface pale green (subglossy to somewhat dull), hairs absent, oil dots absent, domatia absent; stipules absent.

Flowers: Inflorescence axillary, flowers arising from a single point; flowers bisexual, with pedicel 5–6 mm long, with many planes of symmetry, c. 6 mm long, small, c. 6 mm diam.; perianth present, with distinct sepals and petals, yellow, pale green, or cream-coloured; inner perianth 5, some or partly joined; stamens 5, filaments present, free of each other, joined to perianth; ovary superior, carpels joined, locules 5; styles joined, 1.

Fruits: Arising from a single point, fruit 20–30 mm long, dark red, not spiny, fleshy, simple, indehiscent, berry. Seeds black, usually 1–5, as wide as long, c. 15 mm long, not winged.

Distribution: Morobe, Milne Bay.

Fig. 348. *Planchonella solida*. Bark, leaves, fruit and seeds

Planchonella torricellensis (K.Schum.) H.J.Lam

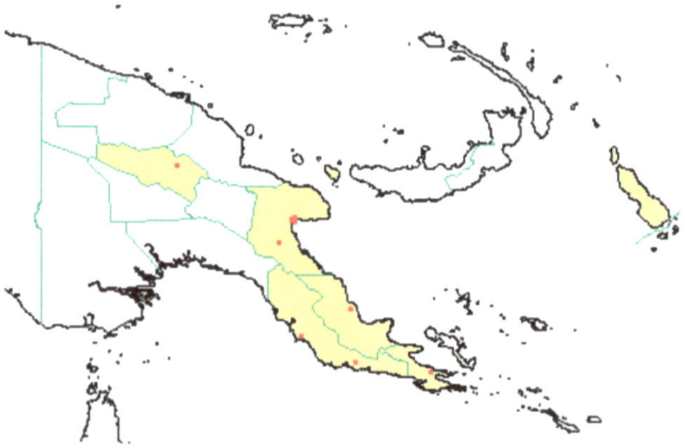

Nova Guinea Vol. 14: 562 (1932)
Timber Group: Major exportable hardwoods

Field Characters: Canopy trees, up to 40 m high; bole cylindrical, up to c. 80 cm diam., straight, up to c. 22 m long; buttresses up to 2 m high; spines absent; aerial roots absent; stilt roots absent. Bark brown or purplish, rough, fissured or pustular; lenticels elongated vertically (within fissures); bark 9–16 mm thick; under-bark brown or mottled; faintly or non-aromatic; blaze consisting of one layer, pink or brown, with stripes, granular with splinters (white to yellow-brown streaks); exudate present, white, not readily flowing, not changing colour on exposure to air, sticky. Terminal buds not enclosed by leaves.

Indumentum: Complex hairs absent; stinging hairs absent; mature twig without hairs.

Leaves: Spaced along branches, leaves spiral, simple; petiole 10–15 mm long, not winged, attached to base of leaf lamina, not swollen; lamina broadest above middle or broadest at or near middle, 7–20 cm long, (1.5–)3–7.5 cm wide; base symmetric, margin entire, not dissected or lobed, apex obtuse, sub-acute, or acuminate, venation pinnate, secondary veins open, prominent, intramarginal veins absent; lower surface pale green or green, upper surface dark green (subglossy to somewhat dull), hairs absent, oil dots absent, domatia absent; stipules absent.

Flowers: Inflorescence axillary, or on the trunk or branches (particularly on branchlets below leaves), flowers arising from a single point; flowers bisexual, with pedicel 5–7 mm long, with many planes of symmetry, c. 6 mm long, small, c. 6 mm diam.; perianth present, with distinct sepals and petals, yellow, pale green, or cream-coloured; inner perianth 5, some or partly joined; stamens 5, filaments present, free of each other, joined to perianth; ovary superior, carpels joined, locules 5; styles joined, 1.

Fruits: Arising from a single point, fruit c. 20 mm long, dark red or purple, not spiny, fleshy, simple, indehiscent, berry. Seeds usually 1–5, as wide as long, not winged.

Distribution: Morobe, Western Highlands, Central, Northern, Milne Bay.

Notes: Pennington (1991) transferred all species of *Planchonella* to the genus *Pouteria*. Therefore, he regarded this species as *Pouteria torricellensis*; however, it is here retained in the genus *Planchonella* until the results of further molecular work resolve the taxonomic status of these two genera.

Pouteria lauterbachiana (H.J.Lam) Baehni

Candollea Vol. 9: 314 (1942)
Timber Group: Non-timber species

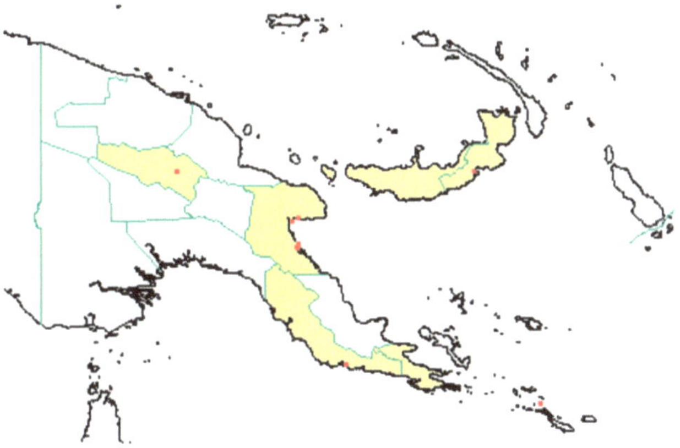

Field Characters: Subcanopy trees, 10–12 m high; bole cylindrical, 20 cm diam., sometimes slightly fluted, straight, 6 m long; buttresses absent or occasionally present; spines absent; aerial roots absent; stilt roots absent. Bark grey or brown, rough, slightly scaly or flaky, slightly fissured, or pustular; lenticels irregular; bark 5–6 mm thick; under-bark red; faintly or non-aromatic; blaze consisting of one layer, pale red or pink, markings absent, fibrous; exudate present, white, not readily flowing, not changing colour on exposure to air, sticky. Terminal buds not enclosed by leaves.

Indumentum: Complex hairs absent; stinging hairs absent; mature twig without hairs.

Leaves: Spaced along branches, leaves sub-opposite, simple; petiole c. 15 mm long, not winged, attached to base of leaf lamina, not swollen; lamina broadest at or near middle, 15–24 cm long, 6.5–8.5 cm wide; base almost symmetric to slightly asymmetric, margin entire, not dissected or lobed, apex acuminate, venation pinnate, secondary veins open, prominent, intramarginal veins absent; lower surface pale green, upper surface green, hairs absent, oil dots absent, domatia absent; stipules absent.

Flowers: Inflorescence axillary, flowers on a branched axis; flowers bisexual, not stalked, with many planes of symmetry, 5–6 mm long, small, 5–6 mm diam.; perianth present, with distinct sepals and petals sepals with brown hairs, white, yellowish brown, or yellow; inner perianth 5, some or partly joined forming a tube with 5 lobes; stamens 5, filaments present, free of each other, joined to perianth; ovary superior, carpels joined, styles joined, 1.

Fruits: arranged on branched axis, fruit purple or brown, not spiny, fleshy, simple, *indehiscent*, drupe. Seeds 1 or 2, as wide as long, >10 mm diam., not winged.

Distribution: Morobe, Western Highlands, Central, Milne Bay, Papuan Islands, New Britain.

Pouteria luzoniensis (Merr.) Baehni var. *papuana* Erlee Fig. 349

Blumea Vol. 8: 502 (1957)
Timber Group: Occasional timber species

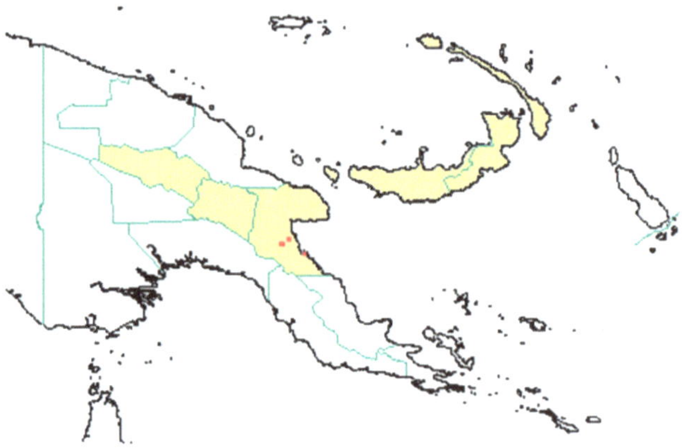

Field Characters: Canopy trees, up to c. 26 m high; bole markedly fluted, 25–30 cm diam., straight, up to c. 20 m long; buttresses up to c. 1 m high; spines absent; aerial roots absent; stilt roots absent. Bark grey or brown, rough, scaly or flaky or slightly tessellated; bark 3 mm thick; under-bark brown with pale reddish tinge; faintly or non-aromatic; blaze consisting of one layer, pink or brown, markings absent, smooth or slightly fibrous; exudate present, white, not readily flowing, not changing colour on exposure to air, sticky. Terminal buds not enclosed by leaves.

Indumentum: Complex hairs absent; stinging hairs absent; mature twig without hairs.

Leaves: Spaced along branches, leaves spiral, simple; petiole present, not winged, attached to base of leaf lamina, not swollen; lamina rarely broadest above middle, broadest at or near middle, or broadest below middle, 3–18 cm long, 1.8–6.5 cm wide; base symmetric, margin entire, not dissected or lobed, apex rounded, obtuse, sub-acute, or acuminate, venation pinnate, secondary veins open, not prominent, but visible, intramarginal veins absent; lower surface dull red caused by presence of reddish hairs, upper surface dark green, hairs present, dense with reddish hairs, oil dots absent, domatia absent; stipules absent.

Flowers: Inflorescence axillary, flowers arising from a single point (2–6-flowered); flowers bisexual, not stalked or shortly with pedicel, with many planes of symmetry, 4–5 mm long, small, 4–5 mm diam.; perianth present, with distinct sepals and petals, white or cream-coloured; inner perianth 5, some or partly joined; stamens 5, filaments present, free of each other, joined to perianth; ovary superior, carpels joined, locules 4 or 5; styles joined, 1.

Fruits: Arising from a single point, fruit 20–23 mm long, brown or purple, not spiny, fleshy, simple, indehiscent, berry. Seeds 1 or 2, 12–16 mm long, as wide as long, 10–14 mm diam., not winged.

Distribution: Morobe, Western Highlands, Eastern Highlands, New Britain, New Ireland.

Notes: It is not clear if this variety should be transferred to the genus *Planchonella* or remain in *Pouteria*. It is here maintained within the genus *Pouteria* until the relationship between these two genera is resolved. However, it is expected that this taxon will probably be transferred to the genus *Planchonella*.

Fig. 349. *Pouteria luzoniensis* var. *papuana*. Bark, leaves and flower buds

Pouteria obovata Pierre

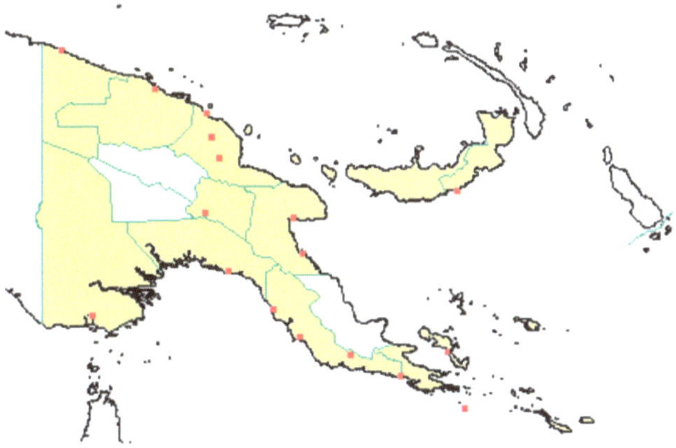

Candollea Vol. 9: 324 (1942)
Timber Group: Major exportable hardwoods

Field Characters: Canopy trees, up to 35 m high; bole cylindrical, up to 50 cm diam., straight, up to 20 m long; buttresses up to 2 m high; spines absent; aerial roots absent; stilt roots absent. Bark pale brown, rough, pustular; lenticels elongated vertically; bark 10 mm thick; under-bark yellow; faintly or non-aromatic; blaze consisting of one layer, yellow or orange, with stripes, granular with splinters; exudate present, colourless, not readily flowing, not changing colour on exposure to air, sticky. Terminal buds not enclosed by leaves.

Indumentum: Complex hairs absent; stinging hairs absent; mature twigs with hairs.

Leaves: Spaced along branches, leaves spiral, simple; petiole up to 50 mm long, not winged, attached to base of leaf lamina, not swollen; lamina broadest above middle, 17–29 cm long, 8–12 cm wide; base symmetric, margin entire, not dissected or lobed, apex rounded, venation pinnate, secondary veins open, prominent, intramarginal veins absent; lower surface pale green, upper surface dark green, hairs absent, oil dots absent, domatia absent; stipules absent.

Flowers: Inflorescence axillary, often also occurring below leaves, flowers on unbranched axis, in clusters arising from a single point; flowers bisexual, with pedicel 6–8 mm long, with many planes of symmetry, 2–4 mm long, small, 2–4 mm diam.; perianth present, with distinct sepals and petals, greenish white; inner perianth 5, some or partly joined; stamens 5, filaments present, free of each other; ovary superior, carpels joined, locules 1; styles joined, 1.

Fruits: Arising from a single point, in clusters; fruit 6–8 mm long, 5–7 mm wide, not spiny, fleshy, simple, indehiscent, berry.

Distribution: West Sepik, East Sepik, Madang, Morobe, Eastern Highlands, Western, Gulf, Central, Milne Bay, Papuan Islands, New Britain.

70. Ebenaceae

Trees and shrubs. Stipules absent. Leaves well-developed, usually spiral, opposite, or whorled, simple, not dissected or lobed; margin entire; venation pinnate. Inflorescences axillary. Bracts present. Flowers unisexual, then plant dioecious, regular, with distinct calyx and corolla. Sepals 3–7. Petals 3–7, joined, at least in part; tube present. Stamens 3–at least–20, free or fused to corolla; filaments present; staminodes absent or occasionally present. Gynoecium with carpels at least partially joined, superior; styles free. Fruit simple, rarely dehiscent or indehiscent, rarely capsule, drupe or berry, fleshy. Seeds without wings.

PNG genera: ***Diospyros***

References: Kostermans (1977)

Diospyros ellipticifolia Bakh.
Fig. 350

The Gardens' Bulletin, Straits Settlement Vol. 7: 162 (1933)
Timber Group: Occasional timber species

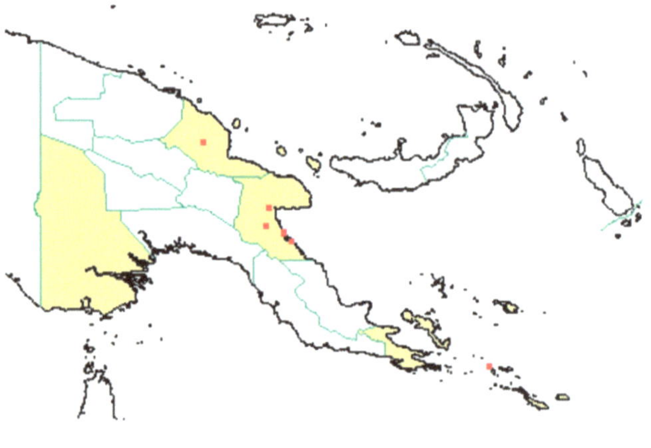

Field Characters: Subcanopy trees, up to 10 m high; bole cylindrical, up to 15 cm diam., straight, 1–1.5 m long; buttresses shortly present or absent; spines absent; aerial roots absent; stilt roots absent. Bark grey or black, rough, pustular; lenticels rounded/swelling or irregular; bark 1–4 mm thick; under-bark red or brown; faintly or non-aromatic; blaze consisting of one layer, red or brown, markings absent, fibrous; exudate present, colourless, not readily flowing, not changing colour on exposure to air, slightly sticky. Terminal buds not enclosed by leaves.

Indumentum: Complex hairs absent; stinging hairs absent; mature twig without hairs.

Leaves: Spaced along branches, leaves spiral, simple; petiole 4–5 mm long, not winged, attached to base of leaf lamina, not swollen; lamina broadest at or near middle, 8.5–19 cm long, 3.5–5.5 cm wide; base symmetric, margin entire, not dissected or lobed, apex acuminate, venation pinnate, secondary veins open, not prominent, but visible or not visible, intramarginal veins absent; lower surface grey or green, upper surface dark green or green, hairs absent, oil dots absent, domatia absent; stipules absent.

Flowers: Inflorescence axillary, flowers on an unbranched axis; flowers bisexual, almost sessile or with pedicel c. 1 mm long, with many planes of symmetry perianth present, with distinct sepals and petals; ovary superior, carpels joined, styles joined, 1.

Fruits: single, 10–15 mm long, 8–10 mm diam., orange, red, not spiny, fleshy, simple, indehiscent, drupe. Seeds 6 or 7, about 10 mm long, as wide as long, c. 8 mm diam., not winged.

Distribution: Madang, Morobe, Western, Papuan Islands.

Notes: Often referred to as *D. elliptica* (J.R.Forst. & G.Forst.) P.S.Green, but this is an invalid name.

Fig. 350. *Diospyros ellipticifolia*. Bark, leaves and fruit

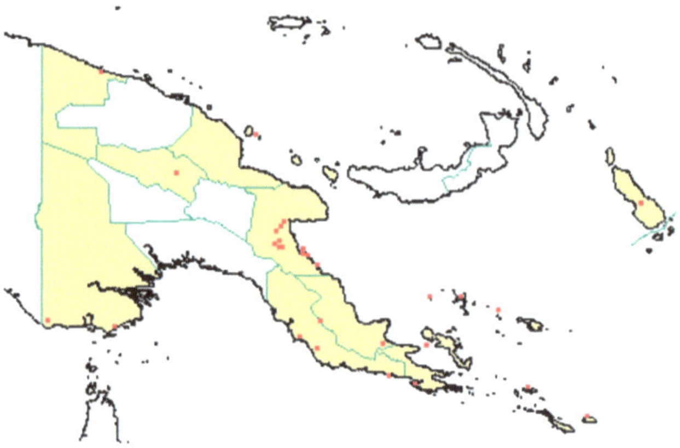

Diospyros hebecarpa Benth.
Fig. 351

Flora Australiensis Vol. 4: 286 (1868)
Timber Group: Occasional timber species

Field Characters: Canopy trees, up to 25 m high or subcanopy trees; bole cylindrical, up to c. 42 cm diam., straight, up to 15 m long; buttresses absent; spines absent; aerial roots absent; stilt roots absent. Bark dark grey, brown, or almost black, smooth; bark 10–12 mm thick; under-bark dark brown or black; faintly or non-aromatic; blaze consisting of one layer, pale orange or pale brown, markings absent; inner blaze pale orange or pale brown, markings absent. Terminal buds not enclosed by leaves.

Indumentum: Complex hairs absent; stinging hairs absent; mature twig without hairs.

Leaves: Spaced along branches, leaves spiral, simple; petiole 4–8 mm long, not winged, attached to base of leaf lamina, not swollen; lamina broadest above middle or broadest at or near middle, (7–)11–18 cm long, (4–)5–6 cm wide; base symmetric, margin entire, not dissected or lobed, apex obtuse, venation pinnate, secondary veins open, prominent, intramarginal veins absent; lower surface pale green, upper surface dark glossy green, hairs present, dense, oil dots absent, domatia absent; stipules absent.

Flowers: Inflorescence axillary, flowers on an unbranched axis, single, unisexual, with male and female flowers on different plants, flowers with pedicel 3–4 mm long, with many planes of symmetry, 10–15 mm long, small, c. 5 mm diam.; perianth present, with distinct sepals and petals, white or pale yellow; inner perianth 4, some or partly joined; stamens 4–8 (male flowers; female flowers with staminodes), filaments present, free of each other, joined to perianth; ovary superior, carpels joined, locules 4–6; styles joined, 1.

Fruits: single, c. 20 mm long, pale dull green, not spiny, fleshy, simple, indehiscent, berry. Seeds black, 4–6, c. 12 mm long, longer than wide, c. 7 mm diam., not winged.

Distribution: West Sepik, Madang, Morobe, Western Highlands, Western, Central, Northern, Milne Bay, Papuan Islands, Bougainville.

Fig. 351. *Diospyros hebecarpa*. Bark, leaves, fruit and seeds

Diospyros lolin Bakh.
Fig. 352

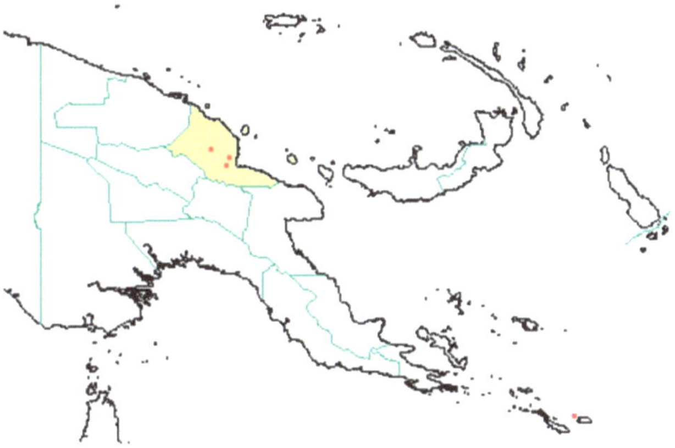

Gardens' Bulletin, Singapore Vol. 7: 175 (1933)
Timber Group: Major exportable hardwoods
Trade Name: Black Ebony

Field Characters: Canopy trees, up to 30 m high; bole cylindrical, 40–55 cm diam., straight; buttresses absent; spines absent; aerial roots absent; stilt roots absent. Bark black, rough, tessellated or pustular; lenticels irregular; bark 5 mm thick; under-bark red or brown; strongly aromatic; pleasant; blaze consisting of one layer, red or brown, markings absent, fibrous; exudate present, colourless, not readily flowing, not changing colour on exposure to air, sticky. Terminal buds not enclosed by leaves.

Indumentum: Complex hairs absent; stinging hairs absent; mature twig hairy tomentose; hairs dense.

Leaves: Spaced along branches, leaves spiral, simple; petiole present, not winged, attached to base of leaf lamina, not swollen; lamina equally broad throughout much of length, 21–26 cm long, 8.5–11 cm wide; base symmetric, margin entire, not dissected or lobed, apex obtuse, venation pinnate, secondary veins open, prominent, intramarginal veins absent; hairs present, dense, oil dots absent, domatia absent; stipules absent.

Flowers: Inflorescence axillary, flowers on an unbranched axis, single, unisexual, with male and female flowers on different plants, flowers subsessile or with pedicel <2 mm long, densely hairy (hairs red-brown), flowers with many planes of symmetry, c. 8 mm long, small, c. 8 mm diam.; perianth present, with distinct sepals and petals, white or pale yellow; inner perianth 4, some or partly joined; stamens 4–8 (male flowers; female flowers with staminodes), filaments present, free of each other, joined to perianth; ovary superior, carpels joined, locules 4–6; styles joined, 1.

Fruits: arranged on unbranched axis, c. 40 mm long, c. 50 mm diam., green, densely hairy (hairs, short, brown), not spiny, fleshy, simple, indehiscent, berry. Seeds black, 4–6, c. 20 mm long, longer than wide, c. 10 mm diam., not winged.

Distribution: Madang, Milne Bay, Papuan Islands.

Notes: *Diospyros lolinopsis* Kosterm. *Blumea* 23(2): 461 (1977) is here treated as a synonym of *D. lolin*.

Fig. 352. *Diospyros lolin*. Bark and leaves

Diospyros papuana Valeton ex Bakh. Fig. 353

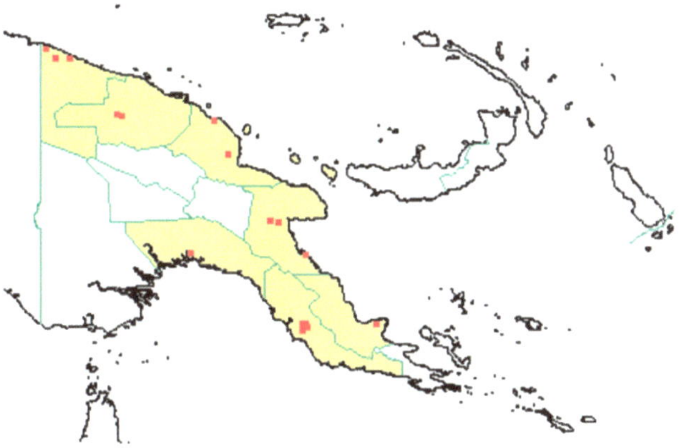

Gardens' Bulletin. Straits Settlements. Singapore Vol. 7: 180 (1933) [*Bulletin de Département de l'Agriculture aux Indes Néerlandaises* 10: 45 (1907, no description)]
Timber Group: Minor commercial hardwoods

Field Characters: Subcanopy trees, 8–12 m high; branches black; bole cylindrical, 15–18 cm diam., straight, 7–8 m long; buttresses absent; spines absent; aerial roots absent; stilt roots absent. Bark black (grey-brown when a sapling or a shrub), when scraped sounds very prominent like metal, rough, slightly flakey to slightly longitudinally fissured, black (wood white, turing black when matured, hard); bark 10–12 mm thick; under-bark black; faintly or non-aromatic; blaze consisting of 2 layers, pink, markings absent, granular without splinters; exudate present, colourless, not readily flowing, not changing colour on exposure to air, not sticky. Terminal buds not enclosed by leaves.

Indumentum: Complex hairs absent; stinging hairs absent.

Leaves: Spaced along branches, leaves spiral, simple; petiole c. 10 mm long, not winged, attached to base of leaf lamina, not swollen; lamina broadest below or near middle; 18–24 cm long, 10–13 cm wide; base symmetric, margin entire, not dissected or lobed, apex obtuse, venation pinnate, secondary veins open, not prominent, but visible, intramarginal veins absent; lower surface green to yellow-green, upper surface glossy dark green, hairs absent, oil dots absent, domatia absent; stipules absent.

Flowers: Inflorescence terminal, flowers on an unbranched axis, single, unisexual, with male and female flowers on different plants, flowers subsessile or with pedicel short, hairs absent, flower buds blackish green; flowers with many planes of symmetry, c. 8 mm long, small, c. 8 mm diam.; perianth present, with distinct sepals and petals, white or pale yellow; inner perianth 4, some or partly joined; stamens 4–8 (male flowers; female flowers with staminodes), filaments present, free of each other, joined to perianth; ovary superior, carpels joined, locules 4–6; styles joined, 1.

Fruits: terminal, arranged on unbranched axis, fruit slightly flattened globular, 7–10 mm long, 6.5–8 mm diam., yellow or orange to brown, with black dots, not spiny, fleshy, simple, indehiscent, berry; calyx persistent. Seeds c. 10, 40–45 mm long, longer than broad, flattened, c. 40 mm wide., not winged.

Distribution: West Sepik, East Sepik, Madang, Morobe, Gulf, Central, Northern.

Fig. 353. *Diospyros papuana*. Bark, fruit, seeds and leaves

Diospyros sogeriensis Kosterm.
Fig. 354

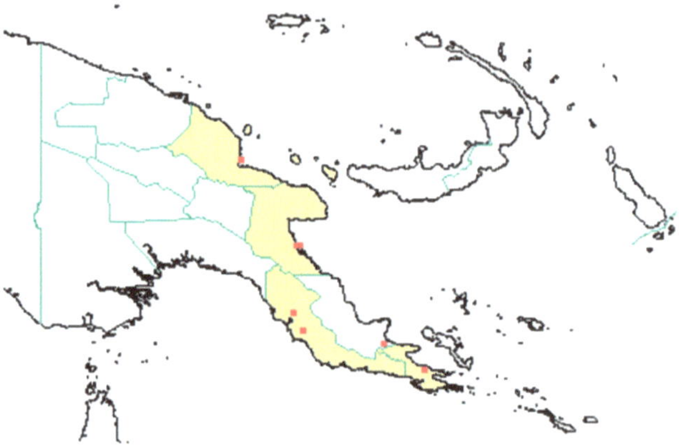

Gardens' Bulletin. Straits Settlements. Singapore Vol. 7: 185 (1933)
Timber Group: Major exportable hardwoods

Field Characters: Subcanopy trees, 15 m high; bole cylindrical, 15 cm diam., straight, 7 m long; buttresses absent; spines absent; aerial roots absent; stilt roots absent. Bark black, rough, pustular; lenticels irregular; bark 2 mm thick; under-bark pink; faintly or non-aromatic; blaze consisting of one layer, pink, markings absent, granular without splinters; exudate present, colourless, not readily flowing, not changing colour on exposure to air, not sticky. Terminal buds not enclosed by leaves.

Indumentum: Complex hairs absent; stinging hairs absent.

Leaves: Spaced along branches, leaves spiral, simple; petiole c. 10 mm long, not winged, attached to base of leaf lamina, not swollen; lamina broadest at or near middle; base symmetric, margin entire, not dissected or lobed, apex obtuse, venation pinnate, secondary veins open, not prominent, but visible, intramarginal veins absent; lower surface green, upper surface glossy green, hairs absent, oil dots absent, domatia absent; stipules absent.

Flowers: Inflorescence terminal, flowers on an unbranched axis, single, unisexual, with male and female flowers on different plants, flowers subsessile or with pedicel <2 mm long, hairs absent, flowers with many planes of symmetry, c. 8 mm long, small, c. 8 mm diam.; perianth present, with distinct sepals and petals, white or pale yellow; inner perianth 4, some or partly joined; stamens 4–8 (male flowers; female flowers with staminodes), filaments present, free of each other, joined to perianth; ovary superior, carpels joined, locules 4–6; styles joined, 1.

Fruits: arranged on unbranched axis, fruit 15–30 mm long, 15–30 mm diam., yellow or orange, not spiny, fleshy, simple, indehiscent, berry. Seeds 6, c. 10 mm long, as long as broad, c. 10 mm diam., not winged.

Distribution: Madang, Morobe, Central, Milne Bay.

Fig. 354. *Diospyros sogeriensis*. Bark, leaves and fruit

71. Primulaceae *sensu lato*

Notes: Primulaceae, in the broad sense, can be recognised by leaves that are usually spiral, sometimes with dark dots or lines; flowers with united petals; stamens opposite petals; ovary with several to many ovules; and stigma unlobed.

Three subfamilies are recognised as occurring in Papua New Guinea.

1. subfamily Primuloideae
2. subfamily Maesoideae
3. subfamily Myrsinoideae

1. subfamily Primuloideae

Notes: Previously regarded as Primulaceae, in the narrow sense.

Trees, shrubs, and lianas. Stipules absent. Leaves well-developed, spiral, opposite, or whorled, simple, dissected or lobed or usually not dissected or lobed; margin entire or usually toothed; venation pinnate or palmate. Inflorescences axillary or commonly terminal. Bracts absent. Flowers bisexual, regular, with distinct calyx and corolla, with tepals (not readily resolvable as calyx and/or corolla), or rarely with petals absent. Sepals (3–)5(–9). Petals (3–)5(–9), joined, at least in part; tube present. Stamens (3–)5(–9), free or fused to corolla; filaments present; staminodes absent or present. Gynoecium with carpels at least partially joined, superior or partially inferior; styles partially or fully joined. Fruit simple, usually dehiscent or indehiscent, capsule, dry, at least non-fleshy. Seeds without wings.

PNG genera: *Androsace, Primula*

References: Bentvelzen (1962), Steenis (1972b)

1a. Corolla shorter than calyx .... *Androsace* (not treated here)

1b. Corolla longer than calyx .... *Primula umbellata* (Lour.) Bentv. (not treated here)

2. subfamily Maesoideae

Notes: Previously the genus *Maesa* was included in the Myrsinaceae, in the narrow sense.

Trees and lianas. Stipules absent. Leaves well-developed, spiral, simple, not dissected or lobed; margin toothed or entire; venation pinnate. Inflorescences axillary, often branched. Bracts present. Flowers small, bisexual or unisexual, then plant monoecious, regular, with distinct calyx and corolla. Sepals usually 4 or 5. Petals usually 4 or 5, joined, at least in part; tube present. Stamens usually 4 or 5, fused at base, joined to middle of corolla tube, opposite corolla lobes; filaments present; staminodes absent. Gynoecium with carpels joined, semi-inferior; styles joined, 1; stigma truncate or capitate and lobed. Fruit simple, indehiscent, drupe-like, fleshy (calyx persistent). Seeds many, without wings.

PNG genera: ***Maesa*** (see key to genera of subfamily Myrsinoideae, below).

References: Sleumer (1987)

Maesa bismarckiana Mez
Fig. 355

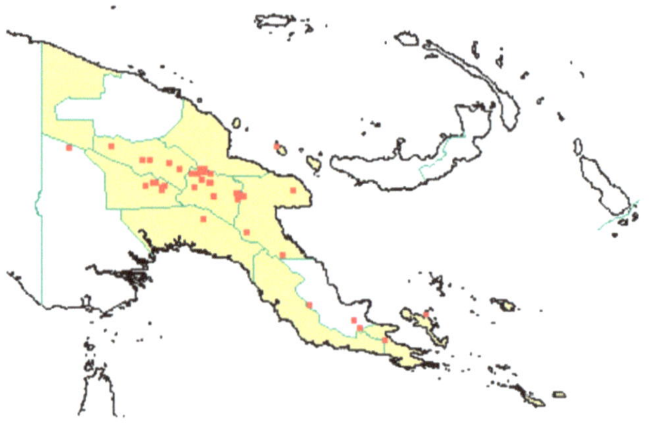

Botanisches Archiv. Zeitschrift für die gesamte Botanik. Königsberg and Dahlem bei Berlin Vol. 1: 125 (1922)
Other Literature: Royen P, van (1982a) Myrsinaceae. In Royen P, van (ed.). 'The alpine flora of New Guinea. Vol. 3.' pp. 1949–1990; Sleumer HO (1987) A revision of the genus *Maesa* Forsk. (Myrsinaceae) in New Guinea, the Moluccas and the Solomon Islands. *Blumea* 32: 39–65
Timber Group: Non-timber species

Field Characters: Subcanopy slender trees or shrubs, (2–)7–10(–15) m high; bole cylindrical, up to c. 20 cm diam., straight, 2–4 m long; buttresses absent; spines absent; aerial roots absent; stilt roots absent. Bark grey or grey-brown, rough, pustular, lenticels white; bark <25 mm thick; under-bark green; faintly or non-aromatic; blaze consisting of two layers, inner blaze pale red-brown, markings absent, outer blaze fainter, with faint streaks and/or speckles; exudate absent. Terminal buds not enclosed by leaves.

Indumentum: Complex hairs absent; stinging hairs absent; mature twig without hairs, distally more or less densely ferrugineous-lepidote, mostly roughly verruculose.

Leaves: Spaced along branches, leaves spiral, simple; petiole (4–)6–10 mm long, not winged, attached to base of leaf lamina, not swollen or only slightly so; lamina broadest at or near middle, 3.5–9.5(–14) cm long, 2–4(–6.5) cm wide; base symmetric, margin entire, or slightly dissected, apex sub-acuminate, venation pinnate, secondary veins open, prominent, with reddish tinge, intramarginal veins absent; lower surface pale green, upper surface green, young leaves densely covered with reddish scales, mature leaves only with reddish scales on lower surface; gland lines dark, short, irregular; oil dots absent; stipules absent.

Flowers: Inflorescence axillary, and occurring on branches, on an unbranched axis; flowers unisexual, occurring on separate plants, with pedicel short (1–1.5 mm long), with many planes of symmetry, c. 2.5 mm long, small, 2.5–3 mm diam.; perianth present, with distinct sepals and petals, yellowish green; inner perianth 4, partly joined; stamens 4, filaments very short, free of each other, joined to perianth; ovary semi-inferior, carpels joined, locules 4; styles joined, 1, short, grooved.

Fruits: arranged on unbranched axis, fruit 2.5(–3) mm long, as wide as long, pink to brownish, not spiny, fleshy, simple, indehiscent, drupe. Seeds many, not winged.

Distribution: West Sepik, Madang, Morobe, Western Highlands, Eastern Highlands, Southern Highlands, Gulf, Central, Milne Bay, Papuan Islands.

Notes: This species is cultivated by Papua New Guineans for decorating purposes (Sleumer 1987).

Fig. 355. *Maesa bismarckiana*. Bark, leaves and immature fruit

3. subfamily Myrsinoideae

Notes: Previously regarded as Myrsinaceae, in the narrow sense.

Trees, shrubs, and sometimes lianas. Stipules absent. Leaves well-developed, spiral, simple, not dissected or lobed; margin usually entire; venation pinnate. Inflorescences axillary or terminal. Bracts present or usually absent. Flowers bisexual or unisexual, then plant monoecious, regular, with distinct calyx and corolla. Sepals (3 or)4 or 5. Petals (3 or)4 or 5(or 6), free or usually joined, at least in part; tube rarely absent or present. Stamens (3 or)4 or 5(or 6), free or fused with corolla; filaments present; staminodes absent or present. Gynoecium with carpels at least partially joined, usually superior or partially inferior; styles partially or fully joined. Fruit simple, indehiscent, drupe or berry, fleshy. Seeds without wings.

PNG genera: *Aegiceras, Amblyanthus,* ***Ardisia, Conandrium,*** *Discocalyx, Embelia, Fittingia, Grenacheria, Loheria, Lysimachia,* ***Myrsine, Tapeinosperma*** [note: *Rapanea* is now regarded as *Myrsine*]

References: Royen (1982a), Sleumer (1988), Smith (1973a, 1973b), Takeuchi (2010)

1a. Ovary semi-inferior; fruits with many seeds .... *Maesa* (subfam. Maesoideae, see above)

1b. Ovary superior; fruits with 1 seed........ 2

2a. Anthers transversely septate; seeds sickle-shaped; trees of mangroves with seed germinating before leaving fruit .... *Aegiceras* (not treated here)

2b. Anthers not transversely septate........ 3

3a. Lianas; flowers unisexual........ 4

3b. Trees, shrubs, sub-shrubs or herbs; flowers unisexual or bisexual........ 5

4a. Petals free .... *Embelia* (not treated here)

4b. Petals joined .... *Grenacheria* (not treated here)

5a. Herbs, less than 1 m high; flowers yellow .... *Lysimachia* (not treated here)

5b. Trees, shrubs or subshrubs........ 6

6a. Usually subshrubs, sometimes small trees; flowers bisexual........ *Ardisia*

6a. Trees or shrubs; flowers unisexual or bisexual........ 7

7a. Stamens joined, or anthers touching; flowers bisexual 8

7b. Stamens free; flowers usually unisexual, rarely bisexual 10

8a. Petals joined to middle or higher; ovules 3 or 4; inflorescences a panicle with flowers in umbels at end of branchlets........ *Amblyanthus polyantha* Laut. (not treated here)

8b. Petals joined at base; ovules many; inflorescences a panicle with long lateral branches 9

9a. Leaves 10–13 cm long, < 6 cm wide; inflorescences axillary; flowers 4–5 mm long .... *Conandrium polyanthum* (Laut. & K.Schum.) Mez

9b. Leaves > 27 cm long, > 11 cm wide; inflorescences terminal; flowers 7–8 mm long... *Tapeinosperma magnifica* Pipoly & Takeuchi

10a. Corolla segments twisted in bud..*Ardisia*

10b. Corolla segments overlapping in bud...11

11a. Inflorescences very short, umbel-like, densely covered with scales .... *Myrsine*

11b. Inflorescences distinct, raceme-like, umbel-like, or paniculate, never short; scales absent 12

12a. Fruit (drupe) with exocarp spongy or fleshy, soft, thick; endocarp ridged or tuberculate .... *Fittingia* (not treated here)

12b. Fruit (drupe) with exocarp thin, not spongy or fleshy; endocarp usually smooth............................ 13

13a. Petals recurved; stamens with distinct filaments... *Loheria* (not treated here)

13b. Petals spreading; stamens with anthers sessile.. *Discocalyx* (not treated here)

Ardisia imperialis K.Schum.
Fig. 356

Botanische Jahrbücher für Systematik, Pflanzengeschichte und Pflanzengeographie 9(2): 213 (1887)
Timber Group: Non-timber species

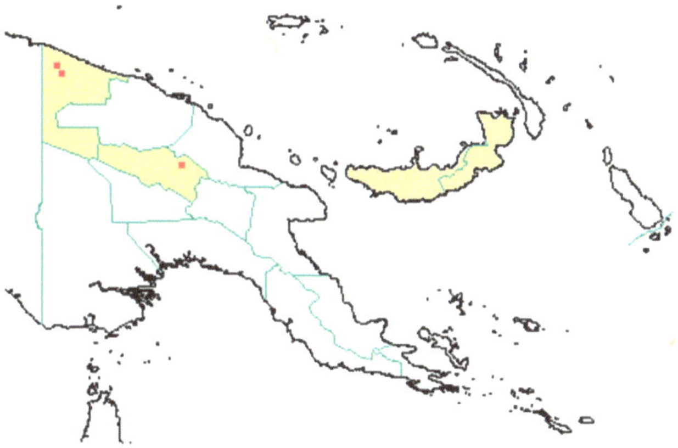

Field Characters: Subcanopy slender trees, up to c. 9 m high; bole cylindrical, narrow (c. 7–10 cm diam., straight; buttresses absent; spines absent; aerial roots absent; stilt roots absent. Bark grey-brown, slightly rough; bark 10–15 mm thick; under-bark dark red-brown, usually with green tinge; blaze consisting of one layer, pale red to pale brown, often with purple tinge, brittle, markings absent; exudate colourless, not readily flowing, not changing colour on exposure to air, not sticky. Terminal buds not enclosed by leaves.

Indumentum: Complex hairs absent; stinging hairs absent; mature twig without hairs.

Leaves: spaced along branches, leaves spiral, simple; petiole present, not winged, attached to base of leaf lamina, not swollen; lamina broadest at or near middle to slightly below middle; base symmetric, margin entire, not dissected or lobed, apex shortly sub-acuminate, venation pinnate, secondary veins open, not prominent, but visible, intramarginal veins absent; lower surface subglossy to dull green, upper surface glossy mid to pale green, hairs absent, oil dots absent, domatia absent; stipules absent.

Flowers: inflorescence axillary, dull dark pink to red, with flowers on a branched axis; flowers bisexual, with pedicel, with many planes of symmetry, small; perianth present, with distinct sepals and petals, cream-coloured with tinge of pink to red; inner perianth 5, free; stamens 5, filaments present, free of each other, free of perianth; ovary superior, carpels joined, locules 1; styles joined, 1.

Fruits: arranged on branched axis, fruit ovoid, red, not spiny, fleshy, simple, indehiscent, drupe (berry-like).

Distribution: West Sepik, Western Highlands, New Britain.

Fig. 356. *Ardisia imperalis.* Bark, flowers and leaves

Conandrium polyanthum (Laut. & K.Schum.) Mez

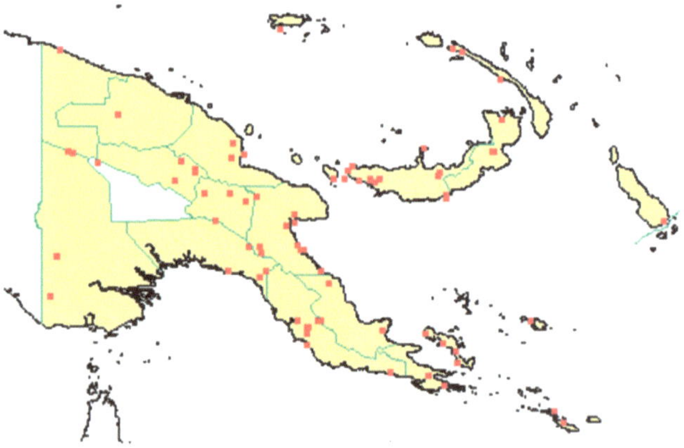

in Engler, H.G.A., Das Pflanzenreich 157 (1902)
Timber Group: Non-timber species

Field Characters: Subcanopy trees, 7–10 m high; bole cylindrical, 45–50 cm diam., straight, 2–4 m long; buttresses absent; spines absent; aerial roots absent; stilt roots absent. Bark grey or brown, smooth; bark <25 mm thick; under-bark yellow or green; faintly or non-aromatic; blaze consisting of one layer, red or brown (to straw-coloured), markings absent; exudate absent. Terminal buds not enclosed by leaves.

Indumentum: Complex hairs absent; stinging hairs absent; mature twig without hairs.

Leaves: spaced along branches, leaves spiral, simple; petiole present, winged, attached to base of leaf lamina, not swollen; lamina broadest at or near middle, 10–13 cm long, 4–5 cm wide; base symmetric, margin entire, not dissected or lobed, apex obtuse or sub-acuminate, venation pinnate, secondary veins open, not prominent, but visible, intramarginal veins absent; lower surface green, upper surface green, hairs absent, oil dots absent, domatia absent; stipules absent.

Flowers: inflorescence axillary, flowers on a branched axis; flowers bisexual, with pedicel, with many planes of symmetry, 4–5 mm long, small, c. 5 mm diam.; perianth present, with distinct sepals and petals, red or purple; inner perianth 5, free; stamens 5, filaments present, free of each other, free of perianth; ovary superior, carpels joined, locules 1; styles joined, 1.

Fruits: arranged on branched axis, fruit 5–8 mm long, dark green or black, not spiny, fleshy, simple, indehiscent, drupe (berry-like). Seed 1, c. 2 mm long, as wide as long, 3–5 mm diam., not winged.

Distribution: West Sepik, East Sepik, Madang, Morobe, Western Highlands, Eastern Highlands, Western, Gulf, Central, Northern, Milne Bay, Papuan Islands, New Britain, New Ireland, Manus, Bougainville.

Myrsine brassii (P.Royen) B.J.Conn

Telopea 21: 157–159 (2018)
Timber Group: Non-timber species

Field Characters: Subcanopy trees, 3–15 m high; bole cylindrical, crooked or straight; buttresses absent; spines absent; aerial roots absent; stilt roots absent. Bark pale brown, slightly rough or smooth, slightly pustular; lenticels rounded/swelling; bark <25 mm thick; under-bark green; faintly or non-aromatic; blaze consisting of one layer, pale orange or pink, markings absent; exudate absent. Terminal buds not enclosed by leaves.

Indumentum: Complex hairs absent; stinging hairs absent; mature twig without hairs.

Leaves: Spaced along branches, leaves spiral, simple; petiole present, not winged, attached to base of leaf lamina, not swollen; lamina broadest above middle, (1–)1.5–2.5(–3.8) cm long, 0.8–1.5 cm wide; base symmetric, margin entire, not dissected or lobed, apex often emarginate or retuse, or rounded, venation pinnate, secondary veins open, prominent, intramarginal veins absent; lower surface pale green, upper surface dark glossy green, hairs absent, oil dots present (with round and elongate dark oil dots, and with scattered red-brown scales), domatia absent; stipules absent.

Flowers: Inflorescence axillary, flowers on an unbranched axis or sometimes on branched axis; flowers bisexual, not stalked, with many planes of symmetry, 1.3–2(–3) mm long, small, c. 1.5 mm diam.; perianth present, with distinct sepals and petals, red or purple; inner perianth 4, some or partly joined; stamens 4, filaments absent (by misinterpretation) or present (very short, < 0.5 mm long), free of each other, joined to perianth; ovary superior, carpels joined, locules 4–6; styles joined, 1.

Fruits: arranged on unbranched axis, fruit 2–3 mm long, dark blue or purple, not spiny, fleshy, simple, indehiscent, drupe. Seed 1, c. 2 mm long, as wide as long, c. 2 mm diam., not winged.

Distribution: West Sepik, Morobe, Western Highlands, Eastern Highlands, Southern Highlands, Northern, Milne Bay.

Notes: Since *Rapanea* is now included within *Myrsine*, the specific epithet of this species has been transferred to the genus *Myrsine* (Conn 2018). It was previously known as *Rapanea brassii* P.Royen (Royen 1982a: refer p. 1979, fig. 604D–J).

Tapeinosperma magnifica Pipoly & Takeuchi

Harvard Papers in Botany Vol. 8: 153–156 (2004) Figs 1 & 2.

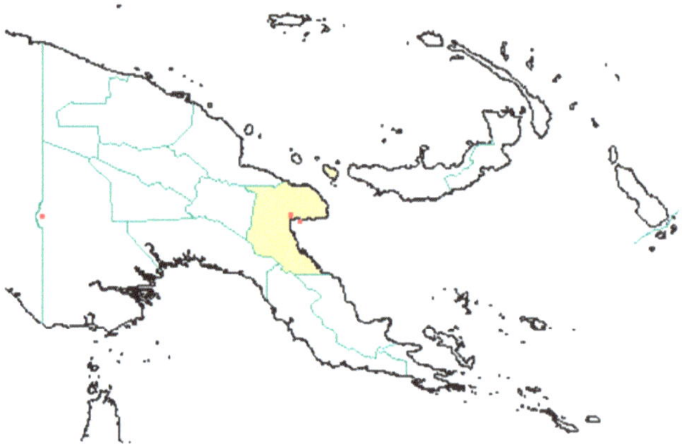

Field Characters: Subcanopy trees, up to 12 m high; bole cylindrical, up to 13 cm diam., straight, up to c. 8 m long; buttresses absent; spines absent; aerial roots absent; stilt roots absent. Bark light brown, rough, pustular; lenticels elongated vertically or rounded/swelling; bark 10 mm thick; under-bark dark red; faintly or non-aromatic; pleasant; blaze consisting of one layer, dark red, with stripes, fibrous; exudate present, colourless, not readily flowing, changing to dark red on exposure to air, sticky. Terminal buds not enclosed by leaves.

Indumentum: Complex hairs absent; stinging hairs absent; mature twig hairy; hairs dense or in older parts usually sparse (glabrescent).

Leaves: Spaced along branches, leaves spiral, simple; petiole present, not winged, attached to base of leaf lamina, not swollen; lamina broadest at or near middle or equally broad throughout much of length, (27–)30–44 cm long, (11–)12–16.5 cm wide; base symmetric, margin entire, not dissected or lobed, apex obtuse or sub-acuminate, venation pinnate, secondary veins open, prominent, intramarginal veins absent; lower surface green, upper surface dark green, hairs present, dense or usually sparse, oil dots present (conspicuously punctate), domatia absent; stipules absent.

Flowers: Inflorescence terminal, flowers on a branched axis; flowers bisexual, with pedicel, with many planes of symmetry, 7–8 mm long, small, c. 8 mm diam.; perianth present, with distinct sepals and petals, purple; inner perianth 5, some or partly joined; stamens 5, filaments present, joined (staminal column c. 1.5 mm long), free of perianth; ovary superior, carpels joined, styles joined, 1.

Fruits: arranged on branched axis, fruit 5–7 mm long, not spiny, fleshy, simple, indehiscent, drupe. Seed 1, c. 5 mm long, as wide as long, c. 5 mm diam., not winged.

Distribution: Morobe (known only from the area around the Lae municipality).

72. Symplocaceae

Trees and shrubs. Stipules absent. Leaves well-developed, spiral, simple, not dissected or lobed; margin entire; venation pinnate. Inflorescences axillary or terminal. Bracts present. Flowers bisexual, regular, with distinct calyx and corolla. Sepals (3–)5. Petals (3–)5–10(–11), joined, at least in part; tube present. Stamens (4–)5–35 (or more), free or fused; filaments present; staminodes absent. Gynoecium with carpels at least partially joined, usually inferior or partially inferior; styles partially or fully joined. Fruit simple, indehiscent, usually drupe or berry, fleshy. Seeds without wings.

PNG genera: *Cordyloblaste*, ***Symplocos***

References: Nooteboom (1977)

Symplocos cochinchinensis (Lour.) S.Moore subsp. *leptophylla* var. *leptophylla* (Brand) Noot. Figs 357, 358

Leiden Botanical Series Vol. 1: 162 (1975)
Timber Group: Non-timber species

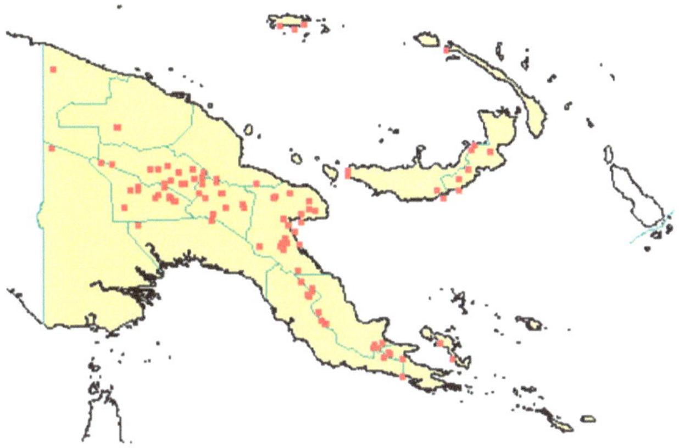

Field Characters: Subcanopy trees, 11–15 m high; bole cylindrical, 15–29 cm diam., crooked, 7–10 m long; buttresses absent; spines absent; aerial roots absent; stilt roots absent. Bark brown, rough, pustular; lenticels elongated vertically or irregular; bark 5 mm thick; under-bark pale green; strongly aromatic; pleasant; blaze consisting of one layer, white or pale yellow cream-coloured, speckled, fibrous; exudate present, colourless, not readily flowing, not changing colour on exposure to air, not sticky. Terminal buds not enclosed by leaves.

Indumentum: Complex hairs absent; stinging hairs absent; mature twig without hairs.

Leaves: Spaced along branches, leaves spiral, simple; petiole present, not winged, attached to base of leaf lamina, not swollen; lamina broadest at or near middle, 7.5–15 cm long, 2.5–5(–9) cm wide; base symmetric, margin entire, not dissected or lobed, venation pinnate, secondary veins open, prominent, intramarginal veins absent; lower surface pale green, upper surface blue-green, hairs sparse on lower surface, oil dots absent, domatia absent; stipules absent.

Flowers: Inflorescence axillary, flowers on a branched axis; flowers bisexual, shortly with pedicel c. 1 mm long, with many planes of symmetry; ovary inferior, carpels joined, style joined, 1.

Fruits: 10–12 mm long, 8–10 mm diam., fruit green when immature, not spiny, fleshy, simple, indehiscent, drupe.

Distribution: West Sepik, East Sepik, Madang, Morobe, Western Highlands, Eastern Highlands, Southern Highlands, Western, Gulf, Central, Northern, Milne Bay, Papuan Islands, New Britain, New Ireland, Manus.

Notes: *Symplocos cochinchinensis* is regarded as an extremely variable species. A taxonomic re-evaluation of the taxonomy of this species is urgently required because the amount of variation makes it difficult to identify the different subspecies and varieties that occur within Papua New Guinea. With respect to this plant, the amount of morphological variation currently included in *S. cochinchinensis* subsp. *leptophylla* and within var. *leptophylla* makes it extremely difficult to define the characteristics of this plant.

The variant that was collected from Mt Wilhelm represents the longer and broader leaf form (8.5–12 cm long; 5–5.5 mm wide) that appears to be also common in the Western Highlands Province.

Fig. 357. *Symplocos cochinchinensis* subsp. *leptophylla* var. *leptophylla*. Bark, flowers, fruit and leaves

Fig. 358. *Symplocos cochinchinensis* subsp. *leptophylla* var. *leptophylla*. Leaves and fruit

Symplocos cochinchinensis (Lour.) S.Moore subsp. *leptophylla* (Brand) Noot. var. *reginae* (Brand) Noot.

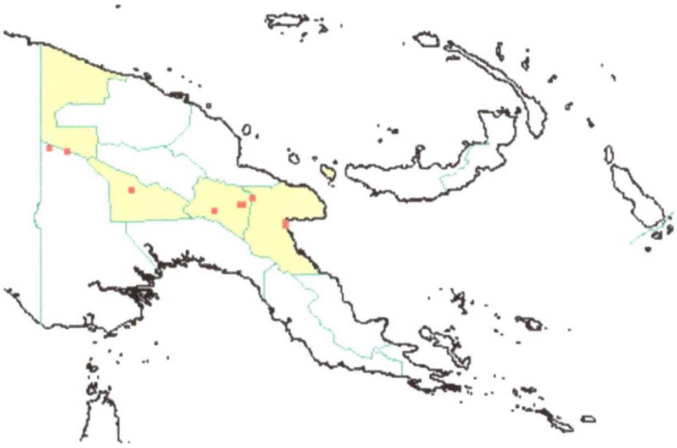

Leiden Botanical Series Vol. 1: 162 (1975)
Timber Group: Non-timber species

Field Characters: Subcanopy trees; bole cylindrical, straight; buttresses absent; spines absent; aerial roots absent; stilt roots absent. Bark brown or black, almost smooth, slightly pustular; lenticels elongated laterally slight horizontal rings; bark 3–4 mm thick; under-bark green; strongly aromatic; pleasant like freshly cut grass; blaze consisting of one layer, white or pale yellow cream-coloured, slightly speckled, smooth; exudate present, colourless, not readily flowing, not changing colour on exposure to air, not sticky. Terminal buds not enclosed by leaves.

Indumentum: Complex hairs absent; stinging hairs absent; mature twig without hairs.

Leaves: Spaced along branches, leaves spiral, simple; petiole present, not winged, attached to base of leaf lamina, not swollen; lamina sometimes broadest above middle, broadest at or near middle, or sometimes broadest below middle, 7.5–10 cm long, 3–6 cm wide; base symmetric, margin entire or crenate (sometimes teeth minute and indistinct), not dissected or lobed, apex acuminate, venation pinnate, secondary veins open, prominent, intramarginal veins absent; lower surface pale green, upper surface dark green, hairs present on lower surface, somewhat dense or sparse, oil dots absent, domatia absent; stipules absent.

Flowers: Inflorescence leaf-opposed or axillary, flowers on a branched axis; flowers bisexual, shortly with pedicel c. 1 mm long, with many planes of symmetry perianth present; ovary inferior, carpels joined, style joined, 1.

Fruits: arranged on branched axis, fruit 15–20 mm long, 10 mm diam., purplish blue, not spiny, hairy to almost glabrous, fleshy, simple, indehiscent, drupe.

Distribution: West Sepik, Morobe, Eastern Highlands, Southern Highlands.

73. Theaceae

Trees and shrubs. Stipules absent. Leaves well-developed, spiral, simple, not dissected or lobed; margin entire or toothed; venation pinnate. Inflorescences axillary. Bracts present. Flowers bisexual, regular, with distinct calyx and corolla or with sepals grading into petals. Sepals 5–7. Petals 5(–50), free or joined, at least in part; tube present or absent. Stamens 5–many, free or fused; filaments present; staminodes absent. Gynoecium with carpels at least partially joined, inferior, usually superior, or partially inferior; styles free or partially or fully joined. Fruit simple, dehiscent or indehiscent, capsule, drupe or berry, dry, at least non-fleshy, or fleshy. Seeds without wings.

PNG genera: ***Gordonia***

References: Barker (1980)

Gordonia papuana Kobuski

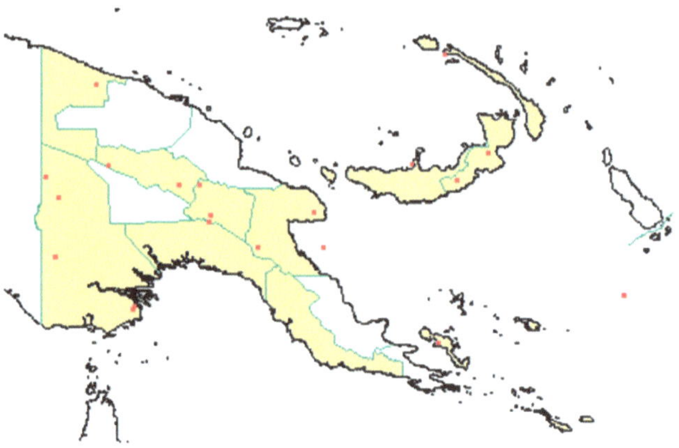

Journal of the Arnold Arboretum Vol. 21: 136 (1940)
Other Literature: W.R. Barker, *Brunonia* Vol. 3: 8–14 (1980) Fig. 1.
Timber Group: Commercial hardwoods

Field Characters: Canopy trees, up to 36 m high, or subcanopy trees; bole cylindrical, up to 130 cm diam., straight, up to 27 m long; buttresses up to 1 m high, or absent; spines absent; aerial roots absent; stilt roots absent. Bark brown, almost black (occasionally), grey, or white, smooth or slightly rough, sometimes scaly or flaky, finely fissured, or slightly pustular; lenticels elongated vertically; bark <25 mm thick; under-bark brown, red, yellow, mottled, or green; faintly or non-aromatic; blaze consisting of one layer, white, yellow, pale red, or pale brown, markings absent; exudate present, colourless, not readily flowing, not changing colour on exposure to air, not sticky. Terminal buds not enclosed by leaves.

Indumentum: Complex hairs absent; stinging hairs absent; mature twig hairy (when young) or without hairs; hairs dense or sparse with fine short white hairs.

Leaves: Spaced along branches, leaves spiral, simple; petiole present, not winged, attached to base of leaf lamina, not swollen; lamina rarely broadest above middle, broadest at or near middle, or slightly broadest below middle, (3.5–)7–13(–21) cm long, (1.5–)2.5–5(–8.5) cm wide; base symmetric, margin entire, not dissected or lobed, apex rarely rounded, rarely obtuse, or acuminate (short- to long-acuminate), venation pinnate, secondary veins open, prominent, intramarginal veins absent; lower surface pale green or green (dull to glossy), upper surface dark green (dull to glossy), hairs absent or present (sometimes glabrescent at base of lower surface), sparse, oil dots absent, domatia absent; stipules absent.

Flowers: Inflorescence axillary, and extra-axillary, flowers single (strongly and sweetly aromatic); flowers bisexual, with pedicel, with many planes of symmetry, 10–23 mm long, large, 20–30 mm diam.; perianth present, with distinct sepals and petals, white, sometimes yellow, or rarely pink; inner perianth 5–7, free; stamens 50–120 (arranged in 3 whorls), filaments present, free of each other or at base joined, free of perianth; ovary superior, carpels joined, locules (4 or)5; styles free, (4 or)5.

Fruits: single, (15–)20–35 mm long, 5–15 mm diam., brown, not spiny (covered with short appressed hairs), non-fleshy, simple (rarely 4-, mostly 5-angled), dehiscent, capsule (mostly separating into 5 valves). Seeds 2 or 3 (per locule), 8–10 mm long, longer than wide, 3–5 mm diam., winged (with one membranous vertical wing; wing up to 2 times length of seed).

Distribution: West Sepik, East Sepik, Madang, Morobe, Western Highlands, Eastern Highlands, Southern Highlands, Western, Central, Milne Bay, Papuan Islands, New Britain, New Ireland.

74. Styracaceae

Trees and shrubs. Stipules absent. Leaves well-developed, spiral, simple, not dissected or lobed; margin entire; venation pinnate. Inflorescences axillary or terminal. Bracts absent. Flowers bisexual, regular, with distinct calyx and corolla. Sepals (2–)4 or 5(–7). Petals (2–)4 or 5(–7), rarely free or joined, at least in part; tube present or absent. Stamens (5–)8–10(–20), free or fused; filaments present; staminodes absent. Gynoecium with carpels at least partially joined, partially inferior, inferior, or superior; styles partially or fully joined. Fruit simple, dehiscent or indehiscent, capsule, samara or rarely drupe, dry, at least non-fleshy or fleshy. Seeds with or without wings.

PNG genera: ***Bruinsmia, Styrax***

Reference: Hwang and Grimes (1996)

1a. Ovary with 3 locules, reducing to 1 when mature; seeds 1 or 2, rounded, large............. *Styrax argestis*

1b. Ovary usually with 5 locules; seeds many, minute, pointed at each end.............. *Bruinsmia styracoides*

Bruinsmia styracoides Boerl. & Koord. Fig. 359

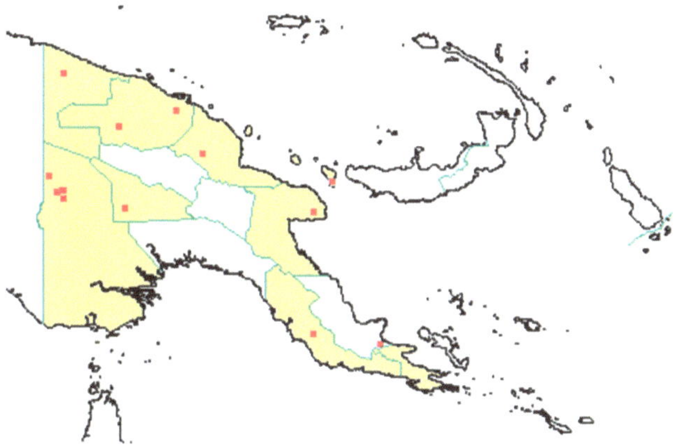

Natuurkundig Tijdschrift voor Nederlandsch-Indië Vol. 53: 69, plate (1893)
Other Literature: C.G.G.J. van Steenis, *Flora Malesiana* Vol. 4: 50 (1949) Fig. 1
Timber Group: Occasional timber species

Field Characters: Canopy trees, 20 m high; bole cylindrical, 40–50 cm diam., straight bole, 12 m long; buttresses absent; spines absent; aerial roots absent; stilt roots absent. Bark greyish brown, rough, slightly cracked, pustular; lenticels elongated vertically; bark 10 mm thick; under-bark red; faintly or non-aromatic; blaze consisting of one layer, orange, red, with stripes yellow, granular without splinters; exudate present, colourless, not readily flowing, changing to brown or orange on exposure to air, sticky. Terminal buds not enclosed by leaves.

Indumentum: Complex hairs absent; stinging hairs absent; mature twigs without hairs.

Leaves: Spaced along branches, leaves simple; petiole present, not winged, attached to base of leaf lamina, not swollen; lamina broadest at or near middle, 14–19 cm long, 5.5–8.5 cm wide; base symmetric, margin crenate, not dissected or lobed, apex acuminate, venation pinnate, secondary veins open, prominent, intramarginal veins absent; lower surface pale green, upper surface dark green, hairs absent, oil dots absent, domatia absent; stipules absent.

Flowers: Inflorescence axillary, flowers on a branched axis; flowers unisexual, with male and female flowers on the same plant, with pedicel; with many planes of symmetry, 8–10 mm long, large, c. 1.5 mm diam.; perianth present, with distinct sepals and petals sepals cup-like, white, green; inner perianth 5, some or partly joined; stamens many, filaments present, free of each other, free of perianth; ovary superior, carpels 4 or 5, joined, styles joined, 1.

Fruits: arranged on branched axis, c. 10 mm long, c. 10 mm diam., green (immature), not spiny, fleshy, simple, indehiscent, drupe-like. Seeds many (c. 50), pointed at each end, not winged, broad as long.

Distribution: West Sepik, East Sepik, Madang, Morobe, Southern Highlands, Western, Central, Northern, Milne Bay.

Notes: The genus *Bruinsmia* is monotypic (consisting of only one species) and is endemic to the Malesian region.

Fig. 359. *Bruinsmia stracoides*. Habit, bark, flowers and leaves

Styrax argestis (Lour.) G.Don Fig. 360

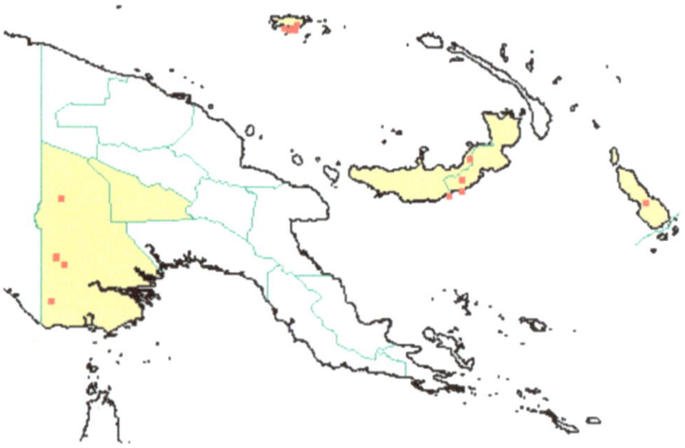

A General History of the Dichlamydeous Plants … Vol. 4: 5 (1837)
Other Literature: C.G.G.J. van Steenis, *Flora Malesiana* Vol. 4: 51 & 52 (1949) Figs 2 (in part) & 3; P.G. Peekel, *Flora of the Bismarck Archipelago for Naturalists* 433 (1984) Fig. 694.
Timber Group: Not a timber species

Field Characters: Sub-canopy trees, 3–12 m high, or shrub up to 2 m high; bole cylindrical, c. 5 cm diam., straight bole, up to c. 5 m long; buttresses absent; spines absent; aerial roots absent; stilt roots absent. Bark dark brown, smooth; lenticels absent; bark thin; under-bark dark maroon-red; faintly or non-aromatic; blaze consisting of one layer, pale red to pink, with faint whitish stripes, granular without splinters; exudate absent. Terminal buds not enclosed by leaves.

Indumentum: Complex hairs absent; stinging hairs absent; mature twigs without hairs.

Leaves: Spaced along branches, leaves simple; petiole present, 2.5–6 cm long, not winged, attached to base of leaf lamina, not swollen; lamina broadest below middle, 3.5–13 cm long, 2–6 cm wide; base symmetric, margin very faintly toothed, sometimes appearing almost entire, apex acuminate, venation pinnate, secondary veins open, prominent, intramarginal veins absent; lower surface dull green, with pale brown hairs (lepidote), upper surface dark green, glossy, hairs absent, oil dots absent, domatia absent; stipules absent.

Flowers: Inflorescence axillary and terminal, flowers on a branched axis; flowers unisexual, with male and female flowers on the same plant, with pedicel; with many planes of symmetry, 8–10 mm long, large; perianth present, with distinct sepals and petals sepals cup-like, white, green; inner perianth (corolla) usually 5, some or partly joined; stamens 10, 7–10 mm long, hairy below, filaments present, free of each other, free of perianth; ovary superior, style 3-angular, carpels imperfectly 3, joined, styles joined, 1.

Fruits: arranged on branched axis, c. 10 mm long, c. 10 mm diam., green (immature), not spiny, fleshy, simple, indehiscent, drupe-like. Seeds 1 or 2, 7–13 mm long, pointed at each end, not winged, broad as long.

Distribution: Southern Highlands, Western, New Britain. Manus, Bougainville.

Notes: The distribution of this species in Papua New Guinea is very incompletely known.

Fig. 360. *Styrax argestis*. Bark, fruit, leaves and flowers

75. Actinidiaceae

Trees, shrubs, and lianas. Stipules present (minute). Leaves well-developed, spiral, simple, not dissected or lobed; margin entire or toothed; venation pinnate. Inflorescences axillary. Bracts often present or absent. Flowers bisexual or unisexual (then plant monoecious or dioecious), regular, with distinct calyx and corolla. Sepals (4 or)5(–7). Petals (4 or)5(–7), free; tube absent. Stamens (10–)18–many, free; filaments present; staminodes absent. Gynoecium with carpels at least partially joined, carpels 5–20 or more, superior; styles partially or fully joined or free. Fruit simple, dehiscent or indehiscent, capsule, berry, dry, at least non-fleshy, or fleshy. Seeds without wings.

PNG genera: *Saurauia*

Notes: *Saurauia* has previously been classified in the Family Saurauiaceae.

References: Backer and Bakhuizen van den Brink (1963), Conn and Damas (2013), Royen (1982b), Takeuchi (2008)

Saurauia conferta Warb.
Fig. 361

Botanische Jahrbücher für Systematik, Pflanzengeschichte und Pflanzengeographie Vol. 13: 379 (1891)
Timber Group: Non-timber species

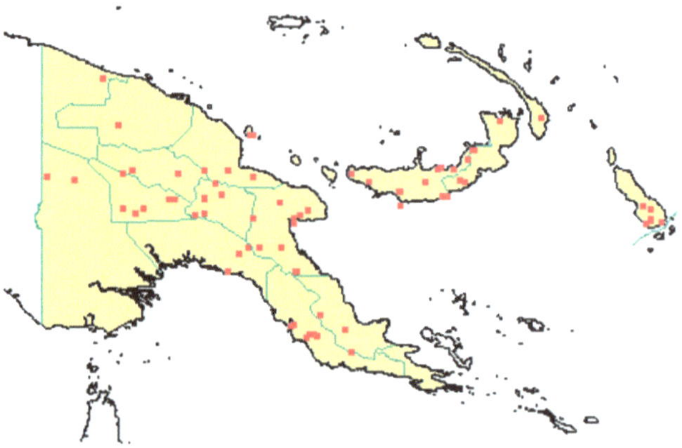

Field Characters: Subcanopy trees, 5–8 m high; bole cylindrical, 6–8 cm diam., straight; buttresses absent; spines absent; aerial roots absent; stilt roots absent. Bark brown, slightly rough or smooth, slightly pustular; lenticels elongated vertically often not distinct; bark 3 mm thick; under-bark yellow or green; faintly or non-aromatic; unpleasant; blaze consisting of one layer, white or pale yellow cream-coloured, markings absent, fibrous; exudate present, colourless, not readily flowing, changing to dark orange on exposure to air, slightly sticky. Terminal buds not enclosed by leaves.

Indumentum: Complex hairs absent; stinging hairs absent.

Leaves: Spaced along branches, leaves spiral, simple; petiole 25 mm long, not winged, attached to base of leaf lamina, not swollen; lamina broadest above middle, 24–26 cm long, 8–11 cm wide; base symmetric, margin serrate to dentate (toothed), not dissected or lobed, apex acuminate, venation pinnate, secondary veins open, prominent, intramarginal veins absent; lower surface pale green, upper surface dark green, hairs present, sparse, oil dots absent, domatia absent; stipules absent.

Flowers: Inflorescence axillary, flowers on a branched axis condensed; inflorescence with gelatinous exudate or flowers on an unbranched axis (by misinterpretation); flowers unisexual, with male and female flowers on same plant, with pedicel 70 mm long, with many planes of symmetry, 40–45 mm long, large, 50 mm diam.; perianth present, with distinct sepals and petals, white; inner perianth 5, free or some or partly joined at base; stamens many (yellow-orange), filaments present, joined, joined to perianth; ovary inferior, carpels joined, locules 5; styles free, 5.

Fruits: arranged on branched axis, condensed, or arranged on unbranched axis (by misinterpretation), indehiscent.

Distribution: West Sepik, East Sepik, Madang, Morobe, Western Highlands, Eastern Highlands, Southern Highlands, Western, Gulf, Central, Northern, New Britain, New Ireland, Bougainville.

Fig. 361. *Saurauia conferta.* Bark, leaves and flowers

Saurauia congestiflora A.C.Sm.
Fig. 362

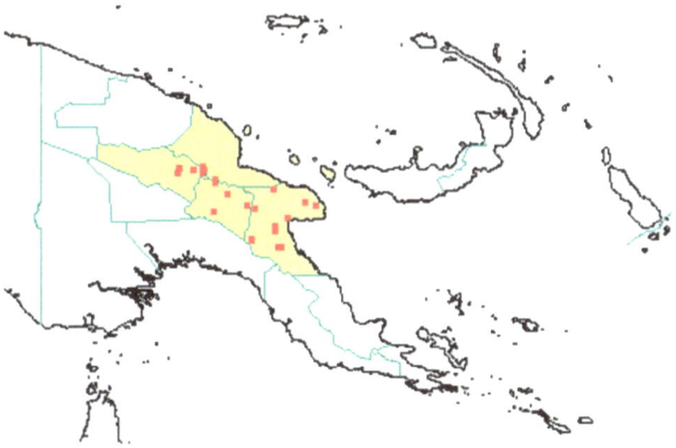

Journal of the Arnold Arboretum Vol. 22: 519 (1941)
Timber Group: Occasional timber species

Field Characters: Subcanopy trees, c. 15 m high; bole cylindrical, 20 cm diam., straight; buttresses absent; spines absent; aerial roots absent; stilt roots absent. Bark brown or grey, rough, fissured; bark 8–10 mm thick; under-bark yellow or green; faintly or non-aromatic; unpleasant or pleasant; blaze consisting of one layer, pale yellow cream-coloured, markings absent, fibrous; exudate present, colourless, not readily flowing, changing to pale brown or pale orange on exposure to air, slightly sticky. Terminal buds not enclosed by leaves.

Indumentum: Complex hairs present, star-like; stinging hairs absent; mature twig hairy; hairs dense.

Leaves: Spaced along branches, leaves spiral, simple; petiole 18–20 mm long, not winged, attached to base of leaf lamina, not swollen; lamina broadest at or near middle, sometimes broadest below middle, or sometimes broadest above middle, (9–)11–15.5(–20) cm long, (4.5–)6–9.5 cm wide; base symmetric, margin crenate or entire, not dissected or lobed, apex slightly emarginate or retuse, rounded, obtuse, or acuminate, venation pinnate, secondary veins open, prominent, intramarginal veins absent; lower surface pale brown or red, upper surface glossy green, hairs present, dense, oil dots absent, domatia absent; stipules absent.

Flowers: Inflorescence axillary, on long stalks (peduncles), flowers arising from a single point (by misinterpretation) or on a branched axis (branches short); flowers bisexual, with pedicel short, with many planes of symmetry, 12–20 mm long, large, 12–14 mm diam.; perianth present, with distinct sepals and petals, white; inner perianth 5, free; stamens many, filaments very short, joined at base, free of perianth; ovary superior, carpels joined, styles joined, 1.

Fruits: Arising from a single point (by misinterpretation) or arranged on branched axis (branches very short), fruit 8–10 mm long, 7–8 mm diam., blue, red, green, or brown, not spiny, fleshy, simple, indehiscent. Seeds many, not winged.

Distribution: Madang, Morobe, Western Highlands, Eastern Highlands.

Fig. 362. *Saurauia congestiflora.* Bark, leaves and flowers

Saurauia plurilocularis C.T.White & W.D.Francis Fig. 363

Proceedings of the Royal Society of Queensland 244 (1927)
Timber Group: Non-timber species

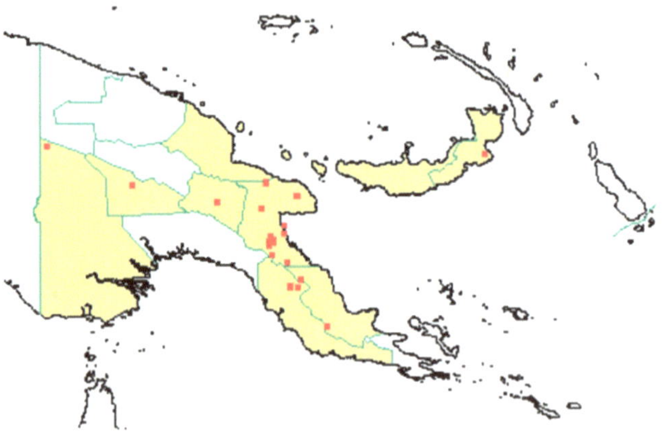

Field Characters: Subcanopy trees, 4–8 m high; bole markedly fluted, c. 20 cm diam., straight, 1.5 m long; buttresses absent; spines absent; aerial roots absent; stilt roots absent. Bark brown, rough, fissured; lenticels elongated vertically; bark 8–9 mm thick; under-bark brown; faintly or non-aromatic; pleasant; blaze consisting of 2 layers; outer blaze pale brown or white, with stripes, granular without splinters; inner blaze white, markings absent, granular without splinters; exudate present, slightly white or colourless, not readily flowing or flowing, not changing colour on exposure to air, not sticky. Terminal buds not enclosed by leaves.

Indumentum: Complex hairs absent; stinging hairs absent.

Leaves: Spaced along branches, leaves spiral, simple, lamina broadest above middle, c. 50 cm long, c. 10 cm wide; base symmetric, margin serrate to dentate (toothed), with teeth dark brown, not dissected or lobed, apex obtuse or acuminate; lower surface green, upper surface dark green, domatia absent; stipules absent.

Flowers: Inflorescence axillary, flowers bisexual; perianth present, with distinct sepals and petals, white.

Fruits: bright red (cherry-red), simple, indehiscent.

Distribution: Madang, Morobe, Eastern Highlands, Southern Highlands, Western, Central, Northern, New Britain.

Fig. 363. *Saurauia plurilocularis.* Bark, leaves and flowers

Saurauia rufa Burkill
Fig. 364

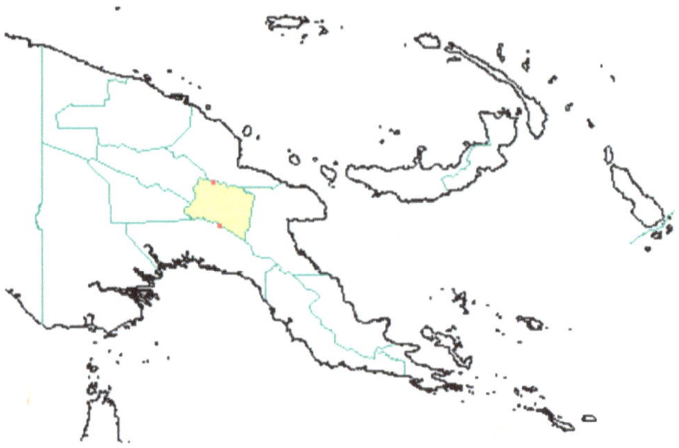

Bulletin of Miscellaneous Information, Royal Gardens, Kew 97 (1988)
Timber Group: Non-timber species

Field Characters: Subcanopy trees, 6–15 m high; bole cylindrical, 15–25 cm diam., straight, 3–4 m long; buttresses absent; spines present broad at base, on branches leaves and inflorescences; aerial roots absent; stilt roots absent. Bark brown or dull grey, rough, fissured or slightly pustular; lenticels irregular; bark 8–12 mm thick; under-bark yellow cream-coloured or yellowish green; faintly or non-aromatic; pleasant; blaze consisting of one layer, white, pale yellow cream-coloured, or pale orange, markings absent, fibrous; exudate present, colourless, not readily flowing, changing to orange or brown on exposure to air or not changing colour, slightly sticky. Terminal buds not enclosed by leaves.

Indumentum: Complex hairs absent; stinging hairs absent; mature twig without hairs.

Leaves: Spaced along branches, leaves spiral, simple; petiole 10 mm long, not winged, attached to base of leaf lamina, not swollen; lamina broadest at or near middle or broadest below middle, 14–21 cm long, 6.5–8 cm wide; base symmetric, margin serrate to dentate (toothed), not dissected or lobed, apex obtuse, venation pinnate, secondary veins open, prominent, intramarginal veins absent; lower surface pale green, upper surface dark green, hairs absent, oil dots absent, domatia absent; stipules absent.

Flowers: Inflorescence axillary, usually flowers on an unbranched axis flower clusters surrounded by reddish bracts on a long stalk (peduncle 9–17 mm long) or flowers single, unisexual, with male and female flowers on same plant, flowers with pedicel 10–15 cm long, with many planes of symmetry, 25–30 mm long, large, 20 mm diam.; perianth present, with distinct sepals and petals, white; inner perianth 5, free; stamens many, filaments present, joined, joined to perianth; ovary inferior, carpels joined, locules 5; styles free, 5.

Fruits: usually arranged on unbranched axis or single, green, spiny, coarsely hair-like, non-fleshy, simple.

Distribution: Eastern Highlands.

Fig. 364. *Saurauia rufa*. Bark, leaves, flowers and developing fruit

unplaced asterid I

76. Boraginaceae

Trees, shrubs, lianas, and herbs. Stipules absent. Leaves well-developed or much reduced, spiral or opposite, simple, not dissected or lobed; margin entire; venation pinnate or palmate (3-veined at base). Inflorescences axillary, terminal, or leaf-opposed. Bracts absent or present. Flowers bisexual, slightly zygomorphic or slightly irregular, with distinct calyx and corolla. Sepals usually 5–8. Petals 5, joined, at least in part; tube present. Stamens 5, free or fused; filaments present; staminodes absent. Gynoecium with carpels at least partially joined, superior; styles partially or fully joined. Fruit simple, dehiscent or indehiscent, drupe, 1–4-seeded, dry, at least non-fleshy, or fleshy. Seeds without wings.

PNG genera: *Bothriospermum, Carmona, Coldenia,* ***Cordia****, Cynoglossum, Echium, Ehretia, Halgania, Heliotropium, Myosotis, Pectocarya, Tournefortia, Trichodesma, Trigonotis.*

References: Royen (1975)

1a. Corolla with distinct scales in throat; fruits always breaking into 4 nutlets.. 2

1b. Corolla without scales in throat.. 4

2a. Corolla lobes twisted in bud; hairs on upper surface of rosulate leaves directed towards apex, with hairs on lower surface directed towards base .... *Myosotis scorpioides* L. (not treated here)

2b. Corolla lobes not twisted in bud... 3

3a. Nutlets smooth or with straight hairs .... *Trigonotis* (not treated here)

3b. Nutlets with hooded bristles that attached to objects; flowers white to blue.. .... *Cynoglossum javanicum* (Lehm.) Thumb. (not treated here)

4a. Prostrate or creeping herbs, with leaves folded like a fan, densely hairy ...... *Coldenia* (not treated here)

4b. Trees, shrubs or herbs, with leaves not folded like a fan 5

5a. Style distinctly 4-branched; flowers male (unisexual) or bisexual; trees or robust shrubs............ *Cordia*

5b. Style not 4-branched; flowers all bisexual 6

6a. Style 2-branched, without annular stigma below apex; inflorescences many-flowered.......................... ....*Ehretia* (not treated here)

6b. Style entire or shortly 2-toothed, if toothed then depressed at apex and with annular stigma below apex; inflorescences many-flowered or solitary 7

7a. Stamens with connective prolonged into a very long point, the points of 5 stamens twisted into 1 cone far exserted from corolla throat.................. *Trichodesma zeylanicum* (Burm.f.) R.Br. (not treated here)

7b. Stamens with connective straight 8

8a. Erect or prostrate herbs, or ornamental shrubs; fruits with 2 lobes or breaking into segments .... *Heliotropium* (not treated here)

8b. Erect or climbing shrubs, or small trees; fruits not lobed .... *Tournefortia* (not treated here)

Cordia dichotoma G.Forst.
Figs 365, 366

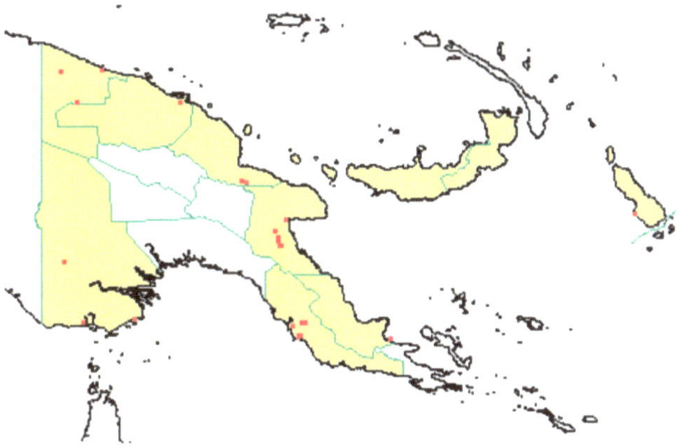

Florulae Insularum Australium Prodromus 18 (1786)
Other Literature: J.J. Havel, *Forest Botany, Part 2 Botanical Taxonomy* 277 (1975) Fig. 79; P.G. Peekel, *Flora of the Bismarck Archipelago for Naturalists* 469 (1984) Fig. 752 (as *C. myxa* L.).
Timber Group: Minor hardwoods

Field Characters: Canopy trees, 15–30 m high; bole cylindrical, 25–50 cm diam., straight mostly short, up to c. 10 m long; buttresses absent; spines absent; aerial roots absent; stilt roots absent. Bark grey, rough, strongly fissured and ridged; bark 18–20 mm thick; blaze consisting of 2 layers; outer blaze white, pale yellow, or greyish green, markings absent, fibrous; inner blaze white or pale yellow, markings absent, fibrous; exudate present, colourless, not readily flowing, changing to brown on exposure to air, sticky. Terminal buds not enclosed by leaves.

Fig. 365. *Cordia dichotoma*. Bark

Indumentum: Complex hairs absent; stinging hairs absent.

Leaves: Spaced along branches, leaves spiral, simple; petiole present, not winged, attached to base of leaf lamina, not swollen; lamina broadest below middle, 8 cm long, 5 cm wide; base symmetric, margin entire, not dissected or lobed, apex sub-acute or acuminate, venation pinnate, or at base trinerved, secondary veins open, prominent, intramarginal veins absent; lower surface pale green, upper surface green, oil dots absent, domatia absent; stipules absent.

Flowers: Inflorescence terminal, flowers on a branched axis; flowers bisexual, with many planes of symmetry, 5–6 mm long, small, c. 2 mm diam., with pedicel; perianth present, with distinct sepals and petals, white; inner perianth 5, some or partly joined forming a corolla tube; stamens 5, filaments present, free of each other, joined to perianth; ovary superior, carpels joined, locules 2; styles free, 2.

Fruits: arranged on branched axis, fruit 10–12 mm long, brown, not spiny, fleshy, simple, indehiscent, drupe. Seed 1, 5–6 mm long, longer than wide, c. 2 mm diam., not winged.

Distribution: West Sepik, East Sepik, Madang, Morobe, Western, Central, Northern.

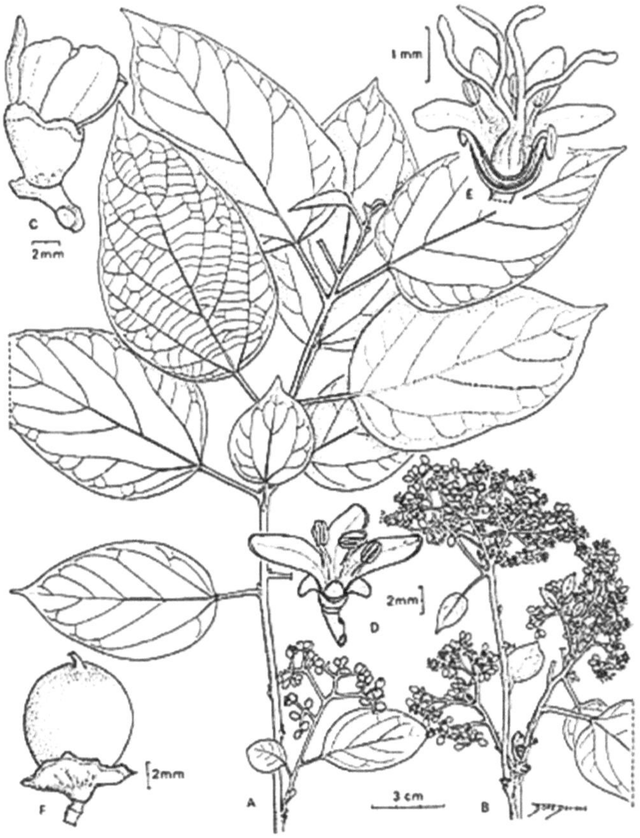

Fig. 366. *Cordia dichotoma*. Illustration of branchlet showing flowers and fruit (© Papua New Guinea National Herbarium, Lae)

Cordia subcordata Lam.
Fig. 367

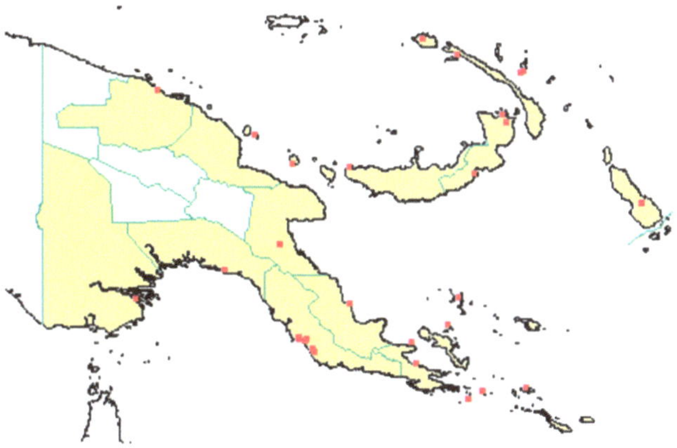

Tableau Encyclopédique et Méthodique ... Botanique 1 (1792)
Other Literature: P.G. Peekel, *Flora of the Bismarck Archipelago for Naturalists* 469 (1984) Fig. 751.
Timber Group: Non-timber tree

Field Characters: Coastal or near-coastal subcanopy to canopy trees, 7–10(–15) m high; bole cylindrical, crooked, mostly short; buttresses absent; spines absent; aerial roots absent; stilt roots absent. Bark grey, rough, strongly fissured and ridged; bark 10–18 mm thick; blaze consisting of 1 layer; under-bark dark brown; blaze pale brown to cream-coloured, with brown streaks, fibrous; exudate unknown. Terminal buds not enclosed by leaves.

Indumentum: Complex hairs absent; stinging hairs absent.

Leaves: Spaced along branches, leaves spiral (sometimes sub-opposite), simple; petiole 4–6 cm long, not winged, attached to base of leaf lamina, not swollen; lamina broadest below middle, 8–25 cm long, 5–17 cm wide; base symmetric, rounded to subcordate, margin entire, not dissected or lobed, apex sub-acute to acuminate, venation pinnate, secondary veins open, prominent, intramarginal veins absent; lower surface pale green, upper surface green, oil dots absent, domatia absent; stipules absent.

Flowers: Inflorescence axillary, towards ends of branchlets, flowers on a branched axis; flowers bisexual, with many planes of symmetry, (18–)20–40 mm long, large, 35–50 mm diam., with pedicel; perianth present, with distinct sepals and petals; inner perianth orange, sometimes yellow, 5–7, forming a long corolla tube; stamens 5, filaments present, free of each other, joined to perianth; ovary superior, carpels joined, locules 4; styles joined, 1.

Fruits: arranged on branched axis, fruit 20–30 mm long, 15–20 mm diam., brown, not spiny, woody when mature, simple, indehiscent, drupe. Seeds up to 4, 10–13 mm long, longer than wide, not winged.

Distribution: East Sepik, Madang, Morobe, Western, Gulf, Central, Northern, Milne Bay, Papuan Islands, New Britain, New Ireland, Bougainville.

One collection, *J.C. Saunders 148*, from the Eastern Highlands, appears to be a misidentification.

Notes: This species appears to produce fruit throughout much of the year. These fruits are buoyant and may be carried long distances by ocean currents.

Fig. 367. *Cordia subcordata.* Habit, leaves, bark, flowers and fruit

Heliotropium foertherianum Diane & Hilger Fig. 368

Botanische Jahrbücher für Systematik, Pflanzengeschichte und Pflanzengeographie 125: 46 (2003)
Timber Group: Non-timber product

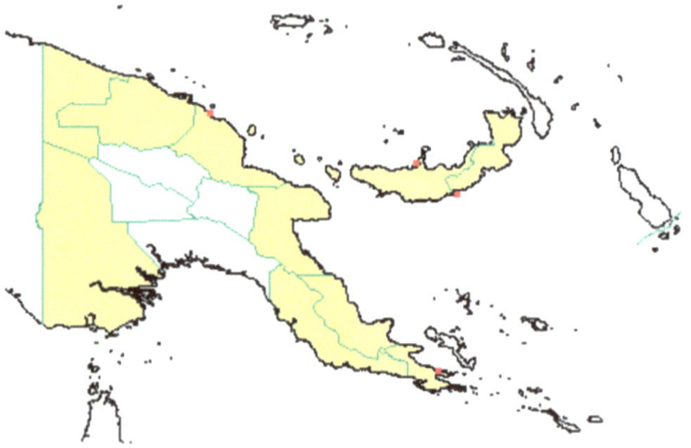

Field Characters: Rare small, sub-canopy trees, up to 5 m high, or usually shrubs 1–5 m tall; bole cylindrical, c. 25 cm diam., crooked, mostly short, up to c. 1 m long; branchlets stout; buttresses absent; spines absent; aerial roots absent; stilt roots absent. Bark grey, coarsely rough, strongly fissured and ridged, bark 18–20 mm thick; under-bark pale brown; blaze consisting of 2 layers; outer blaze mid-yellow, markings absent; inner blaze pale yellow, markings absent; exudate not known. Terminal buds not enclosed by leaves.

Indumentum: Branchlets densely hairy, with hairs rust-coloured or white; complex hairs absent; stinging hairs absent.

Leaves: terminating branches, spiral, simple; petiole present, not winged, attached to base of leaf lamina, not swollen; lamina broadest above middle, 7–13 cm long, 2–4 cm wide, densely covered with yellowish white 'hair-like' hairs, base tapering (attenuate); margin entire, not dissected or lobed, apex obtuse to rounded; venation pinnate, secondary veins open, prominent, pale yellow, intramarginal veins absent; lower surface pale green, upper surface sub-glossy green, oil dots absent, domatia absent; stipules absent.

Flowers: Inflorescence terminal, flowers on a branched axis, corymbose, 5–10 cm diam., densely rust-coloured hairy, cymes scorpoid; flowers bisexual, with many planes of symmetry, 2.5–3 mm long, small, c. 2.5 mm diam.; pedicel absent (flowers sessile); perianth present, with distinct sepals and petals; calyx (outer perianth) fleshy, 1.5–2 mm long, densely hairy with rust-coloured hairs; inner perianth (Corolla) white, forming a corolla tube, with 5 lobes; stamens 5, filaments present, free of each other, joined to perianth (c. 4 mm above base of corolla); ovary superior, subglobose, glabrous, carpels joined, locules 2; styles joined, 1.

Fruits: arranged on branched axis, fruit c. 5 mm diam., brown, not spiny, fleshy, simple, indehiscent, drupe.

Distribution: West Sepik, East Sepik, Madang, Morobe, Western, Central, Northern.

Notes: Previously known as *Argusia argentea* (L.f.) Heine *Flore de la Nouvelle-Calédonie et Dépendances* Vol. 7: 109 (1976).

Fig. 368. *Heliotropium foertherianum*. Habit, bark, leaves, flowers and fruit

Icacinales

PNG families: Icacinaceae

77. Icacinaceae

Trees, sometimes shrubs. Stipules absent. Leaves well-developed, spiral, simple, not dissected or lobed; margin entire; venation pinnate. Inflorescences axillary or arising from old wood of trunk and/or branches, opening branched. Bracts absent. Pedicel articulated with calyx. Flowers bisexual, regular, with distinct calyx and corolla. Sepals free or joined at base, usually 4 or 5. Petals free, (4 or) 5; tube absent. Stamens free, 5; filaments present, usually shorter than anthers; staminodes absent. Gynoecium with 1 carpel, superior; style 1. Fruit simple, ± compressed, ridged, indehiscent, large, drupe, becoming woody. Seed 1, without wings.

PNG genera: ***Merrilliodendron***

References: Hua and Howard (2008), Sleumer (1942, 1969, 1972a), Utteridge (2007a)

Merrilliodendron megacarpum (Hemsl.) Sleum. Fig. 369

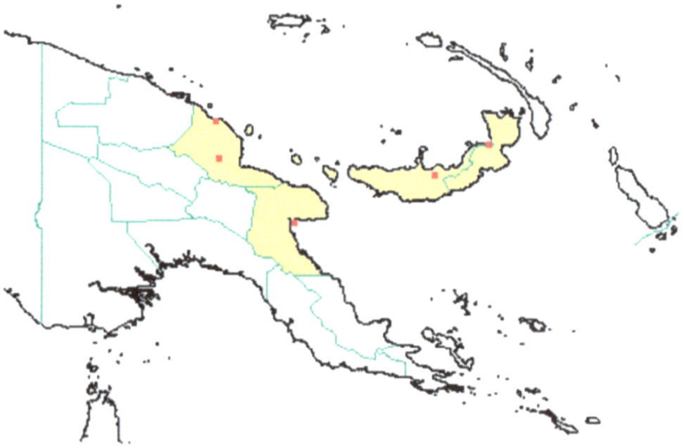

Notizblatt des Botanischen Gartens und Museums zu Berlin-Dahlem Vol. 15: 243 (1940)
Other Literature: H. Sleumer, *Flora Malesiana Series 1* Vol. 7: 50 & 51 (1972) Fig. 19.
Timber Group: Non-timber species

Field Characters: Subcanopy trees, (5–)6–16(–25) m high, or shrub up to 3 m high; bole cylindrical and often fluted, 30–55 cm diam., straight, (3–)5–10 m long; buttresses absent; spines absent; aerial roots absent; stilt roots absent. Bark dark brown, brown, white, green-grey to pale brown, rough, pustular; lenticels elongated vertically (ridged, with fissures narrow); bark 10–15 mm thick; under-bark dark brown; not known if aromatic; blaze consisting of one layer, pale brown to cream-coloured, speckled, fibrous; exudate present, clear, turning brown on exposure to the air, slightly sticky. Terminal buds not enclosed by leaves.

Indumentum: Complex hairs absent; stinging hairs absent; mature twig without hairs.

Leaves: Spaced along branches, leaves spiral, simple; petiole present, 15–20 mm long, not winged, attached to base of leaf lamina, not swollen; lamina broadest at or near middle, (15–)20–30 cm long, 7–11(–16) cm wide; base symmetric, rounded to cuneate, margin entire, not dissected or lobed, apex shortly tapered, or blunt venation pinnate, secondary veins open, usually 10–12 per side, prominent, intramarginal veins absent; lower surface pale green, upper surface dark green, hairs absent, oil dots present, many but minute, domatia absent; stipules absent.

Flowers: Inflorescence axillary, however, often in defoliated axes or from wood of trunck or branches, 7–20 cm long, flowers on a branched axis, many-flowered; flowers bisexual, with pedicel 4–6 mm long, flowers with many planes of symmetry, 3–5 mm long, small, 1.5–2 mm diam.; perianth present, with distinct sepals and petals, cream-coloured or pale yellow to purplish; inner perianth 5, 3–4 mm long, free, inner surface hairy; stamens 5, filaments short, without hairs (anthers with connective hairy), free of each other, free from perianth; ovary superior, carpels solitary, locules 1; style 1.

Fruits: arranged on branched axis, pendulous, fruit (40–)50–100 mm long, (20–)30–60 mm diam., white or yellow to purple (when ripe and fresh), becoming purple to black (when older), not spiny, leathery to woody (endocarp), simple, indehiscent, drupe. Seed 1, 40–60 mm long, longer than wide, 20–25 mm wide, not winged.

Distribution: Madang, Morobe, New Britain.

Fig. 369. *Merrilliodendron megacarpum*. Bark, fruit, leaves and seedling

Metteniusales

PNG families: Metteniusaceae

78. Metteniusaceae

Trees, shrubs, and lianas. Stipules absent. Leaves well-developed, usually spiral or opposite, simple, not dissected or lobed; margin usually entire or toothed; venation pinnate. Inflorescences axillary or terminal. Bracts absent. Flowers unisexual, then plant dioecious, regular, with distinct calyx and corolla male flowers or perianth absent female flowers. Sepals absent or (4 or)5(or 6). Petals absent or (4 or)5(or 6), free or joined, at least in part; tube absent or present. Stamens absent or (4 or)5(or 6), fused to perianth or free; filaments present; staminodes absent. Gynoecium with carpels at least partially joined, superior; styles partially or fully joined. Fruit simple, indehiscent, drupe, fleshy. Seeds without wings.

PNG genera: ***Platea.***

References: Sleumer (1972b)

Notes: *Platea* has previously been included in the Icacinaceae.

1a. Stamens with filaments joined for almost their entire length to the corolla tube; leaves without scales .... *Gonocaryum litorale* (Cardiopteridaceae) (see below)

1b. Stamens with filaments free, joined to the very base of the corolla; leaves with a layer of scales on lower surface, at least when young; scales appressed, rounded to star-shaped .... *Platea*

Platea excelsa Blume var. *borneensis* (Heine) Sleumer Fig. 370

Blumea Vol. 17: 246 (1969)
Other Literature: H. Sleumer, *Flora Malesiana Series 1* Vol. 7: 13 & 14 (1971) Fig. 6.
Timber Group: Non-timber species

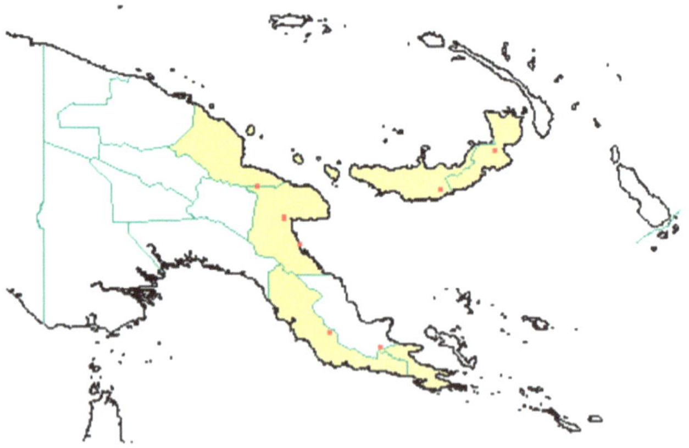

Field Characters: Canopy trees, 20–25 m high, or subcanopy trees; bole cylindrical, 30–35 cm diam., straight; buttresses present; spines absent; aerial roots absent; stilt roots absent. Bark brown, rough, pustular; lenticels elongated vertically; bark 10 mm thick; under-bark green; strongly aromatic; pleasant; blaze consisting of one layer, red, with stripes, fibrous; exudate absent. Terminal buds not enclosed by leaves.

Indumentum: Complex hairs absent; stinging hairs absent; mature twig without hairs.

Leaves: Spaced along branches, leaves spiral, simple; petiole present, not winged, attached to base of leaf lamina, not swollen; lamina broadest at or near middle, (9–)12–23(–26) cm long, (4.5–)5–10(–12) cm wide; base very asymmetric, margin entire, not dissected or lobed, apex acuminate, venation pinnate, secondary veins open, prominent, intramarginal veins absent; lower surface green or greenish red (hairs reddish), upper surface glossy green, hairs absent upper surface or present lower surface, dense, oil dots absent, domatia absent; stipules absent.

Flowers: Inflorescence axillary, flowers on a branched axis; flowers unisexual, with male and female flowers on different plants, with pedicel, with many planes of symmetry, 1.5–2 mm long, small, 1.5–2 mm diam.; perianth present (male flowers) or absent (female flowers), with distinct sepals and petals, pale green; inner perianth 5, some or partly joined at base; stamens absent (female flowers) –5 (male flowers), filaments short, free of each other, joined to perianth; ovary superior, carpels solitary, locules 1; styles absent.

Fruits: arranged on branched axis, fruit 35–40 mm long, 20–25 mm diam., dark green or red, not spiny, fleshy, simple, indehiscent, drupe. Seed 1, c. 15 mm long, longer than wide, c. 10 mm wide, not winged.

Distribution: Madang, Morobe, Central, Milne Bay, New Britain.

Fig. 370. *Platea excelsa* var. *borneensis*. Bark, leaves and fruit

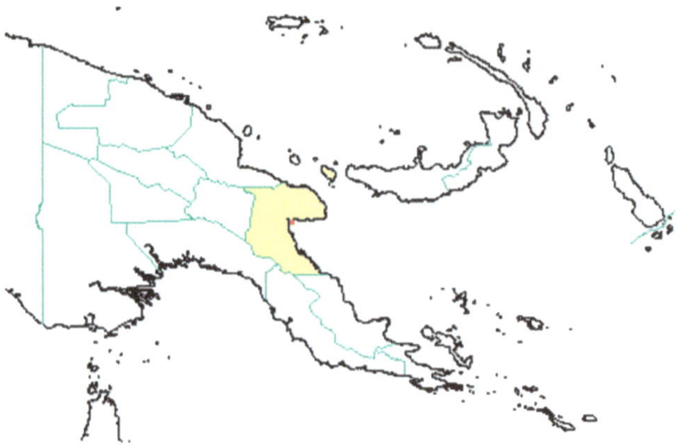

Platea latifolia Blume

Flora van Nederlandsch Indië 647 (1825)
Other Literature: H. Sleumer, *Flora Malesiana* Vol. Series 1, 7: 11 (1971)
Timber Group: Non-timber species

Field Characters: Canopy trees, mostly 20–25(–30) m high; bole cylindrical, up to c. 45 cm diam., straight, up to c. 20 m long; buttresses absent, or sometimes up to 0.5 m high; spines absent; aerial roots absent; stilt roots absent. Bark grey, rough, pustular; lenticels elongated vertically; bark 7–9 mm thick; under-bark green; strongly aromatic; unpleasant; blaze consisting of one layer, yellow or yellowish brown, with stripes, granular without splinters; exudate present or absent, colourless, not readily flowing, changing to pale brown on exposure to air, not sticky. Terminal buds not enclosed by leaves.

Indumentum: Complex hairs present, star-like; stinging hairs absent; mature twig hairy; hairs sparse.

Leaves: Spaced along branches, leaves spiral, simple; petiole present, not winged, attached to base of leaf lamina, not swollen; lamina broadest below middle, 7–17 cm long, 2.5–8 cm wide; base symmetric, margin entire, not dissected or lobed, apex acuminate, venation pinnate, secondary veins open, prominent, intramarginal veins absent; lower surface brown, with rusty brown hairs, upper surface dark green, hairs present (on lower surface), sparse, oil dots absent, domatia absent; stipules absent.

Flowers: Inflorescence axillary, flowers on an unbranched axis; bisexual, with pedicel, with many planes of symmetry, c. 5 mm long, small, c. 5 mm diam.; perianth present, with distinct sepals and petals, white or yellow; inner perianth 4, free; stamens 4, filaments present, free of each other, free of perianth; ovary superior, carpels joined, locules 2; styles absent.

Fruits: arranged on unbranched axis, fruit 25–40 mm long, 15–20 mm diam., fruit dark blue or purple, not spiny, slightly fleshy, simple, indehiscent, drupe. Seeds 1 or 2, at least 20 mm long, longer than wide, c. 10 mm diam., not winged.

Distribution: Morobe.

Gentianales

PNG families: Apocynaceae, Gentianaceae, Loganiaceae, Rubiaceae

1a. Stipules absent .... 82. Apocynaceae

1b. Stipules usually large and ± persistent 2

2a. Flowers with carpels inferior (often becoming superior in fruit); corolla tube often narrow and lobes spreading .... 79. Rubiaceae

2b. Flowers with carpels superior; corolla tube mostly broad and lobes spreading to recurved 3

3a. Corolla lobes valvate; fruit dehiscent, 2-valve capsule .... 81. Loganiaceae

3b. Corolla lobes contorted or imbricate; fruit indehiscent, berry-like .... 80. Gentianaceae

79. Rubiaceae

Trees, shrubs, lianas, and herbs. Stipules present. Leaves well-developed, spiral (by misinterpretation) one leaf of pair not developed, opposite, or whorled, simple, not dissected or lobed; margin entire or toothed; venation pinnate or one-veined. Inflorescences terminal. Bracts absent or present. Flowers bisexual or unisexual, then plant monoecious or sometimes dioecious, regular, with distinct calyx and corolla or sometimes with sepals absent. Sepals 4 or 5. Petals (3 or)4–10, joined, at least in part; tube present. Stamens 4 or 5, fused to corolla; filaments present; staminodes absent. Gynoecium with carpels at least partially joined, inferior (in fruit often becoming superior); styles free or partially or fully joined. Fruit simple, dehiscent or indehiscent, capsule, achene, drupe, or berry, dry, at least non-fleshy, or fleshy. Seeds without wings or rarely with wings.

PNG genera: *Adina, Aidia, Airosperma, Amaracarpus, Anotis, Anthocephalus, Anthorrhiza, Antirhea, Arcytophyllum, Argostemma, Atractocarpus, Badusa, Bikkia, Borreria, Calycosia, Cephaelis, Chomelia, Cinchona, Coelospermum, Coffea* (introduced), *Coprosma, Coptosapelta, Cowiea,* ***Cyclophyllum****, Dentella, Diodia, Diplospora, Dolicholobium, Gaertnera, Galium,* ***Gardenia****, Geophila, Guettarda, Gynochthodes, Hedyotis, Hydnophytum, Hypobathrum,* ***Ixora****, Kajewskiella, Knoxia, Lasianthus, Litosanthes, Lucinaea, Maschalodesme,* ***Mastixiodendron****, Metadina, Mitracarpus, Mitragyna, Morinda, Mussaenda, Mycetia, Myrmecodia, Myrmephytum,* ***Nauclea****, Neolamarckia,* ***Neonauclea****, Nertera, Oldenlandia, Ophiorrhiza, Pachystylus, Paederia, Pavetta, Pentas, Pertusadina, Plectroniella, Pogonolobus, Porterandia, Psilanthus,* ***Psychotria****,* ***Psydrax****, Randia, Rhadinopus, Richardia, Saprosma, Sarcocephalus, Scyphiphora, Spermacoce,* ***Tarenna****,* ***Timonius****, Uncaria, Urophyllum,* ***Versteegia****, Wendlandia, Xanthophytum*

References: Bremer (2009), Bremer *et al.* (1995), Bremer and Eriksson (2009), Davis *et al.* (2009), Robbrecht (1988)

1a. Leaves with tertiary venation, finely and regularly parallel (visible at least on lower surface); inflorescences axillary; fruits a drupe 2

1b. Leaves with tertiary venation not visible or variously areolate; inflorescences axillary, terminal or other; fruit dry or fleshy, drupe-like, baccate, capsule, schizocarp, or other 3

2a. Fruit with 1 pyrene, containing 2–5 seeds; corolla with 4 or 5 lobes .... *Antirhea* (not treated here)

2b. Fruit with at least 50 pyrenes, each with 1 seed; corolla with 6 lobes .... *Timonius*

3a. Mangroves, growing in areas regularly inundated with sea water; stilt roots usually present .... *Scyphiphora* (not treated here)

3b. Terrestrial or plants of freshwater habitats; stilt roots absent 4

4a. Flowers fused together by their ovaries, at least at their bases; fruits multiple, formed from more than 1 flower 5

4b. Flowers not joined to each other, but sometimes tightly clustered together; fruits free 6

5a. Stipules forming a hemispherical to conical bud; fruit drupe-like, each with 2 or 4 pyrenes; each pyrene with 1 seed .... *Morinda* (not treated here)

5b. Stipules held erect and pressed together in a flattened bud; fruit baccate, each fruit with many seeds.. .... *Nauclea*

6a. Flowers in 1 to several symmetrical globose heads 7

6b. Flowers variously arranged in cymes, panicles or other branched arrangements, if in heads, then not symmetrically globose 12

7a. Lianas; spines present, recurved .... *Uncaria* (not treated here)

7b. Trees or shrubs; spines absent 8

8a. Fruits indehiscent .... *Neolamarckia* (not treated here)

8b. Fruits dehiscent, a capsule 9

9a. Stipules held erect and pressed together for form a flattened bud 10

9b. Stipules forming a conical or hemispherical bud 11

10a. Inflorescence heads sessile or subsessile; peduncles up to 5 mm long; stigmas cylindrical .... *Mitragyna* (not treated here)

10b. Inflorescence heads stalked; peduncles at least 10 mm long; stigmas globose to ovoid .... *Neonauclea*

11a. Seeds not winged; stipules triangular, not lobed .... *Metadina* (not treated here)

11b. Seeds winged; stipules deeply 2-lobed .... *Adina* (not treated here)

12a. Inflorescences axillary (in both axils at a node), super-axillary, and/or appearing axillary because on regularly produced axillary or lateral short shoots 13

12b. Inflorescences terminal, pseudo-axillary because borne in only 1 axil at a node, or pseudo-axillary because leaves of very different size such that one leaf not distinct 16

13a. Branchlets and lower surface of leaves densely hairy with long hairs...*Xanthophytum* (not treated here)

13b. Branchlets and lower surface of leaves without hairs or if hairy, then hairs not dense nor long 14

14a. Petioles and inflorescence axes articulate at their bases; stigmas not lobed .... *Ixora*

14b. Petioles and inflorescence axes not articulate; stipules lobed 15

15a. Srubs or small trees; plants without an unpleasant aroma (when crushed); corolla salverform with slender tube; corolla lobes convolute (in bud) .... *Pavetta* (not treated here)

15b. Erect shrubs; plants with or without unpleasant aroma when crushed; corolla campanulate, tubular, or funnelform, with lobes valvate or valvate-induplicate (in bud) .... *Saprosma* (not treated here)

15c. Subcanopy to canopy trees; plants without unpleasant aroma (when crushed); corolla campanulate, with lobes valvate .... *Mastixiodendron*

16a. Woody twiners or climbers; fruits a woody capsule, subglobose; seeds winged ....
.... *Coptosapelta* (not treated here)

16b. Trees and erect shrubs; fruits feshy, indehiscent or capsule-like, flattened; seeds not winged 17

17a. Fruit capsule-like, papery to cartilage-like, mitre-shaped and laterally flattened ....
.... *Ophiorrhiza* (not treated here)

17b. Fruit indehiscent, fleshy.. 18

18a. Corolla lobes imbricate (in bud); fruit a drupe with 1 pyrene; pyrenes sub-globular, with 4–9 locules
.... *Guettardia* (not treated here)

18b. Corolla lobes usually convolute or valvate (in bud); fruit baccate with many seeds or drupe-like, with 1-celled pyrenes 2 to many 19

19a. Fruits a berry; seeds many 20

19b. Fruits a drupe, with 2 to many pyrenes, each containing 1 seed 23

20a. Seeds many; corolla lobes valvate (in bud) .... *Urophyllum* (not treated here)

20b. Seeds 3 – 8; corolla lobes convolute (in buds) 21

21a. Plants often with strong unpleasant aroma when crushed; fruits with pyrenes flattened to triangular; flower buds subacute to rounded .... *Lasianthus* (not treated here)

21b. Plants without an unpleasant aroma; fruits with pyrenes plano-convex to ± ellipsoid; flower buds sharply acute to acuminate.. *Psydrax*

22a. Corolla lobes convolute (in bud); fruits a berry, fleshy to leathery on outer surface 23

22b. Corolla lobes valvate, imbricate or convolute (in bud), but if convolute than fruit not berry; fruits a drupe, berry, capsule or schizocarp 27

23a. Fruits ridged or winged, ridges continuous with midrib of each calyx lobe........................... *Gardenia*

23b. Fruit smooth to warty, never ridged.. 24

24a. Inflorescences all apparently leaf-opposed or borne at leafless nodes; stems with leaves opposite or apparently alternate .... *Aidia* (not treated here)

24b. Inflorescences mostly borne on apparently 3-leaved nodes; stems with some 3-leaved nodes............ 25

25a. Petioles articulate; fruit with 2 seeds, 1 in each locule; stigma not lobed .... *Ixora*

25b. Petioles not articulate; fruit with 2– many seeds, 1– many in each locule; stigma lobed 26

26a. Ovary with 2 locules; ovules 1 in each locule; fruits drupe-like; seeds 2, plano-convex .... *Pavetta* (not treated here)

26b. Ovary with 2 locules; ovules 2 or more in each locule; fruits baccate; seeds 2 or more, ellipsoid, obovoid, or compressed globose .... *Tarenna*

27a. Fruits with 4 or 5 locules; stigmas 4 or 5 .... *Mycetia* (not treated here)

27b. Fruits usually with 2 locules; stigmas 1 or 2 28

28a. Fruits indehiscent, drupe-like or baccate, fleshy or leathery 29

28b. Fruits a dry, dehiscent capsule or schizocarp, or indehiscent... 35

29a. Stigma not lobed; leaves with petioles articulate at base.. *Ixora*

29b. Stigma with 2 or 3 lobes; leaves with petiole not articulate 30

30a. Fruits baccate; seeds many in each locule, enclosed in fleshy cells..31

30b. Fruits indehiscent or drupe-like; seeds 1 in each locule, enclosed in a pyrene 32

31a. Corolla lobes valvate-reduplicate; seeds flattened; plants not succulent .... *Mussaenda* (not treated here)

31b. Corolla lobes valvate-induplicate; seeds anged; plants often succulent .... *Mycetia* (not treated here)

32a. Stipules caducous, often exposing a ring of persistent hairs.. *Psychotria*

32b. Stipules persistent to caducous, not enclosing persistent hairs or if present, then hairs reduced........ 33

33a. Corolla lobes convolute (in buds)... *Pavetta* (not treated here)

33b. Corolla lobes valvate (in buds) 34

34a. Stipules persistent, becoming hardened, often fragmenting .... *Psychotria*

34b. Stipules caducous, or if persistent then not becoming hardened or fragmented .... *Saprosma* (not treated here)

35a. Fruits mitre-shaped and laterally flattened.. *Ophiorrhiza* (not treated here)

35a. Fruits ellipsoid to sub-globular 36

36a. Fruits dehiscent, a capsule, at least 8 mm long.. *Cinchona* (not treated here)

36b. Fruit indehiscent, a schizocarp or capsule, up to 8 mm 37

37a. Corolla lobes imbricate (in bud); fruits dehiscent, a capsule.................. *Wendlandia* (not treated here)

37b. Corolla lobes valvate (in bud); fruits indehiscent, a schizocarp or capsule.... *Hedyotis* (not treated here)

Cyclophyllum brevipes (Merr. & L.M.Perry) S.T.Reynolds & R.J.F.Hend.

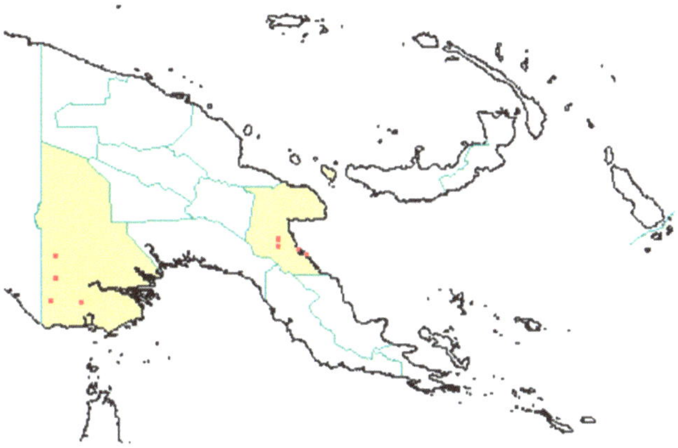

Austrobaileya Vol. 6: 62 (2001)
Timber Group: Non-timber species

Field Characters: Subcanopy trees, up to 20 m high; bole cylindrical, 60 cm diam., straight, c. 7 m long; buttresses absent; spines absent; aerial roots absent; stilt roots absent. Bark grey or dark brown, rough, scaly or flaky or pustular; lenticels irregular; bark c. 5 mm thick; under-bark dark green; faintly or non-aromatic; blaze consisting of one layer, white or pink, markings absent; exudate absent. Terminal buds not enclosed by leaves.

Indumentum: Complex hairs absent; stinging hairs absent; mature twig without hairs.

Leaves: Spaced along branches, leaves opposite, simple; petiole present, not winged, attached to base of leaf lamina, not swollen; lamina broadest at or near middle, 6–13 cm long, 4–5 cm wide; base symmetric, margin entire, not dissected or lobed, apex acuminate, venation pinnate, secondary veins open, prominent, intramarginal veins absent; lower surface yellowish green, upper surface glossy green, hairs absent, oil dots absent, domatia absent; stipules present, joined, joined across twigs, encircling the twig, collar-like, not fringed, large, persistent.

Flowers: Inflorescence axillary, flowers single or flowers on an unbranched axis; flowers bisexual (pleasantly aromatic), with pedicel, with many planes of symmetry, 2–3 mm long, small, c. 1.5 mm diam.; perianth present, with distinct sepals and petals, white, yellow, or cream-coloured; inner perianth 5, some or partly joined; stamens 5, filaments present, free of each other, joined to perianth; ovary inferior, carpels joined, locules 2; styles joined, 1.

Fruits: single or arranged on unbranched axis, fruit 8–12 mm long, c. 10 mm diam., fruit red, not spiny, fleshy, simple, indehiscent, drupe. Seed 1, 8–10 mm long, as wide as long, c. 8 mm diam., not winged.

Distribution: Morobe, Western.

Notes: Previously known as *Canthium brevipes* Merr. & L.M.Perry.

Gardenia kamialiensis W.N.Takeuchi Fig. 371

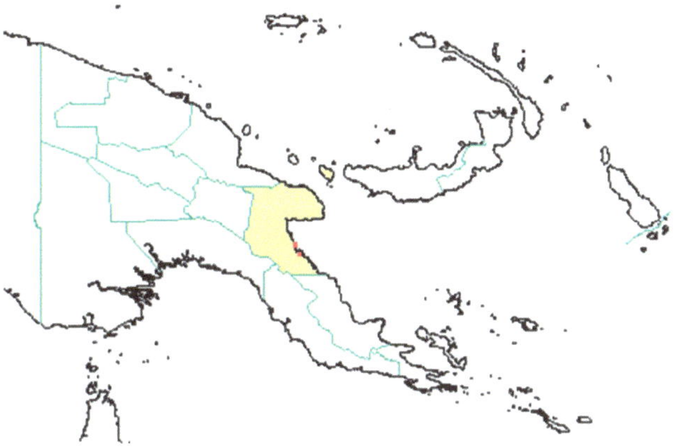

Harvard Papers in Botany Vol. 9: 232–236 (2004) Figs 2–5.
Timber Group: Non-timber species

Field Characters: Canopy trees, 25–30 m high, or subcanopy trees, up to 18 m high; bole cylindrical, 20 cm diam., straight; buttresses absent; spines absent; aerial roots absent; stilt roots absent. Bark grey, rough, pustular; lenticels elongated laterally or irregular; bark 5 mm thick; under-bark green; faintly or non-aromatic; pleasant; blaze consisting of one layer, pale yellow, with stripes, granular without splinters; exudate absent. Terminal buds enclosed by leaves.

Indumentum: Complex hairs absent; stinging hairs absent; mature twig without hairs.

Leaves: Spaced along branches, leaves opposite, simple; petiole present short or almost absent, winged lamina extending along edge of petiole, attached to base of leaf lamina, not swollen; lamina broadest above middle, (15–)35–40 cm long (leaves unequal in size), (8–)13.5–17 cm wide; base symmetric to slightly asymmetric, margin entire, not dissected or lobed, apex abruptly acuminate, venation pinnate, secondary veins open, prominent, intramarginal veins absent; lower surface green or pale green, upper surface glossy green, hairs absent, oil dots absent, domatia absent; stipules present, joined, joined across twigs, encircling the twig, leafy, not fringed, large, 4–10(–14) mm long, not persistent.

Flowers: Inflorescence terminal, flowers single, bisexual, with pedicel up to 16 mm long, with many planes of symmetry, 40–75 mm long, large, 50–60 mm diam.; perianth present, with distinct sepals and petals, white, aromatic; inner perianth 6–9, some or partly joined forming a corolla tube; stamens 6–9 (same number as corolla lobes), filaments short, 1 mm long, free of each other, joined to perianth; ovary inferior, carpels joined, locules 1; styles joined, 1 (30–35 mm long).

Fruits: single, 55–90 mm long, 50–65 mm diam., green (immature), not spiny, fleshy, simple, indehiscent, drupe. Seeds many (held within bright red placentae), 3–6 mm long, as wide as long, 3–6 mm wide, not winged.

Distribution: Morobe.

Fig. 371. *Gardenia kamialiensis*. Bark, leaves and fruit

Gardenia papuana F.M.Bailey
Fig. 372

Queensland Agriculture Journal Vol. 23: 218 (1909)
Timber Group: Occasional timber species

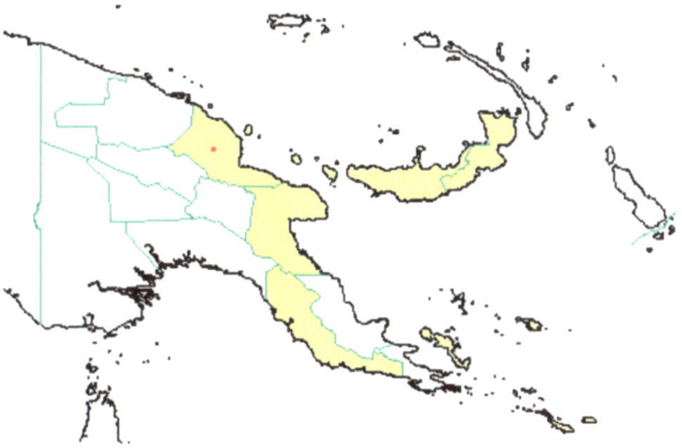

Field Characters: Canopy trees, 20–25 m high; bole cylindrical, 40–45 cm diam., straight; buttresses absent; spines absent; aerial roots absent; stilt roots absent. Bark pale brown, rough, pustular or tessellated; lenticels irregular; bark 10 mm thick; under-bark yellow or green; strongly aromatic; pleasant; blaze consisting of one layer, yellow, with stripes (in form of rings), granular with splinters (brittle); exudate present, colourless, not readily flowing, changing to dark yellow on exposure to air, sticky. Terminal buds enclosed by leaves.

Indumentum: Complex hairs absent; stinging hairs absent; mature twig without hairs.

Leaves: Spaced along branches, leaves opposite, simple; petiole present, not winged, attached to base of leaf lamina, not swollen; lamina broadest at or near middle, 14–24 cm long, 8–13.5 cm wide; base symmetric, margin entire, not dissected or lobed, apex slightly acuminate, venation pinnate, secondary veins open, prominent, intramarginal veins absent; lower surface pale green, upper surface glossy green, hairs absent, oil dots absent, domatia present, scattered along mid-vein; stipules present, joined, joined across twigs, encircling the twig, leafy, not fringed, large, persistent.

Flowers: Inflorescence axillary, flowers single, bisexual, with pedicel, with many planes of symmetry perianth present, with distinct sepals and petals, white; inner perianth 5, some or partly joined; stamens 5, filaments present, free of each other, joined to perianth; ovary inferior, carpels joined, styles joined, 1.

Fruits: single, (30–)40–50 mm long, (25–)30–40 mm diam., yellow, not spiny (ridged, sepals persistent), fleshy, simple, indehiscent, berry. Seed c. 3 mm long, as wide as long, c. 3 mm diam., not winged.

Distribution: Madang, Morobe, Central, Milne Bay, Papuan Islands, New Britain.

Fig. 372. *Gardenia papuana*. Bark, leaves and fruit

Ixora amplexifolia K.Schum. & Lauterb.

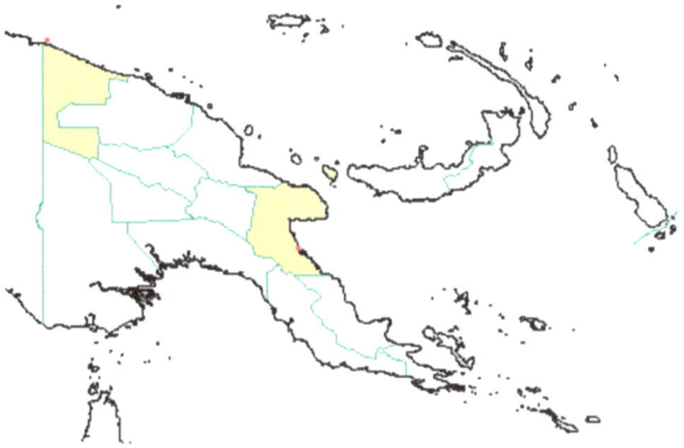

Flora der deutschen Schutzgebiete in der Südsee 572 (1901)
Timber Group: Non-timber species

Field Characters: Subcanopy trees, up to 15 m high; bole cylindrical, 25 cm diam., straight, 8 m long; buttresses absent; spines absent; aerial roots absent; stilt roots absent. Bark brown, rough, fissured or pustular; lenticels irregular; bark 5 mm thick; under-bark yellow; faintly or non-aromatic; blaze consisting of one layer, pale yellow cream-coloured, slightly speckled, fibrous or slightly granular with splinters; exudate present, colourless, not readily flowing, changing to orange on exposure to air, not sticky. Terminal buds not enclosed by leaves.

Indumentum: Complex hairs absent; stinging hairs absent; mature twig without hairs.

Leaves: Spaced along branches, leaves opposite, simple; petiole 15–25 mm long, not winged, attached to base of leaf lamina, not swollen; lamina broadest above middle or broadest at or near middle, 12–19 cm long, 4–6 cm wide; base symmetric, margin entire, not dissected or lobed, apex acuminate, venation pinnate, secondary veins open, prominent or not prominent, but visible, intramarginal veins absent; lower surface pale green, upper surface green, hairs absent, oil dots absent, domatia absent; stipules absent.

Flowers: Inflorescence axillary, flowers on a branched axis; flowers bisexual, with pedicel, 8–10 mm long, flowers with many planes of symmetry, 20–22 mm long, large, 15–18 mm diam.; perianth present, with distinct sepals and petals, white, cream-coloured; inner perianth 4, joined for a tube and separate lobes; stamens 4, filaments present (anthers long, narrow), free of each other, free of perianth; ovary partly inferior or inferior, carpels joined, locules 2; styles joined, 1.

Fruits: arranged on branched axis, fruit 6–8 mm long, c. 8 mm diam., fruit pale red, pink, not spiny, fleshy, simple, indehiscent, drupe. Seed 1, 4–5 mm long, as long as broad, slightly flattened, 4–5 mm diam., not winged.

Distribution: West Sepik, Madang, Morobe.

Notes: The taxonomy of this species is not well-understood and is sometimes treated as part of the broader taxonomic concept of the *I. amplexifolia-I. subauriculata* complex.

Mastixiodendron pachyclados (K.Schum.) Melch. Fig. 373

Botanische Jahrbücher für Systematik, Pflanzengeschichte und Pflanzengeographie Vol. 60: 168 (1925)
Timber Group: Commercial hardwoods

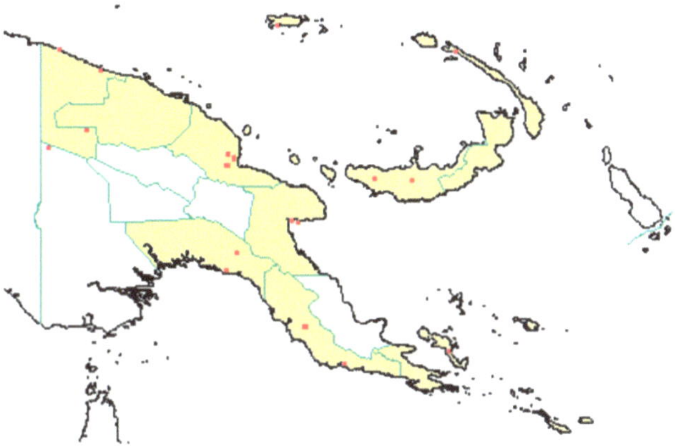

Field Characters: Canopy trees, up to 35 m high, or subcanopy trees; bole cylindrical, up to 120 cm diam., straight, up to c. 20 m long; buttresses absent or when present, usually small, up to 2 m high; spines absent; aerial roots absent; stilt roots absent. Bark brown or grey, rough, scaly or flaky; bark 10–14 mm thick; under-bark pale yellow (cream-coloured), mottled, dark red, or dark brown; faintly or non-aromatic; blaze consisting of 2 layers; outer blaze pale brown or yellow (cream-coloured), with stripes orange, fibrous; inner blaze white, pink, or pale yellow (cream-coloured), with stripes orange, fibrous; exudate present, colourless, not readily flowing, changing to dark brown or black on exposure to air, slightly sticky or not sticky. Terminal buds enclosed by leaves.

Indumentum: Complex hairs absent; stinging hairs absent; mature twig without hairs.

Leaves: Spaced along branches, leaves opposite, simple; petiole present, not winged, attached to base of leaf lamina, slightly swollen towards base and towards tip, or not swollen; lamina broadest above middle, 13–28 cm long, 5.5–18 cm wide; base symmetric, margin entire, not dissected or lobed, apex sub-acute or shortly acuminate, venation pinnate, secondary veins open, prominent, intramarginal veins absent; lower surface pale green or green, upper surface dark glossy green, hairs absent, oil dots absent, domatia absent; stipules present, joined, joined across twigs (slightly twisted), not encircling the twig or almost encircling the twig, leafy, not fringed, large, (15–)20–40 mm long, not persistent.

Flowers: Inflorescence axillary, flowers on a branched axis; flowers bisexual, with pedicel, with many planes of symmetry, 10–22 mm long, large, 9–24 mm diam.; perianth present, with distinct sepals and petals, white, whitish yellow, or pale green; inner perianth 4 (inner surface densely covered with white hairs), free; stamens 4, filaments present, free of each other, free of perianth; ovary partly inferior or inferior, carpels joined, locules 2; styles joined, 1.

Fruits: arranged on branched axis, fruit (12–)20–35(–45) mm long, (8–)10–20 mm diam., fruit dark yellow or green (probably immature), not spiny, fleshy, simple, indehiscent, drupe. Seed 1, 12–20 mm long, longer than wide, 4–5 mm diam., not winged.

Distribution: West Sepik, East Sepik, Madang, Morobe, Gulf, Central, Milne Bay, Papuan Islands, New Britain, New Ireland, Manus.

Fig. 373. *Mastixiodendron pachyclados.* Bark, leaves and flower buds

Mastixiodendron plectocarpum S.P.Darwin

Journal of the Arnold Arboretum Vol. 58: 370 (1977)
Timber Group: Non-timber species

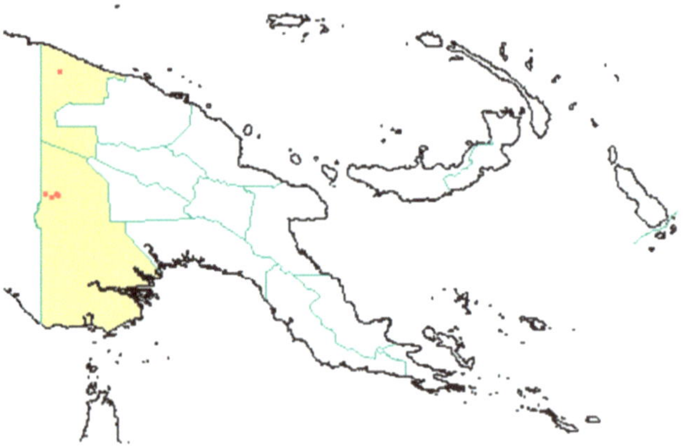

Field Characters: Canopy trees, up to 35 m high, or subcanopy trees; bole cylindrical, up to 60 cm diam., straight, up to 25 m long; buttresses up to 1.5 m high, or absent; spines absent; aerial roots absent; stilt roots absent. Bark brown or dark grey, slightly rough or smooth, fissured or scaly or flaky; bark <25 mm thick; faintly or non-aromatic; blaze consisting of one layer, white or pale yellow, markings absent; exudate present, colourless, not readily flowing, not changing colour on exposure to air, not sticky or sticky. Terminal buds enclosed by leaves.

Indumentum: Complex hairs absent; stinging hairs absent; mature twig without hairs.

Leaves: Spaced along branches, leaves opposite, simple; petiole present, not winged, attached to base of leaf lamina, not swollen; lamina broadest below middle or broadest at or near middle, 6–19 cm long, 1.5–6.5 cm wide; base symmetric, margin entire, not dissected or lobed, apex rarely acuminate or sub-acute, venation pinnate, secondary veins open, not prominent, but visible, intramarginal veins absent; lower surface green, upper surface sub-glossy green, hairs absent, oil dots absent, domatia absent; stipules present, joined, joined across twigs (slightly twisted), not encircling the twig or almost encircling the twig, leafy, not fringed, large, 12–20 mm long, not persistent.

Flowers: Inflorescence axillary, flowers on a branched axis; flowers bisexual, with pedicel, with many planes of symmetry, (6–)8–11 mm long, small, 5–12 mm diam.; perianth present, with distinct sepals and petals, pale yellow or yellowish green; inner perianth 4, free; stamens 4, filaments present, free of each other, free of perianth; ovary inferior, carpels joined, locules 2; styles joined, 1.

Fruits: arranged on branched axis, fruit (20–)25–30 mm long, 10–16 mm diam., black (when mature) or pale green, not spiny, fleshy, simple, indehiscent, drupe. Seed 1, 10–12 mm long, longer than wide, 2–3 mm diam., not winged.

Distribution: Western, West Sepik.

Notes: Steven P. Darwin (1977), in *Journal of the Arnold Arboretum*, Vol. 58, 349–381, describes this species from Geelvink Bay (Indonesian Papua) and from the Western region of Papua New Guinea. One collection, *D.B. Foreman and M. Kumul NGF48218*, from the West Sepik region is here regarded as possibly also belonging to this species.

Mastixiodendron smithii Merr. & L.M.Perry

Journal of the Arnold Arboretum Vol. 26: 255 (1945)
Timber Group: Non-timber species

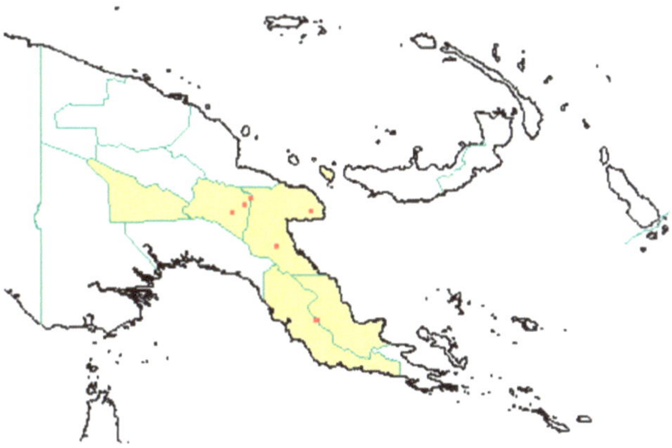

Field Characters: Canopy trees, up to 40 m high, or subcanopy trees; bole cylindrical, up to c. 100 cm diam., straight, up to c. 20 m long; buttresses up to 3(–4) m high; spines absent; aerial roots absent; stilt roots absent. Bark pale brown or dark grey, rough, scaly or flaky; bark <25 mm thick; under-bark green; almost strongly aromatic or faintly or non-aromatic; pleasant (fruit-like); blaze consisting of one layer, white or pale yellow (straw-coloured), markings absent, fibrous; exudate present, colourless, not readily flowing, changing to green on exposure to air, sticky or not sticky. Terminal buds enclosed by leaves.

Indumentum: Complex hairs absent; stinging hairs absent; mature twig without hairs.

Leaves: Spaced along branches, leaves opposite, simple; petiole present, slightly winged (with lamina slightly extended down petiole) or not winged, attached to base of leaf lamina, not swollen or slightly swollen; lamina broadest at or near middle, 11–20(–36) cm long, 4–10(–20) cm wide; base symmetric, margin entire, not dissected or lobed, apex obtuse, venation pinnate, secondary veins open, not prominent, but visible, intramarginal veins absent; lower surface pale green, upper surface dark glossy green, hairs absent, oil dots absent, domatia absent; stipules present, joined, joined across twigs (slightly twisted), almost encircling the twig or not encircling the twig, leafy, not fringed, large, 18–35 mm long, not persistent.

Flowers: Inflorescence axillary, flowers on a branched axis; flowers bisexual, with pedicel, with many planes of symmetry, (6–)9–12 mm long, small, 5–10 mm diam.; perianth present, with distinct sepals and petals, pale yellow or yellowish green (towards base); inner perianth 4, free; stamens 4, filaments present, free of each other, free of perianth; ovary inferior, carpels joined, styles joined, 1.

Fruits: arranged on branched axis, fruit 35–50(–70) mm long, 12–25(–30) mm diam., green (probably immature), not spiny, fleshy, simple, indehiscent, drupe. Seed 1, 20–25 mm long, longer than wide, c. 10 mm diam., not winged.

Distribution: Morobe, Eastern Highlands, Southern Highlands, Central.

Nauclea orientalis L. Figs 374, 375

Species Plantarum, edition 2 243 (1762)
Timber Group: Commercial hardwoods

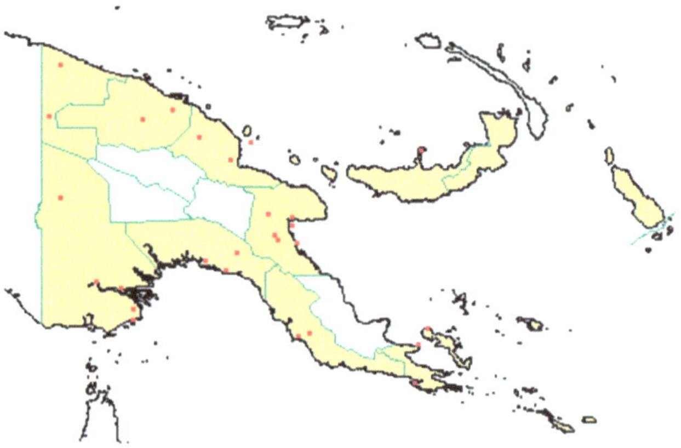

Field Characters: Subcanopy trees, up to c. 20 m high; bole cylindrical, slightly crooked or straight; buttresses absent; spines absent; aerial roots absent; stilt roots absent. Bark pale grey, slightly rough, slightly furrowed cork or tessellated; bark <25 mm thick.

Indumentum: Complex hairs absent; stinging hairs absent; mature twig hairy or mature twig without hairs; hairs dense or sparse.

Leaves: Spaced along branches, leaves opposite, simple; petiole present, not winged, attached to base of leaf lamina, not swollen; lamina broadest at or near middle or broadest below middle, 12–21 cm long, 7–15 cm wide; base symmetric, margin entire, not dissected or lobed, apex obtuse or sub-acute, venation pinnate, secondary veins open, prominent, intramarginal veins absent; lower surface pale green or green, upper surface dark green, hairs absent or present (on lower surface), sparse, oil dots absent, domatia absent; stipules present, free, laterally placed, not encircling the twig, leafy, not fringed, large, not persistent.

Flowers: Inflorescence terminal (on short branchlets), flowers arising from a single point (flowers arranged in globular clusters 20–60 mm diam.); flowers bisexual, not stalked, with many planes of symmetry, 8–11 mm long, small, 3–5 mm diam.; perianth present, with distinct sepals and petals, yellow or orange (sweetly aromatic); inner perianth 5, some or partly joined (forming a long corolla tube and 5 lobes); stamens 5, filaments present (short), free of each other, joined to perianth; ovary inferior, carpels joined, locules 2; styles joined, 1.

Fruits: Arising from a single point, fruit 20–40 mm long, 20–40 mm diam., fruit brown (strongly aromatic), not spiny, fleshy, multiple (fruits joined by their calyces into an indehiscent fleshy syncarp), indehiscent, drupe. Seeds 1 (per fruitlet; many per fruiting head), to about 5 mm long, as wide as long (slightly compressed), 1–10 mm diam., not winged.

Distribution: West Sepik, East Sepik, Madang, Morobe, Western, Gulf, Central, Milne Bay, Papuan Islands, New Britain, Bougainville.

Notes: Previously known as *Sarcocephalus orientalis* (L.) Merr., *Nauclea coadunata* Roxb. ex Sm., *Sarcocephalus coadunatus* (Roxb. ex Sm.) Druce, and *Sarcocephalus cordatus* Miq.

Fig. 374. *Nauclea orientalis.* Leaves, fruit and bark

Fig. 375. *Nauclea orientalis.* Habit, leaves and fruit

Neonauclea acuminata C.E.Ridsdale

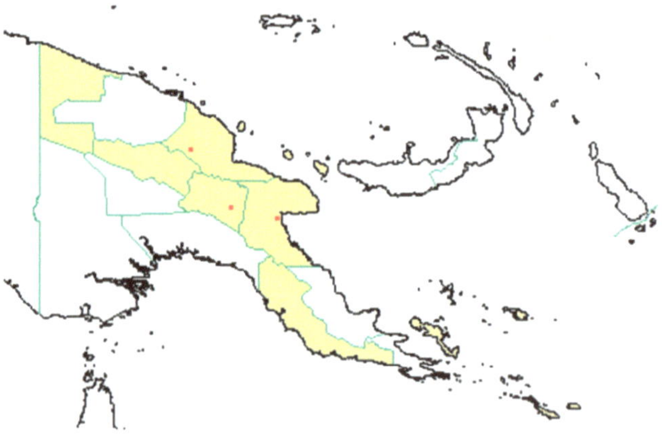

Gardens' Bulletin, Singapore Vol. 15: 279 (1970)
Other Literature: C.E. Ridsdale, *Blumea* Vol. 34: 234 & 235 (1989) Fig. 11.
Timber Group: Commercial hardwoods

Field Characters: Canopy trees, up to 35 m high, or subcanopy trees; bole cylindrical, up to c. 50 cm diam., straight, 15–20 m long; buttresses absent; spines absent; aerial roots absent; stilt roots absent. Bark brown or grey, rough, fissured (thinly to coarsely), rarely pustular, or slightly scaly or flaky; lenticels slightly irregular; bark 16–20 mm thick; under-bark green, yellowish brown, yellow, or orange; faintly or non-aromatic; blaze consisting of one layer, white or pale yellow (straw-coloured), markings absent, fibrous; exudate absent. Terminal buds enclosed by leaves.

Indumentum: Complex hairs absent; stinging hairs absent; mature twig without hairs.

Leaves: Spaced along branches, leaves opposite, simple; petiole present, not winged, attached to base of leaf lamina, not swollen; lamina rarely broadest above middle or broadest at or near middle, (10–)20–36 cm long,

(5–)12–20(–22) cm wide; base symmetric, margin entire, not dissected or lobed, apex sub-acute or shortly acuminate, venation pinnate, secondary veins open, prominent, intramarginal veins absent; lower surface green, upper surface dark glossy green, hairs absent, oil dots absent, domatia absent; stipules present, joined, joined across twigs, not encircling the twig, leafy, not fringed, large, 12–28 mm long, not persistent.

Flowers: Inflorescence axillary, flowers arising from a single point; flowers bisexual, not stalked or with short pedicel (flower subsessile), with many planes of symmetry, 11–16 mm long, small, 5–6 mm diam.; perianth present, with distinct sepals and petals, cream-coloured or white; inner perianth 5, some or partly joined; stamens 5, filaments present (short), free of each other, joined to perianth (exserted beyond corolla); ovary inferior, carpels joined, locules 2; styles joined, 1.

Fruits: Arising from a single point (forming a globular fruiting head 8–12 mm diam.), fruit 3–5 mm long, c. 2 mm diam., pale brown, not spiny, non-fleshy, multiple, dehiscent (each fruitlet), capsule (each fruitlet splitting into 4 valves). Seeds 1 (per fruitlet; many per globular fruiting head), to about 5 mm long, longer than wide (somewhat bilaterally flattened), c. 2 mm diam., shortly winged at both ends.

Distribution: West Sepik, Madang, Morobe, Western Highlands, Eastern Highlands, Central, Papuan Islands.

Neonauclea glabra (Roxb.) Bakh.f. & Ridsdale

Blumea Vol. 34: 240–242 (1989) Fig. 13.
Timber Group: Non-timber species

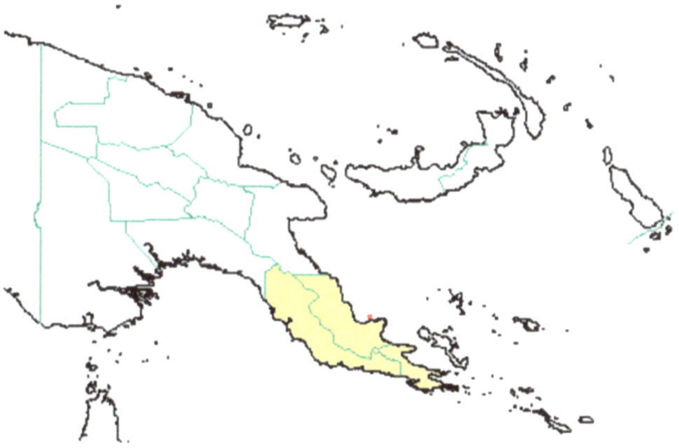

Field Characters: Canopy trees, up to 45 m high; bole cylindrical, straight, up to 18 m long; buttresses absent or rarely present; spines absent; aerial roots absent; stilt roots absent. Bark grey or brown, slightly rough, scaly or flaky or cracked; bark <25 mm thick; under-bark pink; faintly or non-aromatic; blaze consisting of one layer, brown or yellow, markings absent; exudate absent. Terminal buds enclosed by leaves.

Indumentum: Complex hairs absent; stinging hairs absent; mature twig without hairs.

Leaves: Spaced along branches, leaves opposite, simple; petiole present, not winged, attached to base of leaf lamina, not swollen; lamina broadest at or near middle, 10–18(–22) cm long, (4–)5–10 cm wide; base symmetric, margin entire, not dissected or lobed, apex sub-acute, venation pinnate, secondary veins open, not prominent, but visible, intramarginal veins absent; lower surface pale green, upper surface dark green, hairs absent, oil dots absent, domatia absent; stipules present, joined, joined across twigs, not encircling the twig, leafy, not fringed, large, 10–20(–28) mm long, not persistent.

Flowers: Inflorescence terminal, flowers arising from a single point; flowers bisexual, shortly with pedicel (subsessile), with many planes of symmetry, 6–9 mm long, small, 3–4 mm diam.; perianth present, with distinct sepals and petals, cream-coloured or white; inner perianth 5, some or partly joined; stamens 5, filaments present (short), free of each other, joined to perianth; ovary inferior, carpels joined, locules 2; styles joined, 1.

Fruits: Arising from a single point (forming a globular fruiting head 10–20 mm diam.), fruit 4–5 mm long, c. 2 mm diam., pale brown, not spiny, non-fleshy, multiple, dehiscent (each fruitlet), capsule (each fruitlet splitting into 4 values). Seeds 1 (per fruitlet; many per globular fruiting head), to about 5 mm long, longer than wide (somewhat bilaterally flattened), c. 2 mm diam., shortly winged at both ends.

Distribution: Central, Northern, Milne Bay.

Neonauclea hagenii (Lauterb. & K.Schum.) Merr.

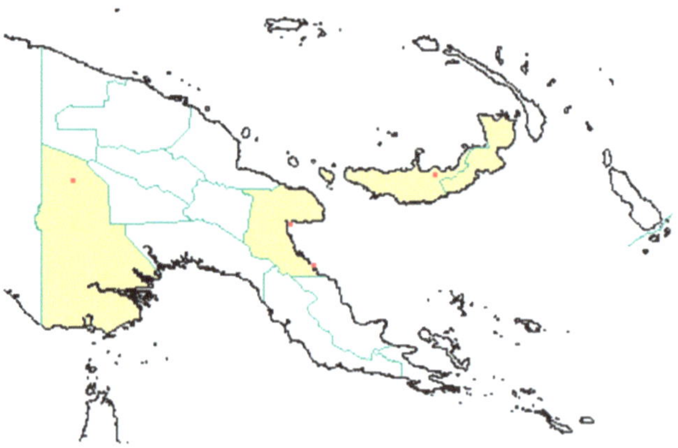

Journal of the Washington Academy of Science Vol. 5: 540 (1915)
Other Literature: C.E. Ridsdale, *Blumea* Vol. 34: 230–234 (1989) Fig. 11.
Timber Group: Non-timber species

Field Characters: Subcanopy trees, 10–20 m high, or canopy trees, up to 30 m high; bole cylindrical, up to c. 50 cm diam., straight, up to c. 12 m long; buttresses present (short); spines absent; aerial roots absent; stilt roots absent. Bark grey or brown, rough, often pustular, sometimes scaly or flaky, or slightly fissured; lenticels elongated vertically; bark <25 mm thick; under-bark pink; faintly or non-aromatic; blaze consisting of one layer, white, pale yellow, pink, or yellowish brown, markings absent, fibrous; exudate absent. Terminal buds enclosed by leaves.

Indumentum: Complex hairs absent; stinging hairs absent; mature twig without hairs.

Leaves: Spaced along branches, leaves opposite, simple; petiole present, not winged, attached to base of leaf lamina, not swollen; lamina broadest at or near middle, (8–)12–20(–23) cm long, (3–)5–9(–12) cm wide; base symmetric, margin entire, not dissected or lobed, apex sub-acute, venation pinnate, secondary veins open, not prominent, but visible, intramarginal veins absent; lower surface pale green, upper surface dark green, hairs absent, oil dots absent, domatia absent; stipules present, joined, joined across twigs, not encircling the twig, leafy, fringed (minutely and finely hairy or with only a few minute scattered hairs), large, 8–16(–20) mm long, not persistent.

Flowers: Inflorescence terminal, flowers arising from a single point; perianth present, with distinct sepals and petals, white or cream-coloured; inner perianth 5, some or partly joined; stamens 5, filaments present (short), free of each other, joined to perianth; ovary inferior, carpels joined, locules 2; styles joined.

Fruits: Arising from a single point (forming a globular fruiting head 25–30 mm diam., sometimes as small as 20 mm), fruit pale brown, not spiny, non-fleshy, dehiscent (each fruitlet), capsule (each fruitlet splitting into 4 values). Seeds 1 (per fruitlet; many per globular fruiting head), to about 5 mm long, longer than wide (somewhat bilaterally flattened), c. 2 mm diam., shortly winged at both ends.

Distribution: West Sepik, Madang, Morobe, Western Highlands, Western (subsp. *papuana*), Northern, New Britain.

Notes: Two subspecies occur in Papua New Guinea, namely subsp. *hagenii* and subsp. *papuana* (Valeton) Ridsdale. *Neonauclea hagenii* subsp. *hagenii* has flowers with a glabrous corolla, 9–12 mm long and mature fruiting heads (20–)25–30 mm diam., whereas, subsp. *papuana* has a hairy corolla 7–9 mm long, and mature fruiting heads 20–25 mm diam.

Neonauclea lanceolata (Blume) Merr. subsp. *gracilis* (Vidal.) Ridsdale

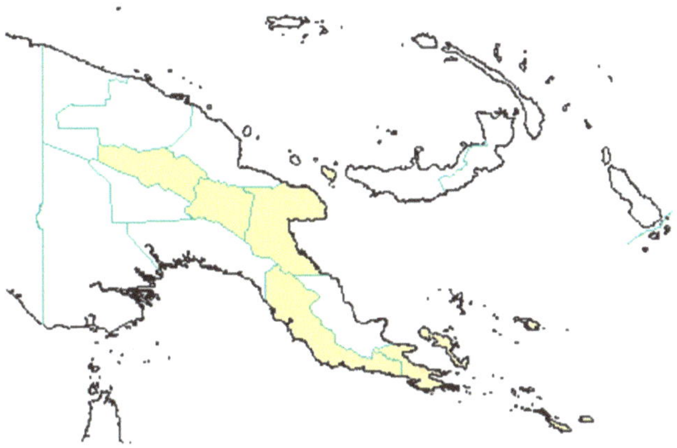

Blumea Vol. 34: 225 & 226 (1989) Fig. 19 (map).
Timber Group: Non-timber species

Field Characters: Subcanopy trees, up to c. 25 m high; bole cylindrical, straight; buttresses absent or sometimes present (short); spines absent; aerial roots absent; stilt roots absent. Bark grey or brown, rough, scaly or flaky or cracked (vertically); bark <25 mm thick; under-bark pink; faintly or non-aromatic; blaze consisting of one layer, pink or white, markings absent; exudate absent. Terminal buds enclosed by leaves.

Indumentum: Complex hairs absent; stinging hairs absent; mature twig without hairs.

Leaves: Spaced along branches, leaves opposite, simple; petiole present, not winged, attached to base of leaf lamina, not swollen; lamina rarely broadest above middle or usually broadest at or near middle, (3–)7–12(–20) cm long, (2–)4–7(–8) cm wide; base symmetric, margin entire, not dissected or lobed, apex acuminate, venation pinnate, secondary veins open, not prominent, but visible, intramarginal veins absent; lower surface pale green, upper surface dark green, hairs absent, oil dots absent, domatia absent; stipules present, joined, joined across twigs, not encircling the twig, leafy, not fringed, large, 4–8(–10) mm long, not persistent.

Flowers: Inflorescence terminal, flowers arising from a single point; flowers bisexual, with pedicel short (flowers subsessile), with many planes of symmetry perianth present, with distinct sepals and petals, white or cream-coloured; inner perianth 5, some or partly joined; stamens 5, filaments present (short), free of each other, joined to perianth; ovary inferior, carpels joined, locules 2; styles joined, 1.

Fruits: Arising from a single point (forming a globular fruiting head 10–12 mm diam., sometimes as small as 7 mm or as large as 15 mm diam.), fruit 3–5 mm long, c. 3 mm diam., pale brown, not spiny, non-fleshy, multiple, dehiscent (each fruitlet), capsule (each fruitlet splitting into 4 values). Seeds 1 (per fruitlet; many per globular fruiting head), to about 5 mm long, longer than wide (somewhat bilaterally flattened), c. 2 mm diam., shortly winged at both ends.

Distribution: West Sepik, Madang, Morobe, Western Highlands, Eastern Highlands, Central, Milne Bay, Papuan Islands.

Neonauclea obversifolia (Valeton) Merr. & L.M.Perry Fig. 376

Journal of the Arnold Arboretum Vol. 25: 188 (1944)
Other Literature: C.E. Ridsdale, *Blumea* Vol. 34: 242 (1989) Fig. 28 (map).
Timber Group: Commercial hardwoods

Field Characters: Canopy trees, up to 46 m high; bole cylindrical, up to c. 50 cm diam., straight, up to c. 20 m long; buttresses usually absent, or up to 2 m high; spines absent; aerial roots absent; stilt roots absent. Bark grey or brown, slightly rough, scaly or flaky or sometimes pustular; lenticels slightly irregular; bark 20–25 mm thick; under-bark white or pale brown (silvery brown); faintly or non-aromatic; blaze consisting of one layer, white, pale yellow (straw-coloured), or pale brown, markings absent; exudate absent. Terminal buds enclosed by leaves.

Indumentum: Complex hairs absent; stinging hairs absent; mature twig without hairs.

Leaves: Spaced along branches, leaves opposite, simple; petiole present, not winged, attached to base of leaf lamina, not swollen; lamina broadest at or near middle, 7–11(–16) cm long, 3–6 cm wide; base symmetric, margin entire, not dissected or lobed, apex acuminate or obtuse, venation pinnate, secondary veins open, not prominent, but visible, intramarginal veins absent; lower surface pale green, upper surface dark green, hairs absent, oil dots absent, domatia absent; stipules present, joined, joined across twigs, not encircling the twig, leafy, fringed (finely hairy), large, 6–10 mm long, not persistent.

Flowers: Inflorescence terminal, flowers arising from a single point (flowering globular clusters occurring singly or in threes); flowers bisexual, not stalked or shortly with pedicel (subsessile), with many planes of symmetry, 6–9 mm long, small, 4–5 mm diam.; perianth present, with distinct sepals and petals, white or cream-coloured; inner perianth 5, some or partly joined; stamens 5, filaments present (short), free of each other, joined to perianth; ovary inferior, carpels joined, locules 2; styles joined, 1.

Fruits: Arising from a single point (forming a globular fruiting head 12–15 mm diam.), fruit 3–5 mm long, c. 2 mm diam., pale brown, not spiny, non-fleshy, multiple, dehiscent (each fruitlet), capsule (each fruitlet splitting into 4 values). Seeds 1 (per fruitlet; many per globular fruiting head), to about 5 mm long, longer than wide (somewhat bilaterally flattened), c. 2 mm diam., winged at both ends.

Distribution: West Sepik, East Sepik, Madang, Morobe, Eastern Highlands, Western, Milne Bay, New Britain, New Ireland.

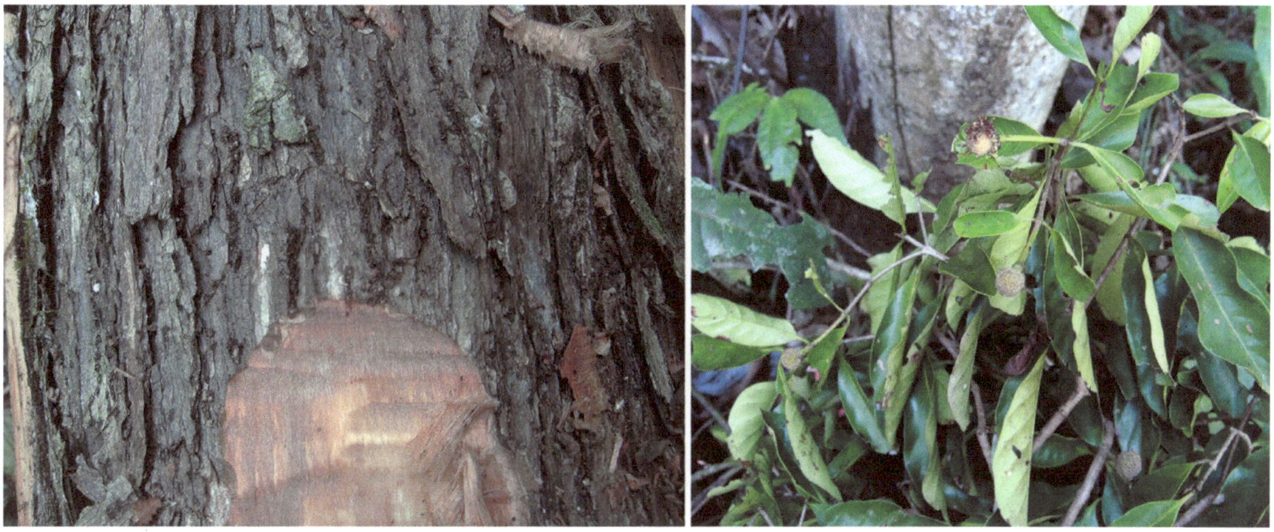

Fig. 376. *Neonauclea obversifolia.* Bark, leaves and fruit

Neonauclea purpurea (Roxb.) Merr. Fig. 377

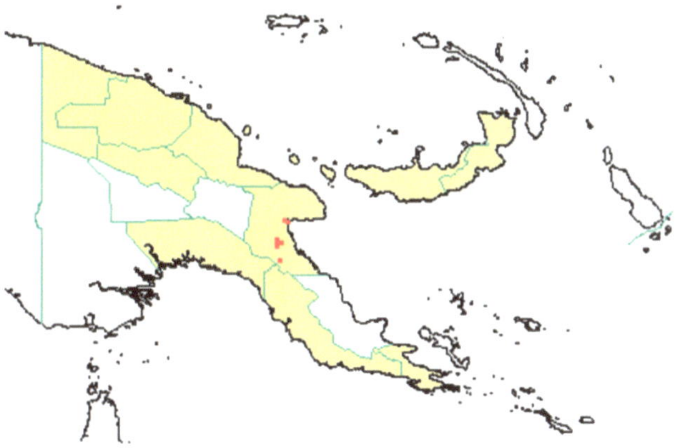

An Interpretation of Rumphius's Herbarium Amboinense 483 (1917)
Other Literature: C.E. Ridsdale, *Blumea* Vol. 24: (1979)
Timber Group: Major exportable hardwoods
Trade Name: Labula

Field Characters: Canopy trees, 10–40 m high, or subcanopy trees; bole cylindrical, up to 90 cm diam., crooked, usually 25–30 m long; buttresses slightly present or absent; spines absent; aerial roots absent; stilt roots absent. Bark grey or brown, rough, fissured; bark <25 mm thick; under-bark brown; strongly aromatic; pleasant; blaze consisting of one layer, light yellow or pale brown, markings absent, fibrous; exudate present, colourless, not readily flowing, changing to light brown on exposure to air, not sticky. Terminal buds not enclosed by leaves.

Indumentum: Complex hairs absent; stinging hairs absent; mature twig without hairs.

Leaves: Spaced along branches, leaves opposite, simple; petiole present, not winged, attached to base of leaf lamina, not swollen; lamina broadest at or near middle, 18–32 cm long, 11–18 cm wide; base symmetric to slightly asymmetric, margin entire, not dissected or lobed, apex acute or shortly acuminate, venation pinnate, secondary veins open, prominent, intramarginal veins absent; lower surface green (whitish to yellowish green), upper surface green, hairs absent on upper surface or present on lower surface (hairs white), dense, oil dots absent, domatia absent; stipules present, free, laterally placed, encircling the twig, collar-like, not fringed, large, not persistent.

Fig. 377. *Neonauclea purpurea*. Leaves, showing stipules

Flowers: Inflorescence terminal, flowers arising from a single point; flowers bisexual, not stalked, with many planes of symmetry, c. 10 mm long, small (< or =10 mm diam.); perianth present, with distinct sepals and petals, white; inner perianth 5, some or partly joined; stamens 5, filaments absent, free of each other, joined to perianth; ovary inferior, carpels joined, locules 5; styles joined, 1.

Fruits: Arising from a single point, fruit 30–50 mm long, greenish yellow (when immature) or brown (greenish-brown), not spiny, fleshy, multiple, dehiscent, capsule. Seeds 1 (per fruitlet; many per globular fruiting head), barely visible (to 1 mm long), as wide as long, < 1 mm diam., not winged.

Distribution: West Sepik, East Sepik, Madang, Morobe, Western Highlands, Eastern Highlands, Western, Gulf, Central, Milne Bay, New Britain.

Notes: Previously known as *Anthocephalus chinensis* (Lamk) Rich. ex Walp.

Neonauclea solomonensis Ridsdale

Garden's Bulletin Singapore Vol. 25: 274 (1970)
Other Literature: C.E. Ridsdale, *Blumea* Vol. 34: 254 (1989) Fig. 15.
Timber Group: Non-timber species

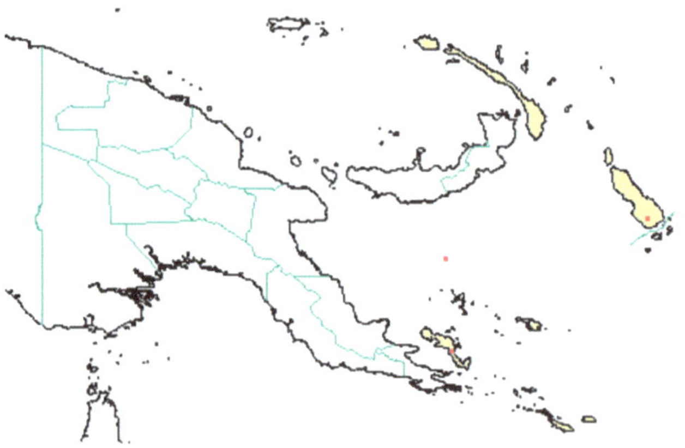

Field Characters: Canopy trees, up to 30 m high, or subcanopy trees; bole cylindrical, rarely fluted, up to 80 cm diam., straight; buttresses usually present; spines absent; aerial roots absent; stilt roots absent. Bark grey or pale brown, slightly rough, slightly scaly or flaky, finely fissured, or slightly pustular; lenticels irregular; bark <25 mm thick; under-bark yellow; faintly or non-aromatic; blaze consisting of one layer, yellow or yellowish brown (on exposure), markings absent; exudate absent. Terminal buds enclosed by leaves.

Indumentum: Complex hairs absent; stinging hairs absent; mature twig without hairs.

Leaves: Spaced along branches, leaves opposite, simple; petiole present, not winged, attached to base of leaf lamina, not swollen; lamina broadest above middle or broadest at or near middle, 10–20 cm long, (4–)5–10 cm wide; base symmetric, margin entire, not dissected or lobed, apex sub-acute, venation pinnate, secondary veins open, not prominent, but visible, intramarginal veins absent; lower surface pale green, upper surface dark green, hairs absent, oil dots absent, domatia absent; stipules present, joined, joined across twigs, not encircling the twig, leafy, not fringed, large, 10–15 mm long, not persistent.

Flowers: Inflorescence terminal, flowers arising from a single point (flowering globular clusters occurring singly or in threes); flowers bisexual, with pedicel short (subsessile), with many planes of symmetry, 7–8 mm long, small, c. 4 mm diam.; perianth present, with distinct sepals and petals, white or cream-coloured; inner perianth 5, some or partly joined; stamens 5, filaments present (short), free of each other, joined to perianth; ovary inferior, carpels joined, locules 2; styles joined, 1.

Fruits: Arising from a single point (forming a globular fruiting head 10–15 mm diam.), fruit 4–6 mm long, c. 2 mm diam., pale brown (greenish brown), not spiny, non-fleshy, multiple, dehiscent (each fruitlet), capsule (each fruitlet splitting into 4 valves). Seeds 1 (per fruitlet; many per globular fruiting head), to about 5 mm long, longer than wide (somewhat bilaterally flattened), c. 2 mm diam., shortly winged at both ends.

Distribution: Milne Bay, Papuan Islands, New Ireland, Bougainville.

Psychotria micralabastra Valeton
Fig. 378

Botanische Jahrbücher für Systematik, Pflanzengeschichte und Pflanzengeographie Vol. 61: 88 (1927)
Timber Group: Non-timber species

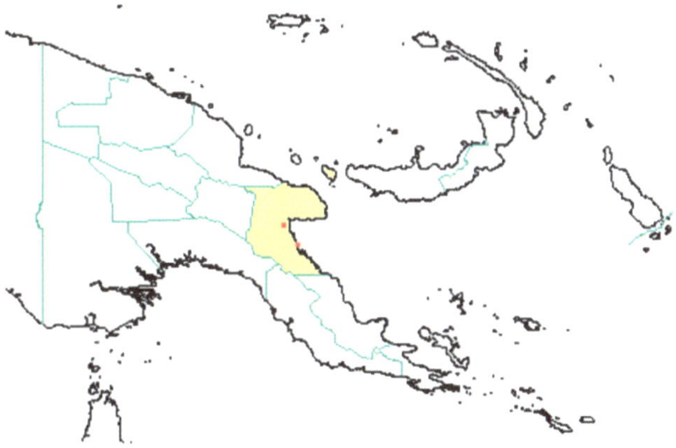

Field Characters: Subcanopy trees, 12 m high; bole cylindrical, 20 cm diam., straight, 2 m long; buttresses absent; spines absent; aerial roots absent; stilt roots absent. Bark brown or pale green, slightly rough or smooth, slightly pitted; bark 6 mm thick; under-bark green; faintly or non-aromatic; blaze consisting of one layer, pale red or brown, markings absent, slightly fibrous; exudate present, colourless, flowing, not changing colour on exposure to air, not sticky. Terminal buds enclosed by leaves.

Indumentum: Complex hairs absent; stinging hairs absent; mature twig without hairs.

Leaves: Spaced along branches, leaves opposite, simple; petiole present, not winged, attached to base of leaf lamina, not swollen; lamina broadest at or near middle, 10–13 cm long, 6–7.5 cm wide; base symmetric, margin entire, not dissected or lobed, apex acuminate, venation pinnate, secondary veins open, prominent, intramarginal veins absent; lower surface pale green, upper surface green, hairs absent, oil dots absent, domatia absent; stipules present, joined, joined across twigs, encircling the twig, leafy, not fringed, large, not persistent.

Flowers: Inflorescence terminal, flowers on a branched axis; flowers bisexual, with pedicel, with many planes of symmetry or slightly asymmetric, 2.5 mm long, small, 3.5 mm diam.; perianth present, with all sepals and/or petals (hence tepals) similar sepals small or possibly absent, pale yellow often with greenish tinge; inner perianth 6, free or some or partly joined; stamens 6, filaments present, free of each other, joined to perianth; ovary inferior largely superior in fruit, carpels joined, styles joined, 1.

Fruits: arranged on branched axis, fruit 6–10 mm long, 5–8 mm diam., red, not spiny, slightly fleshy, simple, indehiscent, drupe. Seed 1, to about 5 mm long, not winged.

Distribution: West Sepik, Madang, Morobe, Gulf, Central, Milne Bay, Papuan Islands, New Britain, New Ireland.

Fig. 378. *Psychotria micralabastra*. Leaves and flower buds

Psychotria micrococca Valeton

Botanische Jahrbücher für Systematik, Pflanzengeschichte und Pflanzengeographie Vol. 61: 89 (1927)
Timber Group: Non-timber species

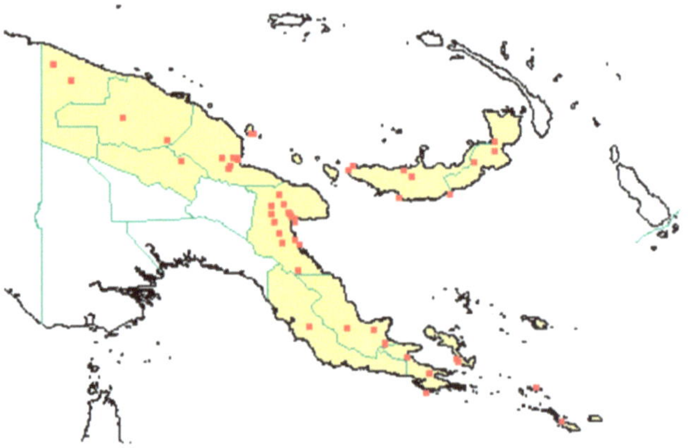

Field Characters: Subcanopy trees, 4 m high; bole cylindrical, 10 cm diam., straight, 1 m long; buttresses absent; spines absent; aerial roots absent; stilt roots absent. Bark brown, rough, pustular; lenticels irregular; bark 5 mm thick; under-bark pale orange; faintly or non-aromatic; blaze consisting of one layer, orange, with stripes, fibrous;

inner blaze orange, with stripes, fibrous; exudate present, colourless, not readily flowing, not changing colour on exposure to air, not sticky. Terminal buds not enclosed by leaves.

Indumentum: Complex hairs absent; stinging hairs absent; mature twig without hairs.

Leaves: Spaced along branches, leaves opposite, simple; petiole present, not winged, attached to base of leaf lamina, not swollen; lamina broadest at or near middle; base symmetric, margin entire, not dissected or lobed, apex acuminate or obtuse, venation pinnate, secondary veins open, prominent or not prominent, but visible, intramarginal veins absent; lower surface dull green, upper surface dull dark green, hairs absent, oil dots absent, domatia absent; stipules present, joined, joined across twigs, encircling the twig, leafy, not fringed, large, not persistent.

Flowers: Inflorescence terminal, flowers on a branched axis; flowers bisexual, with pedicel, with many planes of symmetry perianth present, with distinct sepals and petals; ovary inferior, carpels joined, styles joined, 1.

Fruits: arranged on branched axis, fruit 8–10 mm long, 8–10 mm diam., red, not spiny, fleshy, simple, indehiscent, drupe. Seed 1, not winged.

Distribution: West Sepik, East Sepik, Madang, Morobe, Central, Northern, Milne Bay, Papuan Islands, New Britain.

Psydrax cymigera (Valeton) S.T.Reynolds & R.J.F.Hend.

Austrobaileya Vol. 22: 97 (2004)
Timber Group: Occasional timber species

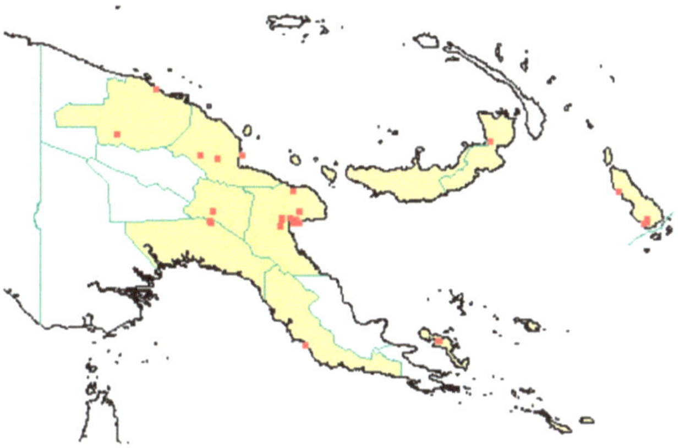

Field Characters: Subcanopy trees, up to 18 m high; bole cylindrical, up to 20 cm diam., straight, 5 m long; buttresses absent; spines absent; aerial roots absent; stilt roots absent. Bark grey or brown, rough, slightly scaly or flaky; lenticels irregular; bark 10 mm thick; under-bark brown or grey; strongly aromatic; pleasant; blaze consisting of one layer, orange or brown, with stripes, granular with splinters; exudate present, colourless, not readily flowing, changing to brown on exposure to air, not sticky. Terminal buds not enclosed by leaves.

Indumentum: Complex hairs absent; stinging hairs absent; mature twig without hairs.

Leaves: Spaced along branches, leaves opposite, simple; petiole present, not winged, attached to base of leaf lamina, not swollen; lamina broadest at or near middle, 15–16.5 cm long, 4.5–6 cm wide; base symmetric, margin entire, not dissected or lobed, apex acuminate, venation pinnate, secondary veins open, prominent, intramarginal veins absent; lower surface pale green, upper surface glossy dark green, hairs absent, oil dots absent, domatia absent; stipules present, joined, joined across twigs, encircling the twig, collar-like, not fringed, large, persistent.

Flowers: Inflorescence axillary, flowers on a branched axis, bisexual, with pedicel 3–4 mm long, with many planes of symmetry, 6–7 mm long, small, c. 3 mm diam.; perianth present, with distinct sepals and petals, white at least on inner surface of lobes, often with purple tinge or greenish purple (especially in older flowers); inner perianth 4, some or partly joined to form a long corolla tube; stamens 4, filaments present short, free of each other, joined to perianth; ovary inferior, carpels joined, styles joined, 1, long-exserted beyond corolla.

Fruits: arranged on branched axis, (5–)8–10 mm long, 8–10 mm diam., green (probably immature), not spiny, fleshy, simple, indehiscent, berry

Distribution: East Sepik, Madang, Morobe, Eastern Highlands, Gulf, Central, Papuan Islands, New Britain, Bougainville.

Notes: Previously known as *Canthium cymigerum* (Valeton) B.L.Burtt. Although several species have been classified as belonging to the genus *Canthium*, this genus does not occur in Papua New Guinea.

Tarenna sambucina var. *buruensis (Miq.)* Fosberg & Sachet Fig. 379

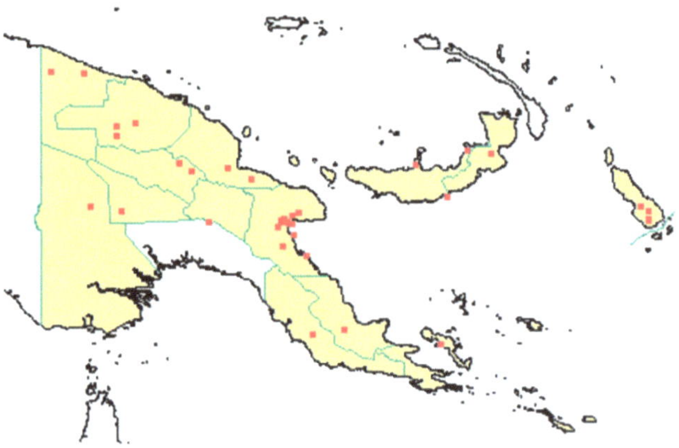

Allertonia Vol. 6: 272 (1991)
Other Literature: A.C. Smith, *Flora Vitiensis Nova. A new flora of Fiji (Spermatophytes only)* Vol. 4: 196 (1988).
Timber Group: Non-timber species

Field Characters: Subcanopy trees, 8–20 m high, or shrubs; bole cylindrical, (10–)30–35 cm diam., straight; buttresses absent; spines absent; aerial roots absent; stilt roots absent. Bark pale brown to green-brown, smooth to slightly rough, pustular; lenticels irregular; bark 5 mm thick; under-bark dark maroon; faintly or non-aromatic; pleasant; blaze consisting of one layer, pink to pale yellow, with stripes, granular without splinters; exudate absent. Terminal buds enclosed by leaves.

Indumentum: Complex hairs absent; stinging hairs absent; mature twig without hairs.

Leaves: Spaced along branches, tending to cluster towards distal ends of branches, leaves opposite, simple; petiole present, 25–35 mm long, shortly winged near base of lamina, not swollen; lamina broadest above middle, 18–25 cm long, 7–14 cm wide; base symmetric to slightly asymmetric, margin entire, not dissected or lobed, apex shortly acuminate, venation pinnate, secondary veins open, prominent, intramarginal veins absent; lower surface green or pale green, upper surface glossy or subglossy mid-green, hairs absent, oil dots absent, domatia present on abaxial surface; stipules present, joined across twigs, leafy, not fringed, large, usually persistent.

Flowers: Inflorescence terminal, sometimes on short lateral branches, 9–15 cm long, many-flowered, flowers single, bisexual, with pedicel 30–45 mm long, with many planes of symmetry, c. 130–140 mm long, large, 70–80 mm diam.; perianth present, with distinct sepals and petals, white (turning yellow), aromatic; inner perianth usually 5, some or partly joined forming a long corolla tube; stamens usually 5 (same number as corolla lobes), filaments free of each other, joined to perianth (to throat of corolla, usually with anthers exserted from corolla); ovary inferior, carpels joined, locules 2 (ovules 1–many per locule); styles joined, 1 (30–35 mm long).

Fruits: single, globular, c. 5 mm long, c. 5 mm diam., purple-green to black, not spiny, fleshy but hard, simple, indehiscent, drupe. Seeds many, angular, not winged.

Distribution: West Sepik, East Sepik, Madang, Morobe, Western Highlands, Eastern Highlands, Southern Highlands, Western, Central, Northern, Milne Bay, Papuan Islands, New Britain, Bougainville.

Notes: Previously known as *Tarenna buruensis* (Miq.) Merr.

Fig. 379. *Tarenna sambucina* var. *buruensis*. Habit, bark, leaves and fruit

Timonius belensis Merr. & L.M.Perry

Journal of the Arnold Arboretum Vol. 26: 236 (1945)
Timber Group: Non-timber species

Field Characters: Subcanopy trees, 14–20 m high, often much shorter; bole cylindrical, 15–30 cm diam., slightly crooked or almost straight, up to c. 10 m long; buttresses absent; spines absent; aerial roots absent; stilt roots absent.

Bark brown or grey, rough, pustular; lenticels irregular; bark 5 mm thick; under-bark white or pale yellow cream-coloured; faintly or non-aromatic; unpleasant; blaze consisting of one layer, orange or brown, markings absent, granular with splinters; exudate present, colourless, not readily flowing, changing to dark orange or brown on exposure to air, not sticky. Terminal buds enclosed by leaves.

Indumentum: Complex hairs absent; stinging hairs absent; mature twig without hairs.

Leaves: Spaced along branches, leaves opposite, simple; petiole 12–15 mm long, not winged, attached to base of leaf lamina, not swollen; lamina broadest at or near middle, (4–)7–8.5 cm long, (1.6–)4–4.5 cm wide; base symmetric, margin entire, not dissected or lobed, apex sub-acute, slightly sharp-pointed or obtuse, venation pinnate, secondary veins open, not prominent, but visible, intramarginal veins absent; lower surface green, upper surface dark green, hairs absent, oil dots absent, domatia absent; stipules present, joined, joined across twigs, encircling the twig, leafy narrow, not fringed, large, (15–)40–70 mm long, not persistent.

Flowers: Inflorescence axillary, flowers single, bisexual, with pedicel 6–7 mm long, with many planes of symmetry, 14–16 mm long, small, 4–5 mm diam.; perianth present, with distinct sepals and petals, white at least on inner surface of lobes, often with purple tinge or greenish purple (especially in older flowers); inner perianth (4 or)8, some or partly joined to form a long corolla tube; stamens 4, filaments present short, free of each other, joined to perianth; ovary inferior, carpels joined, styles joined, 1.

Fruits: single, 10–15 mm long, slightly flattened, 8–14 mm diam., green, not spiny, fleshy, simple, indehiscent, berry.

Distribution: West Sepik, East Sepik, Madang, Morobe, Western Highlands, Eastern Highlands, Southern Highlands, Western, Central, Milne Bay.

Versteegia cauliflora Valeton
Fig. 380

Nova Guinea Vol. 8: 484 (1911)
Timber Group: Non-timber species

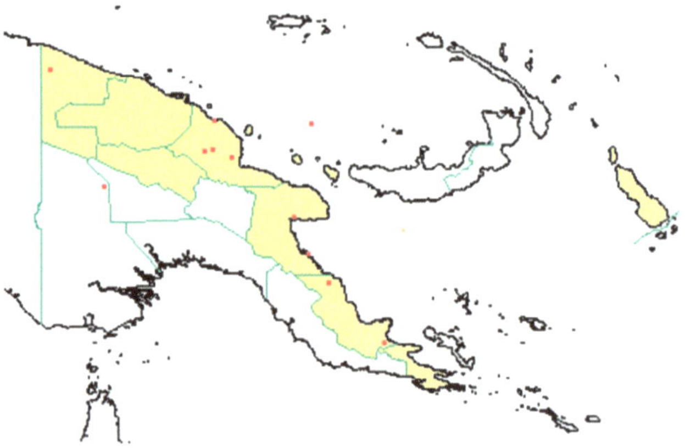

Field Characters: Subcanopy trees, 4–8 m high; bole cylindrical, c. 10 cm diam., straight 4–8 m long; buttresses absent; spines absent; aerial roots absent; stilt roots absent. Bark brown, slightly rough, slightly fissured or slightly pustular; lenticels irregular scattered; faintly or non-aromatic; blaze consisting of one layer, pink or brown pale to dark, markings absent, fibrous; exudate present, colourless, not readily flowing, not changing colour on exposure to air, sticky. Terminal buds not enclosed by leaves.

Indumentum: Complex hairs absent; stinging hairs absent; mature twig without hairs.

Leaves: Spaced along branches, leaves opposite, simple; petiole present, not winged, attached to base of leaf lamina, not swollen; lamina broadest above middle, 28–35 cm long, 11–14 cm wide; base symmetric, margin entire, not dissected or lobed, apex obtuse, venation pinnate, secondary veins open, prominent, intramarginal veins absent; lower surface pale green, upper surface dark green, hairs absent, oil dots absent, domatia absent; stipules present, joined, joined across twigs, encircling the twig, leafy, not fringed, large, up to c. 10 mm long, persistent.

Flowers: Inflorescence on the trunk or branches, flowers on an unbranched axis in clusters on trunk; flowers bisexual, not stalked or shortly with pedicel up to c. 3 mm long, with many planes of symmetry, 6–10 mm long, small, 5–8 mm diam.; perianth present, with distinct sepals and petals, white, brown perianth becoming darker with age, yellow, or red; inner perianth 5, some or partly joined; stamens 5, filaments present, free of each other, joined to perianth; ovary inferior, carpels joined, locules 5; styles joined, 1.

Fruits: arranged on unbranched axis, fruit 14–22 mm long, 14–15 mm diam., red, broadest at or near middle, or below middle, not spiny, fleshy, simple, indehiscent, drupe. Seed 1, c. 10 mm long, as wide as long, c. 10 mm diam., not winged.

Distribution: West Sepik, Madang, Morobe, Eastern Highlands, Western, Central, Northern, Milne Bay, Bougainville.

Fig. 380. *Versteegia cauliflora*. Habit of small tree with fruit

80. Gentianaceae

Trees, shrubs, and herbs. Stipules absent or present. Leaves well-developed, rarely spiral, opposite, or whorled, simple, not dissected or lobed; margin entire; venation palmate or pinnate. Inflorescences axillary or terminal. Bracts absent or present. Flowers bisexual, regular, slightly irregular, or zygomorphic, with distinct calyx and corolla. Sepals 4 or 5(–12). Petals 4 or 5(–12), joined, at least in part; tube present. Stamens 4 or 5(–12), free or fused to corolla; filaments present; staminodes absent. Gynoecium with carpels at least partially joined, superior; styles partially or fully joined. Fruit simple, dehiscent or indehiscent, capsule, berry, dry, at least non-fleshy, or fleshy. Seeds without wings.

PNG genera: *Cyrtophyllum, Exacum,* ***Fagraea****, Gentiana,* ***Picrophloeus****, Swertia,* ***Utania***

References: Conn (1995), Conn and Brown (1993), Leenhouts (1962), Sugumaran and Wong (2012), Wong (2012), Wong and Sugumaran (2012a, 2012b)

1a. Saprophytes; leaves reduced to scales; inflorescences axillary .... *Exacum tenue* (Blume) Klack. (not treated here)

1b. Terrestrial or hemi-epiphytic, not saprophytes; leaves normal; inflorescences usually terminal.......... 2

2a. Inflorescences axillary.. *Cyrtophyllum* (not treated here)

2b. Inflorescences usually terminal.. 3

3a. Ovary with 1 locule.. 4

3b. Ovary with >1 locule.. 5

4a. Small herbs, <20 cm high; flowers solitary; corolla lobes without glands at base, with membrane between petals; ovules >4... *Gentiana* (not treated here)

4b. Tall herbs, up to 80 cm high; flowers in branched inflorescences; corolla lobes with distinct glands at base; withut membrane between petals; ovule 4 .... *Swertia papuana* Diels (not treated here)

5a. Herb.. *Exacum* (not treated here)

5b. Woody shrub or tree, not herbaceous 6

6a. Petiolar sheaths at base of each leaf-pair fused to form a cup-like ochrea; stigma capitate, not expanding conspicuously at base; stamens and style distinctly exserted from corolla tube.................. *Picrophloeus*

6b. Petiolar sheaths at base of each leaf-pair not fused or only slightly so, not forming an ochrea; stigma appearing peltate, expanded at base into a circular plate-like rim; stamen and style not or only slightly exserted from corolla tube 4

6a. Leaf arrangement on branches distichous; vegetative terminal buds not resinous; inflorescence a pendulous cyme, with all branches condensed along rachis. Surface of dried fruits firm and smooth, with epidermis not detaching from pericarp.. *Utania racemosa*

6b. Leaf arrangement on branches decussate; vegetative terminal buds covered with cream-coloured to yellowish resin; inflorescence without any branching (flowers solitary) or an erect cyme with well-developed branches; surface of dried fruits wrinkled, with epidermis detaching from pericarp........... .... *Fagraea*

Fagraea berteroana Benth.
Fig. 381

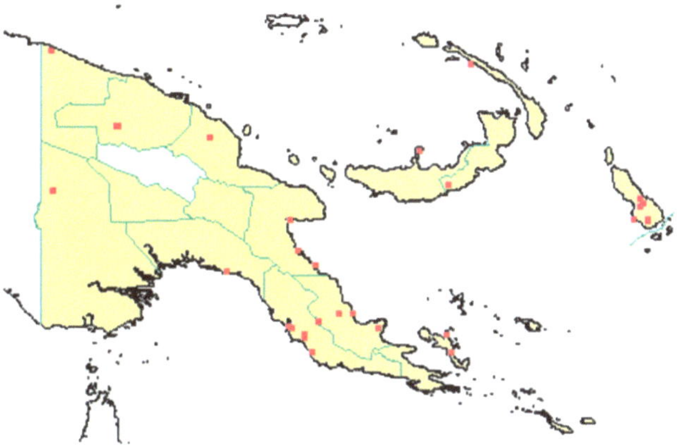

Journal of the Proceedings of the Linnean Society. Botany Vol. 1: 98 (1857)
Other Literature: B.J. Conn, *Handbooks of the Flora of Papua New Guinea* Vol. 3: 136 & 137 (1995) Fig. 31.
Timber Group: Non-timber species

Field Characters: Usually subcanopy trees, up to 10(–20) m high; buttresses absent; spines absent; aerial roots absent; stilt roots absent. Bark sometimes grey or dark brown, rough, sometimes scaly or flaky or fissured; bark <25 mm thick; faintly or non-aromatic; blaze consisting of one layer, pale brown, markings absent; inner blaze pale brown, markings absent; exudate absent. Terminal buds not enclosed by leaves.

Indumentum: Complex hairs absent; stinging hairs absent; mature twig without hairs.

Leaves: Spaced along branches, leaves opposite, simple; petiole (15–)25–40(–50) mm long, not winged, attached to base of leaf lamina, not swollen; lamina rarely broadest above middle, broadest at or near middle, or rarely broadest below middle, (8–)10–16(–19) cm long, (4.5–)6–10.5(–12) cm wide; base symmetric, margin entire, not dissected or lobed, apex rounded or shortly acuminate, venation pinnate, secondary veins open, not prominent, but visible, intramarginal veins absent; lower surface green, upper surface green, hairs absent, oil dots absent, domatia absent; stipules present, joined, joined across twigs, not encircling the twig, collar-like, not fringed, large, persistent.

Flowers: Inflorescence terminal, flowers on a branched axis; flowers bisexual, with pedicel, with many planes of symmetry, (40–)45–100 mm long, large, c. 30 mm diam.; perianth present, with distinct sepals and petals, white or pale yellow to orange to cream-coloured; inner perianth 5, some or partly joined; stamens 5, filaments present, free of each other, joined to perianth; ovary superior, carpels joined, locules 2; styles joined, 1.

Fruits: arranged on branched axis, fruit 30–60 mm long, orange or red, not spiny, fleshy, simple, indehiscent, berry. Seeds many, barely visible, c. 1 mm long, irregular (angular), c. 1 mm diam., not winged.

Distribution: West Sepik, East Sepik, Madang, Morobe, Eastern Highlands, Southern Highlands, Western, Gulf, Central, Northern, Milne Bay, Papuan Islands, New Britain, New Ireland, Bougainville.

Notes: The name of this species is frequently misspelt as *Fagraea berteriana*.

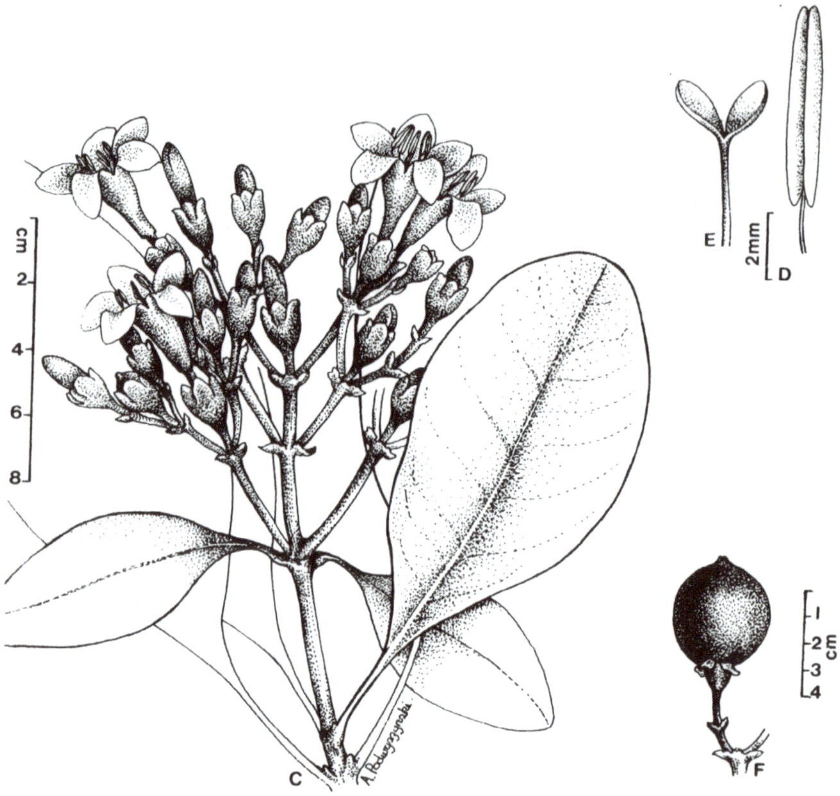

Fig. 381. *Fagraea berteroana.* Illustration of branchlet with flowers and fruit (© Royal Botanic Gardens Melbourne)

Fagraea bodenii Wernham

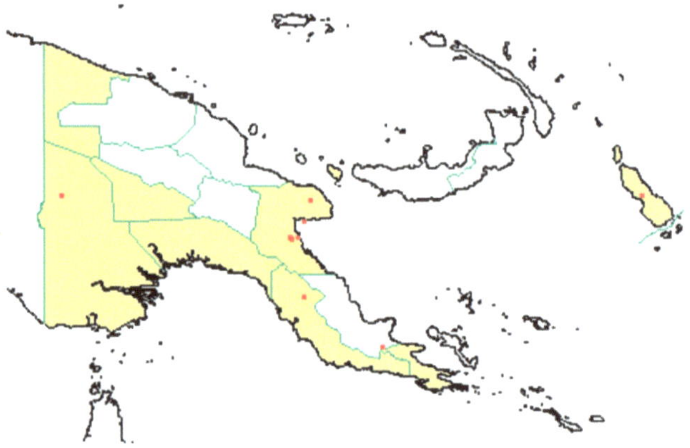

Transactions of the Linnean Society. Botany Vol. 9: 111 (1916)
Other Literature: B.J. Conn, *Handbooks of the Flora of Papua New Guinea* Vol. 3: 139 (1995) Fig. 29.
Timber Group: Non-timber species

Field Characters: Occasionally canopy trees, up to 30(–40) m high, or subcanopy trees, up to 15 m high; bole cylindrical, 10–50(–100) cm diam., straight, 8–20(–30) m long; buttresses present or absent; spines absent; aerial roots absent; stilt roots absent. Bark cream to grey; thickness <25 mm thick; faintly or non-aromatic; blaze consisting of one layer, white or pale yellow (cream-coloured), markings absent; exudate absent. Terminal buds not enclosed by leaves.

Indumentum: Complex hairs absent; stinging hairs absent; mature twig without hairs.

Leaves: Spaced along branches, leaves opposite, simple; petiole 8–20(–30) mm long, not winged, attached to base of leaf lamina, not swollen; lamina slightly broadest above middle or broadest at or near middle, 5–16 cm long, 2.5–8 cm wide; base symmetric, margin entire, not dissected or lobed, apex rounded, obtuse, or slightly mucronate, venation pinnate, secondary veins open, occasionally prominent or not prominent, but visible, intramarginal veins absent; lower surface pale green, upper surface green, hairs absent, oil dots absent, domatia absent; stipules present, joined, joined across twigs, encircling the twig, collar-like, not fringed, large, persistent.

Flowers: Inflorescence terminal, flowers on a branched axis; flowers bisexual, with pedicel, with many planes of symmetry, 20–25(–45) mm long, large, c. 15 mm diam.; perianth present, with distinct sepals and petals, green (outer surface) or cream-coloured (inner surface); inner perianth 5, some or partly joined; stamens 5, filaments present, free of each other, joined to perianth; ovary superior, carpels joined, locules 2; styles joined, 1.

Fruits: arranged on branched axis, fruit c. 40 mm long, yellow, orange, or red, not spiny, fleshy, simple, indehiscent, berry. Seeds many, barely visible, c. 1 mm long, irregular (angular), c. 1 mm diam., not winged.

Distribution: Morobe, Western, Central, Milne Bay, Bougainville.

Fagraea ceilanica Thunb.
Figs 382, 383

Kongl. Vetenskaps Academiens Handlingar Vol. 3: 132 (1782) Fig. 4.
Other Literature: B.J. Conn, *Handbooks of the Flora of Papua New Guinea* Vol. 3: 140–142 (1995) Fig. 30.
Timber Group: Occasional timber species

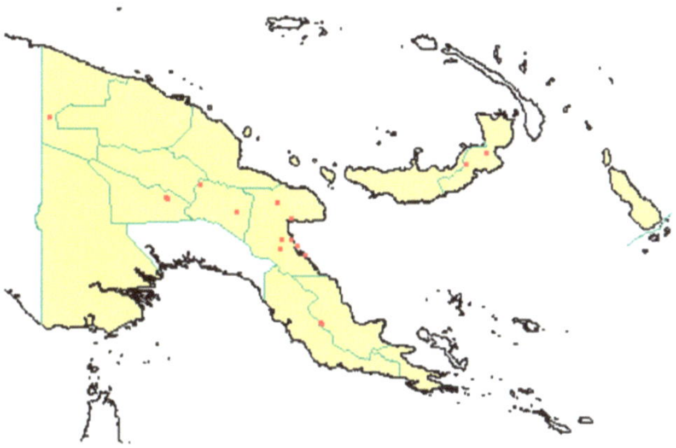

Field Characters: Subcanopy trees, 8–12(–20) m high, often a large shrub to small treelet; bole cylindrical, rarely > c. 20 cm diam., straight, usually up to c. 3 m long, often branching from near base of tree; buttresses absent; spines absent; aerial roots absent; stilt roots absent. Bark brown; thickness <25 mm thick; under-bark green; faintly or non-aromatic; blaze consisting of one layer, white, pale yellow (straw-coloured), or pale orange (tinge); exudate absent. Terminal buds not enclosed by leaves.

Indumentum: Complex hairs absent; stinging hairs absent; mature twig without hairs.

Leaves: Spaced along branches, leaves opposite, simple; petiole 10–20(–30) mm long, not winged, attached to base of leaf lamina, not swollen; lamina broadest above middle, 8–15(–24) cm long, 3–6(–10) cm wide; base symmetric, margin entire, not dissected or lobed, apex obtuse, sub-acute, or sometimes mucronate, venation pinnate, secondary veins open, not prominent, but visible, intramarginal veins absent; lower surface pale green, upper surface dark green, hairs absent, oil dots absent, domatia absent; stipules present, joined, joined across twigs, encircling the twig or soon not encircling the twig, collar-like, not fringed, large, persistent.

Flowers: Inflorescence terminal, flowers on a branched axis; flowers bisexual, with pedicel, with many planes of symmetry, (25–)35–75 mm long, large, 35–45 mm diam.; perianth present, with distinct sepals and petals, white (sometimes with greenish tinge) or cream-coloured; inner perianth 5, some or partly joined; stamens 5, filaments present, free of each other, joined to perianth; ovary superior, carpels joined, locules 2; styles joined, 1.

Fruits: arranged on branched axis, fruit c. 25 mm long, c. 35 mm diam., orange or red, not spiny, fleshy, simple, indehiscent, drupe. Seeds many, < 2 mm long, irregular (angular), c. 2 mm diam., not winged.

Distribution: West Sepik, East Sepik, Madang, Morobe, Western Highlands, Eastern Highlands, Southern Highlands, Western, Central, New Britain.

Fig. 382. *Fagraea ceilanica.* Leaves, fruit and flowers

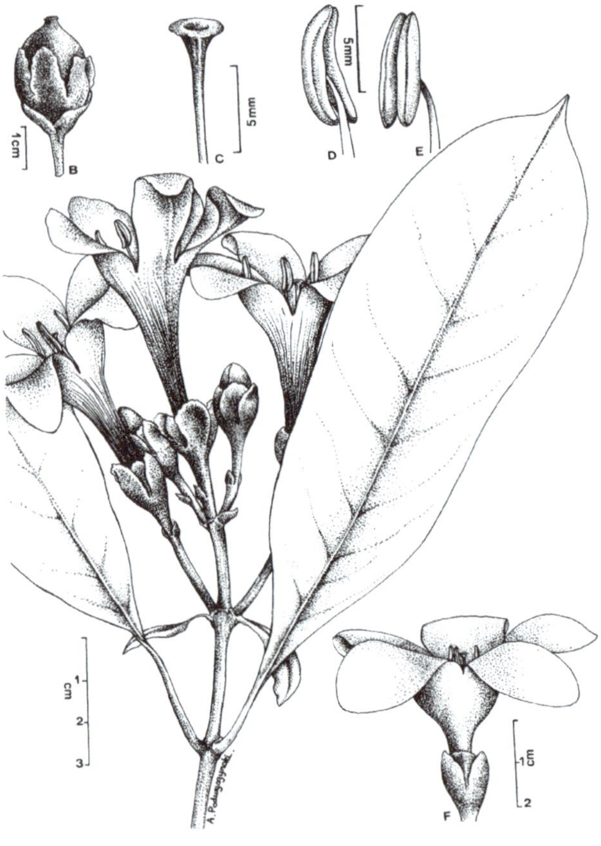

Fig. 383. *Fagraea ceilanica.* Illustration of branchlet showing flowers and fruit (© Royal Botanic Gardens Melbourne)

Fagraea dolichopoda Gilg & Benedict

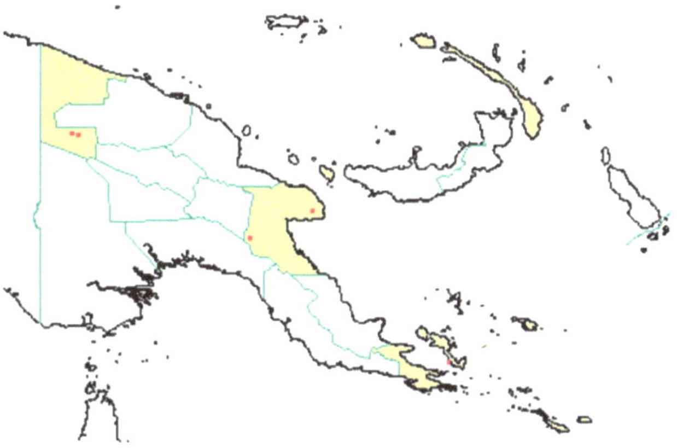

Botanische Jahrbücher für Systematik, Pflanzengeschichte und Pflanzengeographie Vol. 54: 196 (1916)
Other Literature: B.J. Conn, *Handbooks of the Flora of Papua New Guinea* Vol. 3: 147 & 148 (1995) Fig. 32.
Timber Group: Non-timber species

Field Characters: Canopy trees, up to 30 m high, or subcanopy trees; bole cylindrical, c. 35 cm diam., straight; buttresses absent; spines absent; aerial roots absent; stilt roots absent. Bark cream or light grey to brown, rough, fissured; bark <25 mm thick; faintly or non-aromatic; blaze consisting of one layer, white or pale yellow (straw-coloured), markings absent, fibrous or granular without splinters; inner blaze white or pale yellow (straw-coloured), markings absent, fibrous or granular without splinters; exudate absent. Terminal buds not enclosed by leaves.

Indumentum: Complex hairs absent; stinging hairs absent; mature twig without hairs.

Leaves: Spaced along branches, leaves opposite, simple; petiole 13–27 mm long, not winged, attached to base of leaf lamina, not swollen; lamina broadest above middle or broadest at or near middle, (5.5–)8.5–12.5 cm long, 2.1–4(–5) cm wide; base symmetric, margin entire, not dissected or lobed, apex distinctly acuminate or long-tapering, venation pinnate, secondary veins open, not prominent, but visible, intramarginal veins absent; lower surface pale green, upper surface dark dull green, hairs absent, oil dots absent, domatia absent; stipules present, joined, joined across twigs, encircling the twig, or soon not encircling twig, collar-like, not fringed, often small, persistent.

Flowers: Inflorescence terminal, flowers on a branched axis; flowers bisexual, with pedicel, with many planes of symmetry, 30–36 mm long, large, c. 20 mm diam.; perianth present, with distinct sepals and petals, white, greenish yellow (tinge), or cream-coloured; inner perianth 5, some or partly joined; stamens 5, filaments present, free of each other, joined to perianth; ovary superior, carpels joined, locules 2; styles joined, 1.

Fruits: arranged on branched axis, fruit c. 15 mm long, white, not spiny, fleshy, simple, indehiscent, berry. Seeds many, barely visible, c. 1 mm long, irregular (angular), c. 1 mm diam., not winged.

Distribution: West Sepik, Morobe, Milne Bay, Papuan Islands.

Notes: *Fagraea dolichopoda* is now regarded as restricted to New Guinea (Conn & Brown 1993).

Fagraea salticola Leenh. Figs 384, 385

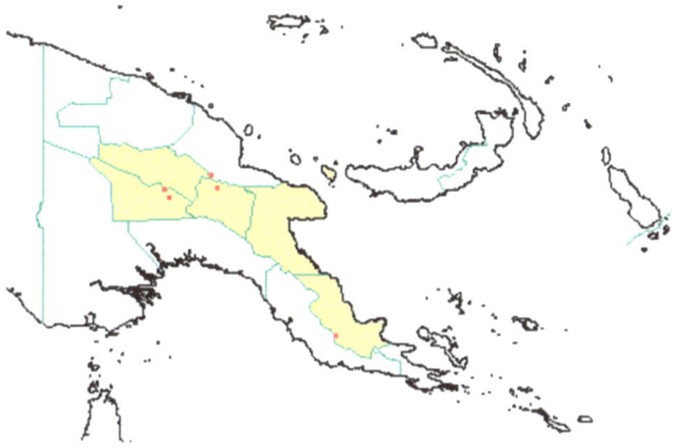

Bulletin du Jardin Botanique de l'État. Bulletin van den Rijksplantentuin Vol. 32: 429 & 430 (1962)
Other Literature: B.J. Conn, *Handbooks of the Flora of Papua New Guinea* Vol. 3: 153 & 154 (1995) Fig. 33.
Timber Group: Non-timber species

Field Characters: Canopy trees, up to 27 m high, or subcanopy trees; bole cylindrical or often markedly fluted, 25–40(–70) cm diam., crooked or straight, 7–13 m long; buttresses absent; spines absent; aerial roots absent; stilt roots absent. Bark grey, dark brown, or almost black, rough, scaly or flaky or fissured; bark (2–)5–8 mm thick; under-bark green; faintly or non-aromatic, pleasant; blaze consisting of one layer, pale pink, white, or pale yellow (straw-coloured), markings absent, fibrous with some splinters; exudate present, colourless, not readily flowing, changing to pale brown on exposure to air, not sticky. Terminal buds not enclosed by leaves.

Indumentum: Complex hairs absent; stinging hairs absent; mature twig without hairs.

Leaves: Spaced along branches, leaves opposite, simple; petiole 5–15 mm long, not winged, attached to base of leaf lamina, not swollen; lamina broadest above middle or broadest at or near middle, (4–)5–12(–14) cm long, (3–)5–8(–10.5) cm wide; base symmetric, margin entire, not dissected or lobed, apex rounded or rarely obtuse, venation pinnate, secondary veins open, not visible or not prominent, but visible, intramarginal veins absent; lower surface pale green, upper surface dark green, hairs absent, oil dots absent, domatia absent; stipules present, joined, joined across twigs, encircling the twig, or soon not encircling the twig, collar-like, not fringed, large, persistent.

Flowers: Inflorescence terminal, flowers on an unbranched axis or flowers on a branched axis; flowers bisexual, not stalked or with pedicel, with many planes of symmetry, 25–40 mm long, large, 20–25 mm diam.; perianth present, with distinct sepals and petals, white (inner surface), greenish yellow (outer surface), or cream-coloured (inner surface); inner perianth 5, some or partly joined; stamens 5, filaments present, free of each other, joined to perianth; ovary superior, carpels joined, locules 2; styles joined, 1.

Fruits: arranged on unbranched axis or Arranged on branched axis, fruit 35–40 mm long, c. 20 mm diam., orange, red, or brown, not spiny, fleshy, simple, indehiscent, berry. Seeds many, barely visible, c. 1 mm long, irregular (angular), c. 1 mm diam., not winged.

Distribution: Madang, Morobe, Western Highlands, Eastern Highlands, Southern Highlands, Northern.

Fig. 384. *Fagraea salticola*. Branchlet with leaves and fruit

Fig. 385. *Fagraea salticola*. Bark, flowers, fruit and seeds

Picrophloeus javanensis Blume

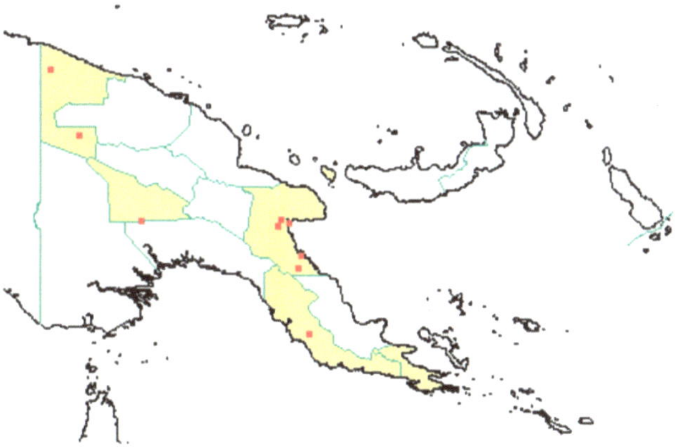

Bijdragen tot de Flora van Nederlandsch Indie Vol 16: 1020 (1827)
References: Wong (2012)
Other Literature: B.J. Conn, *Handbooks of the Flora of Papua New Guinea* Vol. 3: 144 (1995) (as *Fagraea elliptica* Roxb.)
Timber Group: Non-timber species

Field Characters: Small subcanopy trees, c. 8 m high; bole cylindrical, c. 20 cm diam., crooked, c. 4 m long; buttresses absent; spines absent; aerial roots absent; stilt roots absent. Bark brown or grey, rough, pustular; lenticels irregular, c. 10 mm thick; under-bark white, faintly or non-aromatic, pleasant; blaze consisting of one layer; strongly aromatic; unpleasant, yellow, with stripes, granular with splinters; exudate colourless, not readily flowing, changing colour to green or black on exposure to air, sticky. Terminal buds not enclosed by leaves

Indumentum: Complex hairs absent; stinging hairs absent; mature twig without hairs.

Leaves: Spaced along branches, leaves opposite, simple; petiole present, not winged, attached to base of leaf blade, not swollen; lamina broadest above middle, 11–23 cm long, 5–8 cm wide; lamina symmetric, margin entire, not dissected or lobed, apex acuminate, venation pinnate, secondary veins open, not prominent, but visible, intramarginal veins absent; lower surface pale green, upper surface dark green, hairs absent; oil dots absent; domatia absent; stipules present, joined, joined across twigs, encircling the twig, collar-like, not fringed, large, persistent.

Flowers: Inflorescence terminal, flowers on a branched axis, with petiole absent; flowers bisexual, stalked, with many planes of symmetry, c. 15 mm long, small, 10 mm diam.; perianth present, with distinct sepals and petals, white; inner perianth 5, some or partly joined; stamens 5, filaments present, free of each other, joined to perianth; ovary superior, carpels joined (when more than one); styles solitary, 1.

Fruits: arranged on branched axis, fruit 4–5 mm long, c. 4 mm diam., not spiny, fleshy, simple, indehiscent, drupe; seeds many, 0.5–1 mm long, not winged, irregular *angular*, c. 1 mm diam.

Distribution: West Sepik, Morobe, Southern Highlands, Central, Milne Bay.

Notes: This species has previously been referred to by the name *Fagraea elliptica*; however, this name is regarded as dubious (Wong 2012).

Utania racemosa (Jack ex Wall.) M.Sugumaran Fig. 386

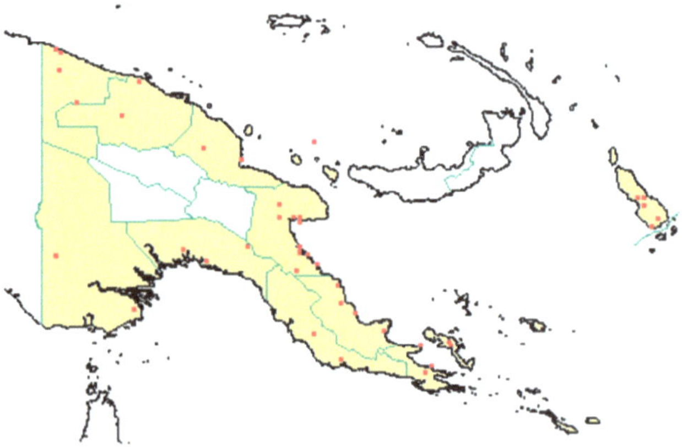

Plant Ecology and Evolution Vol. 147(2): 220 (2014)
Other Literature: B.J. Conn, *Handbooks of the Flora of Papua New Guinea* Vol. 3: 151–153 (1995) Fig. 33 (as *Fagraea racemosa*).
Timber Group: Non-timber species

Field Characters: Subcanopy trees, 2–10(–16) m high; bole cylindrical, slightly crooked or straight; buttresses absent; spines absent; aerial roots absent; stilt roots absent. Bark grey or light brown, slightly rough, fissured; bark 15 mm thick; under-bark yellow or green; faintly or non-aromatic; pleasant; blaze consisting of one layer, white or pale yellow (straw-coloured), markings absent, fibrous; exudate present, colourless, not readily flowing, changing to red or orange on exposure to air, not sticky. Terminal buds not enclosed by leaves.

Indumentum: Complex hairs absent; stinging hairs absent; mature twig without hairs.

Leaves: Spaced along branches, leaves opposite, simple; petiole 10–20 mm long, not winged, attached to base of leaf lamina, not swollen; lamina occasionally broadest above middle, broadest at or near middle, broadest below middle, or equally broad throughout much of length, 15–30 cm long, 8–15 cm wide; base symmetric, margin entire, not dissected or lobed, apex usually rounded to obtuse, venation pinnate, secondary veins open, prominent, intramarginal veins absent; lower surface pale green, upper surface dark green, hairs absent, oil dots absent, domatia absent; stipules present, joined, joined across twigs, encircling the twig, collar-like, not fringed, large, persistent.

Flowers: Inflorescence terminal, flowers on a branched axis; flowers bisexual, not stalked or with pedicel, with many planes of symmetry, 20–40 mm long, large, 20–30 mm diam.; perianth present, with distinct sepals and petals, white or sometimes pink at base; inner perianth 5, some or partly joined; stamens 5, filaments present, free of each other, joined to perianth; ovary superior, carpels joined, locules 2; styles joined, 1.

Fig. 386. *Utania racemosa*. Flowers and leaves

Fruits: arranged on branched axis, fruit 10–25 mm long, 10–24 mm diam., fruit orange, blue, or red, not spiny, fleshy, simple, indehiscent, berry. Seeds many, barely visible, c. 1 mm long, irregular (angular), c. 1 mm diam., not winged.

Distribution: West Sepik, East Sepik, Madang, Morobe, Western, Gulf, Central, Northern, Milne Bay, Papuan Islands, Bougainville.

Notes: *Utania racemosa* is here applied in a broad sense, not as used by Sugumaran and Wong (2014) who regarded this species as restricted to Indo-China, Thailand, Malay Peninsula (Malaysia) and Sumatera (Indonesia). As here applied in this account, there is considerable morphological variation within this species, often within very small geographical areas. Therefore, if this species complex is to be divided into several distinct species, it will require considerable field studies, morphological analyses and other research techniques.

Previously known as *Fagraea racemosa* Jack ex Wall.

81. Loganiaceae

Trees, shrubs, lianas, and herbs. Stipules present sometimes reduced to stipular lines. Leaves well-developed or much reduced, opposite, simple, not dissected or lobed; margin entire; venation pinnate, palmate, or one-veined. Inflorescences axillary or terminal. Bracts present. Flowers bisexual or unisexual, then plant dioecious, regular, with distinct calyx and corolla. Sepals (4 or)5. Petals (4 or)5, joined, at least in part; tube present. Stamens (4 or)5, free of one another or fused to corolla; filaments present; staminodes absent or present. Gynoecium with carpels at least partially joined, superior; styles partially or fully joined. Fruit simple, dehiscent or indehiscent, capsule, schizocarp, dry, at least non-fleshy. Seeds without wings.

PNG genera: *Geniostoma, Mitrasacme, Mitreola,* ***Neuburgia****, Spigelia, Strychnos*

References: Conn (1979b, 1995), Leenhouts (1962)

1a. Herbaceous plants, annual or perennial, up to 0.5(–0.7) m high 2

1b. Woody plants, shrubs or trees, usually at least 2 m high, or climbers, epiphytes or hemi-epiphytes ... 4

2a. Stem with pseudowhorl of 4 large leaves at base of inforescence; capsue 2-lobed, not horned distally; style 1 .... *Spigelia* (not treated here)

2b. Stem with rosette of leaves basally and/or leaves in pairs along stem, never pseudowhorled; capsule 2-hrned distally; style 2, ± joined 3

3a. Calyx, corolla and stamens 4-merous; style free basally, joined distally... *Mitrasacme* (not treated here)

3b. Calyx, corolla and stamens 5-merous; styles free .... *Mitreola* (not treated here)

4a. Leaves with 3–5(–7) veins arising from the base; tendrils present; woody climber .... *Strychnos* (not treated here)

4b. Leaves with pinnate venation; tendrils absent; habit various, mostly shrubs or trees 5

5a. Fruits dehiscent, 2-valved capsule; seeds many, embedded in juicy orange or red pup; inflorescences axillary and/or on branches or stem; shrub .... *Geniostoma* (not treated here)

5b. Fruits indehiscent, drupe-like; seeds 1(or 2), not embedded in juicy pulp; inflorescences usually terminal, sometimes axllary; large shrubs or trees .... *Neuburgia*

Neuburgia corynocarpa (A.Gray) Leenh. var. *corynocarpa* Fig. 387

Flora Malesiana, Series 1 Vol. 6: 363 (1963)
Other Literature: B.J. Conn, *Handbooks of the Flora of Papua New Guinea* Vol. 3: 177–179 (1995) Fig. 40 & 41.
Timber Group: Occasional timber species

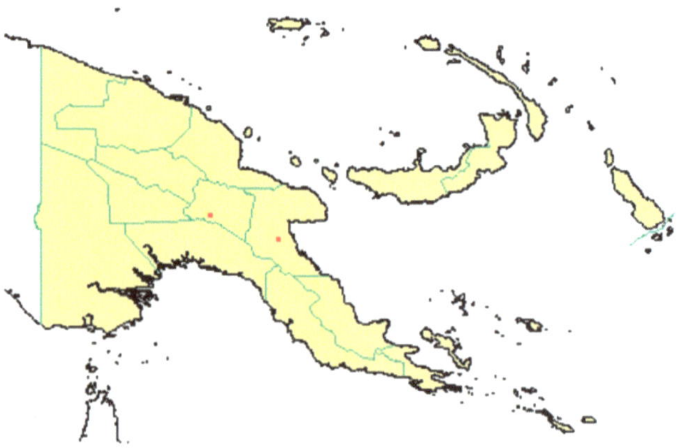

Field Characters: Canopy trees, 20–30 m high; bole cylindrical, 40–60 cm diam., straight, 10–15 m long; buttresses sometimes present or usually absent; spines absent; aerial roots absent; stilt roots absent. Bark dark brown, slightly rough to smooth, scaly or flaky or fissured; bark c. 6 mm thick; under-bark green; faintly or non-aromatic; blaze consisting of one layer, white or pale yellow, markings absent; exudate absent. Terminal buds not enclosed by leaves.

Indumentum: Complex hairs absent; stinging hairs absent; mature twig without hairs.

Leaves: Spaced along branches, leaves opposite, simple; petiole 3–10(–25) mm long, not winged, attached to base of leaf lamina, not swollen; lamina broadest above middle or broadest at or near middle, (6–)8–16(–28) cm long, (2–)4–7(–11) cm wide; base symmetric, margin entire, not dissected or lobed, apex rounded to obtuse or sub-acuminate, venation pinnate, secondary veins open, prominent, intramarginal veins absent; lower surface pale green, upper surface green, hairs absent, oil dots absent, domatia absent; stipules present, joined, joined across twigs, encircling the twig, collar-like to leafy, not fringed, large, persistent.

Fig. 387. *Neuburgia corynocarpa*. Habit, bark and leaves

Flowers: Inflorescence terminal, flowers on a branched axis; flowers bisexual, not stalked, with many planes of symmetry, (2–)2.5–4(–4.5) mm long, small, 3–4 mm diam.; perianth present, with distinct sepals and petals, white; inner perianth 5, some or partly joined; stamens 5, filaments present, free of each other, joined to perianth; ovary superior, carpels joined, locules 2; styles joined, 1.

Fruits: arranged on branched axis, fruit 15–25(–50) mm long, white or rarely red, not spiny, non-fleshy, simple, indehiscent, drupe. Seeds 1(or 2), up to 15 mm long, longer than wide, c. 6 mm diam., not winged.

Distribution: West Sepik, East Sepik, Madang, Morobe, Western Highlands, Eastern Highlands, Southern Highlands, Western, Gulf, Central, Northern, Milne Bay, Papuan Islands, New Britain, New Ireland, Manus, Bougainville.

Notes: The second variety of this species (var. *sarcantha* (Gilg & Bened.) B.J.Conn) tends to have a longer corolla tube (4–8 mm long cf. var. *corynocarpa* (2–)2.5–4(–4.5) mm long) and longer corolla lobe (1.5–4 mm long cf. (0.5–)0.8–1.5(–2) mm long). Other parts of the flower tend to be larger in var. *sarcantha* than in var. *corynocarpa*; however, there is considerable overlaps in most of these features (Conn 1995, pp. 177–180).

82. Apocynaceae

Trees, shrubs, lianas, and herbs. Stipules absent or rarely present. Leaves well-developed or much reduced, opposite, whorled, with 3 leaves per whorl, or spiral, simple, often with miky exudate, not dissected or lobed; margin entire; venation pinnate. Inflorescences axillary. Bracts present. Flowers bisexual, regular, with distinct calyx and corolla. Sepals 5. Petals 5, joined, at least in part; tube present. Stamens 5, free or fused with gynoecium or to one another; filaments present; staminodes absent. Gynoecium with carpels at least partially joined, but sometimes only by styles, superior or partially inferior; styles partially or fully joined. Fruit simple or aggregate, dehiscent or indehiscent, follicle, drupe or berry, dry, at least non-fleshy or fleshy. Seeds without wings or with wings, often conspicuousy hairy.

PNG genera: *Allamanda, Allowoodsonia,* ***Alstonia****, Alyxia, Anodendron, Asclepias, Bleekeria, Brachystelma, Calotropis, Carissa, Carruthersia, Cascabela, Catharanthus,* ***Cerbera****, Ceropegia, Chenemorpha, Clitandropsis, Cryptolepis, Cynanchum, Delphyodon, Dischidia, Ecdysanthera, Ervatamia, Finlaysonia, Gymnanthera, Heterostemma, Hoya, Ichnocarpus, Kentrochrosia, Kopsia, Lepinia,* ***Lepiniopsis****, Marsdenia, Melodinus, Neisosperma, Nerium, Ochrosia, Odontadenia, Pagiantha, Papuechites, Parsonsia, Phyllanthera, Plumeria* (introduced), *Rauvolfia, Rejoua, Roupellia, Sarcolobus, Secamone, Tabernaemontana, Thevetia, Toxocarpus, Trachelospermum, Tylophora, Urceola,* ***Voacanga****,* ***Wrightia***

References: Endress and Bruyns (2000), Forster (1992a–f), Markgraf

1a. Pollen not aggregated into pollinia; leaves never reduced nor scale-like, upper surface lacking raised glands .... subfamily Apocynoideae

1b. Pollen aggregated into pollinia; leaves with base of upper surface containing a cluster of 2–20 minute raised glands or glands absent, or leaves reduced and scale-like .... subfamilies Asclepiadoideae and Secamonoideae (neither subfamily treated here)

Key to subfamily Apocynoideae

1a. Stamens free or joined with stigma; anthers with long appendage at base 2

1b. Stamens free; anthers without a long appendage at base 13

2a. Anthers free; fruit fleshy; seeds glabrous; shrubs with opposite leaves 3

2b. Anther joined to stigma; fruit always dry; seeds with a tuft of hairs at apex; mostly lianas 5

3a. Calyx lobes joined for at least half their length .... *Voacanga*

3b. Calyx lobes divided almost to base 4

4a. Corolla lobes widened at base; stamens inserted below middle of corolla tube; fruit large .... *Rejoua* (not treated here)

4b. Corolla lobes narrow at base; stamens at least at middle of corolla tube; fruit small .... *Ervatamia* (not treated here)

5a. Stamens exserted from corolla tube 6

5b. Stamens included within corolla 9

6a. Erect shrubs to small trees; flowers with corolla and corona; disc absent .... *Wrightia*

6b. Lianas; flowers with corolla, without corona; disc present 7

7a. Climbing plants; corolla lobes distorted, hairy at base; disc 5-lobed; ovary and fruiting locules consisting of separate carpels (apocarpous) .... *Ichnocarpus* (not treated here)

7b. Twining plants; corolla lobes not distorted, without hair; disc ring-shaped; ovary and fruiting locules fused (syncarpous) 8

8a. Corolla lobes circular, strongly overlapping in bud; stigma with 5 teeth; fruit ellipsoid, with hooks; seeds with brown hairs .... *Delphyodon* (not treated here)

8b. Corolla lobes narrowly ovate in bud, scarcely overlapping; stigma with horizontal ring at base; fruit cylindrical, smooth; seeds with white or brown hairs .... *Parsonsia* (not treated here)

9a. Corolla tube with appendages on inner surface 10

9b. Corolla tube without appendages, but often hairy on inner surface 11

10a. Shrub; leaves whorled; flowers large; disc absent .... *Nerium* (not treated here)

10b. Lianas; leaves opposite; flowers small; disc 5-lobed .... *Papuechites* (not treaed here)

11a. Flowers minute; stigma ± sessile; disc not 5-lobed or toothed .... *Ecdysanthera* (not treated here)

11b. Flowers medium-sized; stigma on a distinct style; disc 5-lobed or 5-toothed 12

12a. Stigma with collar; disc ring-shaped, 5-toothed; ovary without hairs .... *Anodendron oblongifolium* Hemsl. (not treated here)

12b. Stigma without a collar; disc 5-lobed; ovary hairy .... *Ichnocarpus* (not treated here)

13a. Ovary with 3–5 locules (often becoming 1-loculate at maturity) .... *Lepiniopsis ternatensis* Valeton

13b. Ovary with 1 or 2 locules 14

14a. Ovary and fruiting locules joined (syncarpous), with 1 or 2 locules 15

14b. Ovary and fruiting locules free (apocarpous), with 2 locules 19

15a. Ovary with 2 locules 17

15a. Ovary with 1 locule 18

17a. Shrubs or sometimes lianas, with stipular thorns; throat of corolla without cales; leaves with a few curved longitudinal veins .... *Carissa papuana* Markg. (not treated here)

17b. Lianas without thorns; corolla throat with scales; leaves with many, parallel, lateral veins .... *Melodinus* (not treated here)

18a. Ornamental shrubs; leaves whorled; flowers large, yellow .... *Allamanda* (not treated here)

18b. Lianas; leaves opposite; flowers small, white.. *Melodinus* (not treated here)

19a. Ovules in each locule usually >6 20

19b. Ovules in each locule 2–6, in pairs 22

20a. Herbs; leaves opposite; flowers white or pink, with dark red or yellow centres (cultivated).................. .... *Catharanthus roseus* (L.) G.Don (not treated here)

20b. Trees; leaves whorled or opposite 21

21a. Leaves alternate; seeds winged; cultivated trees.. *Plumeria* (not treated here)

21b. Leaves in whorls of 3 or more rarely opposite; seeds without wing, sometimes with long hairs; forest trees.. *Alstonia*

21c. Leaves opposite; seeds without wing. Embedded in sticky red pulp; shrubs to small trees .... *Tabernaemontana* (not treated here)

22a. Inflorescences terminal.. 23

22b. Inflorescences axillary, sometimes pseudo-terminal.. 25

23a. Leaves opposite; corolla without appendages in throat............ *Kopsia flavidus* Blume (not treated here)

23b. Leaves alternate; corolla with 5 appendages in throat 24

24a. Fowers white; disc absent; leaves broad, rounded at apex; tree .... *Cerbera*

24b. Flowers red; disc present; leaves narrow, pointed; ornamental shrub............ *Thevetia* (not treated here)

25a. Trees or shrubs; flowers without a disc.. 26

25b. Lianas or shrubs; flowers with a disc.. 28

26a. Fruits consisting of 2 mericarps; inflorescences thyrsoid; stigma without a collar of hairs at base .... *Alyxia* (not treated here)

26b. Fruits drupe-like; inflorescences cyme-like; stigma with a collar of hairs at base............................. 27

27a. Ovary superior, gradually tapering into style; mericarps with solid endocarp surrounding 2 lateral spongy cavities.. *Ochrosia* (not treated here)

27b. Ovary half-immerged, abruptly rounded below style; endocarp with coarse fibres penetrating mesocarp .... *Neisosperma* (not treated here)

28a. Lianas or shrubs; stigma head without collar at base; inforescences thyrsoid; fruit consisting of 2 mericarps.. *Alyxia* (not treated here)

28b. Shrubs; stigma head with collar at base; inflorecences cyme-like; fruit consisting of 2 free drupelets or a single, entire or 2-lobed drupe .... *Rauvolfia* (not treated here)

Alstonia brassii Monach.
Fig. 388

Pacific Science Vol. 3: 166 (1949)
Timber Group: Minor hardwoods
Trade Name: Hard Alstonia

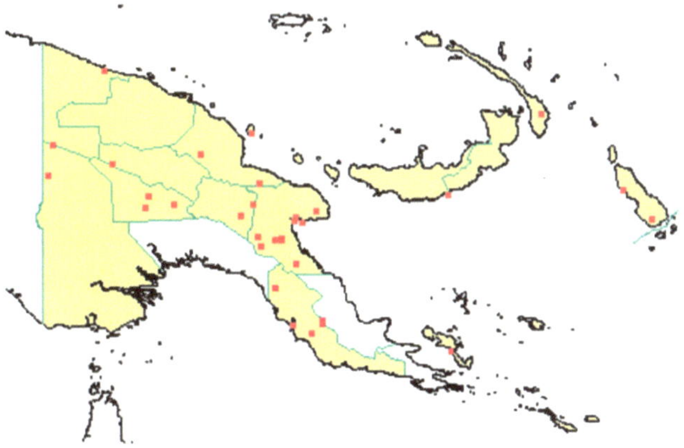

Field Characters: Canopy trees or subcanopy trees, up to 25 m high; bole cylindrical, 30 cm diam., straight, up to 5 m long; buttresses present; spines absent; aerial roots absent; stilt roots absent. Bark white or greenish grey, slightly rough or almost smooth, pustular; lenticels rounded/swelling; bark c. 8 mm thick; under-bark green; strongly aromatic; unpleasant; blaze consisting of 2 layers; outer blaze white (cream-coloured), markings absent, fibrous or granular with splinters and granular without splinters; inner blaze yellow to orange, markings absent, fibrous to granular with splinters and granular without splinters; exudate colourless (twigs with white exudate), not readily flowing, not changing colour on exposure to air, not sticky. Terminal buds not enclosed by leaves.

Indumentum: Complex hairs absent; stinging hairs absent; mature twig without hairs.

Leaves: Spaced along branches, leaves spiral, simple; petiole present, not winged, attached to base of leaf lamina, not swollen; lamina broadest above middle, 11–15 cm long, 4.5–5 cm wide; base symmetric, margin entire, not dissected or lobed, apex obtuse, venation pinnate, secondary veins open, prominent, intramarginal veins absent; lower surface pale green, upper surface green, hairs absent, oil dots present, domatia absent; stipules absent.

Flowers: Inflorescence terminal and axillary (near end of branches), flowers on a branched axis; flowers bisexual, with pedicel, with many planes of symmetry, 5 mm long, small, 4–5 mm diam.; perianth present, with distinct sepals and petals with corolla lobes twisted in bud, white; inner perianth 5, some or partly joined; stamens 5, filaments present, free of each other, joined to perianth; ovary superior, carpels joined, locules 2; styles joined, 1.

Fruits: arranged on branched axis, fruit 350–750 mm long, brown, not spiny, non-fleshy, simple, dehiscent, legume. Seeds many, 8–10 mm long, longer than wide, c. 3 mm diam., not winged (with tuft of dark red-brown hairs, to 10 mm long).

Distribution: West Sepik, East Sepik, Madang, Morobe, Western Highlands, Eastern Highlands, Southern Highlands, Western, Central, Papuan Islands, New Britain, New Ireland, Bougainville.

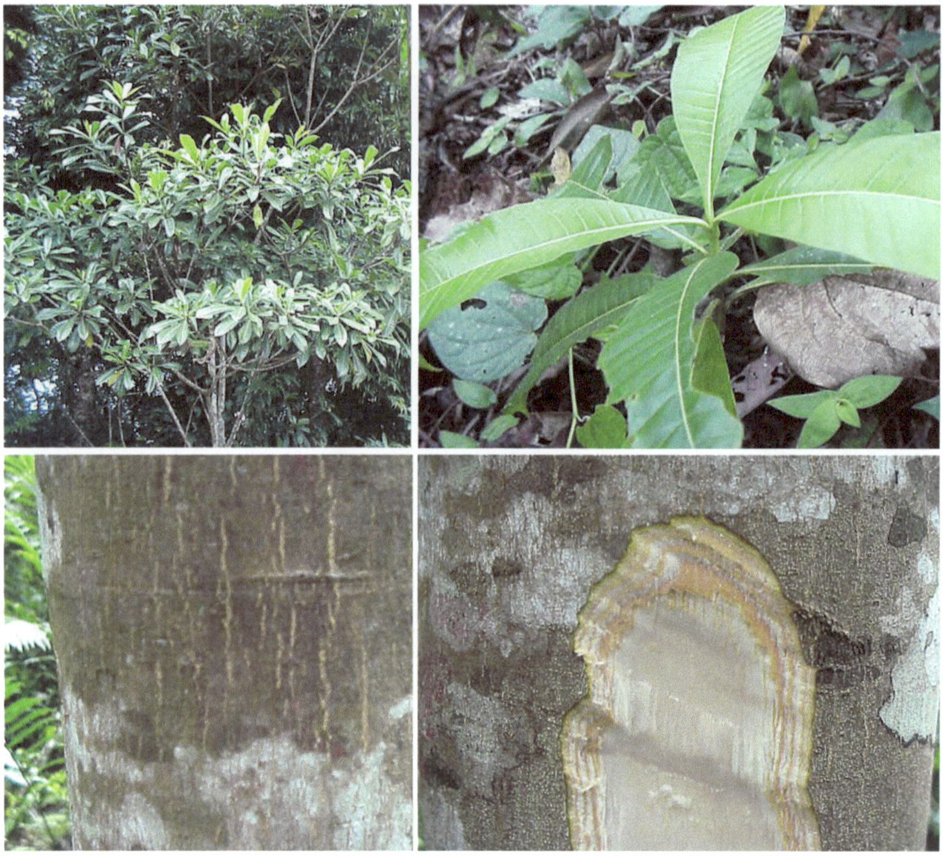

Fig. 388. *Alstonia brassii.* Bark, leaves and habit

Alstonia scholaris (L.) R.Br. Fig. 389

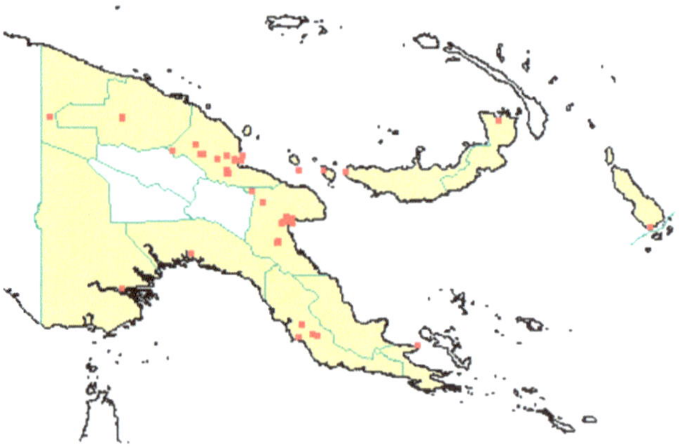

Memoirs of the Wernerian Natural History Society Vol. 1: 76 (1811)

Other Literature: D.J. Boyland et al., *Forest Trees of Australia, 4th edn* 78 & 79 (1984)

Timber Group: Major exportable hardwoods

Trade Name: White Cheesewood

Field Characters: Canopy trees, up to 20(–40) m high; bole cylindrical, usually flanged basally, 60–100 cm diam., straight, 10–25 m long; buttresses present; spines absent; aerial roots absent; stilt roots absent. Bark cream, light yellow, rarely grey, or rarely brown, slightly rough, fissured, pustular, or slightly tessellated; lenticels elongated laterally or sometimes elongated vertically; bark 8–12 mm thick; under-bark yellow; strongly aromatic; resinous/liniment-like or spice-like slightly; blaze consisting of one layer, yellowish white cream-coloured or yellowish brown, speckled, granular without splinters; inner blaze yellowish white cream-coloured or yellowish brown, speckled, granular without splinters; exudate present, white, flowing, not changing colour on exposure to air, sticky. Terminal buds not enclosed by leaves.

Indumentum: Complex hairs absent; stinging hairs absent; mature twig without hairs.

Leaves: Spaced along branches, leaves whorled, 4–8, simple; petiole 1–1.5 cm long, not winged, attached to base of leaf lamina, not swollen; lamina broadest above middle or broadest at or near middle, 7.5–15.5 cm long, 3–5 cm wide; base symmetric, margin entire, not dissected or lobed, apex obtuse, venation pinnate, secondary veins closed, not prominent, but visible, intramarginal veins present; lower surface blue-green, upper surface dark green, hairs absent, oil dots absent, domatia absent; stipules absent.

Flowers: Inflorescence terminal or axillary (appearing terminal in upper axils), flowers on a branched axis; flowers bisexual sweetly aromatic, with pedicel, with many planes of symmetry, 10–12 mm long, small (< or =10 mm diam.); perianth present, with distinct sepals and petals, cream-coloured or white; inner perianth 5, some or partly joined; stamens 5, filaments present, free of each other, joined to perianth; ovary superior, carpels joined, locules 2; styles joined, 1.

Fruits: arranged on branched axis, fruit up to 300 mm long, greenish yellow or green, not spiny, non-fleshy, simple (2 follicles), dehiscent, follicle. Seeds many, to about 5 mm long, longer than wide (with tufts of long hairs), c. 4 mm diam., not winged.

Distribution: West Sepik, East Sepik, Madang, Morobe, Western, Gulf, Central, Northern, Milne Bay, New Britain.

Fig. 389. *Alstonia scholaris*. Bark and habit

Alstonia spectabilis R.Br.
Figs 390, 391

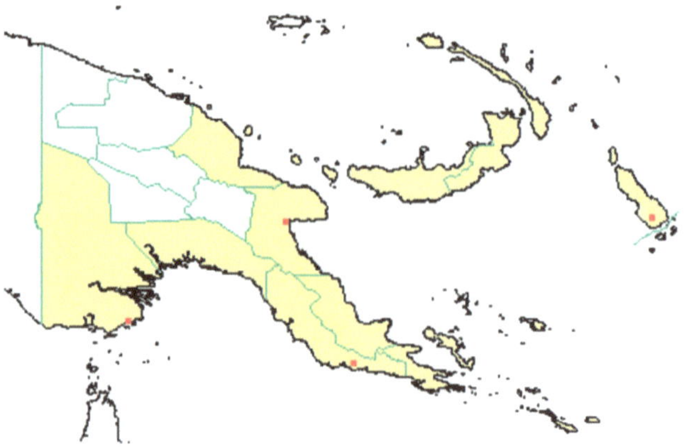

Memoirs of the Wernerian Natural History Society Vol. 1: 76 (1811)
Timber Group: Minor hardwoods

Field Characters: Canopy trees, 25–30 m high; bole cylindrical, up to 60 cm diam., straight or sometimes crooked, up to 20 m long; buttresses up to 2 m high; spines absent; aerial roots absent; stilt roots absent. Bark brown or grey, rough, pustular; lenticels elongated vertically; bark 10–12 mm thick; under-bark green, orange, or yellow; faintly or non-aromatic; blaze consisting of one layer, orange or brown, with stripes orange-white, granular with splinters; inner blaze brown or orange, with stripes orange-white, granular with splinters; exudate present, colourless, not readily flowing, changing to grey or green on exposure to air, slightly sticky. Terminal buds not enclosed by leaves.

Indumentum: Complex hairs absent; stinging hairs absent; mature twig without hairs.

Leaves: Spaced along branches, leaves whorled, 3, simple; petiole present, 8 mm long, not winged, attached to base of leaf lamina, not swollen; lamina broadest above middle, 11–20 cm long, 4.5–7.5 cm wide; base symmetric, margin entire, not dissected or lobed, apex acuminate, venation pinnate, secondary veins open, prominent, intramarginal veins absent; lower surface pale green, upper surface green, hairs absent, oil dots absent, domatia absent; stipules absent.

Fig. 390. *Alstonia spectabilis.* Bark and leaves

Flowers: Inflorescence axillary, (appearing terminal in upper axils) or terminal, flowers on a branched axis; flowers bisexual, with pedicel, with many planes of symmetry perianth present, with distinct sepals and petals, white; inner perianth 5, some or partly joined; stamens 5, filaments present, free of each other, joined to perianth; ovary superior, carpels partly separate or joined, locules 2; styles joined, 1.

Fruits: arranged on unbranched axis, fruit 40–70 mm long, 5 mm diam., fruit green (immature), not spiny, non-fleshy, simple, dehiscent, follicle. Seeds many.

Distribution: Madang, Morobe, Western, Gulf, Central, Northern, Milne Bay, Papuan Islands, New Britain, New Ireland, Bougainville.

Fig. 391. *Alstonia spectabilis.* Leaves and flowers

Cerbera floribunda K.Schum.
Figs 392, 393

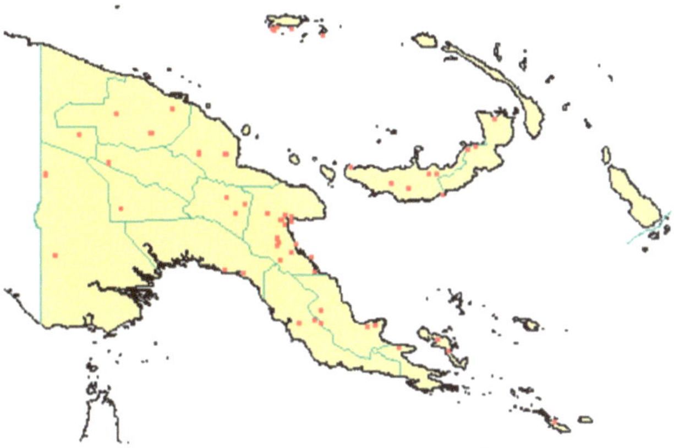

Die Flora von Kaiser Wilhelms Land 111 (1889)
Other Literature: P. van Royen, *Manual of Forest Trees of Papua New Guinea* Vol. 9: 23 (1964)
Timber Group: Minor hardwoods

Field Characters: Canopy trees, up to 25 m high, or subcanopy trees; bole cylindrical, 30–70 cm diam., straight, 8–18 m long; buttresses absent; spines absent; aerial roots absent; stilt roots absent. Bark brown or dark grey, rough, scaly or flaky or coarsely pustular; lenticels rarely rounded/swelling or irregular; bark 6–10 mm thick; under-bark pale yellow (cream-coloured); strongly aromatic; unpleasant or pleasant; blaze consisting of one layer, mixed colours or pale yellow, markings absent or slightly speckled, granular without splinters or granular with splinters; exudate present, white, flowing, not changing colour on exposure to air, slightly sticky. Terminal buds not enclosed by leaves.

Indumentum: Complex hairs absent; stinging hairs absent; mature twig without hairs.

Leaves: Spaced along branches, leaves spiral, simple; petiole present, not winged, attached to base of leaf lamina, not swollen; lamina usually broadest above middle or broadest at or near middle, 13–15 cm long, 3–4.5 cm wide; base symmetric, margin entire, not dissected or lobed, apex rounded, obtuse, or shortly acuminate, venation pinnate, secondary veins open, prominent, intramarginal veins absent; lower surface pale green, upper surface dark glossy green, hairs absent, oil dots absent, domatia absent; stipules absent.

Flowers: Inflorescence terminal, flowers on a branched axis; flowers bisexual, with pedicel, with many planes of symmetry, 50–60 mm long, large, 20–28 mm diam.; perianth present, with distinct sepals and petals with corolla lobes twisted in bud, pale yellow, reddish brown on inner surface of lobes, or white; inner perianth 5, some or partly joined, forming a long corolla tube; stamens 5, filaments present short, free of each other, joined to perianth; ovary superior, carpels joined, locules 2; styles joined, 1.

Fruits: arranged on branched axis (usually in pairs), fruit (70–)80–100(–110) mm long, (40–)50–60 mm diam., dark blue, not spiny, non-fleshy to fleshy with woody fibrous endocarp, simple, indehiscent, drupe (water dispersed). Seeds 1 or 2, up to 70 mm long, longer than wide, (8–)12–30 mm diam., not winged or sometimes slightly winged.

Distribution: West Sepik, East Sepik, Madang, Morobe, Western Highlands, Eastern Highlands, Southern Highlands, Western, Gulf, Central, Northern, Milne Bay, Papuan Islands, New Britain, New Ireland, Manus, Bougainville.

Fig. 392. *Cerbera floribunda*. Bark, leaves, flowers and fruit

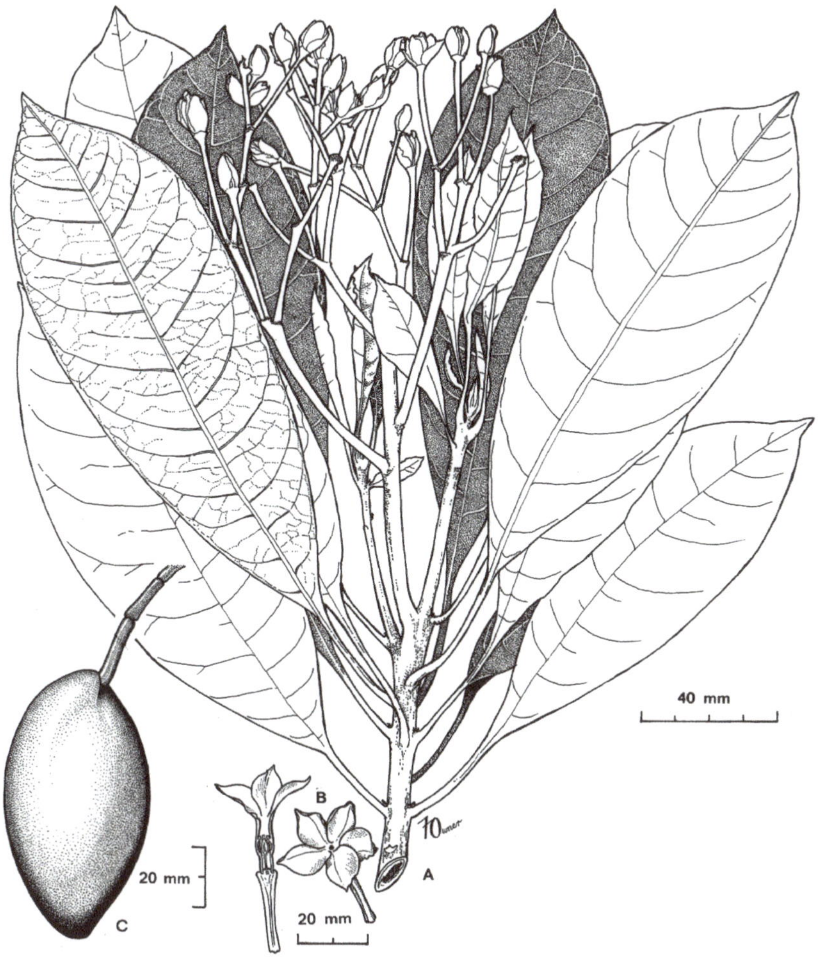

Fig. 393. *Cerbera floribunda*. Illustration of branchlet showing flowers and fruit (© Papua New Guinea National Herbarium, Lae)

Lepiniopsis ternatensis Valeton
Fig. 394

Annales du Jardin Botanique de Buitenzorg Vol. 12: 252–254 (1895) Fig. 28.
Timber Group: Non-timber species

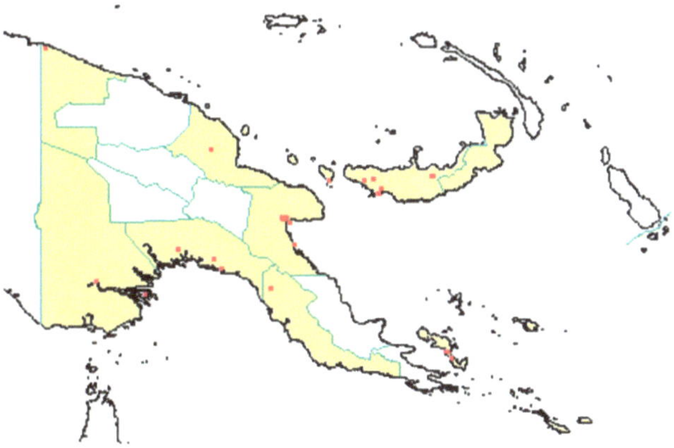

Field Characters: Subcanopy trees, 6–20 m high (with 3-whorled branches); bole cylindrical up to about 45 cm diam., straight, up to about 10 m long; buttresses absent; spines absent; aerial roots absent; stilt roots absent. Bark pale brown to grey, rough to slightly rough, slightly fissured or pustular; lenticels irregular or elongated vertically, or slightly elongated laterally or rounded/swelling; bark 5–10 mm thick; under-bark yellow; faintly or non-aromatic; blaze consisting of one layer, brown or brownish yellow to yellow, with stripes (sometimes faint), granular without splinters; exudate present, also on branchlets and leaves, white, flowing, not changing colour on exposure to air, sticky. Terminal buds not enclosed by leaves.

Indumentum: Complex hairs absent; stinging hairs absent; mature twig without hairs.

Leaves: Clustered at end of branches, leaves opposite or whorled, 4, simple; petiole 1–3.5 cm long, not winged, attached to base of leaf lamina, not swollen; lamina usually broadest above middle or broadest at or near middle, (6.5–)14.5–20(–26) cm long, (2.5–)5–8 cm wide; base slightly asymmetric to strongly so, margin entire, not dissected or lobed, apex acuminate, often abruptly so, venation pinnate, secondary veins open, prominent or not prominent, intramarginal veins absent; lower surface pale green, upper surface green to dark green, hairs absent, oil dots absent, domatia absent; stipules absent.

Fig. 394. *Lepiniopsis ternatensis.* Leaves

Flowers: Inflorescence axillary, terminal or leaf-opposed, flowers on branched or unbranched axis; flowers bisexual, with pedicel, with many planes of symmetry, 16–20 mm long, large, 15–20 mm diam.; perianth present, with distinct sepals and petals, white, sweetly aromatic; inner perianth 5, some or partly joined, with corolla lobes or tube orange; stamens 5, filaments present, short, free of each other, joined to perianth; ovary superior, carpels mostly separate or joined by style, locules 2; styles joined, 1.

Fruits: arranged on unbranched axis, fruit 25–50 mm long, laterally flattened, 15–20 mm diam., almost black (when mature) or red, not spiny, slightly fleshy, simple, indehiscent or tardily dehiscent, drupe-like or follicle. Seeds 1–3, cream-coloured, 20–30 mm long, longer than wide, 8–10 mm diam., not winged.

Distribution: West Sepik, East Sepik, Madang, Morobe, Western, Gulf, Central, Papuan Islands, New Britain.

Voacanga papuana K.Schum.
Fig. 395

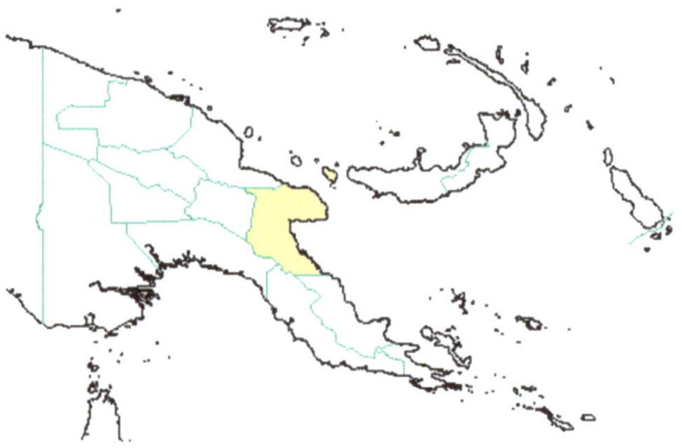

Naturlichen Pflanzenfamilien, iv, 2 (1895) 149
Timber Group: Non-timber species

Field Characters: Small trees 10–20 m high. Bole cylindrical, 12–25 cm diam.; straight, bole 5–8 m high; buttresses absent; spines absent; aerial roots absent; stilt roots absent. Bark grey, slightly rough, pustular; lenticels slightly elongated laterally or rounded/swelling; under-bark yellow; bark thickness c. 5 mm thick; blaze consisting of one layer; faintly to non-aromatic, yellow, with stripes, granular without splinters; exudate absent or present on twigs and leaves. Terminal buds not enclosed by leaves; complex hairs absent; stinging hairs absent; mature twig without hairs.

Leaves: spaced along branches, opposite, simple; petiole present, not winged, attached to base of leaf lamina, not swollen; lamina broadest above middle, 6.5–14 cm long, 2.5–4.5 cm wide, very asymmetric, margin entire, not dissected or lobed, apex abruptly acuminate, venation pinnate, secondary veins open, not prominent, but visible, intramarginal veins absent; lower surface pale green, upper surface green, hairs absent; oil dots absent; domatia absent; stipules absent.

Flowers: Inflorescence usually terminal or leaf-opposed. Flowers on a branched axis; flowers bisexual, stalked, with many planes of symmetry, 16–20 mm long, large, 15–20 mm diam.; perianth present, with distinct sepals and petals, white, sweetly aromatic; inner perianth 5, some or partly joined; stamens 5, filaments short, free of each other, joined to perianth; ovary superior, carpels joined by style or mostly separate (when more than one), locules 2; styles solitary, 1.

Fruit: 30–35 mm long, laterally flattened, 20 mm diam., red, not spiny, slightly fleshy, simple, dehiscent tardily, follicle. Seeds 1 or 2, cream-coloured, c. 20 mm long, not winged, longer than wide, 8-10 mm diam.

Distribution: West Sepik, East Sepik, Madang, Morobe, Western, Gulf, Central, Northern, Milne Bay.

Fig. 395. *Voacanga papuana*. Habit, leaves, flowers and fruit

Wrightia laevis Hook.f.

The Flora of British India Vol. 3: 654 (1882)
Timber Group: Minor hardwoods

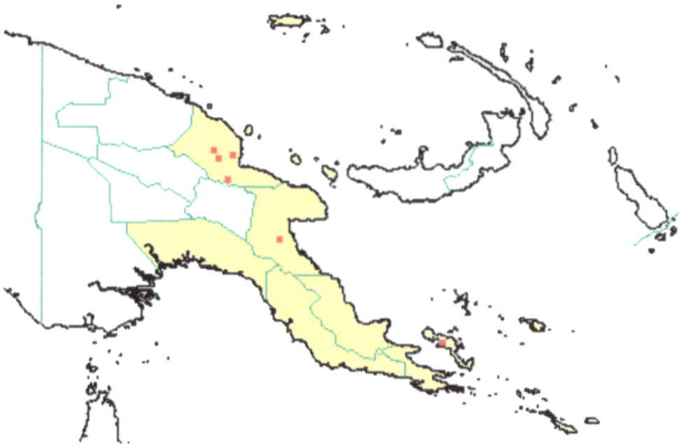

Field Characters: Canopy trees, up to 25 m high; bole cylindrical, 40 cm diam., straight; buttresses present; spines absent; aerial roots absent; stilt roots absent. Bark pale brown, smooth or slightly rough, slightly pustular; lenticels irregular; bark 4–5 mm thick; under-bark brown or green; faintly or non-aromatic; blaze consisting of one layer, pale brown fawn-coloured, slightly speckled; exudate present, white, flowing, not changing colour on exposure to air, sticky. Terminal buds not enclosed by leaves.

Indumentum: Complex hairs absent; stinging hairs absent; mature twig without hairs.

Leaves: Spaced along branches, leaves opposite, simple; petiole 7–10 mm long, not winged, attached to base of leaf lamina, not swollen; lamina broadest at or near middle, 9.5–16 cm long, 3–5.5 cm wide; base symmetric, margin entire, not dissected or lobed, apex acuminate, venation pinnate, secondary veins open, prominent, intramarginal veins absent; lower surface glossy green, upper surface dark green, hairs absent, oil dots absent, domatia absent; stipules absent.

Flowers: Inflorescence terminal, flowers on a branched axis; flowers bisexual, with pedicel 8–10 mm long, with many planes of symmetry, 10–12 mm long, large, 10–13 mm diam.; perianth present, with distinct sepals and petals, slivery green to yellow; inner perianth 5, some or partly joined, with corolla lobes or tube yellow, turning mauve; stamens 5, filaments present, long (anthers long, narrow, hairy), free of each other, joined to perianth; ovary superior, carpels mostly separate or joined by style, locules 2; styles joined, 1.

Fruits: arranged on a branched axis, fruit (70–)100–120 mm long, narrow, 10–15 mm diam., almost black (when mature), not spiny, non-fleshy, simple, indehiscent or tardily dehiscent, drupe-like or follicle. Seeds 1–3, cream-coloured, not winged.

Distribution: Madang, Morobe, Gulf, Central, Northern, Milne Bay, Papuan Islands, Manus.

Lamiales

PNG families: Acanthaceae, Bignoniaceae, Byblidaceae, Gesneriaceae, **Lamiaceae,** Lentibulariaceae, Linderniaceae, Mazaceae, Myoporaceae, Oleaceae, Orobanchaceae, Pedaliaceae, Phrymaceae, Plantaginaceae, Scrophulariaceae, Verbenaceae

1a. Parasitic herbs; ovary with 1 locule .... Orobanchaceae (not treated here)

1b. Non-parasitic plants; ovary with 2 locules 2

2a. Flowers with 1 ovule in each ovary .... Phrymaceae (not treated here)

2b. Flowers with 2 or more ovules in each ovary 3

3a. Mangroves with erect pneumatophores .... *Avicennia* (Acanthaceae)

3b. Plants not mangroves; pneumatophores absent 4

4a. Plants with leaf traps for catching insects 5

4b. Plants without leaf traps 6

5a. Corolla ± actinomorphic, without nectary spur .... Bybilidaceae (not treated here)

5b. Corolla zygomorphic, with nectary spur .... Lentibulariaceae (not treated here)

6a. Corolla thin, dry, membranous .... Plantaginaceae (not treated here)

6b. Corolla normal, not thin or dry 7

7a. Fruits spiny; plants with mucilaginous hairs .... *Josephinia* (Pedaliaceae)

7b. Fruits lacking spines; plants without mucilaginous hairs 8

8a. Corolla with 4 lobes, actinomorphic 9

8b. Corolla usually with 5 lobes, often 2-lipped, zygomorphic 10

9a. Stamens 4; ovules usually >2 per locule .... *Buddleja* (Scrophulariaceae) (not treated here)

9b. Stamens 2; ovules usually 2 per locule .... 83. Oleaceae

10a. Ovary with 1 or 2 ovules in each locule 11

10b. Ovary usually >2 ovules in each locule 12

11a. Stigma lobes slender; stigmatic surface indistinct; style usually gynobasic or ovary distinctly lobed so that style arising from between 4 lobes of the ovary .... 84. Lamiaceae

11b. Stigma lobes thickened; stigmatic surface distinct; style terminal; ovary entire or indistinctly lobed .... Verbenaceae (not treated here)

12a. Seeds explosively released from dehiscent fruits, with enlarged funiculus assisting seed dispersal .... 86. Acanthaceae

12b. Seeds not explosively released from fruit, without an enlarged funiculus 13

13a. Seeds usually flattened, winged .... 85. Bignoniaceae

13b. Seeds not flattened, not winged 14

14a. Leaves alternate throughout 15

14b. Leaves usually opposite or whorled, or at least opposite on lower nodes 16

15a. Plants without oil dots on leaves .... Scrophulariaceae (not treated here)

15b. Plants with ± clear oil dots on leaves .... Myoporaceae (not treated here)

16a. Anthers cohering in pairs or all coherent; flowers usually in pairs, rarely reduced to a single flower .... Gesneriaceae (not treated here)

16b. Anthers usually not coherent; flowers in >2-flowered cyme-like inflorescences, often reduce to 1 flower 17

17a. Lower lip of corolla with projection closing throat; anther locules divergent .... Mazaceae (not treated here)

17b. Lower lip of corolla without projection closing throat 18

18a. Shrubs or herbs; stamens ± equal, or lower pair reduced to staminodes .... Scrophulariaceae (not treated here)

18b. Usually small herbs; lower stamens usually very different to upper stamens .... Linderiaceae (not treated here)

83. Oleaceae

Trees, shrubs, lianas. Stipules absent. Leaves well-developed, opposite, rarely spiral, simple and compound, pinnate, not dissected or lobed and dissected or lobed; margin entire and toothed; venation one-veined, pinnate, and palmate. Inflorescences axillary and terminal. Bracts absent. Flowers bisexual, rarely unisexual (then plants dioecious), regular, with distinct calyx and corolla. Sepals fused (calyx tubular), 4- or 5-lobed. Petals usually fused (corolla usually tubular), usually 4- or 5-lobed, joined, at least in part; tube usually present. Stamens 2(or 4), free, joined to petals; filaments present; staminodes absent. Gynoecium with ovary 2-locular, superior; styles usually fully joined (stigma 2-lobed). Fruit simple, indehiscent, drupe, berry, samara or capsule, slightly fleshy. Seeds usually 1 (sometimes more), without wings.

PNG genera: ***Chionanthus***, *Jasminum*, *Ligustrum*, *Myxopyrum*, *Olea*.

References: Green (1994, 2004), Watson and Dallwitz (1992 onwards)

Notes: *Linociera* is regarded as a synonym of *Chionanthus* (Stearn 1976).

1a. Climbers, scramblers, sometimes multi-stemmed climbing shrubs 2

1b. Trees or shrubs, not climbers 3

2a. Stems ± rounded (in section); leaves non-glandular; fruits deeply bilobed, usually a fleshy berry (often 1-seeded by abortion); calyx 5–10-lobed; corolla at least 5-lobed .... *Jasminum* (not treated here)

2b. Stems strongly 4-angular (in section); leaves glandular on lower surface; fruits not lobed, drupe-like, 1–4-seeded; calyx and corolla 4-lobed .... *Myxopyrum* (not treated here)

3a. Corolla tube absent or no more than 2 mm long; stamens 2 or 4; 1-seeded drupe with hard endocarp .... *Chionanthus*

3b. Corolla tube at least 2 mm long; stamens 2; 1–4-seeded drupe or berry with thin or thick endocarp 4

4a. Fruit a berry or drupe, 1–4-seeded, with thin, membranous to papery endocarp; inflorescences terminal; shrubs .... *Ligustrum* (not treated here)

4b. Fruit a drupe, 1-seeded, with thick, hard endocarp; inflorescences axillary or terminal; shrubs or trees .... *Olea* (not treated here)

Chionanthus riparius (Lingelsh.) Kiew Fig. 396

Blumea Vol. 43(2): 474 (1998)
Timber Group: Non-timber species

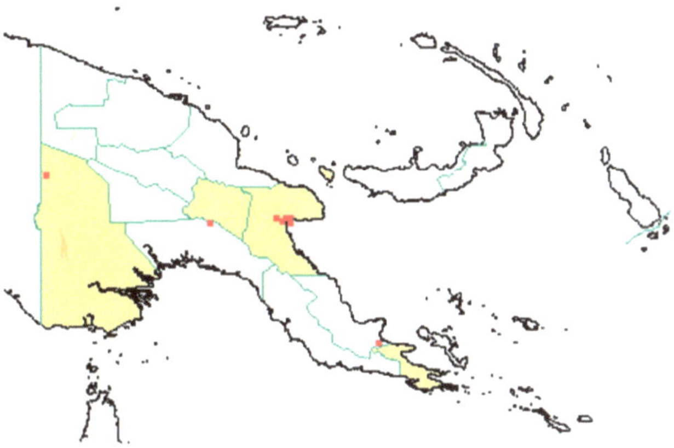

Field Characters: Subcanopy to canopy trees, 10–30 m high; bole cylindrical, 30–75 cm diam., straight, 5–13 m long; buttresses absent, or base of trunk slightly spurred; spines absent; aerial roots absent; stilt roots absent. Bark pale brown to pale grey, rough, pustular with lenticels irregular and rounded; bark 8–15(–30) mm thick; under-bark dark red; faintly aromatic; pleasant; blaze consisting of one layer, orange-red, sometimes yellowish, speckled, granular with splinters; exudate present, colourless, not readily flowing, changing to red-brown on exposure to air, slightly sticky. Terminal buds not enclosed by leaves.

Indumentum: Complex hairs present, star-like; stinging hairs absent; mature twig hairy; hairs dense.

Leaves: Spaced along branches, leaves opposite, simple; petiole 10–20(–36) mm long, not winged, attached to base of leaf lamina, slightly swollen; lamina usually broadest above middle, 16–23(–30) cm long, (7.5–)9–12 cm wide; base symmetric, margin entire, not dissected or lobed, apex shortly acuminate, venation pinnate, secondary veins open, prominent, intramarginal veins absent; lower surface mid green or pale green to glaucous, upper surface dull to glossy dark green, hairs absent; oil dots absent, domatia absent; stipules absent.

Flowers: Inflorescence axillary, flowers on a branched axis; flowers bisexual, with pedicel, almost with many planes of symmetry or with one plane of symmetry, c. 10 mm long (including stamens and style); perianth present, with distinct sepals (4-lobed) and petals, dull, cream-coloured to pale yellow, fragrant; inner perianth 4, less than 5 mm long, free (corolla tube absent), linear; stamens 2, filaments present, free of each other, joined to perianth; ovary superior, carpels joined, locules 4; styles joined (short), 1.

Fruits: arranged on branched axis, fruit dull green with pale yellow dots (warty), maturing to bluish black, subglobular, 50–65 mm long, c. 42 mm diam., not spiny, fleshy, simple, indehiscent, drupe (with blunt point, at least when immature). Seed 1, subglobular, 35 mm long, 32 mm diam., pale yellow, not winged.

Distribution: Morobe, Eastern Highlands, Western, Milne Bay.

Notes: This is a most distinctive species of the genus because of its large, oblong leaves that dry chestnut brown, its shortly stalked panicle with crowded flowers and large fruits. Although the inflorescence is paniculate, as only one or two fruits mature, the thickened infructescence appears unbranched and may be mistaken for a raceme (Kiew 1998).

Fig. 396. *Chionanthus riparius.* Bark, fruit, seed and leaves

84. Lamiaceae

Trees, shrubs, rarely lianas, and herbs. Stipules absent. Leaves well-developed, opposite and whorled, simple and compound, pinnate, not dissected or lobed and dissected or lobed; margin entire and toothed; venation one-veined, pinnate, and palmate. Inflorescences axillary and terminal. Bracts present. Flowers bisexual, slightly irregular and zygomorphic, with distinct calyx and corolla. Sepals 2–5. Petals 4 or 5, joined, at least in part; tube present. Stamens 2–4(or 5), sometimes fused or free; filaments present; staminodes present or absent. Gynoecium with more than one free carpel, superior; styles partially or fully joined. Fruit simple, indehiscent, schizocarp, dry, at least non-fleshy, or fleshy. Seeds without wings.

PNG genera: *Anisomeles, Basilicum,* ***Callicarpa****, Clerodendrum, Clinopodium, Congea, Cymaria, Faradaya, Glossocarya,* ***Gmelina****, Holmskioldia, Hyptis, Leucas, Marsypianthes, Mentha, Ocimum, Orthosiphon, Petraeovitex, Platostoma, Plectranthus, Pogostemon, Premna, Salvia, Satureja, Scutellaria, Tectona,* ***Teijsmanniodendron****, Teucrium,* ***Vitex, Viticipremna***

Notes: *Gmelina*, *Teijsmanniodendron*, *Vitex* and *Viticipremna* were previously included in the family Verbenaceae but are now regarded as part of the Lamiaceae subfamily Viticoideae.

References: Keng (1969, 1978), Munir (1982, 1984a, 1984b, 1985, 1987a, 1987b, 1989)

1a. Style gynobasic 2

1b. Style terminal or subterminal 3

2a. Plants strongly aromatic; herbs or shrubs .... Nepetoideae (not treated here)

2b. Plants rarely aromatic; herbs or shrubs (*Anisomeles, Leucas, Pogostemon*) .... Lamioideae (not treated here)

3a. Cultivated climbing shrubs; calyx 5-lobed, not 2-lipped; corolla 2-lipped, 5-lobed, purple, lilac or pink .... *Congea tomentosa* Roxb. (Symphorematoideae) (not treated here)

3b. Trees, shrubs, herbs; calyx 2-lipped, or actinomorphic and usually 4- or 5-lobed; corolla usually 2-lipped, also actinomorphic or 1-lipped, colour various 4

4a. Calyx usually 2-lipped, with lips entire or shallowly 5-lobed; stamens with anther slits often finely hairy; herbs or shrubs (*Holmskioldia, Scutellaria*) .... Scutellarioideae (not treated here)

4b. Calyx actinomorphic and 4- or 5-lobed, to 2-lipped; stamens with anther slits not hairy; plants woody or herbaceous 5

5a. Corolla ± regular to 1-lipped, rarely 2-lipped (Ajugoideae, plus *Callicarpa* – currently not placed in a subfamily) 6

5b. Corolla often 2-lipped (Viticoideae) 9

6a. Stamens 4; corolla with 4 lobes; small trees, shrubs or lianas 7

6b. Stamens 4; corolla with 5 lobes; trees, shrubs or lianas 8

7a. Calyx leathery, truncate (only 4-lobed in bud), remainly closed until irregularly torn by expanding corolla into 2 – 4 irregular sections; corolla white to cream-coloured; stigma with very short, unequal lobes; fruits with up to 4 fleshy, 1-seeded mericarps .... *Faradaya* (not treated here)

7b. Calyx not leathery, distinctly 4(or 5)-lobed; corolla white, blue, violet, mauve to purple; stigma peltate or capitate; fruits with 4 stony, 1-seeded pyrenes .... *Callicarpa*

8a. Climbing shrubs or lianas; calyx with 5 shallow lobes; fruit a dry schizocarp consisting of 4 mericarps; mericarps basally winged .... *Glossocarya* (not treated here)

8b. Trees, shrubs or lianas; calyx often showy, usually with 5 distinct lobes; fruits fleshy, drupe-like or schizocarp, consisting of 4, 1-seeded pyrenes or 4, 1-seeded mericarps (respectively), not winged........ .... *Clerodendrum* (not treated here)

9a. Calyx and corolla 4-lobed.. 10

9b. Calyx and corolla 5-lobed.. 11

10a. Leaves simple.. *Premna* (not treated here)

10b. Leaves digitately compound with 3–6(–7) leaflets .... *Viticipremna*

11a. Corolla broadly funnel-shaped, noticeably widened at throat; fruits with very fleshy mericarp *Gmelina*

11b. Corolla narrowly funnel-shaped to cylindrical, not noticeably widened at throat; fruits with dry or slightly fleshy mericarps.. 12

12a. Petioles and petiolules articulated, conspicuously swollen; fruits a capsule............ *Teijsmanniodendron*

12b. Petioles not articulated, not noticeably swollen; fruits a drupe.. *Vitex*

Callicarpa farinosa Roxb. ex C.B.Clark
Fig. 397

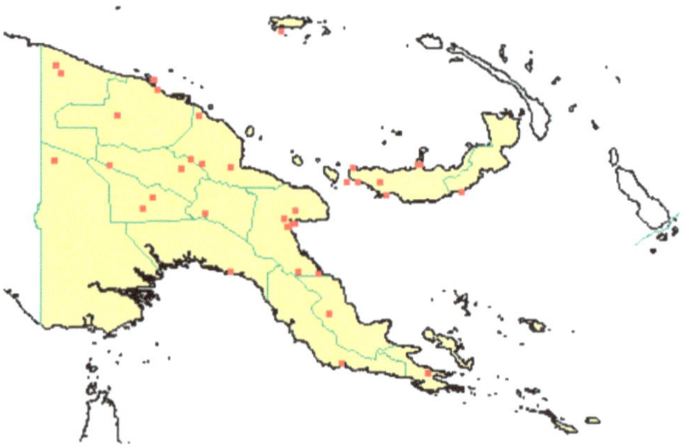

The Flora of British India Vol. 4(12): 567 (1885)
Timber Group: Non-timber species

Field Characters: Subcanopy trees, up to 20 m high; bole markedly fluted, 40 cm diam., crooked, 10 m long; buttresses shortly present or absent; spines absent; aerial roots absent; stilt roots absent. Bark brown, rough, scaly or flaky (papery); bark 4–5 mm thick; under-bark yellow or green; strongly aromatic; unpleasant; blaze consisting of one layer, pale yellow, markings absent, fibrous; exudate present, colourless, not readily flowing, changing to pale red pink on exposure to air, not sticky. Terminal buds not enclosed by leaves.

Indumentum: Complex hairs present, star-like; stinging hairs absent; mature twig hairy; hairs dense.

Leaves: Spaced along branches, leaves opposite, simple; petiole 25–40 mm long, not winged, attached to base of leaf lamina, not swollen; lamina broadest at or near middle, 15–21(–23) cm long, 7–12 cm wide; base symmetric to slightly asymmetric, margin entire, not dissected or lobed, apex usually long-tapering, venation pinnate, secondary veins open, prominent, intramarginal veins absent; lower surface green or brown, upper surface pale green, hairs present, dense, pale brown; oil dots absent, domatia absent; stipules absent.

Flowers: Inflorescence axillary, flowers on a branched axis; flowers bisexual, with pedicel, almost with many planes of symmetry or with one plane of symmetry, c. 10 mm long (including stamens and style); perianth present, with distinct sepals and petals, pale mauve lilac; inner perianth 5, c. 5 mm long, some or partly joined; stamens 4, filaments present, free of each other, joined to perianth; ovary superior, carpels joined, locules 4; styles joined, 1.

Fruits: arranged on branched axis, fruit red, c. 5 mm diam., not spiny, fleshy, simple, indehiscent, drupe. Seeds 4, not winged.

Distribution: West Sepik, East Sepik, Madang, Morobe, Western Highlands, Eastern Highlands, Southern Highlands, Western, Gulf, Central, Northern, Milne Bay, Papuan Islands, New Britain, Manus.

Fig. 397. *Callicarpa farinosa*. Bark, flowers, fruit and leaves

Gmelina ledermannii H.J.Lam

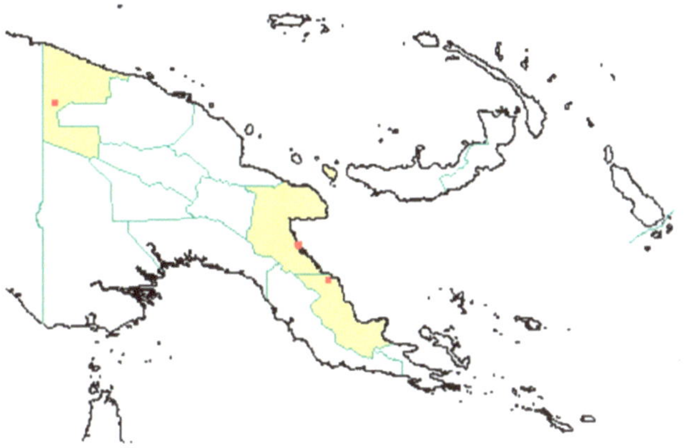

Verbenaceae of the Malayan Archipelago 226 (1919)
Timber Group: Non-timber species

Field Characters: Subcanopy trees, up to 15 m high; bole cylindrical, c. 28 cm diam., straight, 9 m long; buttresses shortly present; spines absent; aerial roots absent; stilt roots absent. Bark brown, rough, fissured; lenticels irregular; bark 5 mm thick; under-bark yellow or brown; strongly aromatic; pleasant; blaze consisting of one layer, yellow or white, speckled, granular without splinters; exudate present, colourless, not readily flowing, changing to brown or red on exposure to air, slightly sticky. Terminal buds not enclosed by leaves.

Indumentum: Complex hairs absent; stinging hairs absent.

Leaves: Spaced along branches, leaves opposite, simple; petiole c. 5 cm long (with 2 glands present), not winged, attached to base of leaf lamina, not swollen; lamina broadest at or near middle, 17–22 cm long, 10–13 cm wide; base symmetric, margin entire, not dissected or lobed, apex acuminate, venation pinnate, secondary veins open, prominent, intramarginal veins absent; lower surface pale green, upper surface dark green, hairs absent, oil dots absent, domatia absent; stipules absent.

Flowers: Inflorescence axillary, flowers on a branched axis; flowers bisexual, with pedicel, with one plane of symmetry, large, c. 15 mm diam.; perianth present, with distinct sepals and petals (sepals and bracts distinctly glandular), white or whitish pink (often with yellow patch on lower lip); inner perianth 5, some or partly joined; stamens 4, filaments present, free of each other, joined to perianth; ovary superior, carpels joined, locules 4; styles joined (with stiff hairs at base of style), 1.

Fruits: arranged on branched axis, fruit 15 mm long, 9 mm diam., glossy, purple or dark blue, not spiny, fleshy, simple, indehiscent, drupe. Seed 1, 11 mm long, as wide as long, 5 mm diam., not winged.

Distribution: West Sepik, Morobe, Northern.

Gmelina macrophylla (R.Br.) Benth. Fig. 398

Flora Australiensis Vol. 5: 65 (1870)
Timber Group: Occasional timber species

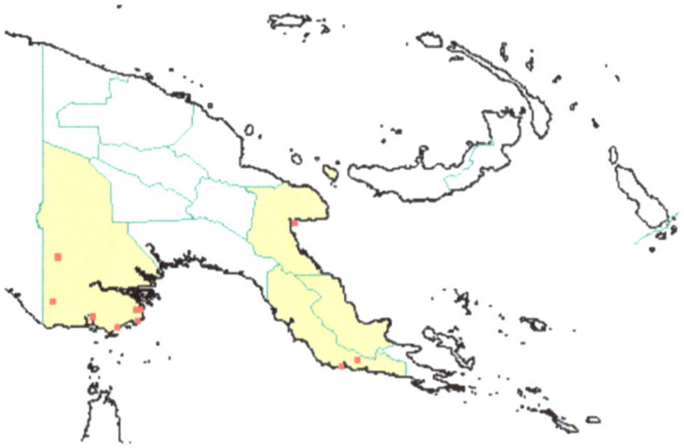

Field Characters: Subcanopy or canopy trees, 5–25(–35) m high, or frequently shrubs; bole cylindrical, (5–)8–20(–100) cm diam., often crooked, usually up to 5 m long, sometimes longer (once recorded as 18 m); buttresses absent or up to 1.5 m high; spines absent; aerial roots absent; stilt roots absent. Bark grey to grey-brown, rough, reticulately, longitudinally fissured (fissure reticulate, with fine cross-fissures), slightly flaky; lenticels irregular; bark 3–5 mm thick; under-bark brown; strongly aromatic; pleasant; blaze consisting of one layer, cale brown to cream-coloured, with yellow flecks, granular without splinters; exudate present, colourless, not readily flowing, changing to orange-brown on exposure to air, slightly sticky. Terminal buds not enclosed by leaves.

Indumentum: Complex hairs absent; stinging hairs absent.

Leaves: Spaced along branches, leaves opposite, simple; petiole c. 5 cm long (with 2 glands present), not winged, attached to base of leaf lamina (with 2 large glands usually visible on lower surface near junction with petiole), not swollen; lamina broadest at or near middle, 15–30 cm long, 7–19 cm wide; base symmetric, margin entire, not dissected or lobed, apex acuminate, venation pinnate, secondary veins open, prominent, intramarginal veins absent; lower surface green, upper surface glossy dark green, hairs absent, oil dots absent, domatia absent; stipules absent.

Flowers: Inflorescence axillary, flowers on a branched axis; flowers bisexual, with pedicel, 18–25 mm long, with one plane of symmetry, large, c. 15 mm diam.; perianth present, with distinct sepals (cream-coloured to dark purple-green or dark red-green) and petals (sepals and bracts distinctly glandular), white, cream-coloured or pink, sometimes purplish (with mauve markings, lower lip with pink apical part and yellow patch at throat); inner perianth 5, some or partly joined, with tube 12–13 mm long, lobes 6–10 mm long; stamens 4, filaments present, free of each other, joined to perianth; ovary superior, carpels joined, locules 4; styles joined (with stiff hairs at base of style), 1; with 1 stigma lobe much longer than the other.

Fruits: arranged on branched axis, fruit 8–18 mm long, 5–12 mm diam., broadest distally, glossy, red to purplish pink, not spiny, fleshy, simple, indehiscent, drupe. Seed 1, 11 mm long, as wide as long, 5 mm diam., not winged.

Distribution: Morobe, Western, Central, Northern.

Notes: Previously known as *Gmelina dalrympleana* (F.Muell.) H.J.Lam (refer Anonymous without date-b)

Fig. 398. *Gmelina macrophylla.* Bark, flowers and leaves

Gmelina moluccana (Blume) Backer ex K. Heyne Fig. 399

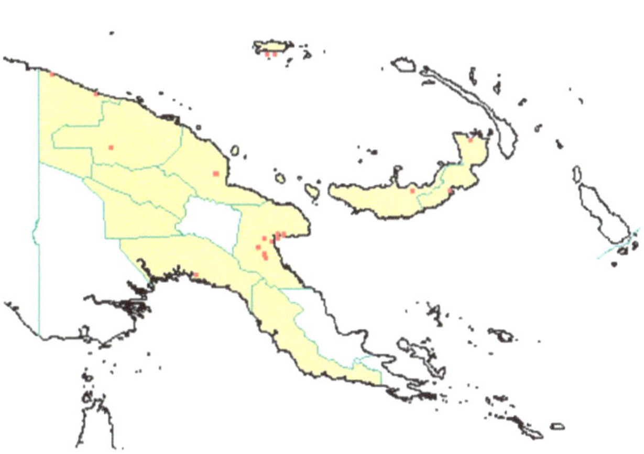

Nuttige Planten van Nederlandsch-Indie tevens Synthetische Catalogus der Verzamelingen van het Museum voor Technische en Handelsbotanie te Buitenzorg Vol. 4: 118 (1917)
Timber Group: Commercial hardwoods

Field Characters: Canopy trees, 20–40 m high; bole cylindrical, up to c. 90 cm diam., straight, 7–12 m long; buttresses present or absent; spines absent; aerial roots absent; stilt roots absent. Bark grey or brown, rough or smooth, slightly tessellated, scaly or flaky (irregular flakes), fissured, or slightly peeling; bark 5–12 mm thick; under-bark pale yellow;

strongly aromatic or faintly or non-aromatic; faintly unpleasant (weak turnip odour); blaze consisting of one layer or faintly consisting of 2 layers; outer blaze brown, orange, or pale yellow, speckled, slightly corky; inner blaze pale yellow, red, or reddish brown (soon turning red-brown on exposure to air), speckled, slightly corky; exudate present, colourless, not readily flowing, changing to dark brown or red on exposure to air, slightly sticky. Terminal buds not enclosed by leaves.

Indumentum: Complex hairs absent; stinging hairs absent; mature twig hairy tomentose; hairs dense.

Leaves: Spaced along branches, leaves opposite, simple; petiole present, not winged, attached to base of leaf lamina, not swollen; lamina broadest below middle, 10–30 cm long, 10–20(–25) cm wide; base symmetric, margin entire, not dissected or lobed, apex rounded, obtuse, or sub-acute, venation pinnate, secondary veins open, prominent, intramarginal veins absent; lower surface dull pale green, upper surface green, hairs present, dense, oil dots absent, domatia absent; stipules absent.

Flowers: Inflorescence terminal or axillary, flowers on a branched axis; flowers bisexual, with pedicel, with one plane of symmetry, 15–20 mm long, large, 15–20 mm diam.; perianth present, with distinct sepals and petals, white, pale purple, or mauve; inner perianth 5, some or partly joined; stamens 4, filaments present, free of each other, joined to perianth; ovary superior, carpels joined, locules 4; styles joined, 1.

Fruits: arranged on branched axis, fruit 20–35 mm long, 20–30 mm diam., blue or purple, not spiny, fleshy, simple, indehiscent, drupe. Seed 1, 12–18 mm long, longer than wide, 10–15 mm diam., not winged.

Distribution: West Sepik, East Sepik, Madang, Morobe, Western Highlands, Southern Highlands, Gulf, Central, Milne Bay, New Britain, Manus.

Fig. 399. *Gmelina moluccana*. Bark, leaves and fruit

Gmelina papuana Bakh.

Journal of the Arnold Arboretum Vol. 10: 71 & 72 (1929)
Timber Group: Occasional timber species

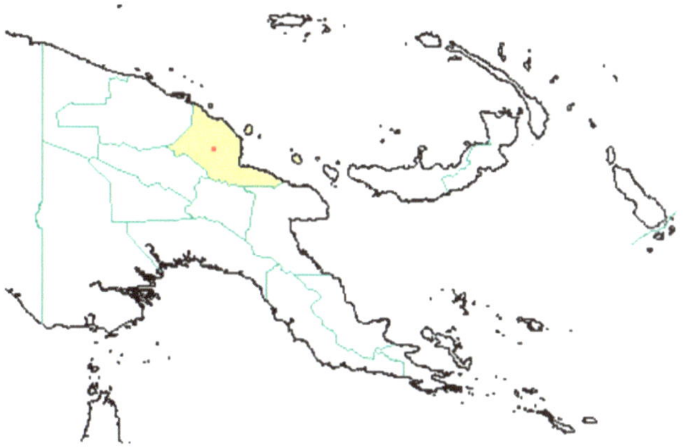

Field Characters: Canopy trees or subcanopy trees, up to 25 m high; bole cylindrical, 50 cm diam., straight; buttresses 1 m high; spines absent; aerial roots absent; stilt roots absent. Bark grey or brown, rough, slightly pustular or tessellated; lenticels irregular; bark 5 mm thick; under-bark pale yellow; strongly aromatic; unpleasant; blaze consisting of one layer, brown or orange, speckled, fibrous; inner blaze orange or brown, speckled, fibrous; exudate present, colourless, not readily flowing, changing to dark brown on exposure to air, slightly sticky. Terminal buds not enclosed by leaves.

Indumentum: Complex hairs absent; stinging hairs absent; mature twig hairy tomentose; hairs dense.

Leaves: Spaced along branches, leaves opposite, simple; petiole present, not winged, attached to base of leaf lamina, swollen; lamina broadest below middle, 11.5–27 cm long, 12.5–25 cm wide; base symmetric to slightly asymmetric, margin entire, not dissected or lobed, apex rounded or obtuse, venation pinnate, secondary veins open, prominent, intramarginal veins absent; lower surface pale green veins pale yellow, upper surface pale green or green, hairs present, dense, oil dots absent, domatia absent; stipules absent.

Flowers: Inflorescence terminal, flowers on a branched axis; flowers bisexual, with pedicel, with one plane of symmetry perianth present, with distinct sepals and petals, white or pale blue; inner perianth 5, some or partly joined 5-lobed; stamens 4, filaments present, free of each other, joined to perianth; ovary superior, carpels joined, locules 4; styles joined, 1.

Fruits: arranged on branched axis, fruit 35 mm long, 30 mm diam., fruit blue, not spiny, fleshy, simple, indehiscent, drupe/berry (1-seeded). Seed 1, 4–20 mm long, longer than wide, c. 15 mm diam., not winged.

Distribution: Madang.

Teijsmanniodendron ahernianum Bakh.
Fig. 400

Journal of the Arnold Arboretum Vol. 16: 74 (1935)
Non-timber species

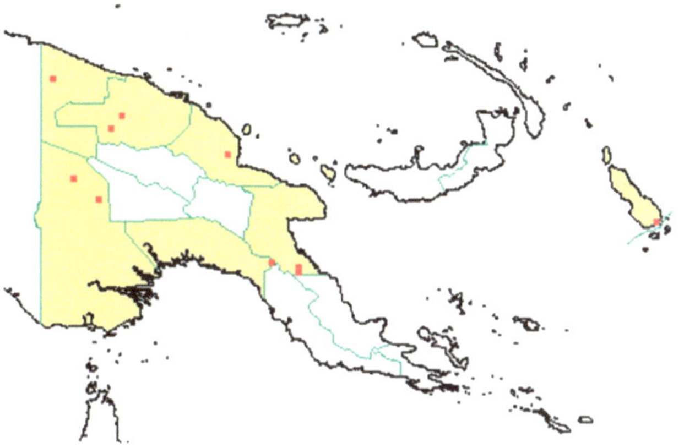

Field Characters: Large trees or small trees, 18–30 m high; bole cylindrical, 15–30 cm diam., straight, 9–10 m long; buttresses absent or present; spines absent; aerial roots absent; stilt roots absent or present. Bark orange, brown, or grey, rough, pustular; lenticels irregular; under-bark green; bark thickness <25 mm thick; blaze consisting of one layer; faintly to non-aromatic; blaze orange or brown, markings absent, granular without splinters; exudate colourless, spotty, changing colour to black or grey on exposure to air, not sticky. Terminal buds not enclosed by leaves.

Indumentum: Complex hairs absent; stinging hairs absent; mature twig without hairs.

Leaves: Spaced along branches, leaves opposite, compound; petiole (25–)50–80(–130) mm long, not winged, attached to base of leaf blade, slightly swollen distally, at point of attachment of petiolules; leaves palmate; petiolule swollen, each leaflet broadest at or near middle, 7–19 cm long, 2.5–6 cm wide, leaflets arranged from one point, symmetric; venation pinnate, secondary veins open, prominent, intramarginal veins absent; lower surface pale green, upper surface dark green, hairs absent; oil dots absent; domatia absent; stipules absent.

Flowers: Inflorescence axillary, flowers on a branched axis; flowers bisexual, shortly stalked (up to 1 mm long) or not stalked, with many planes of symmetry, 8–12 mm long, small, c. 6 mm diam.; perianth with distinct sepals and petals, white; inner perianth 5, some or partly joined; stamens 5, filaments present, free of each other, joined to perianth; ovary superior, carpels joined (when more than one), locules 4; styles solitary, 1.

Fruits: Fruits arranged on branched axis, fruit 12–15 mm long, 5–7 mm diam., brown, black, or dark blue, not spiny, non-fleshy, simple, indehiscent, drupe. Seed 1, c. 10 mm long, not winged, longer than wide, 6–8 mm diam.

Distribution: West Sepik, East Sepik, Madang, Morobe, Western, Gulf, Bougainville.

Fig. 400. *Teijsmanniodendron ahernianum*. Habit, bark, leaves and flower buds

Teijsmanniodendron bogoriense **Koord.** **Fig. 401**

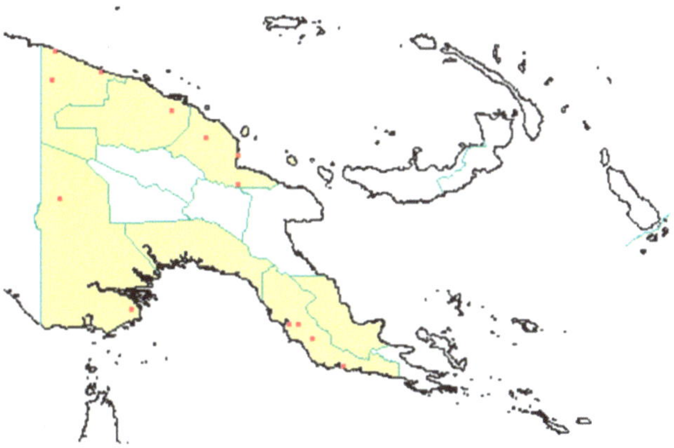

Annales du Jardin Botanique de Buitenzorg Vol. 19: 20 (1904)
Timber Group: Non-timber species

Field Characters: Canopy trees, 15–30 m high, or subcanopy trees; bole cylindrical, 40–127 cm diam., mostly straight, usually 11–23 m long; buttresses to c. 1 m high, or slightly fluted at base, or absent; spines absent; aerial roots absent; stilt roots absent. Bark grey or brown, slightly rough or smooth, pustular, slightly peeling, or slightly scaly or flaky; lenticels irregular; bark 10 mm thick; under-bark yellow or green; faintly or non-aromatic; blaze consisting of one layer, white or pale yellow (cream-coloured), with stripes, granular with splinters, smooth, or slightly fibrous; exudate present or absent (by misinterpretation), colourless, not readily flowing, changing to green or grey on exposure to air, not sticky. Terminal buds not enclosed by leaves.

Indumentum: Complex hairs absent; stinging hairs absent; mature twig without hairs.

Leaves: Spaced along branches, leaves opposite, compound; petiole present, not winged, attached to base of leaf lamina, slightly swollen; leaves with three leaflets or palmate (mostly with 3 leaflets, rarely with 5); petiolule swollen at base; each leaflet sometimes broadest above middle, broadest at or near middle, or sometimes broadest below middle, (10–)13–20(–25) cm long, 4–8 cm wide, leaflets arranged from one point, symmetric to very slightly asymmetric; venation pinnate, secondary veins open, prominent, intramarginal veins absent; lower surface pale green, upper surface dark sub-glossy green, hairs absent, oil dots absent, domatia absent; stipules absent.

Flowers: Inflorescence terminal, flowers on a branched axis; flowers bisexual, with pedicel, with one plane of symmetry, 7–10 mm long, small, 5–7 mm diam.; perianth present, with distinct sepals and petals, mauve, blue, or purple; inner perianth 5, some or partly joined; stamens 4, filaments present, free of each other, joined to perianth; ovary superior, carpels joined, locules 4; styles joined, 1.

Fruits: arranged on branched axis, fruit 15–20 mm long, dark green (possibly immature) or purple, not spiny, non-fleshy, simple, indehiscent or slightly dehiscent, capsule. Seeds 1 (by abortion), 12–15 mm long, longer than wide, c. 6 mm diam., not winged.

Distribution: West Sepik, East Sepik, Madang, Western, Central.

Fig. 401. *Teijsmanniodendron bogoriense.* Habit, bark and leaves

Vitex cofassus Reinw. ex Blume
Fig. 402

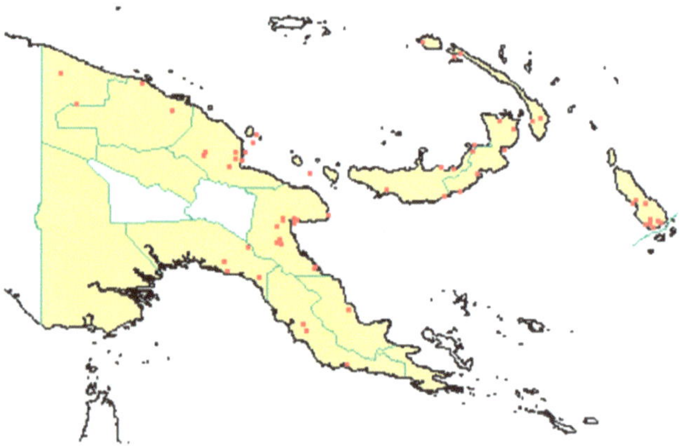

Flora van Nederlandsch Indië 14: 813 (1826)
Other Literature: D.B. Foreman, Checklist of the Vascular Plants of Bougainville 178 (1971) Fig. 178.
Timber Group: Major exportable hardwood
Tradename: New Guinea Teak

Field Characters: Large canopy tree, up to 33 m high; bole cylindrical, 30–170 cm diam. or markedly fluted; crooked or straight, up to 18 m long; buttresses up to 6 m high; spines absent; aerial roots absent; stilt roots absent; bark pale grey or pale brown, slightly rough or mostly smooth, slightly pustular, rarely scaly or flaky, rarely fissured, or peeling, lenticels rounded/swelling; under-bark brown; 6.–10 mm thick; bark blaze consisting of one layer; faintly to non-aromatic; pleasant, white, yellow, orange, or mixed colours, with stripes, rarely smooth or fibrous (with splinters); bark exudate colourless, not readily flowing (spotty), colour changing to black on exposure to air, not sticky; terminal buds not enclosed by leaves.

Indumentum: Complex hairs absent; stinging hairs absent; mature twig indumentum (hairs) present, with hairs short, inconspicuous, sparse (mostly at nodes) or hairs absent.

Leaves: spaced along branches, opposite, compound (often misinterpretated as simple because leaves are unifoliate compound); petiole present, not winged, attached to base of leaf lamina, slightly swollen (at base and tip); leaves with one leaflet; petiolule not swollen; rachis absent; leaves with a terminal leaflet, lamina broadest at or near middle or broadest below middle, (10–)12–22 cm long, 5–10 cm wide, leaflets arranged from one point (only one leaflet), symmetric, terminal developing leaflet buds straight; venation pinnate, secondary veins open, not prominent, but visible, intramarginal veins absent; lower surface green, upper surface sub-glossy green, indumentum (hairs) absent; oil dots absent; domatia absent; stipules absent.

Flowers: Inflorescence terminal or leaf-opposed, flowers on a branched axis; flowers bisexual, stalked, with one plane of symmetry, 4–10 mm long, up to10 mm diam.; perianth present, with distinct sepals and petals, inner perianth pale purple or pale mauve; 5, some or partly joined; stamens 4, filaments present, free of each other, joined to the perianth; ovary superior, carpels joined, locules 5; styles solitary, 1.

Fruits: arranged on branched axis, fruit 10–12 mm long, c. 10 mm diam., green, grey, or black, not spiny, non-fleshy, simple, indehiscent, drupe; seeds usually 1–4, to c. 5 mm long, not winged, narrow (longer than wide), seed c. 4 mm diam.

Distribution: West Sepik, East Sepik, Madang, Morobe, Western Highlands, Gulf, Central, Northern, Milne Bay, New Britain, New Ireland, Bougainville.

Fig. 402. *Vitex cofassus.* Habit, leaves and flower buds

Vitex helogiton K.Schum.
Fig. 403

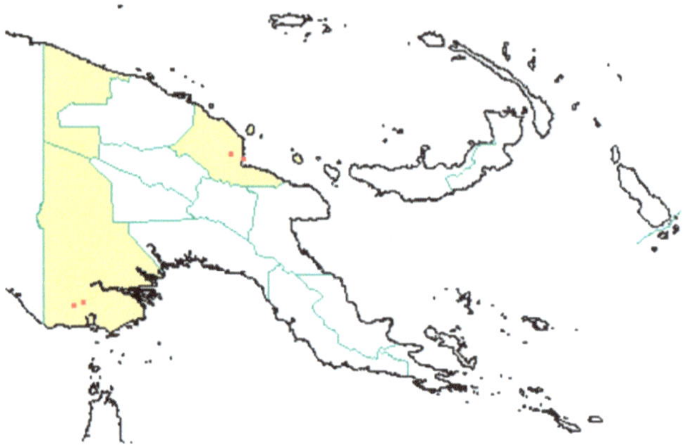

Nachträge zur Flora der Deutschen Schutzgebiete in der Südsee 369 (1905)
Other Literature: A.A. Munir, *Journal of the Adelaide Botanic Gardens* 48–52 (1987) Fig. 4.
Timber Group: Non-timber species

Field Characters: Large canopy tree, rarely up to 30 m high or small sub-canopy tree (up to 20 m high); bole cylindrical, up to c. 70 cm diam.; straight, 8–15 m long; buttresses absent; spines absent; aerial roots absent; stilt roots absent; bark pale brown or brownish grey, rough, scaly, flaky or fissured; under-bark green or brown; less than 25 mm thick; blaze consisting of one layer; faintly to non-aromatic, pale yellow (straw-coloured) or white, markings absent; bark exudate absent; terminal buds not enclosed by leaves.

Indumentum: Complex hairs absent; stinging hairs absent; mature twig indumentum present, with hairs dense, short, adpressed and antrorse.

Leaves: spaced along branches, opposite, compound; petiole present, not winged, attached to base of leaf blade, not swollen; leaves palmate, with 4 or 5 leaflets, or with three leaflets (trifoliate); petiolule not swollen; leaves broadest at or near middle, (3–)5–17(–22) cm long, (2–)3–7(–9) cm wide, leaflets arranged from one point, asymmetric; venation pinnate, secondary veins open, prominent, intramarginal veins absent; leaves with lower surface pale green, upper surface glossy green, indumentum present, with hairs sparse, minute (mostly restricted to midrib and secondary veins); oil dots absent; domatia present, scattered along midrib; stipules absent.

Flowers: Inflorescence axillary, flowers on a branched axis; flowers bisexual, stalked, flowers with one plane of symmetry, 10–12 mm long, 5–6 mm diam.; perianth present, with distinct sepals and petals (both sepals and petals hairy), inner perianth pale mauve, pale purple, or purplish cream-coloured, 5, some or partly joined; stamens 4, filaments present, free of each other, joined to the perianth; ovary superior, carpels joined, locules 2(–4); styles solitary, 1.

Fruits: arranged on branched axis, fruit 8–15(–20) mm long, 6–10(–12) mm diam., purple or purplish red, not spiny, fleshy, simple, indehiscent, drupe; seeds 4, 5–6 mm long, not winged, narrow (longer than wide), seed 3–4 mm diam.

Distribution: Madang, Western.

Notes: This species has frequently been misidentified as *Vitex quinata* or included in a broad concept of *V. glabrata*. *Vitex glabrata* has broadly elliptic leaflets that have more rounded bases and apices than *V. helogiton* and the ovary is glabrous. Whereas, *V. helogiton* has narrowly elliptic leaflets that are gradually tapering to the base and apex, and the ovary is distally hairy. *Vitex glabrata* is restricted to northern Australia. *Vitex quinata* can be distinguished by its obovate leaflets, terminal inflorescence, and glandular ovary.

Fig. 403. *Vitex helogiton*. Bark and leaves

Viticipremna novaepommeraniae (Warb.) H.J.Lam

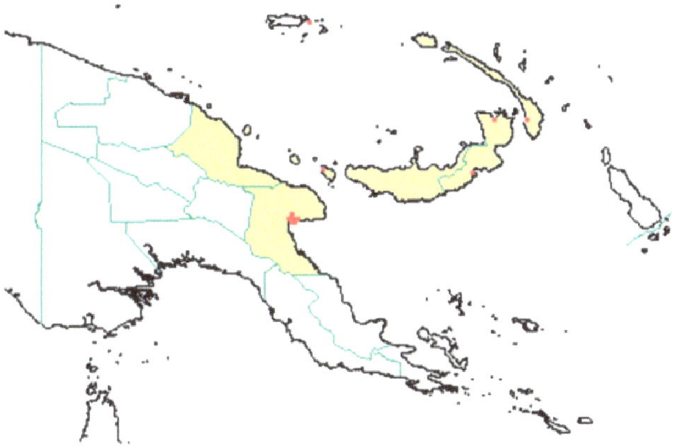

Verbenaceae of the Malayan Archipelago 163 (1919)
Other Literature: A.A. Munir, *Journal of the Adelaide Botanic Gardens* 196–199 (1985) Fig. 5.
Timber Group: Non-timber species

Field Characters: Subcanopy trees, mostly up to 27 m high, or canopy trees, rarely to 34 m high; bole cylindrical, up to 80(–120) cm diam., straight, up to c. 15 m long; buttresses absent; spines absent; aerial roots absent; stilt roots absent. Bark pale brown, rough, peeling; bark <25 mm thick; under-bark pale yellow (cream-coloured), brown, or white; faintly or non-aromatic; pleasant; blaze consisting of one layer, white, pale brown, or pale yellow, with stripes (orange); exudate absent. Terminal buds not enclosed by leaves.

Indumentum: Complex hairs absent; stinging hairs absent; mature twig hairy; hairs dense, with minute rusty red-coloured hairs.

Leaves: Spaced along branches, leaves opposite, compound; petiole present (mostly 3.5–6 cm long), not winged, attached to base of leaf lamina, not swollen; leaves rarely with three leaflets or palmate, with 4 or 5 leaflets; petiolule not swollen; each leaflet broadest above middle or broadest at or near middle, (4–)6–13(–18) cm long, (2.5–)3.5–5.5(–9) cm wide, leaflets arranged from one point, asymmetric; venation pinnate, secondary veins open, prominent, intramarginal veins absent; lower surface pale green, upper surface glossy green, hairs present, sparse (particularly on upper surface) or dense (along veins of lower surface), oil dots present (densely glandular, particularly on lower surface), domatia absent; stipules absent.

Flowers: Inflorescence terminal, flowers on a branched axis; flowers bisexual, with pedicel 10–30 mm long, with one plane of symmetry, 8–12 mm long, small, 2–5 mm diam.; perianth present, with distinct sepals and petals (calyx truncate, not lobed), white or pale yellow with mauve markings; inner perianth 4, some or partly joined; stamens 4, filaments present, free of each other, joined to perianth; ovary superior, carpels joined, locules 4 (often appearing to be 2-locular); styles joined, 1.

Fruits: arranged on branched axis, fruit 5–9 mm long, 5–8 mm diam., black with purple, not spiny, fleshy, simple, indehiscent, drupe. Seeds 4, to about 5 mm long, longer than wide, c. 3 mm diam., not winged.

Distribution: Morobe, New Britain, New Ireland, Manus.

Notes: This species has been frequently misidentified as *Vitex quinata* F.N.Williams . *Viticipremna novaepommeraniae* has leaflets which are unequally obtuse or subtruncate at base; calyx truncate, not lobed; corolla 4-lobed; carpels 4-locular, but often appearing 2-locular; ovary non-glandular. However, *Vitex quinata* has leaflets which are symmetrical at base; calyx minutely 5-lobed; corolla 5-lobed; carpels also 4-locular and often appearing 2-locular; ovary glandular.

Viticipremna tomentosa A.A.Munir

Journal of the Adelaide Botanic Gardens Vol. 7: 184–186 (1985) Fig. 1.
Timber Group: Non-timber species

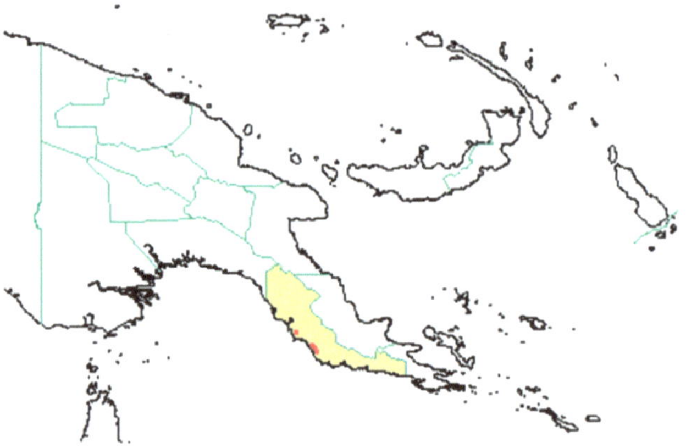

Field Characters: Subcanopy trees, up to 10 m high; bole cylindrical, up to c. 7 cm diam., straight, 3–4 m long; buttresses absent; spines absent; aerial roots absent; stilt roots absent. Bark red or pale brown, rough, irregularly cracked; bark <25 mm thick; under-bark brown; faintly or non-aromatic; pleasant; blaze consisting of one layer, pale yellow (cream-coloured), markings absent; exudate absent. Terminal buds not enclosed by leaves.

Indumentum: Complex hairs absent; stinging hairs absent; mature twig hairy; hairs dense.

Leaves: Spaced along branches, leaves opposite, compound; petiole mostly 4–6.5 cm long, not winged, attached to base of leaf lamina, not swollen; leaves palmate (with 5 leaflets) or with three leaflets; petiolule not swollen; each leaflet broadest below middle, (3.5–)5–12(–18) cm long, (2–)3.5–5(–6.5) cm wide, leaflets arranged from one point, slightly asymmetric; venation pinnate, secondary veins open, prominent or not prominent, but visible, intramarginal veins absent; lower surface pale green, upper surface green, hairs present, dense, especially on lower surface, oil dots absent or present, domatia absent; stipules absent.

Flowers: Inflorescence terminal, flowers on a branched axis; flowers bisexual, with pedicel 1–2(–3) mm long, with one plane of symmetry, 7–8 mm long, small, 3–4 mm diam.; perianth present, with distinct sepals and petals (calyx 4-lobed), white or cream-coloured; inner perianth 4, some or partly joined; stamens 4, filaments present, free of each other, joined to perianth; ovary superior, carpels joined, locules 4; styles joined, 1.

Fruits: arranged on branched axis, fruit 6–8.5 mm long, 5–7 mm diam., brownish red or black, not spiny, fleshy, simple, indehiscent, drupe. Seeds 4, to about 5 mm long, longer than wide, 3–4 mm diam., not winged.

Distribution: Central.

85. Bignoniaceae

Trees, shrubs, lianas, and rarely herbs. Stipules absent. Leaves well-developed, rarely spiral, usually opposite, or whorled, usually compound or simple, bipinnate, pinnate, or palmate, dissected or lobed, or not; margin entire; venation pinnate or palmate. Inflorescences axillary or terminal; Flowers bisexual, zygomorphic or slightly irregular, with distinct calyx and corolla. Sepals 5. Petals 5, joined, at least in part; tube present. Stamens (4 or)5, free; filaments present; staminodes absent. Gynoecium with carpels at least partially joined, superior; styles partially or fully joined. Fruit simple, dehiscent or rarely indehiscent, capsule, rarely berry, dry, at least non-fleshy or rarely fleshy. Seeds with wings, rarely without.

PNG genera: *Deplanchea, Dolichandrone, Jacaranda* (cultivated), ***Lamiodendron****, Neosepicaea, Pandorea, Radermachera, Spathodea* (cultivated), *Tecoma, Tecomanthe*

References: Steenis (1977)

1a. Leaves pinnately or bipinnately compound 2

1b. Leaves palmately compound, unifoliolate, or simple 10

2a. Lianas 3

2b. Trees or shrubs 4

3a. Calyx with 5 lobes or 5 teeth .... *Tecomanthe* (not treated here)

3b. Calyx with 2 or 3 small lobes .... *Pandorea* (not treated here)

4a. Leaves 2 or 3(or 4) pinnate; calyx closed in bud .... *Radermachera* (not treated here)

4b. Leaves pinnate 5

5a. Calyx spathe-like 6

5b. Calyx tubular 7

6a. Corolla broadly campanulate, orange-red with yellow margin; calyx >45 mm long (cultivated).......... .... *Spathodea* (not treated here)

6b. Corolla tubular to campanulate or funnel-shaped, white or lavender; calyx < 30 mm long................ .... *Dolichandrone* (not treated here)

7a. Staminodes present, longer than stamens (cultivated)............................ *Jacaranda* (not treated here)

7b. Staminodes absent or if present, then much shorter than stamens 8

8a. Leaflets variously toothed; extrafloral nectaries present (cultivated) .... *Tecoma* (not treated here)

8b. Leaflets with margin entire; extrafloral nectaries absent.. 9

9a. Calyx thin, with 5 equal lobes.. *Lamiodendron*

9b. Calyx not thin, with lobes unequal and often <5............................ *Radermachera* (not treated here)

10a. Leaves palmately compound.. *Neosepicea* (not treated here)

10b. Leaves simple or unifoliolate..11

11a. Corolla yellow .... *Deplanchea* (not treated here)

11a. Corolla white, red or various colours of blue, never yellow.. 12

12a. Flowers usually blue, lavender or purple-blue; staminodes longer than stamens (cultivated) .... *Jacaranda* (not treated here)

12b. Flowers red, white, lavender or dark red; staminodes much shorter than stamens (cultivated) .... *Tecoma* (not treated here)

Lamiodendron magnificum Steen. Fig. 404

Nova Guinea series 2 Vol. 8: 381 (1957)
Timber Group: Minor hardwoods

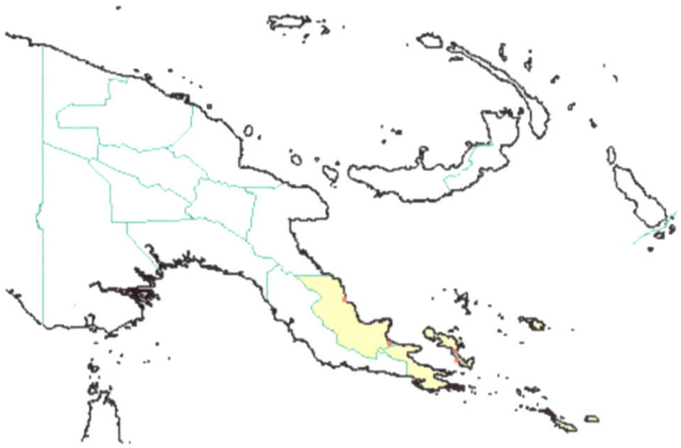

Field Characters: Canopy trees, 15–20 m high; bole markedly fluted, 40–50 cm diam., straight; buttresses slightly present, fluted to c. 2 m high; spines absent; aerial roots absent; stilt roots absent. Bark grey, rough, pustular; lenticels irregular; bark 10 mm thick; under-bark green; strongly aromatic; onion-like; blaze consisting of one layer, white, pale yellow, or pale brown (straw-coloured), markings absent, fibrous; inner blaze pale brown straw-coloured, pale yellow, or white, markings absent, fibrous; exudate present, brown, not readily flowing, changing to orange or brown on exposure to air, not sticky. Terminal buds not enclosed by leaves.

Indumentum: Complex hairs absent; stinging hairs absent; mature twig without hairs.

Leaves: Spaced along branches, leaves opposite, compound; petiole present, not winged, attached to base of leaf lamina, not swollen; leaves pinnate; petiolule swollen, rachis present, not winged, not swollen; leaves with a terminal leaflet, each leaflet broadest below middle, 11–13.5 cm long, 5.5–6 cm wide, leaflets opposite, slightly asymmetric or almost symmetric, terminal developing leaflet buds straight; venation pinnate, secondary veins open, prominent, intramarginal veins present; lower surface pale green, upper surface glossy green, hairs absent, oil dots absent, domatia absent; stipules present, free, laterally placed, not encircling the twig, scale-like, not fringed, large, persistent.

Flowers: Inflorescence axillary, or on branches below leaves, flowers on a branched axis crowded; flowers bisexual, with pedicel, with many planes of symmetry or slightly asymmetric, 50–70 mm long, small, c. 50 mm diam.; perianth present, with distinct sepals and petals, yellow or orange; inner perianth 5, some or partly joined tubing a corolla tube; stamens 4, filaments present, free of each other, joined to perianth; ovary superior, carpels joined, locules 2; styles joined, 1.

Fruits: arranged on branched axis, not spiny, non-fleshy, simple, dehiscent, capsule. Seeds many, winged.

Distribution: Northern, Milne Bay, Papuan Islands.

Fig. 404. *Lamiodendron magnificum*. Trunk, bark, flowers and leaves.

86. Acanthaceae

Trees, shrubs, and herbs. Stipules absent. Leaves well-developed, opposite, simple, not dissected or lobed; margin entire or toothed; venation pinnate. Inflorescences terminal. Bracts present. Flowers bisexual, zygomorphic, with distinct calyx and corolla. Sepals (3 or)4 or 5. Petals (3 or)4 or 5, joined, at least in part; tube present, often split. Stamens 4(or 5), free; filaments present; staminodes present or absent. Gynoecium with two free carpels, superior; styles partially or fully joined. Fruit simple, dehiscent, capsule, dry, at least non-fleshy. Seeds without wings.

PNG genera: *Acanthus, Ancylacanthus, Andrographis, Aphelandra, Asystasia,* ***Avicennia****, Barleria, Blechum, Brunoniella, Calophanoides, Calycacanthus, Cosmianthemum, Dicliptera, Dipteracanthus, Eranthemum, Gendarussa, Graptophyllum, Hemigraphis, Hulemacanthus, Hygrophila, Hypoestes, Jadunia, Justicia, Lepidagathis, Leptophyllum, Leptosiphonium, Odontonema, Oreothyrsus, Peristrophe, Polytrema, Pseuderanthemum, Ptyssiglottis, Rhaphidospora, Rostellularia, Ruellia, Rungia, Sanchezia, Staurogyne, Thunbergia.*

Notes: *Avicennia* was previously placed in the family Verbenaceae and then, more recently, in its own family, the Avicenniaceae.

References: Barker (1986), Bremekamp (1953, 1955a, 1955b, 1957), Bremekamp and Nannenga-Bremekamp (1948), Duke (1990, 1991), Lindau (1905, 1913, 1918), Percival and Womersley (1975)

1a. Mangrove trees or shrubs 2

1b. Herbs or shrubs, sometimes trees, not associated with mangroves 3

2a. Shrub, occurring at the inland-side of mangroves; leaves usually with margin spiny; seedling developing from dispersed fruit; anthers consisting of 1 locule .... *Acanthus* (not treated here)

2b. Subcanopy to canopy trees, mangrove species; leaves with margin entire; seedlings developing on plant; anthers with 2 locules .... *Avicennia*

3a. Fertile stamens 4, sometimes unequal 4

3b. Fertile stamens 2; staminodes present or absent (anthers reduced in size) 15

4a. Upper anthers with 2 locules; lower anthers with 1 locule .... *Hulemacanthus* (not treated here)

4b. Anthers with 2 locules 5

5a. Corolla lobes imbricate 6

5b. Corolla lobes contorted 10

6a. Seed lacking hook-like woody out-growths (jaculators); corolla with upper lip outside other lobes; ovary with at least 20 ovules; capsule 5 or more seeds .... *Staurogyne* (not treated here)

6b. Seed with jaculators; corolla with upper lip inside other lobes; ovary with 1 or 2 ovules per locule; capsule 1–4-seeded 7

7a. Calyx deeply 5-parted; lobes narrow, more or less equal; staminal filaments fused in pairs at base; inflorescence a panicle or raceme 8

7a. Calyx 4- or 5-parted and then lower lobe-pair joined, upper lobes narrower than lower ones; staminal filaments not jointed, free; inflorescence solitary or flowers in spikes, heads, clusters or fascicles 9

8a. Shrubs or trees; capsule with apex entire; corolla dark red .... *Graptophyllum* (not treated here)

8a. Herbs; capsule with apex clavate; corolla white, lilac or violet...................... *Asystasia* (not treated here)

9a. Corolla 40–100 mm long, sometimes yellow; stamens unequal, 2 upper stamens exserted from corolla, lower pair often reduced to staminodes; spiny shrubs .... *Barleria lupulina* Lindl. (not treated here)

9b. Corolla < 20 mm long, never yellow; stamens equal, very short (included in corolla), all fertile; herbs .... *Lepidagathis* (not treated here)

10a. Flowers with long pedicels; staminal filamnets free; seeds without jaculators; ovary with 2 ovules per locule; climbers; calyx with 5–16 teeth; capsules strongly beaked........... *Thunbergia* (not treated here)

10b. Flowers with short or long pedicels; staminal filaments joined in pairs, or all connected at base; seeds with jaculators; ovary with 4 ovules per locule.. 11

11a. Capsule with 1 or 2 seeds per locule; seeds with 1 or 2 jaculators; capsule oblong; stamens all joined together .... *Thunbergia* (not treated here)

11a. Capsule with at least 3 seeds per locules; seeds with 3 or more jaculators; capsule linear or narrowly ellipsoid to obloid-linear 12

12a. Corolla distinctly 2-lipped; flowers sessile or almost so .... *Hygrophila* (not treated here)

12b. Corolla not distinctly 2-lipped, usually more or less actinomorphic.. 13

13a. Flowers in open axillary cymes, sometimes with a large terminal panicle; bracteoles always shorter than calyx; corolla widely funnel-shaped with large spreading lobes; seeds covered with hairs.................... .... *Ruellia tuberosa* L. (not treated here)

13b. Flowers usually in terminal or axillary spikes, not in axillary cymes; bracteoles (when present) shorter or loner than calyx...14

14a. Erect or creeping herb, hairy; ovary with 4–6 ovules per locule; bracteoles present or absent; seeds hairy... *Hemigraphis* (not treated here)

14b. Erect herbs; ovary with 10–20 ovules per locule; bracteoles present.. *Leptosiphonium* (not treated here)

15a. Anthers with 1 locule .... *Hypoestes floribunda* R.Br. (not treated here)

15b. Anthers with 2 locules 16

16a. Anther locules inserted at the same level on the filament; stamens more or less included or exserted from the corolla 17

16b. Anther locules inserted at distinctly different levels on the filament; stamens exserted from the corolla 23

17a. Corolla not distinctly 2-lipped... 18

17b. Corolla distinctly 2-lipped... 20

18a. Calyx with 4 lobes; 2 lateral lobes much narrower than other two lobes...... *Barleria* (not treated here)

18b. Calyx with 5 lobes; lobes more or less equal 19

19a. Weakly stemmed herbs; stamens inserted in middle of corolla tube; introduced, cultivated .... *Odontonema stricta* Kuntz. (not treated here)

19b. Shrubs or woody herbs; stamens inserted near top of corolla tube .... *Pseuderanthemum* (not treated here)

20a. Herbs.. 21

20b. Shrubs 22

21a. Staminodes present (sometimes minute in *Jadunia biroi* Lindau); inflorescence a panicle or raceme.... .... *Jadunia* (not treated here)

21b. Staminodes absent, all stamens fertile; inflorescence with a long peduncle and flowers arranged on a dichotomously branching spike .... *Oreothyrsus* (not treated here – may not be present in PNG)

22a. Staminodes 2; inflorescence a panicle .... *Graptophyllum* (not treated here)

22b. Stamindes absent; inflorescence a spike or dichasium .... *Calycacanthus magnusianus* K.Schum. (not treated here)

23a. Anthers with a basal spur.. 24

23b. Anthers without a basal spur.. 27

24a. Inflorescence axillary, sometimes reduced to a 1 flower; anthers with only lower locule spurred at base 25

24b. Inflorescence mostly terminal, a few are sometimes axillary; anthers with both locules spurred or only lower locule spurred at base 26

25a. Inflorescence usually with 3 flowers; leaves 3.5–9 cm long, 1–3 cm wide; style channel on upper lip with margin hairy; seeds granulate .... *Calophanoides* (not treated here)

25b. Inflorescence with many flowers; leaves 8–25 cm long, 2.5–7.5 cm wide; style channel absent; seeds muricate .... *Rhaphidospora* (not treated here)

26a. Erect shrubs; bracts linear to triangular-subulate; staminal filaments without hairs; anthers with both locules spurred at base .... *Gendarussa vulgaris* Nees (not treated here)

26b. Herbs; bratcs narrowly ovate to obovate; staminal filaments with or without hairs; anthers with only lower locules spurred at base .... *Rungia* (not treated here)

27a. Flowers throughout inflorescences enclosed by an involucre of 2 leaves; corolla tube twisted so that upper lip turned downwards and lower lip turned upwards 28

27b. Flowers not enclosed by an involucre; corolla tube not twisted (as above) 29

28a. One or both of the involucral bracts with a distinct mucro at apex; capsule with side walls remaining attached as a membranous wing after dehiscence...................................... *Dicliptera* (not treated here)

28b. Involucral bracts without mucro at apex; capsule with side walls remaining attached to placentas throughout their length .... *Peristrophe baphica* (Spreng) Bremek. (not treated here)

29a. Flowers white; inflorescences a cyme, with 1–15 flowers, with short pedicels; leaf pairs often unequal .... *Polytrema* (not treated here – possibly not in PNG)

29b. Flowers with violet streaks; inflorescences a spike, with many flowers closely clustered together; leaf pairs more or less equal; introduced weed .... *Justicia* (not treated here)

Avicennia alba Blume
Fig. 405

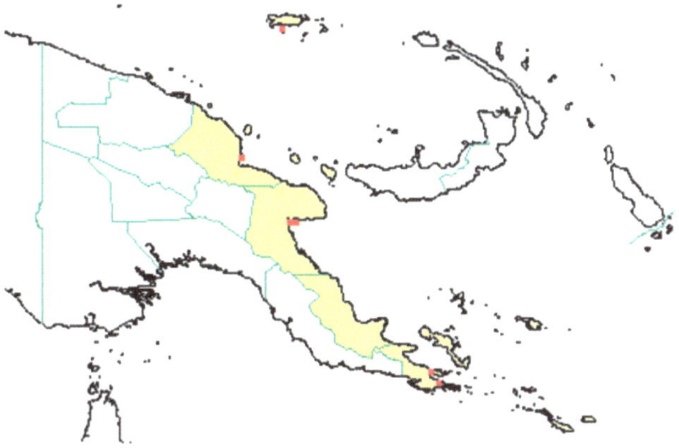

Bijdragen tot de flora van Nederlansch Indië Vol. 14: 821 (1826)
Other Literature: N.C. Duke, *Australian Systematic Botany* Vol. 4: 307–309 (1991) Fig. 5.
Vernacular name: Mangrove.
Timber Group: Occasional timber species

Field Characters: Canopy or subcanopy trees, frequently a shrub, up to 25 m high; bole cylindrical, straight; buttresses absent; spines absent; aerial roots absent or rarely present just above base; pneumatophores c. 20 cm high, 5–10 mm wide near apex; stilt roots absent. Bark black or dark brown, rough or smooth, often fissured forming short longitudinal fissures and very small scales or pustular warty; lenticels elongated vertically; bark <25 mm thick; under-bark green or pale yellow cream-coloured; faintly or non-aromatic; blaze consisting of one layer, white or pale yellow, markings absent, smooth spongy; exudate absent. Terminal buds not enclosed by leaves.

Indumentum: Complex hairs absent; stinging hairs absent; mature twig without hairs.

Leaves: Spaced along branches, leaves opposite, simple; petiole 4–12(–21) mm long, not winged, attached to base of leaf lamina, slightly swollen at base; lamina slightly broadest above middle or broadest at or near middle, 7.5–9(–11) cm long, 3–4(–6) cm wide; base symmetric, margin entire, not dissected or lobed, apex obtuse, venation pinnate, secondary veins open, not prominent, but visible, intramarginal veins absent; lower surface grey silvery green or green, upper surface glossy dark green, hairs often present or absent, sparse minutely hairy on lower leaf surface, oil dots absent, domatia absent; stipules absent.

Flowers: Inflorescence axillary, in distal axils or terminal, flowers on a branched axis in spike-like clusters; flowers bisexual, not stalked, aromatic, with many planes of symmetry, 3–5 mm long, small, 3–4 mm diam.; perianth present, with distinct sepals and petals, yellow or orange; inner perianth 4(–6), some or partly joined lobes 2.5-5 mm long; stamens 4(–6), filaments present, free of each other, joined to perianth; ovary superior, carpels joined, locules 1; styles absent (by misinterpretation) or joined minute, barely extended from ovary, 1.

Fruits: arranged on branched axis, fruit 21–33 mm long, 8–15 mm diam., dull greenish grey or pale green, not spiny, non-fleshy, simple, dehiscent, capsule. Seeds 1(or 2) (seedlings developing on plant), as wide as long, not winged.

Distribution: Madang, Morobe, Northern, Milne Bay, Papuan Islands, Manus.

Notes: The seedling (radicle) of this species is about 9 mm long and is mostly glabrous with a dense hairy collar about 2 mm wide, with hooked hairs.

Fig. 405. *Avicennia alba.* Fruit, pheumatophores, habit, bark, flowers and leaves

Avicennia marina subsp. *australasica* (Walp.) J.Everett Figs 406, 407

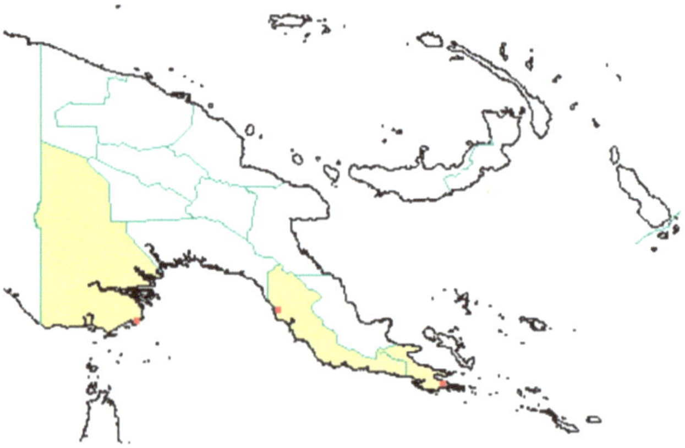

Telopea Vol. 5: 628 & 629 (1994)
Other Literature: N.C. Duke, *Australian Systematic Botany* Vol. 4: 313–315 (1991) Fig. 7.
Vernacular name: Mangrove.
Timber Group: Non-timber species

Field Characters: Subcanopy trees, 5–10(–23) m high, or shrub up to 2 m high; bole cylindrical, up to 35 cm diam., straight; buttresses absent; spines absent; aerial roots absent; stilt roots absent. Bark white, greyish green, grey, or pale brown, smooth or rough, slightly pustular or slightly fissured; lenticels elongated vertically; bark <25 mm thick; under-bark green; faintly or non-aromatic; blaze consisting of one layer, white or pale yellow, markings absent, smooth; exudate absent. Terminal buds not enclosed by leaves.

Indumentum: Complex hairs absent; stinging hairs absent; mature twig without hairs.

Leaves: Spaced along branches, leaves opposite, simple; petiole 7–11(–13) mm long, not winged or winged amplexicaule at base, attached to base of leaf lamina, swollen at base; lamina broadest at or near middle, 4–6(–7) cm long, 1.5–3(–4) cm wide; base symmetric, margin entire, not dissected or lobed, apex obtuse, sub-acute, or acuminate, venation pinnate, secondary veins open, not prominent, but visible, intramarginal veins absent; lower surface pale green, upper surface glossy green, hairs present, sparse finely pubescent on lower surface, oil dots absent, domatia absent; stipules absent.

Flowers: Inflorescence terminal or axillary, in distal axils, flowers on a branched axis; flowers bisexual, not stalked, with many planes of symmetry, 5–7 mm long, small, 5–6 mm diam.; perianth present, with distinct sepals and petals, yellow or orange; inner perianth 4(–6), some or partly joined lobes 2.5–4 mm long; stamens 4(–6), filaments present, free of each other, joined to perianth; ovary superior, carpels joined, locules 1; styles joined, 1.

Fruits: arranged on branched axis, fruit 15–20(–26) mm long, 12–17(–21) mm diam., green or pale brown, not spiny, non-fleshy, simple, dehiscent, capsule. Seeds 1(or 2), as wide as long, not winged.

Distribution: Western, Central, Milne Bay.

Notes: The seedling (radicle) of this species is 5–10(–16) mm long and is mostly glabrous with a dense hairy collar c. 2 mm wide, with hairs straight or wavy. Previously known as *Avicennia marina* var. *resinifera* but this name appears to have not been validly published (refer J. Everett (1994) *Telopea* Vol. 5: 627–629).

Fig. 406. *Avicennia marina* subsp. *australasica*. Habit, bark and leaves

Fig. 407. *Avicennia marina* subsp. *australasica*. Illustration showing branchlet, leaves and flowers (© Papua New Guinea National Herbarium, Lae)

Avicennia marina subsp. *eucalyptifolia* (Zipp.) J.Everett Fig. 408

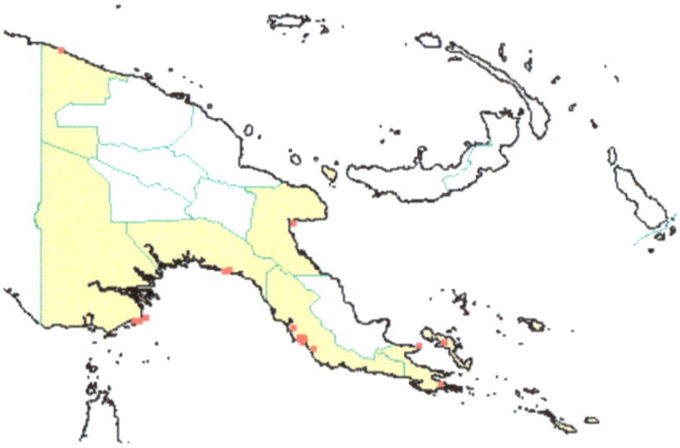

Telopea Vol. 5: 629 (1994)
Other Literature: N.C. Duke, *Australian Systematic Botany* Vol. 4: 315–317 (1991) Fig. 8.
Vernacular name: Mangrove.
Timber Group: Non-timber species

Field Characters: Subcanopy or canopy trees, up to 30 m high; bole cylindrical, up to 46 cm diam., straight, 10–12 m long; buttresses absent; spines absent; aerial roots absent; stilt roots absent. Bark white (when dry), green, greenish grey, or brown, slightly rough or smooth, often scaly or flaky with thin flakes; bark <25 mm thick; under-bark pale yellow or pale brown; faintly or non-aromatic; blaze consisting of one layer, white or pale yellow straw-coloured, markings absent, smooth; exudate absent. Terminal buds not enclosed by leaves.

Indumentum: Complex hairs absent; stinging hairs absent; mature twig without hairs.

Leaves: Spaced along branches, leaves opposite, simple; petiole 7–11(–14) mm long, slightly winged amplexicaul at base, attached to base of leaf lamina, swollen at base; lamina broadest below middle, 5.5–7.5(–9.3) cm long, 1–2.5(–3) cm wide; base symmetric, margin entire, not dissected or lobed, apex slightly acuminate or long-tapering, venation pinnate, secondary veins open, not prominent, but visible, intramarginal veins absent; lower surface grey or green, upper surface dark green, greenish brown, or green, hairs present, sparse finely pubescent on lower surface, oil dots absent, domatia absent; stipules absent.

Flowers: Inflorescence terminal, flowers on a branched axis; flowers bisexual, not stalked, with many planes of symmetry, 5–7 mm long, small, 5–6 mm diam.; perianth present, with distinct sepals and petals, orange; inner perianth 4(–6), some or partly joined lobes 2–3 mm long; stamens 4(–8), filaments present, free of each other, joined to perianth; ovary superior, carpels joined, locules 1; styles joined, 1.

Fruits: arranged on branched axis, fruit 10–16(–20) mm long, 9–15(–19) mm diam., greenish grey, green, or pale brown, not spiny, non-fleshy, simple, dehiscent, capsule. Seeds 1(–2), as wide as long, not winged.

Distribution: West Sepik, Morobe, Western, Gulf, Central, Milne Bay, Papuan Islands.

Notes: The seedlings (radical) of this species are 5–13 mm long, mostly glabrous but with a short densely hairy collar with hairs straight or wavy. Previously known as *Avicennia marina* var. *eucalyptifolia* but to be consistent with the change of rank of other infra-specific taxa within *A. marina*, this taxon is here referred to as a subspecies of this species (refer J. Everett (1994) *Telopea* Vol. 5: 627–629).

Fig. 408. *Avicennia marina* subsp. *eucalyptifolia*. Illustration showing branchlet, leaves and fruits (© Papua New Guinea National Herbarium, Lae)

Avicennia officinalis L.
Fig. 409

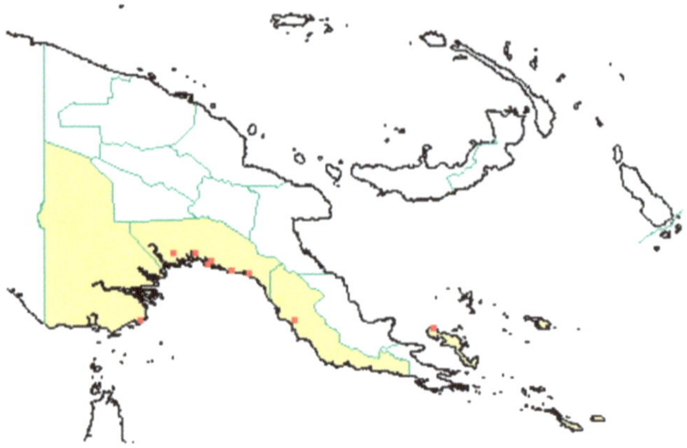

Species Plantarum Vol. 2: 110 (1753)
Other Literature: N.C. Duke, *Australian Systematic Botany* Vol. 4: 319–321 (1991) Fig. 10.
Vernacular name: Mangrove.
Timber Group: Non-timber species

Field Characters: Canopy trees or subcanopy trees, or a shrub, 5–25 m high; bole cylindrical, up to 25 cm diam., straight, up to 7 m long; buttresses absent; spines absent; aerial roots absent or present low-placed aerial roots common; stilt roots absent pneumatophores 20–30 cm high. Bark green, grey, brown, or yellow, slightly rough or smooth in young trees, finely fissured or scattered pustular older trees; lenticels irregular; bark 3–5 mm thick; under-bark red or brown; faintly or non-aromatic or strongly aromatic; pleasant; blaze consisting of one layer, white or pale yellow, markings absent, fibrous; exudate present or absent, colourless, not readily flowing, changing to dark grey on exposure to air, not sticky. Terminal buds not enclosed by leaves.

Indumentum: Complex hairs absent; stinging hairs absent; mature twig hairy or mature twig without hairs; hairs dense or sparse.

Leaves: Spaced along branches, leaves opposite, simple; petiole 8–13(–17) mm long, not winged, attached to base of leaf lamina, not swollen; lamina sometimes broadest above middle or broadest at or near middle, 4–9(–12.5) cm long, 2–4(–6) cm wide; base symmetric, margin entire, not dissected or lobed, apex rounded or obtuse, venation pinnate, secondary veins open, not prominent, but visible, intramarginal veins absent; lower surface pale green or greenish grey, upper surface glossy green shiny or dark green, hairs present, sparse sparsely pubescent on lower surface, oil dots absent, domatia absent; stipules absent.

Flowers: Inflorescence terminal, flowers on a branched axis with 2–12 flowers congested into a compact cluster; flowers bisexual, not stalked, with many planes of symmetry or slightly asymmetric corolla variously zygomorphic, 8–12 mm long, small, 5–12 mm diam.; perianth present, with distinct sepals and petals, yellow or orange; inner perianth 4, some or partly joined lobes 3–5 mm long; stamens 4 (of different lengths), filaments c. 3 mm long, free of each other, joined to perianth; ovary superior, carpels joined, locules 1; styles joined, 1 (short).

Fruits: arranged on branched axis, fruit 12–18(–27) mm long, 8–15 mm diam., pale yellow, pale green, or pale grey, not spiny velvety hairy, non-fleshy, simple, dehiscent, capsule. Seed 1, as wide as long, not winged.

Distribution: Western, Gulf, Central, Papuan Islands.

Notes: The seedlings (radical) of this species are about 13 mm long, densely hairy throughout with hairs straight or wavy.

Fig. 409. *Avicennia officinalis*. Leaves and fruit

Aquifoliales

PNG families: Aquifoliaceae, Cardiopteridaceae, Stemonuraceae

1a. Stipules present; seeds >1 .... Aquifoliaceae

1b. Stipules absent; seeds 1 or 2 2

2a. Seeds 1; fruits not winged .... Stemonuraceae

2b. Seeds 2; fruits with 2 wings .... Cardiopteridaceae

87. Cardiopteridaceae

Trees or climbing shrubs, or lianas. Stipules absent. Leaves well-developed, spiral, simple, not dissected or lobed; margin entire; venation palmate. Inflorescences axillary, branched; Flowers unisexual, then plant dioecious, regular, with distinct calyx and corolla. Sepals (4 or) 5. Petals (4 or) 5, usually joined, at least at base. Stamens 5 (male flowers), free, joined to petals; filaments present; staminodes present or absent (female flowers). Gynoecium consisting of one carpel, superior; styles 1 or 2. Fruit simple, indehiscent, samara, flattened, slightly fleshy, with 2 wings. Seeds 2, without wings.

PNG genera: *Citronella*, ***Gonocaryum***, *Pseudobotrys*

References: Sleumer (1972a)

1a. Flowers unisexual; male flowers with staminal filaments fused for most of their length to lower part of corolla tube .... *Gonocaryum*

1b. Flowers bisexual; stamens not fused to the corolla, except near base 2

2a. Petals free; inflorescences terminal .... *Citronella suaveolens* (Blume) Howard (not treated here)

2b. Petals fused basally to form a corolla tube, distally free; inflorescences arranged on trunk of tree .... *Pseudobotrys* (not treated here)

Gonocaryum litorale (Blume) Sleumer
Fig. 410

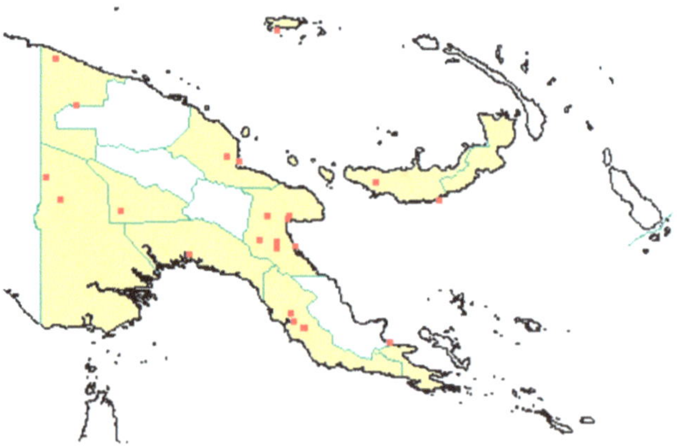

Notizblatt des Botanischen Gartens und Museums zu Berlin-Dahlem Vol. 15: 223 (1940)
Timber Group: Non-timber species

Field Characters: Subcanopy trees, 15 m high; bole cylindrical, 13 cm diam., straight, 7 m long; buttresses absent; spines absent; aerial roots absent; stilt roots absent. Bark brown, rough, pustular; lenticels irregular; bark 3–4 mm thick; under-bark pale green; strongly aromatic; unpleasant; blaze consisting of 2 layers; outer blaze orange, speckled or with stripes, granular without splinters; inner blaze pale yellow, markings absent, fibrous; exudate present, colourless, not readily flowing, changing to brownish grey or pale brown on exposure to air, sticky. Terminal buds not enclosed by leaves.

Indumentum: Complex hairs absent; stinging hairs absent; mature twig without hairs.

Leaves: Spaced along branches, leaves spiral, simple; petiole 8–10 mm long, orange-coloured, not winged, attached to base of leaf lamina, not swollen or swollen throughout; lamina broadest at or near middle, (14–)17–23 mm long, (7–)8–11.5 mm wide; base symmetric, margin entire, not dissected or lobed, apex acuminate, venation pinnate, secondary veins open, prominent, intramarginal veins absent; lower surface green, upper surface green slightly darker than for abaxial surface, hairs absent, oil dots absent, domatia absent; stipules absent.

Flowers: Inflorescence axillary, flowers on an unbranched axis; flowers bisexual, not stalked (sessile), pedicel absent (< 0.5 mm long), flowers with many planes of symmetry perianth present, with distinct sepals and petals, yellowish green or pale yellow; inner perianth 5, free; stamens 5.

Fruits: arranged on an unbranched axis, fruit 40–60 mm long, globular to ellipsoid, 40–50 mm diam., orange, not spiny ridged, slightly fleshy, simple, indehiscent, drupe.

Distribution: West Sepik, Madang, Morobe, Southern Highlands, Western, Gulf, Central, Milne Bay, New Britain, Manus.

Fig. 410. *Gonocaryum litorale.* Bark, leaves, flower buds and fruit

88. Stemonuraceae

Trees. Stipules absent. Leaves well-developed, spiral, simple, not dissected or lobed; margin entire; venation pinnate. Inflorescences axillary; Flowers unisexual, then plant dioecious, regular, with distinct calyx and corolla. Sepals 4 or 5(–7). Petals 4 or 5(–7), usually free or joined, at least in part; tube absent. Stamens 5 (male flowers), free; filaments present; staminodes present female flowers. Gynoecium consisting of one carpel, superior; styles absent. Fruit simple, indehiscent, drupe, slightly fleshy. Seeds without wings.

PNG genera: *Gomphandra, Hartleya, Medusanthera,* ***Stemonurus****, Whitmorea*

References: Sleumer (1972b), Utteridge (2007b)

1a. Flowers unisexual (or functionally so).. 2

1b. Flowers bisexual.. 4

2a. Fruits an ovoid-ellipsoid drupe, without a fleshy lateral appendage....... *Gomphandra* (not treated here)

2b. Fruits a laterally compressed drupe, with a fleshy lateral appendage.. 3

3a. Flowers with disk absent; staminal filaments flattened and fleshy, with long hairs on back of connective and below anthers ventrally........................ *Medusanthera laxiflora* (Miers) Howard (not treated here)

3b. Flowers with thick disk; staminal filaments slightly flattened, slightly fleshy, with short hairs below anthers ventrally, back of connective glabrous................ *Hartleya inopinata* Sleumer (not treated here)

4a. Petals up to 6 mm long, free almost to base; ovary tapering, with stigma at apex.............. *Stemonurus*

4b. Petals greater than 12 mm long, free in distal part only, tubular below; ovary distally inverted and cup-like, with small slightly bilobed stigma on inner edge.. .... *Whitmorea grandiflora* Sleumer (not treated here)

Stemonurus ammui (Kaneh.) Sleumer Fig. 411

Blumea Vol. 17: 260 (1969)
Timber Group: Occasional timber species

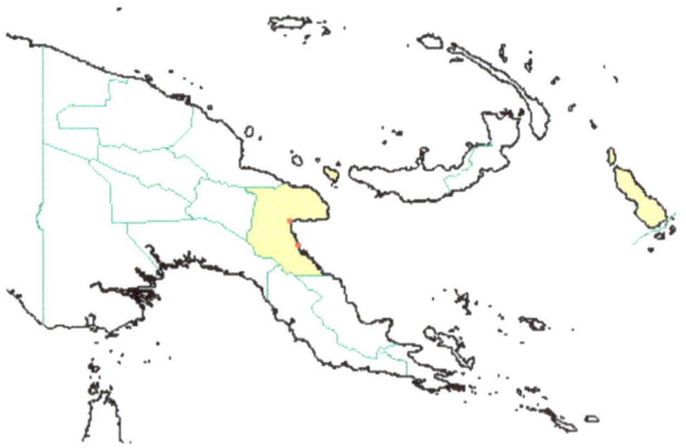

Field Characters: Canopy trees, 25–35 m high; bole cylindrical, 22–50 cm diam., straight, 20–25 m long; buttresses absent; spines absent; aerial roots absent; stilt roots absent. Bark pale grey or brown, rough, slightly scaly or flaky or pustular; lenticels elongated vertically; bark 10–32 mm thick; under-bark orange, brown, with green stripes, or yellow; faintly or non-aromatic; pleasant; blaze consisting of one layer, pale brown, orange, yellow, white, or mixed colours, speckled or with stripes dark red-brown, granular with splinters; exudate present, colourless, not readily flowing, not changing colour on exposure to air, not sticky. Terminal buds not enclosed by leaves.

Indumentum: Complex hairs present or absent; club-shaped on stamens of male flowers; stinging hairs absent; mature twig without hairs.

Leaves: Spaced along branches, leaves spiral, simple; petiole c. 15 mm long, not winged, attached to base of leaf lamina, not swollen; lamina broadest above middle or broadest at or near middle, (10–)12–19 cm long, 5–9.5 cm wide; base very asymmetric, margin entire, not dissected or lobed, apex acuminate or obtuse, venation pinnate, secondary veins open, not prominent, but visible, intramarginal veins absent; lower surface pale green, upper surface green or dark green, hairs absent, oil dots absent, domatia absent; stipules absent.

Flowers: Inflorescence axillary, flowers on a branched axis; flowers unisexual, with male and female flowers on different plants, flowers with pedicel, with many planes of symmetry, 0.7–1.5 mm long, small, c. 1 mm diam.; perianth present, with all sepals and/or petals (hence tepals) similar, yellow, red, or green; inner perianth 5, some or partly joined; stamens absent (female flowers, but staminodes present) or 5 (male flowers), filaments present, free of each other, free of perianth; ovary superior, carpels joined, locules 1; styles absent (male flowers) or free.

Fruits: arranged on branched axis, fruit 28–35 mm long, flattened, 15–25 mm diam., dark dull green, not spiny ridged, slightly fleshy, simple, indehiscent, drupe. Seed 1, 10–15 mm long, as wide as long flattened, 8–10 mm wide, not winged.

Distribution: Morobe.

Notes: This genus was previously placed in the family Icacinaceae.

Fig. 411. *Stemonurus ammui*. Leaves and flowers

89. Aquifoliaceae

Trees. Stipules present. Leaves well-developed, spiral, opposite, or whorled, simple, dissected or lobed, or not; margin entire; venation pinnate. Inflorescences axillary; Flowers unisexual, then plant dioecious, regular, with distinct calyx and corolla. Sepals 4–8. Petals 4–8, joined, at least in part; tube present. Stamens 4–8, free; filaments present; staminodes present in female flowers. Gynoecium with carpels at least partially joined, superior; styles partially or fully joined, 1, very small. Fruit simple, indehiscent, drupe or berry, fleshy. Seeds without wings.

PNG genera: ***Ilex***

References: Cuénoud *et al.* (2000)

Ilex archboldiana Merr. & L.M.Perry

Journal of the Arnold Arboretum Vol. 20: 333 (1939)
Timber Group: Occasional timber species

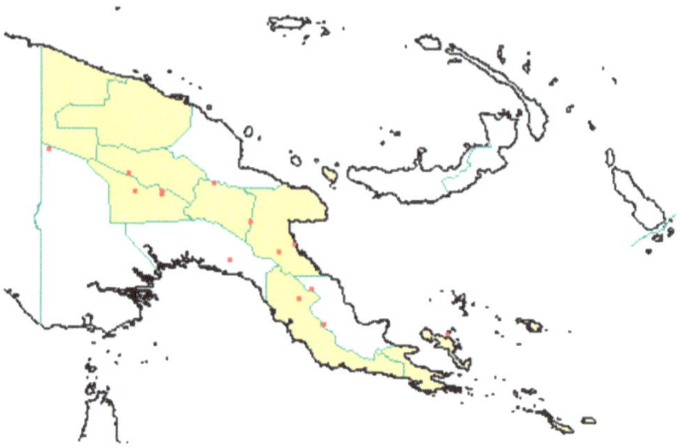

Field Characters: Canopy trees, 20–30 m high; bole cylindrical, 40–94 cm diam., straight, 15 m long; buttresses absent; spines absent; aerial roots absent; stilt roots absent. Bark grey or brown, slightly rough, pustular; lenticels irregular; bark 5 mm thick; under-bark green; faintly or non-aromatic; pleasant like freshly cut grass; blaze consisting of one layer, pale yellow cream-coloured or white, markings absent, granular without splinters; exudate present, colourless, not readily flowing, changing to green on exposure to air, slightly sticky. Terminal buds not enclosed by leaves.

Indumentum: Complex hairs absent; stinging hairs absent; mature twig without hairs.

Leaves: Spaced along branches, leaves spiral, simple; petiole 4–5 mm long, not winged, attached to base of leaf lamina, not swollen; lamina broadest above middle, 2–4.5 cm long, 1.2–3 cm wide; base symmetric, margin entire, often strongly recurved, not dissected or lobed, apex emarginate or retuse, venation pinnate, secondary veins open, not prominent, but visible, intramarginal veins absent; lower surface pale green, upper surface dark green, hairs absent, oil dots absent, domatia absent; stipules absent.

Flowers: Inflorescence axillary, flowers on a branched axis; flowers bisexual, with pedicel 1–2 mm long, with many planes of symmetry, 1.5 mm long, small, 1.5 mm diam.; perianth present, with distinct sepals and petals, white or slightly green; inner perianth 5, free; stamens 5, filaments present, free of each other, free of perianth; ovary superior, carpels joined, style absent, stigma sessile.

Fruits: arranged on branched axis, fruit 5–7 mm long, 5–6 mm diam., red, not spiny, fleshy, simple, indehiscent, berry.

Distribution: West Sepik, East Sepik, Morobe, Western Highlands, Eastern Highlands, Southern Highlands, Central, Milne Bay, Papuan Islands.

Ilex arnhemensis (F.Muell.) Loes.
Fig. 412

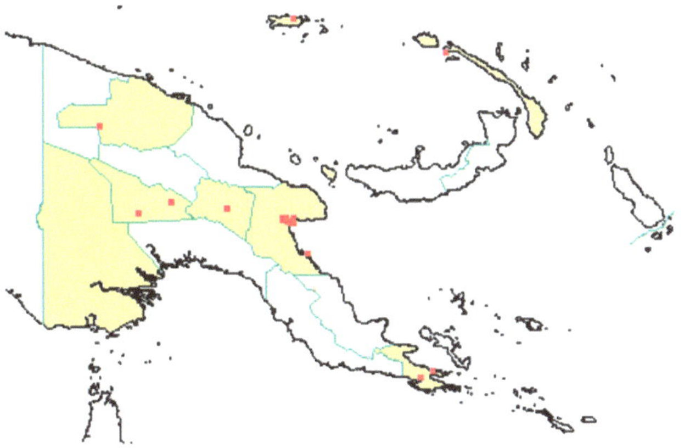

Vorstudien zu einer Monographie der Aquifoliaceen - Inaugural Dissertation (1890); *Naturlichen Pflanzenfamilien. Nachträge zum II bis IV Teil.* Vol. 1: 68 (1901).
Timber Group: Non-timber species

Field Characters: Subcanopy trees, up to 15 m high; bole cylindrical, up to 20 cm diam., crooked, up to 6 m long; buttresses present; spines present; aerial roots absent; stilt roots absent. Bark grey or brown, rough, pustular; lenticels elongated vertically; bark 5 mm thick; under-bark green or red; faintly or non-aromatic; blaze consisting of one layer, yellow or orange, speckled, granular without splinters; exudate present, colourless, not readily flowing, changing to orange or brown on exposure to air, not sticky. Terminal buds not enclosed by leaves.

Indumentum: Complex hairs absent; stinging hairs absent.

Leaves: Spaced along branches, leaves spiral, simple; petiole 5–10 mm long, not winged, attached to base of leaf lamina, not swollen; lamina broadest at or above middle 9–15.5 cm long, 4.5–8.5 cm wide; base symmetric, margin entire, not dissected or lobed, apex acuminate, venation pinnate, secondary veins open, prominent, intramarginal veins absent; lower surface pale green, upper surface dark green, hairs absent, oil dots absent, domatia absent; stipules absent.

Flowers: Inflorescence axillary, flowers on a branched axis; flowers unisexual, with male and female flowers on the same plant, flowers with pedicel 3–4 mm long, with many planes of symmetry; perianth present, with distinct sepals and petals; inner perianth 4 or 5, white, some or partly joined; stamens 8, filaments present, free of each other, free of perianth; ovary superior, carpels joined, locules 4–6; styles absent, stigma sessile.

Fruits: arranged on branched axis, fruits 10–12 mm long, yellow, green, not spiny, fleshy, simple, indehiscent, berry. Seeds many, 3–4 mm long, longer than broad, not winged.

Distribution: East Sepik, Morobe, Eastern Highlands, Southern Highlands, Western, Milne Bay.

Fig. 412. *Ilex arnhemensis*. Bark, leaves and fruit

Ilex ledermannii Loes.

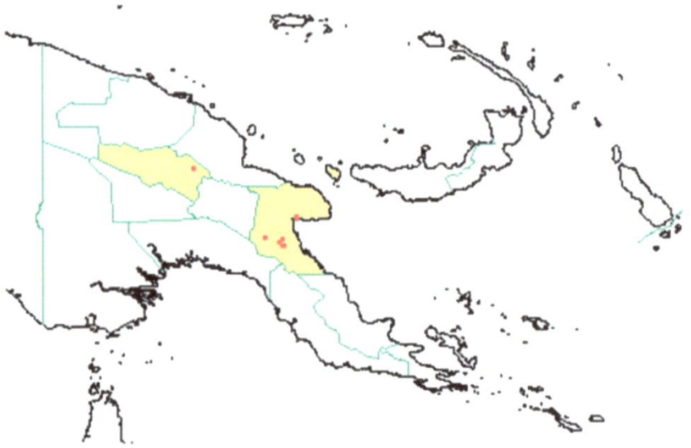

Botanische Jahrbücher für Systematik, Pflanzengeschichte und Pflanzengeographie Vol. 59: 81 (1924)
Timber Group: Occasional timber species

Field Characters: Canopy trees, up to 35 m high; bole cylindrical, 20–40 cm diam., straight, 10–15 m long; buttresses absent; spines absent; aerial roots absent; stilt roots absent. Bark grey, smooth or slightly rough, pustular; lenticels irregular, elongated vertically, or slightly rounded/swelling; bark 5–10 mm thick; under-bark red or green; strongly aromatic or faintly or non-aromatic; pleasant; blaze consisting of 2 layers; outer blaze pink, yellowish white, pale yellow (cream-coloured), pale orange, or pale brown, markings absent or strongly speckled pale brown, granular without splinters; inner blaze red, yellowish white, pale yellow (cream-coloured), or pale brown, markings absent or strongly speckled pale brown, fibrous or granular without splinters; exudate present, colourless, not readily flowing, changing to purple or dark green on exposure to air, not sticky. Terminal buds not enclosed by leaves.

Indumentum: Complex hairs absent; stinging hairs absent; mature twig without hairs simple hairs on axes of inflorescence.

Leaves: Spaced along branches, leaves spiral, simple; petiole present, not winged, attached to base of leaf lamina, not swollen; lamina broadest at or near middle, 7–12 cm long, 3.5–5.5 cm wide; base symmetric, margin entire, not dissected or lobed, apex acuminate, venation pinnate, secondary veins open, prominent, intramarginal veins absent; lower surface pale green, upper surface green glossy, hairs absent, oil dots absent, domatia absent; stipules absent.

Flowers: Inflorescence axillary, often flowers arising from a single point or flowers on a branched axis; flowers unisexual, with male and female flowers on different plants, flowers with pedicel, with many planes of symmetry, 6–7 mm long, small, 6–7 mm diam.; perianth present, with distinct sepals and petals, white; inner perianth 4 or 5, some or partly joined; stamens 8, filaments present, free of each other, free of perianth; ovary superior, carpels joined, locules 4–6; styles absent, stigma sessile.

Fruits: Often arising from a single point or arranged on branched axis, fruit c. 10 mm long, dark red, not spiny, fleshy, simple, indehiscent, berry or drupe. Seeds 3–6, to about 5 mm long, as wide as long, c. 5 mm diam., not winged.

Distribution: Morobe, Western Highlands, Western.

Asterales

PNG families: Alseuosmiaceae, **Asteraceae**, Campanulaceae, Goodeniaceae, Menyanthaceae, Pentaphragmataceae, **Rousseaceae**, Stylidiaceae

1a. Fruits a dehiscent capsule; seeds many; inflorescences with flowers arranged in branched, ± open axes, not in compact heads.. 89. Rousseaceae

1b. Fruits an indehiscent achene; seeds 1; inflorescences with flowers usually arranged in compact heads. .... 90. Asteraceae

90. Rousseaceae

Trees, shrubs, and lianas. Stipules absent. Leaves well-developed, whorled, spiral, or opposite, simple, not dissected or lobed; margin toothed; venation pinnate. Inflorescences axillary; Flowers bisexual, regular, with distinct calyx and corolla. Sepals 4–6. Petals 4–6, joined, at least in part; tube present. Stamens 4 or 5, free; filaments absent; staminodes absent. Gynoecium with carpels at least partially joined, partially inferior; styles partially or fully joined. Fruit simple, dehiscent, capsule, dry, at least non-fleshy. Seeds without wings.

PNG genera: ***Carpodetus***

Notes: The taxonomy of the genus *Carpodetus* in Papua New Guinea requires review. This genus has been previously classified in the Family Escalloniaceae or Grossulariaceae.

References: Reeder (1946)

Carpodetus arboreus (K.Schum. & Lauterb.) Schltr. Fig. 413

Botanische Jahrbücher für Systematik, Pflanzengeschichte und Pflanzengeographie Vol. 52: 136 (1914)
Timber Group: Non-timber species

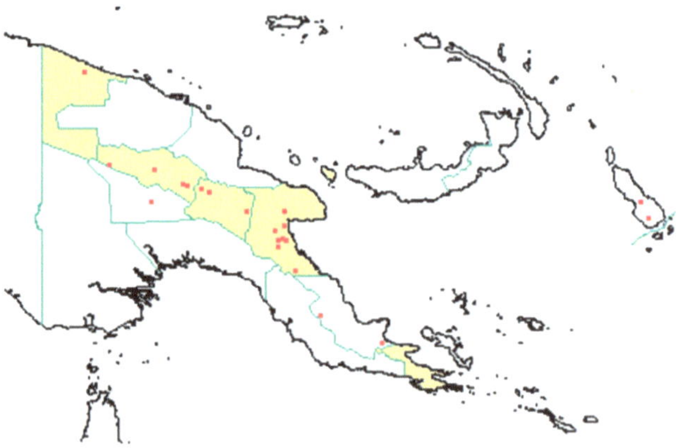

Field Characters: Canopy trees or subcanopy trees, 5–15(–30) m high; bole cylindrical, 20–45 cm diam., straight, 7–20 m long; buttresses usually up to c. 0.5 m high, or sometimes absent; spines absent; aerial roots absent; stilt roots absent. Bark brownish grey or brown, rough, pustular or slightly tessellated sometimes; lenticels elongated vertically or irregular; bark 3–5 mm thick; under-bark pale yellow or green; faintly or non-aromatic or strongly aromatic; faintly unpleasant or pleasant slightly fruity; blaze consisting of one layer, pale brown or pale orange, speckled, fibrous; exudate present, colourless, not readily flowing, changing to pale orange, pale brown, or grey on exposure to air, not sticky. Terminal buds not enclosed by leaves.

Indumentum: Complex hairs absent; stinging hairs absent; mature twig hairy or mature twig without hairs; somewhat hairs dense or sparse.

Leaves: Spaced along branches, leaves spiral, simple; petiole 9–25 mm long, not winged, attached to base of leaf lamina, not swollen; lamina sometimes broadest below middle or broadest at or near middle, 10–20 cm long, 5.5–11.5 cm wide; base symmetric, margin shortly serrate to dentate (toothed) or crenate, not dissected or lobed, apex acuminate, venation pinnate, secondary veins open, prominent, intramarginal veins absent; lower surface pale green, upper surface green or dark glossy green, hairs present or absent, somewhat dense or sparse, oil dots absent, domatia absent; stipules absent.

Flowers: Inflorescence axillary, flowers on a branched axis; flowers bisexual, pleasantly aromatic, shortly with pedicel up to 1 mm long, with many planes of symmetry, 1.5–2 mm long, small, c. 2 mm diam.; perianth present, with distinct sepals and petals (sepals minute), greenish white; inner perianth 4, free; stamens 4, filaments absent, free of each other, free of perianth; ovary partly inferior, carpels joined, locules 2–4; styles joined, 1.

Fruits: arranged on branched axis, fruit 6–10 mm long, 6–10 mm diam., brown, grey (when immature), or dark purple, not spiny, non-fleshy, simple, partly dehiscent, capsule. Seeds many, barely visible, c. 1.5 mm long, longer than wide, 0.5–1 mm diam., not winged.

Distribution: West Sepik, Madang, Morobe, Western Highlands, Eastern Highlands, Southern Highlands, Western, Central, Milne Bay, Bougainville.

Fig. 413. *Carpodetus arboreus.* Bark, leaves and developing fruit

Carpodetus major Schltr.
Fig. 414

Botanische Jahrbücher für Systematik, Pflanzengeschichte und Pflanzengeographie Vol. 52: 137 (1914)
Timber Group: Non-timber species

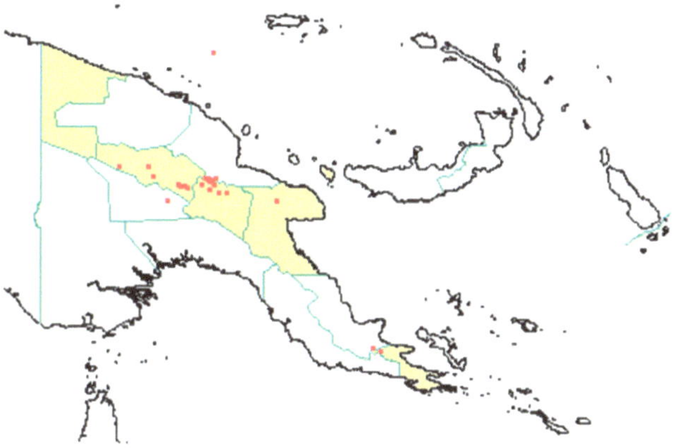

Field Characters: Subcanopy trees, up to 9 m high, often a large shrub, about 2 m high, occasionally recorded as a climber; bole cylindrical, 50–60 cm diam., slightly crooked or straight, 2–3 m long, often branching from near base; buttresses present or absent; spines absent; aerial roots absent; stilt roots absent. Bark grey or greyish brown, rough, pustular or slightly tessellated sometimes; lenticels elongated vertically; bark 3–5 mm thick; under-bark green; faintly or non-aromatic; blaze consisting of one layer, white or pale yellow cream-coloured, with stripes, fibrous; exudate present, colourless, not readily flowing, changing to pale orange or pale brown on exposure to air or not changing colour, not sticky. Terminal buds not enclosed by leaves.

Indumentum: Complex hairs absent; stinging hairs absent; mature twig without hairs.

Leaves: Spaced along branches, leaves spiral, simple; petiole 5–8 mm long, not winged, attached to base of leaf lamina, not swollen; lamina broadest at or near middle stiff, (5–)6.5–10 cm long, (2–)3.2–5 cm wide; base symmetric to very slightly asymmetric, margin finely serrate to dentate (toothed) often recurved, not dissected or lobed, apex sub-acute or acuminate, venation pinnate, secondary veins open, prominent, intramarginal veins absent; lower surface pale green, upper surface dark green or green, hairs absent (by misinterpretation) or present, somewhat dense or sparse hairs minute, appressed to leaf surface, reddish brown on lower surface, oil dots absent, domatia absent; stipules absent.

Flowers: Inflorescence axillary, flowers on a branched axis; flowers bisexual pleasantly aromatic, with pedicel 2–3 mm long, with many planes of symmetry, 6–8 mm long, small, 6–8 mm diam.; perianth present, with distinct sepals and petals sepals minute, pale brown, pale yellow or pale green; inner perianth 5, free; stamens 5, filaments absent, free of each other, free of perianth; ovary partly inferior, carpels joined, locules 4; styles joined, 1.

Fruits: arranged on branched axis, fruit 8–10 mm long, 8–10 mm diam., grey or brown, not spiny but rough, non-fleshy, simple, partly dehiscent, capsule. Seeds many, barely visible, 1.5–2 mm long, as wide as long, 1.5–2 mm diam., not winged.

Distribution: West Sepik, Milne Bay, Morobe, Western Highlands, Eastern Highlands.

Notes: The amount of morphological variation included in material identified as *C. major* suggests that other species may have been included in the concept of this species.

Fig. 414. *Carpodetus major.* Bark

91. Asteraceae

Trees, shrubs, lianas, and herbs. Stipules absent. Leaves well-developed, spiral or opposite, simple, dissected or lobed, or not; margin entire; venation pinnate. Inflorescences axillary or terminal. Bracts present, forming an involucre, 1 to several rows. Flowers bisexual or unisexual, then plant monoecious, zygomorphic or regular, with distinct calyx and corolla, when present, calyx modified as scales, bristles, barbs or horns or with sepals absent. Sepals absent or up to many. Petals 3–5, joined, at least in part; tube present. Stamens 5, fused; filaments present; staminodes absent. Gynoecium with carpels at least partially joined, inferior; styles partially or fully joined. Fruit simple, indehiscent, achene, with pappus persistent, dry, at least non-fleshy. Seeds without wings.

PNG genera: *Abrotanella, Acanthospermum, Achillea, Acmella, Adenostemma, Ageratum, Anaphalioides, Anaphalis, Antennaria, Argyranthemum, Arrhenechthites, Aster, Bedfordia, Bidens, Blumea, Bothriocline, Brachionostylum, Brachyscome, Bracteantha, Camptacra, Carpesium, Centipeda, Centratherum, Chromolaena, Conyza, Coreopsis, Cosmos, Cotula, Crassocephalum, Crepis, Dichrocephala, Dicoma, Eclipta, Elephantopus, Eleutheranthera, Emilia, Epaltes, Erechtites, Erigeron, Ethulia, Euchiton, Galinsoga, Glossocardia, Glossogyne, Gnaphalium, Gynura, Helianthus, Ischnea, Lactuca, Lagenophora, Leptinella, Microglossa, Mikania, Myriactis, Olearia, Papuacalia, Parthenium, Phacellothrix, Piora, Pluchea, Pterocaulon, Rhamphogyne, Senecio, Sigesbeckia, Solidago, Sonchus, Sphaeranthus, Sphaeromorphaea, Sphagneticola, Spilanthes, Struchium, Synedrella, Tagetes, Tanacetum, Tetramolopium, Tithonia, Tridax, Verbesina,* ***Vernonia****, Vittadinia, Wedelia, Wollastonia, Xanthium, Xerochrysum, Youngia, Zinnia*

References: Bremer (1994), Davies (1981), Koster (1966, 1970, 1972, 1975, 1976, 1979, 1980),Randeria (1960), Royen and Lloyd (1975)

Key to Tribes

1a. Heads with flowers all the same, all ligulate..Lactuceae

1b. Heads with flowers all the same or different; disc flowers tubular... 2

2a. Leaves alternate; anthers with a tail-like appendage at base (except *Phacellothrix*)..............................
.... Gnaphaleae, Inuleae, Plucheeae

2b. Leaves opposite or alternate; anthers arrow-shaped or obtuse at base, rarely with a short tail but then (in *Olearia*, tribe Astereae) trees or shrubs; lower surface of leaves with stalked irregularly stellate scale hairs, or with narrowly ellipsoid or T-shaped hairs; head with flowers different................................ 5

3a. Heads radiate, with marginal flowers ligulate..Inuleae

3b. Heads discoid or disc-like, with flowers all ± tubular... 4

4a. Heads with outer flowers often absent, or filiform or radiate when present, then female, yellow or purple to white; disc flowers bisexual or often functionally male; corolla yellow or purple, with erect lobes; cypselas often small, obloid or obovoid, with pappus free or joined, rarely of bristles or scales............
....Gnaphaleae

4b. Heads with outer flowers female, filiform, purple, pink, rarely yellow or whitish 3-lobed; disc flowers bisexual or usually functionally male, purple, or sometimes yellow or whitish, 4- or 5-lobed; cypselas ellipsoid, with pappus free, usually of bristles or scales .... Plucheeae

5a. Leaves mostly opposite; receptacle with chaffy scales..Heliantheae

5b. Leaves opposite or alternate; receptacle without hairs, or rarely with chaffy scales (in some of tribe Anthemideae), but then involucral bracts with scariose margin 6

6a. Leaves alternate; heads with flowers all the same, corolla tubular; anthers arrow-shaped at base, filaments attached higher than at base .... Vernonieae

6b. Leaves opposite or alternate; heads with flowers different or the same; anthers obtuse at base or rarely shortly tailed (in *Olearia*, tribe Astereae) 7

7a. Involucral bracts with margin scarious; style arms of marginal flowers truncate, with a terminal ring of hairs; pappus lacking or sometimes crown-like or consisting of 4 short prickles .... Anthemideae (including *Centipeda*)

7b. Involucral bracts withour scarious margin, or if scarious then style arms narrowly ovate; pappus lacking or consisting of scales, bristles, hairs or prickles 8

8a. Leaves opposite; heads with flowers all the same, with corolla tubular; style arms long, semi-cylindrical or short, club-shaped and obtuse; stigma consisting of 2 marginal, often short rows .... Eupatorieae

8b. Leaves alternate or opposite; heads with flowers different or all the same; style arms fairly short, flat with a narrowly ovate to linear apical appendage, densely hairy on outer surface, or short and truncate with a rin of hairs at apex, sometimes with an apical appendage above ring of hairs 9

9a. Style arms with a narrowly ovate apical appendage, densely hairy on outer surface................ Astereae

9b. Style arms truncate with a ring of hairs at apex, sometimes with an apical appendage above ring of hairs 10

10a. Leaves alternate; pappus of fine fringed hairs..Senecioneae

10b. Leaves opposite, pinnate; pappus of 3–6 scales .... Helenieae

Tribe Anthemideae

(not treated here)

1a. Tall or small herbs; marginal flowers with ligulate corolla 2

1b. Small herbs; marginal flowers with tubular corolla 3

2a. Leaves 2- or 3-pinnatipartite; heads radiate; ligule of corolla (of marginal flowers) short, broad, obtusely 3-toothed; corolla tube dorsally compressed; weed ....*Achillea millefolium* L.

2b. Leaves entire or dissected; head not radiate; corolla of marginal flowers short, tubular; corolla tube of disc flowers 4-toothed.. 3

3a. Corolla of marginal flowers very short, 2- or 3-toothed; cypselas angular; corolla tube of disc flowers very short, bell-shaped, widely spreading; corolla lobe 4-partite; leaves toothed, not dissected............ ....*Centipeda minima* (L.) A.Br. & Ascher

3b. Corolla of marginal flowers very short; disc flowers with corolla 4-lobed, occasionally 3-lobed; cypselas compressed, often winged laterally; leaves dissected (except usually entire in *Cotula wilhelminensis* P.Royen) .... *Cotula*

Tribe Astereae
(not treated here)

1a. Pappus consisting of bristles 2

1b. Pappus absent 8

2a. Trees or shrubs; lower surface of leaves with T-shaped or narrowly ellipsoid hairs, or with irregularly stellate scale-like hairs; anthers shortly arrow-shaped, often with short tail at base .... *Olearia*

2b. Shrubs or herbs; leaves without hairs, or variously hairy on lower surface, if hairs present, then not as above 3

3a. Corolla of marginal flowers filiform, tubular 4

3b. Corolla of marginal flowers ligulate 5

4a. Heads in branched panicle; annual or perennial herbs, sometimes shrubs; cypselas with pappus of many fine, mostly fragile bristles .... *Conzya*

4b. Heads solitary; annual herb; cypselas with pappus of scabrid bristles .... *Phacellothrix cladochaeta* (F.Muell.) F.Muell.

5a. Flowers arranged in a corymb-like inflorescence 6

5b. Flowers arranged in solitary heads 7

6a. Shrubs or large herbs; leaves with petiole; style arms of disc flowers flat, triangular and acute at apex; cypselas angular .... *Microglossa pyrifolia* Kuntze

6b. Herbs; leaves sessile; style arms of disc flowers flat, with a narrowly ovate apex; cypselas 4-angular, laterally compressed .... *Erigeron*

7a. Shrubs or sub-shrubs, often with ericoid appearance; cypselas with 2–4 ribs .... *Tetramolopium*

7b. Herbs; cypselas with 6 or 7 ribs; weed .... *Vittadinia brachycomoides* (F.Muell.) Benth.

8a. Anthers 5; corolla of disc flowers 5-lobed 9

8b. Anthers 4; corolla of disc flowers 4-lobed 10

9a. Involucral bracts herbaceous, with margin clear; cypselas beaked .... *Lagenophora*

9b. Involucral bracts with margin scariose; cypselas without beak .... *Brachyscome*

10a. Flowers arranged in very small heads; heads arranged in branched panicles; corolla of marginal flowers tubular; receptacle hemispherical .... *Dichrocephala*

10b. Flowers arranged in solitary heads; heads small or moderately large; corolla of marginal flowers ligulate or tubular; receptacle flat or convex 11

11a. Corolla of marginal flowers tubular; receptacle flat; heads small .... *Rhamphogyne papuana* Koster

11b. Corolla of marginal flowers ligulate; receptacle flat or convex; heads small or moderately large 12

12a. Shrubs; anthers sub-obtuse at apex, without an apical appendage; cypselas truncate at apex................ .... *Piora ericoides* J.Kost.

12b. Small shrubs or herbs; anthers with a short apical appendage; cypselas with a beak or apical rim.... 13

13a. Small shrubs or low herbs, often with rhizome present; leaves forming a rosette, or crowded or rosette-like at top of stem and branches; heads terminal on scape-like peduncle........................... *Lagenophora*

13b. Herbs; leaves dispersed along stem, sometimes crowded on lower parts; heads terminal on stem and branches .... *Myriactis*

Tribe Eupatorieae
(not treated here)

1a. Involucral bracts in 2 whorls, leaf-like, more or less equal, more or less joined at base; corolla small, tubular, 3–5-partite; anthers without apical appendage; pappus few, club-shaped, bristles absent, joined by a ring at base, glandular on thickened upper-part ....*Adenostemma*

1b. Involucral bracts in 1–many whorls; corolla tubular, funnel-shaped or distally bell-shaped, 5-partite or with 5 lobes; anthers with apical appendage; pappus of bristles or of chaffy scales; bristles 5-merous, slender or narrowly ovate to subulate 2

2a. Climbing herbs or shrubs; heads with 4 flowers; involucre obloid, with bracts in 2 whorls; bracts 4, more or less equal, usually with 1 minute bract at base of involucre; pappus of slender bristles, scabrous...... .... *Mikania*

2b. Erect herbs; heads consisting of many flowers; involucre with bracts in 2 or 3 whorls; bracts overlapping; pappus of chaffy, narrowly ovate to subulate bristles; weed.............................. *Ageratum conyzoides* L.

Tribe Helenieae
(not treated here)

One introduced species, strongly aromatic weed *Tagetes minuta* L.

Tribe Heliantheae
(not treated here)

1a. Leaves alternate; heads unisexual, 2-flowered, with flowers all the same, female flowers in axils of lower leaves; inner bracts of the involucre joined into a 2-loculate body provided with hooks or spines; corolla absent; cypselas enclosed in involucre; male heads terminal and in axils of distal leaves, many-flowered, with cypselas rudimentary; plants monoecious...*Xanthium pungens* Wallr.

1b. Leaves alternate or opposite; heads with flowers different or all the same; inner bracts of the involucre not joined; marginal flowers female or sterile or absent; corolla present; disc flowers bisexual........... 2

2a. Leaves opposite; heads small, sessile or on short peduncles, solitary in axils of leaves and branches; inner bracts of the involucre closely covering the cypselas of the marginal flowers, becoming enlarged in fruit...*Acanthospermum hispidium* DC.

2b. Leaves alternate or opposite; inner bracts of involucre not closely covering cypselas, and not enlarged in fruit 3

3a. Cypsela apex with 2–8 retrorsely hispid awns (forming a crown); pappus absent 4

3b. Cypsela apex not crowned hispid awns; pappus present or absent 7

4a. Cypsela orbicular, dorsally compressed; garden escape .... *Coreopsis tinctpria* Nutt.

4b. Cypsela linear, to narrowly obloid, narrowly ellipsoid, or cuneate, compressed or 3- or 4-lobed 5

5a. Basal leaves dense, with few leaves on stem, alternate or opposite; involucral bracts narrowly ovate; marginal flowers female .... *Glossogyne tenuifolia* (Labill.) Cass. ex Less.

5b. Leaves opposite, distal leaves sometimes alternate; outer bracts of involucre often leaf-like or herbaceous, inner bracts with margin membranous; marginal flowers sterile or absent, rarely female 6

6a. Cypselas linear, narrowly ellipsoid, more or less 4-angled, compressed, with long hispid beak distally .... *Cosmos caudatus* Kunth

6b. Cypselas gradually longer to central part of head, obovoid-obloid, or cuneate or linear, often narrowed in upper part but not beaked .... *Bidens*

7a. Pappus of scales or of many plumose, long hairs 8

7b. Pappus absent or of 1–3 hairs, needles or awns 12

8a. Pappus of many, plumose, long hairs; weed .... *Tridax procumbens* L.

8b. Pappus of scales, sometimes with 2 narrowly ovate awns 9

9a. Pappus of 5–10 scales, with margin fringed, with 2 narrowly ovate awns; introduced .... *Tithonia diversifolia* (Hemsley) A.Gray

9b. Pappus of scales without 2 narrowly ovate awns 10

10a. Cypsela obovoid, thick, rounded at apex; pappus cup-shaped, short, consisting of joined fringed scales; weed .... *Eleutheranthera ruderalis* (Swartz) Schultz.-Bip.

10b. Cypselas turbinate or obloid-obconical; pappus not cup-shaped 11

11a. Pappus with scales narrowly obovoid, long; weed .... *Galinsoga parviflora* Cavanilles

11b. Pappus with scales subdeltoid, short .... *Wedelia*

12a. Cypselas derived from marginal flowers with 2 wings along margin and 2 awns at apex 13

12b. Cypselas without marginal wings 14

13a. Wings of cypselas laciniate (with teeth rigid, flattened and acute); introduced .... *Synedrella nodiflora* (L.) Gaertner

13b. Wings of cypselas not laciniate; introduced .... *Verbesina alata* L.

14a. Cypselas with an irregular, toothed rim at apex .... *Eclipta prostrata* (L.) L.

14b. Cypselas without an irregular, toothed rim at apex 15

15a. Involucral bracts 5, with patent glandular hairs .... *Sigesbeckia orientalis* L.

15b. Involucral bracts in 1–many whorls, without patent glandular hairs 16

16a. Outer bracts of involucre leaf-like .... *Spilanthes*

16b. Outer bracts of involucre not leaf-like 17

17a. Involucral bracts in 2 or 3 whorls, with apex of bracts acute or obtuse .... *Wedelia*

17b. Involucral bracts in 3–many whorls, imbricate, scaly, with apex of bracts rounded and erose; introduced, garden escape .... *Zinnia*

Tribes Gnaphalieae, Inuleae, Plucheeae
(not treated here)

1a. Leaves decurrent (extending down and joined to stem); heads small, densely clustered into glomerules 2

1b. Leaves not decurrent; head solitary or a few clustered together, variously arranged, but not in glomerules 3

2a. Pappus of bristles (Plucheeae) .... *Pterocaulon*

2b. Pappus absent; weed (Plucheeae) .... *Sphaeranthus africanus* L.

3a. Heads small, many, disc-shaped; pappus absent 4

3b. Heads large; pappus present 5

4a. Outer bracts of involucre scariose; cypselas obloid (Plucheeae) .... *Epaltes australis* Less.

4b. Outer bracts of involucre leaf-like or with herbaceous aooendages; cypselas narrowly gourd-shaped and beaked (Inuleae) .... *Carpesium cernuum* L.

5a. Involucre 18–25 mm long; bracts orange-yellow, becoming yellow-brown, glossy; heads large (Gnaphalieae) .... *Xerochrysum bracteolatum* (Vent.) Tzveley

5b. Involucre much shorter then 18 mm long; bracts variously coloured but not yellow 6

6a. Whitish, woolly herbs; involucral bracts rigid, membranous, glossy to sub-glossy, whitish or pale brown 7

6b. Herbs, not whitish; involucral bracts herbaceous or membranous, not whitish or pale brown 8

7a. Heads forming dense corymb-like inflorescences, with a short peduncle; female marginal flowers often many, sometimes absent; disc flowers often male, sometimes bisexual, 1–50; exclusively male heads frequently present (Gnaphalieae) .... *Anaphalis*

7b. Heads clustered or solitary, sessile or sub-sessile; female marginal flowers many; disc flowers bisexual, 1–7; exclusively male flowers absent (Gnaphalieae) .... *Gnaphalium*

8a. Disc flowers few; male flowers with style undevided or shortly 2-armed, and ovary rudimentary (Plucheeae) .... *Pluchea*

8b. Disc flowers few or many, bisexual, with style arms moderately long, ovary developed (Inuleae) .... *Blumea*

Tribe Lactuceae
(not treated here)

1a. Leaves alternate; involucre bell-shaped or ovoid, with involucral bracts imbricate, in many whorls; cypselas narrowly obloid or obovoid, narrowed at both ends, laterally compressed, 10–20-ribbed; hairs of pappus more or less joined at base .... *Sonchus*

1b. Leaves clustered in rosette at base, or rosette and alternate; involucre cylindrical; involucral bracts in a few whorls, imbricate or inner bracts sub-equal and outer ones imbricate and much smaller; cypselas obloid-ellipsoid or linear and beaked, or obloid gourd-shaped and gradually tapering at apex, much compressed, with 1–5 ribs on each side; hairs of pappus not joined at base, inserted in a disk at apex of cypsela 2

2a. Cypselas obloid-ellipsoid .... *Youngia japonica* (L.) DC.

2b. Cypselas ellipsoid or linear and beaked, or narrowly obloid gourd-shaped and gradually tapering at apex .... *Lactuca*

Tribe Senecioneae
(not treated here)

1a. Heads with flowers different 2

1b. Heads with all flowers the same, discoid, many-flowered; disc flowers bisexual 3

2a. Disc flowers female, abortive; cypselas with pappus of many, fine, deciduous bristles .... *Brachionostylum*

2b. Disc flowers bisexual or functionally male; corolla of marginal flowers tubular, female; 4-lobed; cypselas with pappus absent or cypselas crowned with a small rim or with 4 teeth; cushion-like plants in alpine grasslands .... *Abrotanella papuana* S.Moore

3a. Peduncles with 1 or more small linear bracts; style-arms long, acute with a subulate short appendage. .... *Gynura brassii* F.G.Davies

3b. Peduncles without bracts, or rarely with 1 minute filiform bract; style-arms short, acute or obtuse, or truncate with a subulate appendage 4

4a. Inner bracts of involucre in 1 or 2 whorls, equal, cohering, outer bracts much shorter, free; style-arms filiform, with truncate, penicillate apex with a subulate appendage .... *Crassocephalum crepidioides* (Benth.) S.Moore

4b. Bracts of involucre in 1 whorl, or sometimes with a few shorter ones; style-arms acute or obtuse, triangular and penicillate at apex, or truncate.. 5

5a. Involucre without calyx-like bracts; style-arms acute or obtuse, triangular and penicillate at apex... *Emilia*

5b. Involucre sometimes with a few much short bracts; style-arms truncate at apex................................ 6

6a. Heads radiate.. *Senecio*

6b. Heads discoid.. 7

7a. Heads many-flowered; disc flowers many, fertile; introduced.. *Erechtites*

7b. Heads few-flowered; disc flowers solitary or few, sterile, abortive................................. *Arrhenechthites*

Tribe Vernonieae

1a. Cypselas without a pappus.. *Ethulia conyzoides* L.f. ex L. (not treated here)

1b. Cypselas with pappus 2

2a. Anthers 3; pappus of 3 scales, very thick, white, later joined to form a cup-shaped pappus... *Struchium sparganophorum* (L.) Kuntze (not treated here)

2b. Anthers 5; pappus with bristles or consisting of thin, flat scales, never joined to form a cup-shaped pappus.. 3

3a. Heads clustered in great numbers, each cluster surrounded by leaf-like bracts; herb, weeds... *Elephantopus* (not treated here)

3b. Heads arranged in branched panicles or solitary; herbs, shrubs or trees................................. *Vernonia*

Vernonia arborea Buch.-Ham.
Fig. 415

Transactions of the Linnean Society. Botany Vol. 14: 218 (1824)
Timber Group: Non-timber species

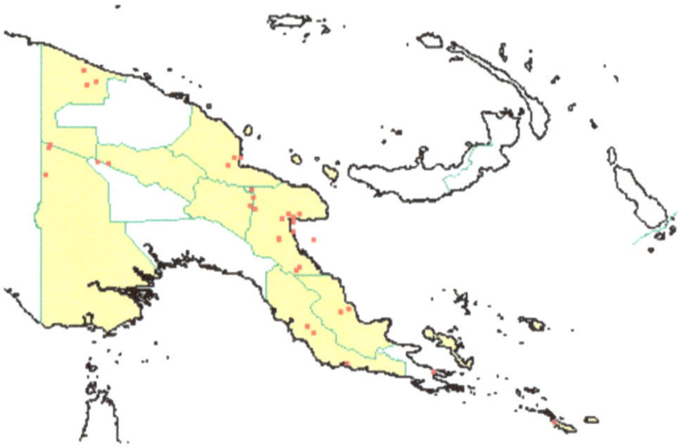

Field Characters: Subcanopy trees, up to 25 m high; bole cylindrical, up to c. 25 cm diam., straight, up to c. 12 m long; buttresses absent; spines absent; aerial roots absent; stilt roots absent. Bark pale brown, rough, slightly pustular to prominently ridged, furrowed cork, or finely cracked; lenticels irregular; bark 5–9 mm thick; under-bark green, yellowish brown, or yellow; strongly aromatic; unpleasant; blaze consisting of one layer, yellow, markings absent or speckled, slightly fibrous, granular without splinters, or granular with splinters; exudate present, colourless, not readily flowing, changing to dark brown or greenish black on exposure to air, not sticky or slightly sticky. Terminal buds not enclosed by leaves.

Indumentum: Complex hairs absent; stinging hairs absent; mature twig hairy (indumentum silky); hairs dense.

Leaves: Spaced along branches, leaves spiral, simple; petiole present, not winged, attached to base of leaf lamina, not swollen; lamina broadest below middle, 4–16.5 cm long, 2.5–6 cm wide; base symmetric to slightly asymmetric, margin entire, not dissected or lobed, apex acute, venation pinnate, secondary veins open, prominent, intramarginal veins absent; lower surface whitish green, upper surface green (rough to touch), hairs present, sparse (hairy on both surfaces, but denser on lower surface) or dense, oil dots absent, domatia absent; stipules absent.

Flowers: Inflorescence terminal, flowers on a branched axis (flower heads arranged in a panicle) or flowers arising from a single point (head); flowers bisexual, not stalked, with many planes of symmetry, 4–5 mm long, small, 3–4 mm diam.; perianth present, with distinct sepals and petals, white or pale purple to lavender on lobes (pappus off-white); inner perianth 5, some or partly joined; stamens many, filaments present, joined, free of perianth; ovary inferior, carpels joined, locules 1; styles joined, 1.

Fruits: Arising from a single point (head) or arranged on branched axis (fruiting heads arranged in a panicle), fruit 3–5 mm long, 1–1.5 mm diam., dark brown, not spiny, non-fleshy, simple, indehiscent, achene (cypsela). Seed 1, barely visible (to 1 mm long), longer than wide, < 1 mm diam., not winged (but single-seeded fruit with white pappus).

Distribution: West Sepik, Madang, Morobe, Western Highlands, Eastern Highlands, Western, Central, Northern, Milne Bay, Papuan Islands.

Fig. 415. *Vernonia arborea*. Bark, flowers and leaves

Escalloniales

92. Escalloniaceae

Trees, shrubs, and lianas. Stipules absent. Leaves well-developed, spiral, opposite, or whorled, simple, not dissected or lobed; margin entire or toothed; venation pinnate. Inflorescences axillary; Flowers bisexual, regular, with distinct calyx and corolla. Sepals (4 or)5(or 6). Petals (4 or)5(or 6), rarely joined, at least in part or free; tube absent or rarely present. Stamens (4 or)5(or 6), free; filaments present; staminodes absent. Gynoecium with carpels at least partially joined or rarely with more than one free carpel, inferior, superior, or partially inferior; styles free. Fruit simple, dehiscent or usually indehiscent, capsule, drupe, fleshy. Seeds without wings.

PNG genera: *Polyosma*

Notes: *Polyosma* has previously been placed in the Cunoniaceae, Grossulariaceae, Polyosmaceae and Saxifragaceae.

References: APG (2003), Francis (1970), Takeuchi (2007)

Polyosma forbesii Valeton ex Lauterb. Fig. 416

Nova Guinea Vol. 8: 821 (1912)
Timber Group: Non-timber species

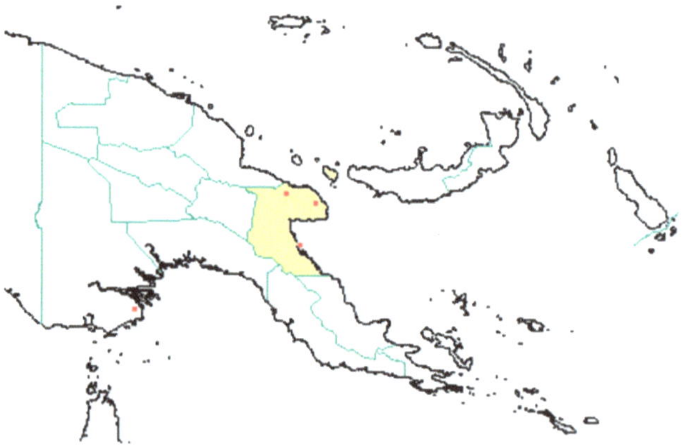

Field Characters: Subcanopy trees, 10–15 m high; bole cylindrical, 10–15 cm diam., straight, up to 10 m long; buttresses up to 0.4 m high, or absent; spines absent; aerial roots absent; stilt roots absent. Bark pale brown, rough, strongly fissured with fissures broad; bark 4–6 mm thick; under-bark dark red; faintly or non-aromatic or strongly aromatic; unpleasant; blaze consisting of one layer, dark red or pale black, markings absent, fibrous, often only slightly so; exudate present, colourless, not readily flowing, not changing colour on exposure to air, not sticky. Terminal buds not enclosed by leaves.

Indumentum: Complex hairs absent; stinging hairs absent; mature twig without hairs.

Leaves: Clustered at end of branches or less often spaced along branches, leaves opposite, simple; petiole 12–18 mm long, not winged, attached to base of leaf lamina, not swollen; lamina broadest above middle or broadest at or near middle, 15–20 cm long, 5–7 cm wide; base symmetric, margin entire, not dissected or lobed, apex slightly acuminate, venation pinnate, secondary veins open, prominent, intramarginal veins absent; lower surface dull green, upper surface green, hairs absent on upper surface or present lower surface, dense, oil dots absent, domatia absent; stipules absent.

Flowers: Inflorescence axillary, in distal leaf axils, flowers on an unbranched axis; flowers bisexual, with pedicel, with many planes of symmetry, 10 mm long, small, 3–5 mm diam.; perianth present densely hairy (at least in bud), with distinct sepals and petals, with the latter narrow, white or pale yellow; inner perianth 4, some or partly joined; stamens 4, filaments present, free of each other, free of perianth; ovary inferior, carpels joined, locules 2; styles joined, 1.

Fruits: arranged on unbranched axis, fruit 10–12 mm long, 6–8 mm diam., green or red maroon, not spiny hairy with off-white hairs, fleshy, simple, indehiscent, drupe. Seed 1, to 5–6 mm long, as wide as long, 4–5 mm diam., not winged.

Distribution: Morobe.

Fig. 416. *Polyosma forbesii*. Habit, bark, flower buds, leaves, flowers and developing fruit

Polyosma integrifolia Blume
Fig. 417

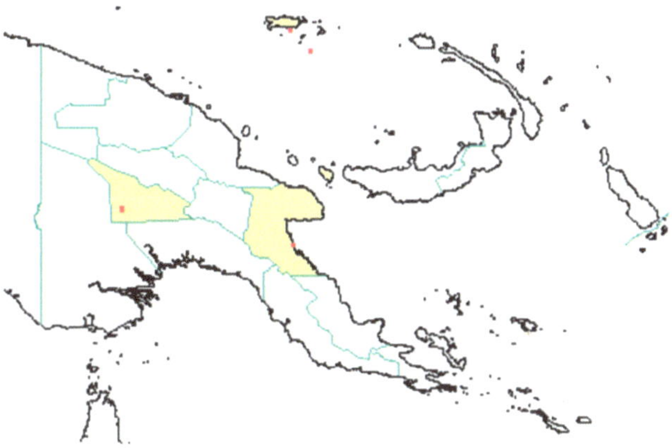

Bijdragen tot de Flora van Nederlandsch Indie Vol. 13: 659 (1826)

Timber Group: Non-timber species

Field Characters: Subcanopy trees, 5–15 m high; bole cylindrical, 10–20 cm diam., straight, up to about 5 m long, or slightly crooked; buttresses absent; spines absent; aerial roots absent; stilt roots absent. Bark grey or brown, rough; bark <25 mm thick; under-bark green. Terminal buds not enclosed by leaves.

Indumentum: Complex hairs absent; stinging hairs absent; mature twig without hairs.

Leaves: Spaced along branches, leaves opposite, simple; petiole 10–25 mm long, not winged, attached to base of leaf lamina, not swollen; lamina broadest at or near middle, (4–)5–18 cm long, 1.5–5(–8) cm wide; base symmetric, margin serrate to dentate (toothed), not dissected or lobed, apex acuminate, venation pinnate, secondary veins open, prominent, intramarginal veins present; lower surface green or pale green, upper surface green, hairs absent, oil dots absent, domatia absent; stipules absent.

Flowers: Inflorescence axillary, flowers on an unbranched axis; flowers bisexual, with pedicel, with many planes of symmetry, 5–8 mm long, small, c. 5 mm diam.; perianth present, with distinct sepals and petals, white or cream-coloured; inner perianth 4, some or partly joined to form a corolla tube; stamens 4 (slightly shorter than petals), filaments present, free of each other; ovary inferior, carpels joined, locules 1; styles joined, 1.

Fruits: arranged on unbranched axis, fruit 5–7(–10) mm long, 3–4 mm diam., purple (mature), green (immature), or blue, not spiny, fleshy, simple, indehiscent, drupe. Seed 1, not winged.

Distribution: East Sepik, Madang, Morobe, Southern Highlands, Western, Northern, Manus.

Fig. 417. *Polyosma integrifolia*. Bark, flower buds, leaves and flowers

Apiales

PNG families: Apiaceae, **Araliaceae**, Myodocarpaceae, **Pittosporaceae**

1a. Ovary superior; stipules absent .... 92. Pittosporaceae

1b. Ovary inferior; stipules present or absent 2

2a. Herbs or small shrubs; flower with disc usually swelling at base of style on fruit; in herbs, petiole often expanded and sheathing at base .... Apiaceae (not treated here)

2b. Trees, shrubs, herbs, rarely climbers or scramblers; flower with disc usually not swollen on fruit; petiole not expanded nor sheathing .... 93. Araliaceae

2c. Trees, usually unbranched; flowers with small, low nectar disc, not swollen in fruit; fruit with large secretory oil ducts in exocarp; petiole sheathing base, with margin membranous or scarious .... Myodocarpaceae (not treated here)

93. Pittosporaceae

Trees, shrubs, and lianas. Stipules absent. Leaves well-developed, spiral or whorled, simple, not dissected or lobed; margin entire; venation pinnate. Inflorescences axillary or terminal; Flowers bisexual, regular, with distinct calyx and corolla. Sepals 5. Petals 5, joined, at least in part or free; tube absent or present. Stamens 5, free or fused; filaments present; staminodes absent. Gynoecium with carpels at least partially joined, superior; styles partially or fully joined. Fruit simple, dehiscent or indehiscent, capsule, berry, dry, at least non-fleshy or fleshy. Seeds without wings, rarely with wings.

PNG genera: *Citriobatus, Hymenosporum,* ***Pittosporum***

References: Bakker and Steenis (1957), Schodde (1972), Steenis (1972a, 1976)

1a. Prickly shrub; fruit a berry, indehiscent; flowers solitary, axillary on very short shoots .... *Citriobatus papuanus* Schodde (not treated here)

1b. Trees or shrubs, without spines; fruit a dehiscent capsule; flowers in cymes or corymbs 2

2a. Corolla up to 15 mm long, glabrous or hairy, cream-coloured, white, purple or purple-red; seeds not winged .... *Pittosporum*

2b. Corolla 30–40 mm long, hairy, yellow; seeds winged .... *Hymenosporum flavum* (Hook.) F.Muell. (not treated here)

Pittosporum ramiflorum Zoll. ex Miq. Fig. 418

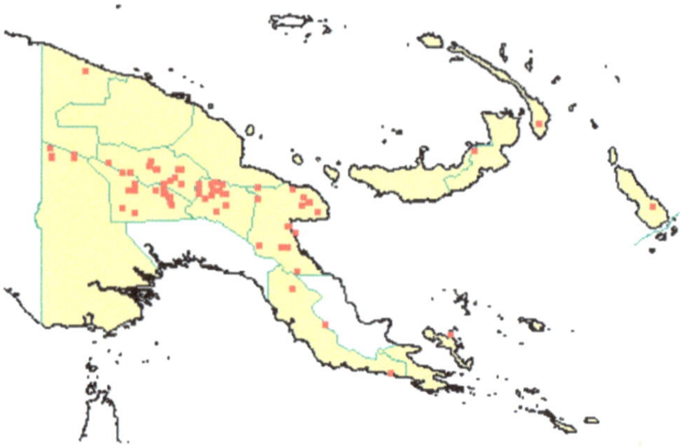

Flora van Nederlandsch Indie Vol. 2: 122 (1859)
Timber Group: Non-timber species

Field Characters: Canopy trees, 15–20 m high; bole cylindrical, 10 cm diam., straight, 8–12 m long; buttresses absent; spines absent; aerial roots absent; stilt roots absent. Bark dark brown or black, rough, slightly fissured or pustular; lenticels irregular; bark 5 mm thick; under-bark white or pale yellow cream-coloured; strongly aromatic; unpleasant; blaze consisting of 2 layers; outer blaze yellow or orange, markings absent, granular without splinters; inner blaze pale yellow or orange cream-coloured but slightly darker than outer blaze, markings absent, fibrous; exudate present, colourless, flowing, changing to black or dark green on exposure to air, sticky. Terminal buds not enclosed by leaves.

Indumentum: Complex hairs absent; stinging hairs absent; mature twig without hairs.

Leaves: Spaced along branches, leaves spiral, simple; petiole 13–20 mm long, not winged, attached to base of leaf lamina, not swollen; lamina broadest above middle or broadest at or near middle, 7.5–9.5 cm long, 4–5 cm wide; base symmetric, margin entire, not dissected or lobed, apex mucronate, venation pinnate, secondary veins open, not prominent, but visible, intramarginal veins absent; lower surface pale green, upper surface green, hairs absent, oil dots absent, domatia absent; stipules absent.

Flowers: Inflorescence leaf-opposed or axillary, flowers on a branched axis, with pedicel, bisexual, with many planes of symmetry, c. 4 mm long, c. 4 mm diam.; perianth present, with distinct sepals and petals, white or cream-coloured; inner perianth 5, some or partly joined to form a corolla tube; stamens 5 (slightly shorter than petals), filaments present, free of each other; ovary inferior, carpels joined, locules 1; styles joined, 1

Fruits: arranged on branched axis, fruit 10–16 mm long, 8–13 mm diam., purple (mature) or dull orange, not spiny, fleshy, simple, dehiscent, capsule. Seed 1, dark red, 8–10 mm long, longer than wide, c. 7 mm diam., not winged.

Distribution: West Sepik, East Sepik, Madang, Morobe, Western Highlands, Eastern Highlands, Southern Highlands, Western, Central, Milne Bay, Papuan Islands, New Britain, New Ireland, Bougainville.

Fig. 418. *Pittosporum ramiflorum*. Fruit, seeds and leaves

94. Araliaceae

Trees, shrubs, lianas, and herbs. Stipules absent or present. Leaves well-developed, spiral, simple or compound, pinnate, palmate, or trifoliate, dissected or lobed or not dissected or lobed; margin entire; venation pinnate or palmate. Inflorescences axillary or terminal; Flowers bisexual or unisexual (then plant monoecious or dioecious),regular, with sepals absent or with distinct calyx and corolla. Sepals 3–5(–12). Petals (3–)5(–12), free or rarely joined, at least in part; tube rarely present. Stamens (3–)5(–12 or more), free; staminodes absent. Gynoecium with more than one free carpel 2–5(–many), rarely superior or inferior; styles free. Fruit simple, indehiscent, drupe or berry, dry, at least non-fleshy, or fleshy. Seeds without wings.

PNG genera: *Anakasia, Anethum, Apium, Aralia, Centella, Ciclospermum, Coriandrum, Daucus, Eryngium,Foeniculum, Harmsiopanax, Hydrocotyle, Mackinlaya, Meryta, Oenanthe, Oreomyrrhis,* ***Osmoxylon****, Petroselinum,* ***Polyscias****, Sanicula, Schefflera, Strobilopanax, Tetraplasandra, Trachymene, Trachyspermum*

Notes: *Delarbrea* was previously included in the Araliaceae (Lowry 1986) but is now classified as part of the Myodocarpaceae.

References: Buwalda (1949, 1951), Cerceau-Larrival (1964), Conn and Frodin (1995), Frodin (1975), Henwood and Hart (2001), Mathias and Constance (1955, 1977), Philipson (1980), Shan and Constance

1a. Herbs..subfamily Hydrocotyloideae (not treated here)

1b. Trees and shrubs..subfamily Aralioideae

Key to subfamily Hydrocotyloideae (not treated here)

1a. Flowers in simple umbels or heads often united in more complex inflorescences, but not in compound umbels.. 2

1b. Flowers arranged in compound umbels which are sometimes united into more complex inflorescences.. 7

2a. Leaves and involucre with prickles; flowers arranged in heads .... *Eryngium*

2b. Leaves and involucre not prickly; flowers in umbels.. 3

3a. Fruits with hooked bristles ....*Sanicula europaea* L.

3b. Fruits without hooked bristles 4

4a. Fruits at least 2X as long as broad, generally not laterally flattened..................................*Oreomyrrhis*

4b. Fruit not longer than broad, laterally flattened 5

5a. Mericarps with 7–9 ribs, with connecting veins between the ribs; leaves simple, shallowly lobed, kidney-shaped ....*Centella asiatica* (L.) Urb.

5b. Mericarps with 3 ribs; leaves not as above.. 6

6a. Leaves with sheaths, with or without torn stipule-like appendages; corolla imbricate......... *Trachymene*

6b. Leaves without shealths; stipules distinct, entire, not torn; corolla valvate ....*Hydrocotyle*

7a. Mericarps winged on margin; leaves 3-pinnate, with ultimate segments almost filiform..................... ....*Anethum graveolens* L.

7b. Mericarp not winged at margin.. 8

8a. Fruits laterally flattened; leaves simple, more or less round ....*Hydrocotyle*

8b. Fruits not laterally flattened; leaves usually compound 9

9a. Calyx with distinct teeth.. 10

9b. Calyx teeth not distinct..11

10a. Mericarps hollow on ventral side, with primary ribs visible as wavy lines, secondary ribs slightly more prominent; flowers spreading (radiating) .... *Coriandrum sativum* L.

10b. Mericarps not hollow on ventral side, with marginal ribs thicker than lateral ribs, secondary ribs absent; flowers not radiating.. *Oenanthe javanica* DC.

11a. Ovary and fruits glabrous.. 12

11b. Ovary and fruits with bristly hairs, or with scale-like trichomes 15

12a. Flowers yellow or yellow-green 13

12b. Flowers white or reddish 14

13a. Involucre absent; leaves 3- or 4-pinnate, with segments ± filiform .... *Foeniculum vulgare* Miller

13b. Involucre 1–3; lower leaves 3-pinnate, with segments almost obovate or cuneate ....
.... *Petroselinum cirspum* (Miller) Nyman

14a. Leaves pinnate, with broad 3-partite to 3-lobed leaflets; leaflets petiolate .... *Apium graveolens* L.

14b. Leaves 2- or 3-pinnate, with segments very narrow to filiform ....
.... *Ciclospermum leptophyllum* (Pers.) Sprague

15a. Involucres pinnatifid .... *Daucus carota* L.

15b. Involucres not pinnatifid .... *Trachyspermum orxburghianum* Craib

Key to subfamily Aralioideae

1a. Petals imbricate 2

1b. Petals valvate; leaves simple or compound 4

2a. Leaves simple, palmately lobed .... *Harmsiopanax* (not treated here)

2b. Leaves pinnately compound 3

3a. Leaves once pinnate .... *Aralia* (not treated here)

3b. Leaves once pinnate (Myodocarpaceae) .... *Delarbrea* (not treated here)

4a. Petals with a narrow base (claw) .... *Mackinlaya* (not treated here)

4b. Petals with a broad base 5

5a. Inflorescence rays 3-fid; central branch shorter bearing 'false fruits" with 2 lateral branches longer with normal flowers .... *Osmoxylon*

5b. Inflorescence branches not as above, 'false fruits' not present 6

6a. Leaves compound, pinnate .... *Polyscias*

6b. Leaves simple, not pinnate, deeply lobed 7

7a. Pedicel articulated below the flower .... *Anakasia* (not treated here)

7b. Pedicel not articulated below the flower .... *Schefflera* (not treated here)

Osmoxylon novoguineense (Scheff.) Becc. Figs 419, 420

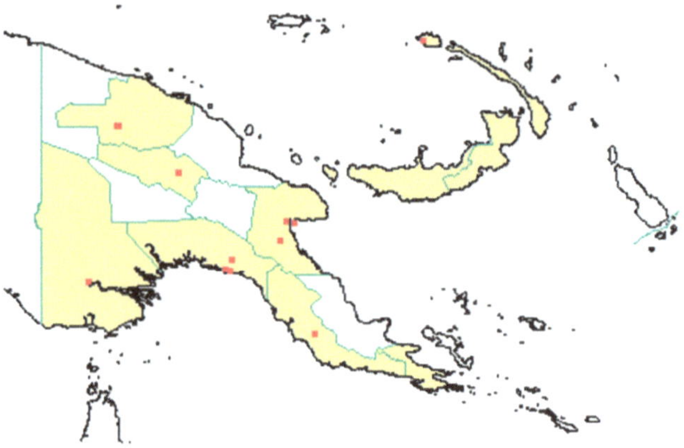

Malesia Vol. 1: 197 (1877)
Other Literature: W.R. Philipson, *Handbooks of the flora of Papua New Guinea* Vol. 3: 24 (1995) Fig. 5.
Timber Group: Non-timber species

Field Characters: Subcanopy trees, 14–18 m high; bole cylindrical, 25 cm diam., straight, 2 m long; buttresses absent; spines absent; aerial roots absent; stilt roots absent. Bark pale brown, rough, pustular; lenticels elongated vertically or rounded/swelling; bark 10 mm thick; under-bark green; faintly or non-aromatic; pleasant; blaze consisting of one layer, pale yellow, slightly speckled or with stripes, granular without splinters; exudate present, colourless, not readily flowing, changing to orange on exposure to air, not sticky. Terminal buds not enclosed by leaves.

Indumentum: Complex hairs absent; stinging hairs absent; mature twig without hairs.

Leaves: Slightly clustered at end of branches or spaced along branches internodes short and leaves forming a terminal 'crown', leaves spiral, sometimes interpreted as compound or simple; petiole 35–50 cm long, not winged, slightly angled, attached to surface of leaf blade or attached to base of leaf lamina (appearing so because leaves deeply lobed), slightly swollen at base and scaly; lamina broadest at or near middle, 85–110 cm long, 90–110 cm wide; base symmetric, margin entire, deeply dissected or lobed almost to base of primary veins, palmately lobed (5–7-lobed and each lobe further dissected), apex acuminate; leaves palmate; venation pinnate on each lobe or palmate (if leaf interpreted as simple), secondary veins open, prominent, intramarginal veins absent; lower surface green, upper surface green, hairs absent, oil dots absent, domatia absent; stipules present, joined, laterally placed, not encircling the twig, leafy, triangular, 2-ridged, not fringed, large, 51–100 mm long, 30–50 mm wide at base, not persistent.

Fig. 419. *Osmoxylon novoguineense.* Bark, leaf, fruit and pseudofruits (with Silva Masbong)

Flowers: Inflorescence terminal, flowers on an unbranched axis, with ultimate axis (peduncles) 90–95 mm long, or flowers arising from a single point; flowers bisexual, not stalked, slightly asymmetric, 12–15 mm long, large, 10–15 mm diam.; perianth present, with distinct sepals and petals, but sepals reduced to a small rim, pale brown or dull red; inner perianth c. 6 (with lobes irregular, erect), some or partly joined forming a tube; stamens 6–10, filaments present, free of each other, free of perianth; ovary inferior (apex of ovary slightly raised above base of perianth), carpels joined, locules 6–14; styles absent with a central double row of pustulate stigmas.

Fruits: Arising from a single point or arranged on unbranched axis, fruit c. 15 mm long, up to 22 mm diam., dark red, not spiny, slightly ribbed, slightly fleshy, simple, indehiscent, drupe. Seeds c. 8 mm long, longer than wide, 2–3 mm wide, not winged.

Distribution: East Sepik, Morobe, Western Highlands, Western, Gulf, Central, Milne Bay, New Britain, New Ireland.

Notes: The inflorescence of this species is a compound umbel, with each axis ending in an umbel of about 20 sterile, fleshy, dark red pseudo-fruits (c. 6 mm long, c. 10 mm diam.) and two lateral branches, each with about 40 bisexual flowers. The function of the pseudo-fruits is unknown.

Fig. 420. *Osmoxylon novoguineense.* Base of petiole, flowers, fruit and pseudofruits

Polyscias belensis Philipson
Fig. 421

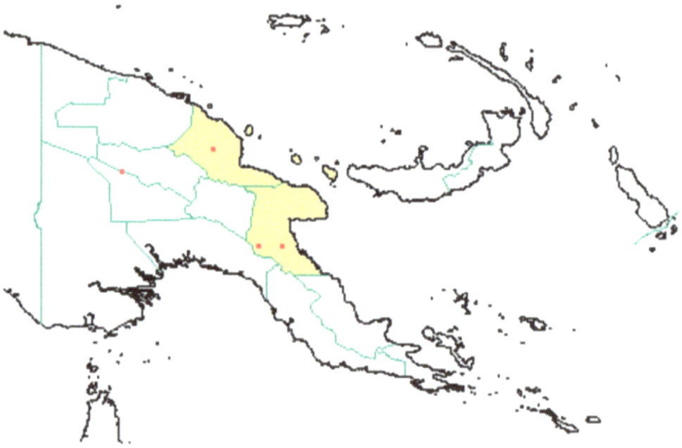

Bulletin of the British Museum (Natural History), Botany Vol. 1: 13 (1951)
Other Literature: W.R. Philipson, *Handbooks of the flora of Papua New Guinea* Vol. 3: 37 (1995)
Timber Group: Occasional timber species

Field Characters: Canopy trees, 15–35 m high; bole cylindrical, c. 40 cm diam., straight; buttresses absent; spines absent; aerial roots absent; stilt roots absent. Bark pale brown, rough, pustular; lenticels elongated vertically; bark 5 mm thick; under-bark yellow; strongly aromatic; spice-like; blaze consisting of one layer, yellow or brown, with stripes, fibrous; exudate present, colourless, not readily flowing, changing to pale yellow on exposure to air, sticky. Terminal buds not enclosed by leaves.

Indumentum: Complex hairs absent; stinging hairs absent; mature twig without hairs.

Leaves: Spaced along branches, leaves spiral, compound; petiole 12–16 cm long, not winged, attached to base of leaf lamina, not swollen; leaves pinnate; petiolule not swollen, up to c. 1 cm long; rachis present, not winged, not swollen; leaves with a terminal leaflet, each leaflet equally broad throughout much of length, (7–)10–12 cm long, (2–)3.5–6 cm wide, leaflets opposite, symmetric, terminal developing leaflet buds straight; venation pinnate, secondary veins open, not prominent, but visible, intramarginal veins absent; lower surface pale green, upper surface dark green, hairs absent, oil dots absent, domatia absent; stipules absent.

Fig. 421. *Polyscias belensis*. Bark and leaves

Flowers: Inflorescence terminal, flowers arising from a single point, in sub-umbellate clusters or flowers on a branched axis; flowers bisexual, with pedicel 5–6 mm long, with many planes of symmetry, 3–5 mm long, small, c. 3 mm diam.; perianth present, with distinct sepals and petals, with calyx a minute rim, pale yellow or green; inner perianth 4, free; stamens 4, filaments present, very short, free of each other, free of perianth; ovary inferior, carpels joined, locules 4 or 5; styles free, 4 or 5.

Fruits: Arising from a single point (as for flowers) or arranged on branched axis, fruit 25–50(–60) mm long, 18–35 mm diam., reddish brown, presumably not spiny, fleshy, simple, dehiscent, capsule. Seed 1, 20–25 mm long, as wide as long (ellipsoid), 15–20 mm diam., not winged.

Distribution: Madang, Morobe, Western Highlands.

Polyscias macranthum (Philipson) Lowry & G.M.Plunkett

Plant Diversity and Evolution Vol. 128: 69 (2010)

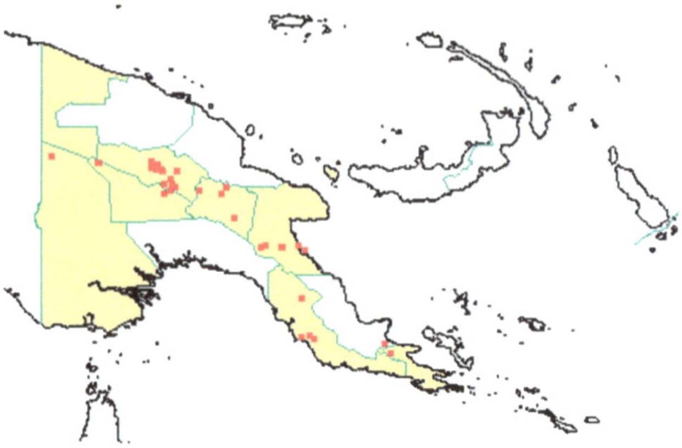

Other Literature: W.R. Philipson, *Handbooks of the Flora of Papua New Guinea* Vol. 3: 4–6 (1995) Fig. 1.

Timber Group: Non-timber species

Field Characters: Canopy trees or subcanopy trees, 8–25(–30) m high; bole cylindrical, up to 25 cm diam., straight, often branching near base, up to 5 m long; buttresses absent; spines absent; aerial roots absent; stilt roots absent. Bark grey, smooth; bark <25 mm thick; under-bark pale brown; faintly or non-aromatic; blaze consisting of one layer, white (cream-coloured), with stripes; exudate present, brown, not changing colour on exposure to air. Terminal buds not enclosed by leaves.

Indumentum: Complex hairs present; stinging hairs absent; mature twig hairy; hairs dense.

Leaves: Clustered at end of branches, leaves spiral, compound; petiole present, not winged, attached to base of leaf lamina, not swollen or swollen; leaves with three leaflets or pinnate; petiolule not swollen; rachis present, not winged, not swollen; leaves with a terminal leaflet, each leaflet broadest at or near middle or broadest below middle, 9–13 cm long, 3.5–5 cm wide, leaflets opposite, symmetric, terminal developing leaflet buds straight; venation pinnate, secondary veins open, not prominent, but visible, intramarginal veins absent; lower surface dull green, upper surface dark glossy green, hairs present, sparse, oil dots absent, domatia absent; stipules absent.

Flowers: Inflorescence terminal, flowers on a branched axis; flowers bisexual, with pedicel, with many planes of symmetry, 6–7 mm long, small, c. 6 mm diam.; perianth present, with distinct sepals and petals, yellow or green; inner perianth 5, free; stamens 4, filaments present, free of each other, free of perianth; ovary inferior, carpels joined, locules 1; styles absent, stigma sessile.

Fruits: arranged on branched axis, fruit 10–12 mm long, c. 8 mm diam., dark green, not spiny, fleshy, simple, indehiscent, drupe. Seed 1, c. 8 mm long, longer than wide, 5–6 mm diam., not winged.

Distribution: West Sepik, Morobe, Western Highlands, Eastern Highlands, Southern Highlands, Western, Central, Milne Bay.

Notes: Previously known as *Arthrophyllum macranthum* Philipson

Polyscias prolifera (Philipson) Lowry & G.M.Plunkett

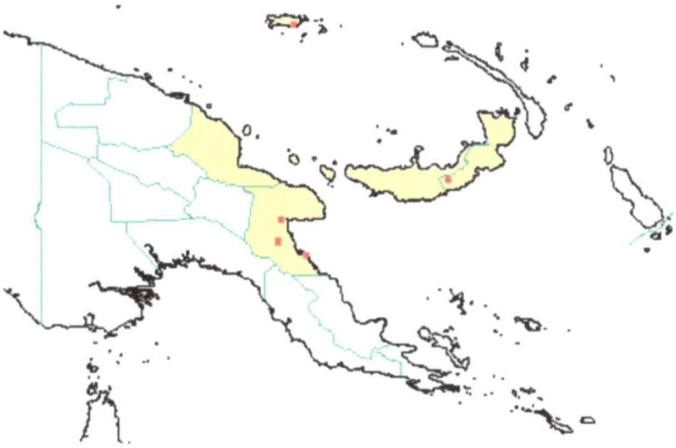

Plant Diversity and Evolution Vol. 128: 70 (2010)
Other Literature: W.R. Philipson, *Handbooks of the Flora of Papua New Guinea* Vol. 3: 7 (1995)
Timber Group: Non-timber species

Field Characters: Subcanopy trees, up to 12 m high; bole cylindrical, 7–10 cm diam., straight, up to 8 m long; buttresses absent; spines absent; aerial roots absent; stilt roots absent. Bark grey or brown, rough, slightly scaly or flaky, fissured, or peeling; bark c. 10 mm thick; under-bark red or brown; faintly or non-aromatic; blaze consisting of one layer, white, light yellow (cream-coloured), or slightly green, markings absent, fibrous; exudate present, colourless, not readily flowing, changing to yellowish golden-coloured on exposure to air, not sticky. Terminal buds not enclosed by leaves.

Indumentum: Complex hairs absent; stinging hairs absent; mature twig without hairs.

Leaves: Spaced along branches, leaves spiral, compound; petiole present, not winged, attached to base of leaf lamina, swollen; leaves pinnate; petiolule not swollen; rachis present, not winged, not swollen; leaves with a terminal leaflet, each leaflet broadest above middle or broadest at or near middle, 90 cm long, 24 cm wide, leaflets opposite, symmetric, terminal developing leaflet buds straight; venation pinnate, secondary veins open, prominent, intramarginal veins absent; lower surface green, upper surface dark glossy green, hairs absent, oil dots absent, domatia absent; stipules absent.

Flowers: Inflorescence terminal, flowers on a branched axis; flowers bisexual, with pedicel, with many planes of symmetry, 5–6 mm long, small (< or =10 mm diam.); perianth present, with distinct sepals and petals, yellow or green; inner perianth 5, free; stamens 5, filaments present, free of each other, free of perianth; ovary inferior, carpels joined, locules 1; styles absent.

Fruits: arranged on branched axis, fruit c. 10 mm long, c. 5 mm diam., dark green, not spiny, fleshy, simple, indehiscent, drupe. Seed 1, c. 8 mm long, longer than wide, 5–6 mm diam.), not winged.

Distribution: Madang, Morobe, New Britain, Manus.

Notes: Previously known as *Arthrophyllum proliferum* Philipson

Polyscias royenii Philipson Fig. 422

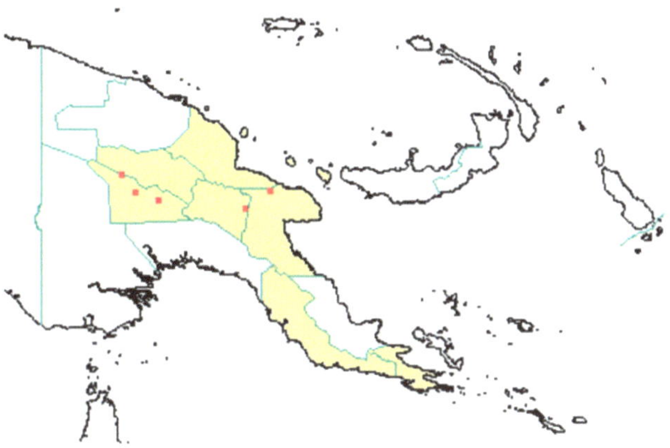

Blumea Vol. 24: 170 (1978)
Other Literature: W.R. Philipson, *Handbooks of the flora of Papua New Guinea* Vol. 3: 42 (1995)
Timber Group: Occasional timber species
Trade Name: Polyscias

Field Characters: Subcanopy trees, up to 20(–28) m high; bole cylindrical, 15–30 cm diam., straight, 6–10 m long; buttresses absent; spines absent; aerial roots absent; stilt roots absent. Bark grey or white, rough, pustular or slightly fissured; lenticels rounded/swelling; bark 6 mm thick; under-bark pale orange; faintly or non-aromatic; blaze consisting of 2 layers; outer blaze white, markings absent, granular without splinters; inner blaze white, yellow, or pink, markings absent, granular without splinters; exudate present, colourless, not readily flowing, not changing colour on exposure to air, not sticky. Terminal buds not enclosed by leaves.

Indumentum: Complex hairs absent; stinging hairs absent; mature twig without hairs.

Leaves: Clustered at end of branches, leaves sub-whorled or spiral, compound; petiole present, not winged, attached to base of leaf lamina, slightly swollen at base; leaves pinnate; petiolule not swollen (short); rachis present, not winged, not swollen; leaves with a terminal leaflet, each leaflet broadest at or near middle or equally broad throughout much of length, 10–20 cm long, 2–4 cm wide, leaflets opposite, almost symmetric, terminal developing leaflet buds straight; venation pinnate, secondary veins open, slightly prominent, intramarginal veins absent; lower surface pale green, upper surface green, hairs absent, oil dots absent, domatia absent; stipules absent.

Flowers: Inflorescence terminal or axillary, flowers on a branched axis; flowers bisexual, with pedicel c. 8 mm long, with many planes of symmetry, c. 5 mm long, small, 5–8 mm diam.; perianth present, with distinct sepals and petals (calyx reduced to a rim), pale yellow or pale green; inner perianth 5, free; stamens 5, filaments present, free of each other, free of perianth; ovary inferior, carpels joined, locules 2 (or 3); styles joined together to form a beak above rim of calyx or absent (by misinterpretation).

Fruits: Arising from a single point (as for flowers) or arranged on branched axis, fruit 7–9 mm long, 7–10 mm diam., brown or green, not spiny, slightly fleshy (leathery), simple, indehiscent, drupe. Seeds not winged.

Distribution: Madang, Morobe, Western Highlands, Southern Highlands, Central, Milne Bay.

Fig. 422. *Polyscias royenii*. Leaves, flowers and developing fruit (with Kiagube Fazang)

Polyscias spectabilis (Harms) Lowry & G.M.Plunkett

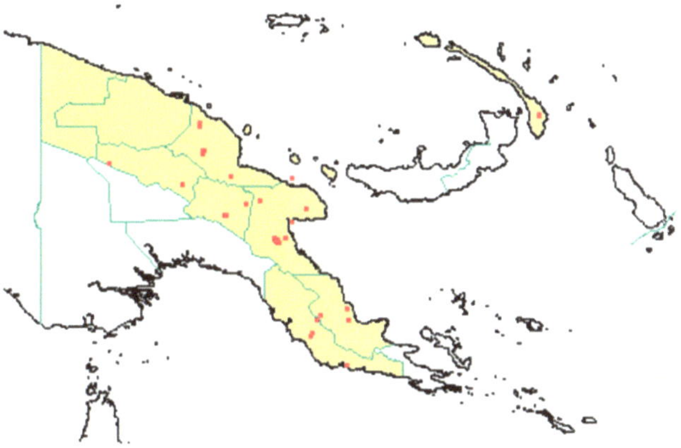

Plant Diversity and Evolution Vol. 128: 74 (2010)
Other Literature: W.R. Philipson, *Handbooks of the Flora of Papua New Guinea* Vol. 3: 10 (1995) Fig. 2.
Timber Group: Occasional timber species

Field Characters: Canopy trees or subcanopy trees, 20–34 m high; bole cylindrical, 50–100 cm diam., straight, 15–20 m long; buttresses absent; spines absent; aerial roots absent; stilt roots absent. Bark grey or brown, rough, slightly scaly or flaky; bark 12–18 mm thick; under-bark brown; faintly or non-aromatic; onion-like (celery-like aroma); blaze consisting of one layer, white or pale yellow, with stripes, fibrous; exudate present, colourless, not readily flowing, not changing colour on exposure to air, sticky. Terminal buds not enclosed by leaves.

Indumentum: Complex hairs absent; stinging hairs absent; mature twig without hairs.

Leaves: Clustered at end of branches, leaves spiral, compound; petiole present, not winged, attached to base of leaf lamina, swollen at point of attachment to branchlet and at node of first leaflets; leaves pinnate; petiolule not swollen but attached to swollen nodes; rachis present, not winged, not swollen; leaves with a terminal leaflet, each leaflet broadest below middle, 7–14 cm long, 4–6.5 cm wide, leaflets opposite, symmetric, terminal developing leaflet buds straight; venation pinnate, secondary veins open, prominent, intramarginal veins absent; lower surface pale green, upper surface dull green, hairs absent, oil dots absent, domatia absent; stipules absent.

Flowers: Inflorescence terminal, flowers on a branched axis arising from a single point (whorl); flowers bisexual, with pedicel, with many planes of symmetry, 10–15 mm long, large, 12–15 mm diam.; perianth present, with distinct sepals and petals, pale green; inner perianth 4, free; stamens many, filaments present, free of each other, free of perianth; ovary inferior, carpels joined, locules (10–)16–22; styles joined (partly joined to form a stylopodium of appressed styles), (10–)16–22.

Fruits: arranged on branched axis arising from a single point (whorl), fruit 7–9 mm long, c. 10 mm diam., black, not spiny, non-fleshy, simple, indehiscent, drupe. Seeds c. 20, c. 6 mm long, longer than wide, 3–4 mm diam., not winged.

Distribution: West Sepik, East Sepik, Madang, Morobe, Western Highlands, Eastern Highlands, Central, Northern, New Ireland.

Notes: Previously known as *Gastonia spectabilis* (Harms) Philipson

Paracryphiales

95. Paracryphiaceae

Trees. Stipules absent. Leaves well-developed, whorled, simple, not dissected or lobed; margin finely toothed; venation pinnate. Inflorescences terminal; Flowers bisexual, regular, with tepals (not readily resolvable as calyx and/or corolla). Sepals 2. Petals 2, free; tube absent. Stamens 8(–11), free; filaments present; staminodes absent. Gynoecium with carpels at least partially joined, superior; styles absent. Fruit simple, dehiscent, follicle, dry, at least non-fleshy. Seeds with wings.

PNG genera: *Quintinia, Sphenostemon*

Notes: *Quintinia* was previously placed in the family Escalloniaceae, Grossulariaceae or Saxifragaceae, whereas *Sphenostemon* was included in the Aquifoliaceae.

References: Bailey (1956), Bernardi (1964)

1a. Leaves spiral, non-aromatic, <3 cm wide; flowers in terminal branched inflorescences; exudate flowing and changing to dark red on exposure to air.. *Sphenostemon pauciflorum*

1b. Leaves sub-opposite or spiral, aromatic, 3–5.5 cm wide; flowers in axillary, unbranched inflorescences; exudate not readily flowing, colourless and not changing colour on exposure to air; bark reddish brown, mostly smooth; under-bark orange or green .... *Quintinia altigena*

1c. Leaves spiral, non-aromatic, 7–20(–30 cm wide; flowers in axillary, unbranched inflorescences; exudate not readily flowing, colourless and not changing colour on exposure to air; bark brown, rough, pustular; under-bark red or brown... Quintinia ledermannii

Quintinia altigena Schltr.

Botanische Jahrbücher für Systematik, Pflanzengeschichte und Pflanzengeographie Vol. 52: 127 (1914)
Timber Group: Non-timber species

Field Characters: Canopy trees, 8–25 m high or subcanopy trees; bole cylindrical, up to 80(–100) cm diam., straight, up to 17 m long; buttresses absent; spines absent; aerial roots absent; stilt roots present. Bark slightly red or reddish brown, mostly smooth; bark 3–5 mm thick; under-bark orange or green; faintly or non-aromatic; blaze consisting of one layer, pink or brown, with stripes (darker pink), fibrous; exudate present, colourless, not readily flowing, not changing colour on exposure to air, not sticky. Terminal buds not enclosed by leaves.

Indumentum: Complex hairs absent; stinging hairs absent; mature twig without hairs.

Leaves: Spaced along branches, leaves sub-opposite or spiral, simple (aromatic); petiole present, not winged, attached to base of leaf lamina, not swollen; lamina broadest above middle, (4.5–)8–10(–15) cm long, 3–5(–5.5) cm wide; base symmetric, margin entire, not dissected or lobed, apex rarely emarginate or retuse, obtuse, or shortly acuminate, venation pinnate, secondary veins open, prominent, intramarginal veins absent; lower surface green, upper surface dark glossy green, hairs absent, oil dots absent, domatia absent; stipules absent.

Flowers: Inflorescence axillary, flowers on an unbranched axis; flowers bisexual, with pedicel, with many planes of symmetry, 3–4 mm long, small, 3–5 mm diam.; perianth present, with distinct sepals and petals, white; inner perianth 4, free; stamens 4, filaments present, free of each other, free of perianth (joined at base of corolla); ovary inferior, carpels joined, locules 5; styles free, 5.

Fruits: arranged on unbranched axis, fruit 4–8 mm long (including persistent sepals), c. 5 mm diam., green or grey, not spiny, non-fleshy, simple, dehiscent, capsule. Seeds 20–many, 1.5–2 mm long, longer than wide, c. 0.5 mm diam., not winged.

Distribution: Morobe, Western Highlands, Eastern Highlands, Southern Highlands.

Notes: High altitude species, above 1800 m elevation.

Quintinia ledermannii Schltr. Fig. 423

Botanische Jahrbucher für Systematik, Pflanzengeschichte und Pflanzengeographie Vol. 52: 125 (1914)
Timber Group: Non-timber species

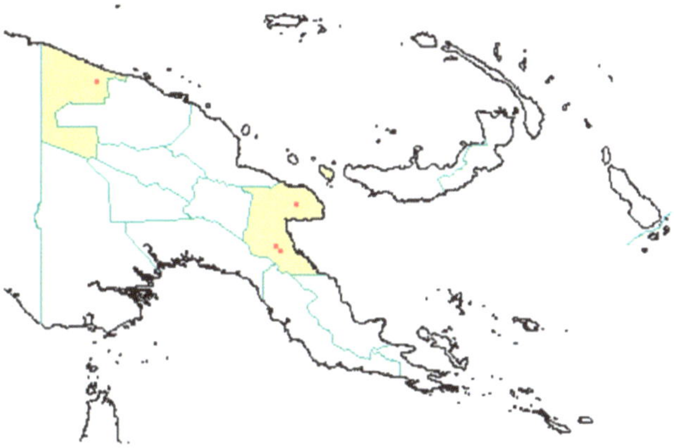

Field Characters: Large canopy tree, up to 30 m high or small sub-canopy tree (up to 10 m high); Bole cylindrical, c. 40 cm diam.; straight, c. 25 m high; buttresses absent; spines absent; aerial roots absent; stilt roots absent; Bark brown, rough, pustular, lenticels elongated vertically; under-bark red or brown; 12 mm thick; bark blaze consisting of one layer; strongly aromatic; pleasant, pale brown, with stripes, slightly fibrous; exudate colourless, not readily flowing (spotty), colour not changing on exposure to air, not sticky; terminal buds not enclosed by leaves.

Indumentum: Complex hairs absent; stinging hairs absent; mature twig indumentum (hairs) absent.

Leaves: spaced along branches, spiral, simple; petiole present, not winged, attached to base of leaf blade, not swollen; lamina sometimes broadest above middle or usually broadest at or near middle, 20–70 cm, 7–20(–30) cm; symmetric, entire, not dissected or lobed, rounded or obtuse, venation pinnate, secondary veins open, prominent or not prominent, but visible, intramarginal veins absent; lower surface pale green, upper surface dark green, indumentum absent; oil dots absent; domatia absent; stipules absent.

Flowers: Inflorescence axillary, flowers on an unbranched axis; flowers bisexual, stalked, flowers with many planes of symmetry, 2–3 mm long, 3–4 mm diam.; perianth present, with distinct sepals and petals, inner perianth white; 4, free; stamens 4, filaments present, free of each other, free of the perianth (joined at base of corolla); ovary partly inferior or inferior, carpels joined, locules 5; styles solitary, 1.

Fig. 423. *Quintinia ledermannii.* Leaves and flowers

Fruits: arranged on unbranched axis, fruit c. 5 mm long (including persistent sepals), c. 4 mm diam., green or brown, not spiny, non-fleshy, simple, dehiscent, capsule; seeds 20–50, to about 5 mm long, not winged, narrow (longer than wide), seed less than 1 mm diam.

Distribution: West Sepik, Morobe, Western Highlands, Western, Central.

Sphenostemon pauciflorum (A.C.Sm.) Steenis & Erdtm.

Svensk Botanisk Tidskrift Utgifven af Svenska Botaniska Foreningen Vol. 49: 22 (1955)
Timber Group: Non-timber species

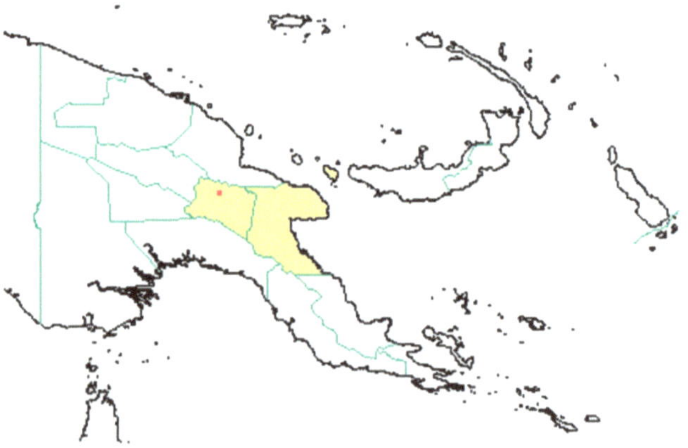

Field Characters: Subcanopy trees, up to c. 20 m high; bole markedly fluted, c. 25 cm diam., crooked; buttresses absent; spines absent; aerial roots absent; stilt roots absent. Bark brown, rough, pustular; lenticels elongated vertically; bark 5–6 mm thick; under-bark green (as stripes) or red; strongly aromatic; pleasant; blaze consisting of one layer, orange or red, with stripes, fibrous; inner blaze orange or red, with stripes, fibrous; exudate present, colourless, not readily flowing, changing to dark red on exposure to air, not sticky. Terminal buds not enclosed by leaves.

Indumentum: Complex hairs absent; stinging hairs absent; mature twig hairy; hairs dense (indumentum silky).

Leaves: Spaced along branches, leaves spiral, simple; petiole present, not winged, attached to base of leaf lamina, not swollen; lamina broadest above middle, 3.5–6.5 cm long, 1.6–2.8 cm wide; base symmetric, margin serrate to dentate (toothed), not dissected or lobed, apex obtuse, venation pinnate, secondary veins open, prominent, intramarginal veins absent; hairs present, sparse, oil dots absent, domatia absent; stipules present, free, laterally placed, not encircling the twig, scale-like, not fringed, small, not persistent.

Flowers: Inflorescence terminal, flowers on a branched axis; flowers unisexual, with male and female flowers on different plants, flowers with pedicel, with many planes of symmetry perianth present, with distinct sepals and petals, white; free; stamens 8, filaments present, free of each other, free of perianth; ovary superior, carpels joined, styles joined, 1.

Fruits: arranged on unbranched axis, fruit c. 20 mm long, c. 15 mm diam., red, not spiny, fleshy, indehiscent, drupe. Seeds 2, 12–15 mm long, as wide as long, c. 10 mm wide, not winged.

Distribution: Morobe, Eastern Highlands.

DATA DICTIONARY

Introduction

The following information has been used to describe and distinguish the important features of the tree species included in this guide to the *Trees of Papua New Guinea*. A brief explanation of each of the terms used in this *Data Dictionary*, together with images, is provided to assist the user to understand the botanical terms as they identify the trees included in this book. Although the *Data Dictionary* can be used as glossary of terms, providing useful definitions, it is included here to assist the users understand the fields of information recorded in the *PNGtrees DELTAaccess* database. In some descriptions, the output from these fields has been reformatted to improve the readability of the plant descriptions. Therefore, the *Data Dictionary* should be consulted when using the *PNGtrees* database and for adding or editing species information in the data-entry forms (refer Appendix 1).

The *Data Dictionary* is based on several interactive identification tools that have been developed. The features used were based on the features used in the following plant keys: Conn (1979a), FloraBase (2003), Hyland *et al.* (1993), Jarvie and Ermayanti (1995–1996), Thiele and Adams (1999), Webb *et al.* (2005), Webb *et al.* (2008+).

Although the complexity of technical terms is reduced to a minimum, the definition of these terms is based, in part, on Conn (1979a), Harden (1990–1993), Radford *et al.* (1998), Womersley (1978). The definitions of these are organised into the following four sections

1. **GROUP NAMES**
2. **GENERAL FEATURES OF THE TREE**
3. **LEAF FEATURES**
4. **FLOWER AND FRUIT FEATURES**

1. GROUP NAMES

The definition of each technical term used for GROUP NAMES is organised into the following four sections

- Group
- Tradename
- Timber Groups
- Timber tree

Group

The two broad groups of trees included in this key are:

Conifer (Pinophyta) This category is used for the Cone-bearing trees, such as the species of *Araucaria* and *Pinus*

Dicotyledon (Magnoliophyta, Class Magnoliopsida) Describes the group of trees that are flowering plants.

Note: Woody monocotyledons (such as, palms) have not been included.

Tradename

These are the non-scientific names used by the forestry and timber industry. Sometimes more than one name is used for the same species. In other cases, one name may refer to more than one species. The names used here are based on the Standard Trade Common Names officially recognised by the *Papua New Guinea Forest Authority* (Eddowes 1977).

Other Vernacular (Common) names

These are the **non-scientific name(s)** used by the community for the plant. Since there are many languages in Papua New Guinea, many plants have several vernacular names. Therefore, it is important to record the language group of the name. Furthermore, some plants are referred to by different names at different phases of the life-cycle. Although the vernacular names are recorded in the *PNGtrees* database, the many names used are not included in this publication.

A complete record would include the: (1) vernacular name; (2) name of language/dialect; (3) name of informant; and, when possible, (4) a recording of the informant pronouncing the vernacular name. Refer 'Standard system of orthography to be used in recording of vernacular names' (see below).

Timber groups

This feature primarily distinguishes between softwood and hardwood timbers. It also distinguishes between the importance of different species as timber trees (such as major, commercial, minor and occasional). Furthermore, the special small group of plantation species has been distinguished by this character.

The six timber groups recognised are based on Eddowes (1977) and include:

Major exportable hardwoods – the timbers in this category of trees are recognised as being the major hardwood timber species harvested from Papua New Guinea.
Commercial hardwoods – many of the timbers in this group have been exported occasionally. However, substantial regular supplies for these species would not be reliable.
Minor hardwoods – this category generally includes locally available species that have currently shown little export potential. Regular supplies of any one of these species is generally not possible. Therefore, they are currently of minor commercial value.
Softwoods – the conifers have been harvested from plantations, mainly at higher altitudes, and are abundant in some areas, for example, in the Bulolo region.
Plantation species – several indigenous and introduced species have been planted in forest plantations throughout Papua New Guinea. *Araucaria* and *Pinus* species are two softwood examples.
Occasional timber – include trees that are currently regarded as of little to no economic significance. Most of these trees are limited in their distribution, but they have been recorded as sawn logs or of other utilitarian value.

Note: the term **"softwood"** refers to the conifers, whereas the **"hardwoods"** are the dicotyledonous (flowering) plants.

Timber tree

This features records if a plant is known to be a timber species. If the species is regarded as a Timber tree, then it would also be classified as belonging to at least one of the categories in the "Timber groups" field. Although the timber of most trees has some local traditional use, such as for the framing of traditional buildings, these examples are not regarded as timber species because they have no known commercial value.

This feature is recorded as either: **yes** or **no**

2. GENERAL FEATURES OF THE TREE

The definition of each technical term used for the general features of the tree is organised into the following three sections

- General features
- Bark
- Indumentum on branches

The information included in GENERAL FEATURES OF THE TREE is the characteristics that can be readily observed in the field. Most of these features are frequently not recorded on the labels of herbarium collections or in the botanical scientific literature.

GENERAL FEATURES

Habit

This feature compares the height of a tree *relative to the overall height* of the forest canopy. The typical height of the mature tree is frequently also given, as a note in the descriptions.

Emergent trees	Trees that noticeably extend beyond the canopy of the forest
Large trees	Trees that make up the canopy of the forest
Small trees	Sub-canopy sized trees

Trunk shape (in section)

The bole of the tree refers to the trunk (or primary axis) of the tree from the base until the first branch. This feature describes the shape of the tree in radial section. This feature is either:

cylindrical (or sub-cylindrical) in cross-section (Fig. 424A)
markedly fluted in cross-section (Fig. 424B)

Fig. 424. General habit. Trunk shape, buttresses, spines, aerial roots and stilt roots

Trunk shape (lengthwise)

The shape of the overall length of the bole (from base of the trunk to the first branch) is categorized as either:

straight (or only very slightly crooked) (Fig. 424C)
(markedly) **crooked** (Fig. 424D)

Buttresses

This feature records the **presence** or **absence of buttresses**. Many tree species develop these support structures at the base of the tree. (Figs 424E & F)

Note: the distance that the buttresses extend away from the centre of the trunk (the width) is usually not recorded.

Spines

This feature records the **presence** or **absence of spines** on trunks and/or branches. It is recorded as either:

present or **absent** (Fig. 424I)

Spines (position)

When spines are **present**, the location of the spines is recorded as either occurring:

on the trunk or **on the branches**

Aerial roots are roots growing from the stem or branches above ground level. They are commonly found in species of *Ficus*. This feature records the **presence** or **absence of aerial roots** as either:

present or **absent** (Fig. 424G)

Stilt roots

Stilt roots are oblique roots that grow from the stem and are frequently supporting structures that are found in mangroves, pandans and palms. This feature records the **presence** or **absence** of **stilt roots** as either:

present or **absent** (Fig. 424H)

Terminal buds

The terminal developing buds are either enclosed by leaves or these enclosing leaves are absent. This is a feature that is common in the Rubiaceae. The terminal developing buds are recorded as either **enclosed** or **not enclosed**.

BARK

Although the term *bark* is used loosely and often inconsistently, it is here regarded as *all tissues outside the vascular cambium*. Therefore, it includes primary and secondary phloem, cortex, periderm and any dead tissues outside the periderm, including the epidermis.

Bark (outer colour)

This feature records the colour of the outer surface of the bark, as seen when looking at the tree. Since the colour of the bark is frequently different in immature trees to that found in mature trees, this character is less reliable when recorded from trees less than 50 cm diameter at breast height (dbh) (approximately 1.3 m above ground). As for other characters that refer to colour, mostly simple colour types are used in this guide to the *Trees of Papua New Guinea*.

The **colour types** include: **white**, **cream-coloured**, **yellow**, **green**, **orange**, **red**, **grey**, **brown**, **black**

Note: a mixture of these colour types is frequently present.

Bark roughness

This feature records whether the outer bark is:

Rough	The surface of the bark should be rough to touch and may vary from finely to coarsely rough (Fig. 425A–G)
Smooth	Frequently, trees that have smooth bark may also be slightly flaky (as in the species illustrated here). However, if most of the surface of the bark is smooth to touch, then it is recorded as 'smooth' (Fig. 425H)

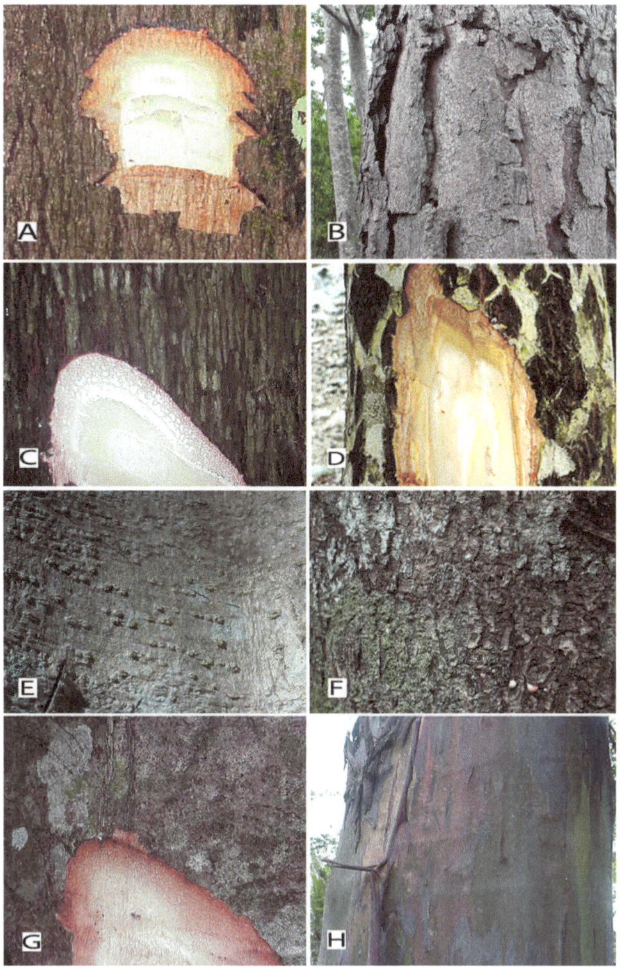

Fig. 425. General bark surface types

Bark texture

When the outer bark is rough, this feature describes the type of roughness.

The following types of roughness are recognised:

scaly or flaky Since these two types of bark roughness are sometimes difficult to distinguish from each other, both categories are here grouped together.

Flaky bark (e.g., *Argyrodendron trifoliolatum*) consists of many regular to slightly irregular, thin flakes. **Scaly bark** (e.g., *Mangifera minor*) is structurally similar, but usually the bark is thinner and not as regular as the flakes of the former example, e.g., *Artocarpus vriesiana* has scaly or flaky bark (Fig. 425C)

fissured bark is finely split into many narrow grooves, e.g., *Dysoxylum inopinatum* (Fig. 425A)

peeling The bark splits or crack and then falls away in thin patches, sheets or long ribbons. The surface of the bark underneath the peeling layer is usually very smooth, e.g., *Eucalyptus deglupta* (Fig. 425H)

cracked The outer surface of the bark is smooth or slightly so, but it is divided into irregular plate-like areas by relatively broad cracks, e.g., *Callophyllum inophyllum* (Fig. 425D)

furrowed cork	Bark with relatively long narrow depressions or grooves, e.g. bark of the introduced *Pinus caribaea* (Fig. 425B)
pustular	bark is more or less covered with raised, rough, irregular bumps or lines of pustules/lenticels. In between the pustules, the surface of the bark is usually smooth or almost smooth, e.g., *Alstonia scholaris* (Fig. 425E)
tessellated	The outer bark is finely divided into more or less regular square-like pieces so that it has a 'chequered' appearance. Note: the pieces do not detach readily, e.g., *Rhus taitensis* (Fig. 425F)
pitted	bark usually has small sunken pits with the general surface of the bark more or less smooth, e.g., *Dracontomelum lenticulatum* (Fig. 425G)

Bark lenticels (pustules)

When the outer bark is pustular, this feature describes the shape of the pustules. The pustules/lenticels are small raised corky bumps or lines through which gaseous exchange occurs. The following types of pustules are recognised:

elongated laterally	The lenticels are arranged laterally across the trunk forming raised more or less horizontal lines of pustules (Fig. 426A)
elongated vertically	Lenticels are arranged vertically along the trunk forming raised more or less vertical lines of pustules (Fig. 426B)
rounded/swellings	Lenticels more or less form globular (rounded) raised swellings on the surface, e.g., *Alstonia scholaris* (Fig. 426E)
irregular	Lenticels do not form any of the above arrangements as they are irregular in shape and orientation

Bark subrhytidome (under-bark) colour

The subrhytidome layer is the thin actively growing layer immediately below the outer surface of the bark. This layer is here referred to as the **under-bark**.

The **colour types** include: **white**, **yellow** or**ange**, **green**, **red**, **brown**, **black**, **mottled** (a mixture of colours)

Fig. 426. Lenticels, under-bark, outer and inner bark blaze, and bark exudate

Bark thickness type

This feature includes the total bark thickness, that is, both outer and inner bark

> This feature records whether the bark is thick or thin:
> **<25 mm thick** (namely, less than 25 mm thick; hence, thin)
> **>25 mm thick** (namely, greater than 25 mm thick; hence, thick)

This standard for differentiating between thick and thin bark, as used in Australia, has proven to be less useful in Papua New Guinea. It has been found that most Papua New Guinean trees have bark that is less than 25 mm thick, hence thin bark, based on this classification system. Although this feature is still included in this first version of the *Trees of Papua New Guinea* it has been replaced by the following more informative '**bark thickness measurement (mm)**'.

Bark thickness measurement (mm)

This feature records the total thickness (in mm) of the outer and inner bark.

Bark blaze layering

The blaze consists of either one or two bark layers as exposed when cut. The bark is recorded as having either **one layer** or **two layers**:

one layer There is no discernible difference between the inner and outer layer of the bark (Fig. 426C)
two layers Both an inner and outer layer can be distinguished. The layers are most commonly discernible because of differences in colour and/or texture (Fig. 426D)

Note: Very occasionally **three layers** of bark are discernible.

Bark blaze aroma

The bark is either recorded as **faintly aromatic or non-aromatic** or as **strongly aromatic**

Note: Since the aroma of the bark is frequently only fully developed in mature trees, it is recommended that caution be used when attempting to categorise the aroma of bark on trees with a trunk of less than 50 cm in diameter at breast height (dbh) (at about 1.3 m above ground). Furthermore, the ability to detect a bark blaze as 'faintly aromatic' can be problematic because of other aromas in the forest and is dependent on the ability of the observer to detect faint aromas. Therefore, 'faintly aromatic' and 'non-aromatic' are treated as the same.

Bark blaze aromatic type

When the bark is aromatic, then the following types of aroma are recognised:

unpleasant **onion-like** **cinnamon-like** **resinous/liniment-like**	**spice-like** **pleasant** **pine-like** **almond-like**

Note: this feature is relatively subjective since the recognition of different aromas is dependent on the perceptions of the observer. Therefore, this character should be used with caution. The two general categories, **pleasant** or **unpleasant** have been included when it is difficult to determine which of the other categories best describe the odour. Please note that the above descriptors are not mutually exclusive.

Bark outer blaze colour

When there is two bark layers recognised, then this is the layer furthest from the wood, or if only one bark layer is present, then this **bark outer blaze colour** and the **bark inner blaze colour** are given the same values.

The **colours of the outer blaze** that are recognised include: **white, yellow, orange, pink, red, brown, black, green, grey, mixed colours.**

Note: the category **mixed colours** is used when several (usually more than 2) different colours are present. Otherwise, several different colours may be selected to represent the main colours.

Bark outer blaze markings

This feature records the **presence** or **absence of markings** in the blaze of the outer bark. The values include:

markings absent (Fig. 426E)
speckled – with marking more or less as wide as long, hence like dots (Fig. 426C)
with stripes – markings distinctly longer than wide, hence like lines (Fig. 426F)

Bark outer blaze texture

The texture of the bark's outer blaze is recorded as either:

smooth – hence, lacking any texture
fibrous – texture consisting of long fibrous groupings of cells (Fig. 426F)
granular with splinters - bark crumbling into small blocks of cells with long splinter-like pieces of bark amongst granules (Fig. 426G)
granular without splinters - all the outer bark crumbles into small blocks of cells. The long splinter-like pieces of bark are absent from this layer
corky – very light, more or less smooth bark, frequently relatively thick, similar in texture to corks used in bottles (Fig. 426H)

Bark inner blaze colour

When there are two bark layers recognised, then this is the layer closest to the wood, or if only one bark layer is present, then this part of the bark is recorded as the same colour as the bark outer blaze.

The **colours of the inner blaze** that are recognised include: **white**, **yellow**, **orange**, **pink**, **red**, **brown**, **black**, **green**, **grey**, **mixed colours**.

Note: the category **mixed colours** is used when several (usually more than 2) different colours are present. Otherwise, several different colours may be selected to represent the main colours.

Bark inner blaze markings

This feature records the **presence** or **absence of markings** in the blaze of the inner bark. The values include:

markings absent;
speckled – marking more or less as wide as long, hence like dots;
with stripes – markings distinctly longer than wide, hence like lines (refer Fig. 426F)

Bark inner blaze texture

The texture of the bark's inner blaze can be:

smooth – hence, lacking any texture
fibrous – texture consisting of long fibrous groupings of cells
granular with splinters – bark crumbling into small blocks of cells with long splinter-like pieces of bark amongst granules

granular without splinters – all the inner bark crumbles into small blocks of cells. The long splinter-like pieces of bark are absent from this layer
corky – very light, more or less smooth bark, frequently relatively thick, similar in texture to corks used in bottles

Bark exudate (sap) presence

The presence of this feature is observed after the bark is cut through to the outer wood. Since the sap often takes a few moments to appear after the bark is cut, wait a minute or two before deciding that sap is absent. When sap is not abundant, it frequently does not appear immediately. Also, remember that small amounts of clear exudate are often difficult to observe. This feature is recorded as either **present** or **absent** (Figs 426I & J)

Bark exudate (sap) colour

When the bark exudate (sap) is **present**, this feature records the colour of the sap when first exposed to the air by the cut. The following **colours** are recognised: **white/milky**, **yellow**, **red**, **brown**, **green**, **blue**, **colourless** (lacking colour or clear, often watery).

Note: Since the colour of the sap may change rapidly once exposed to the air by the cut, the sap colour should be recorded immediately.

Bark exudate (sap) abundance

When the bark exudate (sap) is **present**, this feature records abundance of the sap when the bark is cut. The sap is recorded as:

flowing – Soon after the blaze is cut, the exudate/sap flows abundantly (Fig. 426J)
spotty, not readily flowing – The exudate/sap usually takes some time to appear, but even when it appears immediately, it does not readily flow (hence referred to as spotty) (Fig. 426I)

Bark exudate (sap) colour changing

When the bark exudate (sap) is **present**, this feature records any colour changes of the sap when the bark is cut. This feature is recorded as either: **colour changing on exposure to air** or **colour not changing on exposure to air.**

Note: the sap frequently becomes slight darker, but this is not regarded as a colour change.

Bark exudate (sap) colour change

When the bark exudate (sap) is present and the colour of the sap changes when the bark is cut, the final colour of the sap is recorded.

The following **colours** are recognised: **golden-coloured**, **orange**, **red**, **brown**, **green**, **grey**, **black**.

Bark exudate (sap) stickiness

When the bark exudate (sap) is **present**, this feature records if the exudate is: **sticky** when touched, or **not sticky**.

INDUMENTUM ON BRANCHES

Complex hairs (presence)

This feature records the **presence** or **absence of complex** (not simple – Fig. 427A) **indumentum**. The indumentum either consists of variously branched hairs or trichomes that have been modified into scales. Since these complex hairs are usually very small, a hand lens with at least 10X magnification or a microscope is required for viewing these features. Complex hairs are recorded as either **present** or **absent**.

Complex hairs (type)

When complex hairs are present, then this character records the type of complex hairs. **Note:** A 10X hand lens or microscope is often required. The types of complex hairs recorded include:

Disk-shaped – axis of the hair terminating in a more or less flattened disk of tissue, with the axis attached to the centre of the disk. Also known as peltate hairs (Fig. 427B)
Star-like – the hair is once-branched with each branch radiating out from a single point. Also known as stellate hairs (Fig. 427C)
T-shaped – the hair terminates in two branches that are approximately at right angles to the hairs axis. Hairs are shaped like the uppercase letter 'T'
Club-shaped – hairs are swollen towards the apex of the hair. The hair appears obovoid
Head-like – the hairs terminate in a small more or less globular swelling. Also known as capitate hairs (Fig. 427D)
Awl-like – the hairs are narrow and gradually tapering to a fine point (Fig. 427E)

Stinging hairs This feature records the **presence** or **absence of stinging** (urticating) hairs anywhere on the tree (Fig. 427F). Typically, these hairs are found in certain species of the Family Urticaceae (for example, *Dendrocnide* species). Stinging hairs are recorded as either: **present** or **absent**.

Mature twig indumentum (hairs) presence

This feature records the **presence** or **absence of hairs** on the twigs which are the smallest distal branchlets. Indumentum (hairs) is recorded as either: **present** or, **absent** on the mature twigs.

Mature twig indumentum (hairs) density

When hairs are present on mature twigs, this feature records the density of these hairs as either: **dense** or **sparse**.

Note: It is often best to observe the presence or absence of hairs through a 10X hand lens. When the indumentum is dense, the hairs are usually easily observed, even when short. However, when the indumentum is sparse, hairs may sometimes be difficult to see.

Fig. 427. Indumentum, leaf arrangement and leaf type (diagrams © Royal Botanic Gardens Sydney)

3. LEAF FEATURES

The definition of the technical terms used for the leaf features of the tree are organised into the following five sections:

- General Leaf features
- Simple Leaves
- Compound Leaves
- Venation
- Stipules

General Leaf Features

Leaves (position on branchlet)

The position of the leaves on the branchlets (twigs) are either:

clustered at end of branches with internodes indistinct (Fig. 427G)
spaced along branches with internodes readily visible (Fig. 427H)

Notes: Although most trees tend to have the leaves inserted towards the end of branchlets, the main difference between the two categories of this feature is whether the *internode* (part of the branchlet between the bases of the leaves) is clearly visible or not visible

Leaves (insertion/arrangement)

This feature describes how the leaves are inserted on to the branchlet. The leaves are recorded as:

opposite in pairs, opposite one another on the branch (Fig. 427I)
whorled with more than two leaves inserted at one node of a branch; arising from one level) (Fig. 427J)
spiral leaves occurring singly at a node/level and arranged spirally up the branch (Fig. 427K)

the leaf arrangements of 'opposite and all leaves in one plane' (Fig. 427I – left) and 'opposite and decussate – leaves in two planes' (Fig. 427I – right) are not distinguished in Trees of Papua New Guinea. Both are treated as 'opposite'. Likewise, 'spiral' is here used to include 'spiral – leaves in at least two planes' (Fig. 427K), and 'alternate and leaves

Leaves per whorl

When the **leaves are arranged in a whorl** (three or more leaves arising from a single node/level), then this feature records: - **the number of leaves at each node** (as an integer)

Leaves simple or compound

This feature describes the structure of the leaves as either:

simple – each leaf composed of a single lamina/blade (Fig. 427L)
compound – each leaf made up from two or more leaflets (Fig. 427M)

Note: The modified petioles (phyllodes) of *Acacia* species are recorded as 'simple leaves'. Compound leaves which consist of only one leaflet (unifoliate compound leaves), are frequently difficult to distinguish from simple leaves, except by careful examination. Unifoliate leaves are also scored as 'simple leaves', even though this is a misinterpretation

Petiole presence

This feature records the **presence** or **absence of a petiole** (stalk of a leaf). Sessile leaves lack a petiole, whereas, stalked leaves are petiolate (that is, petiole is present). This feature has the value of either:

absent (Figs 428A & B)
present (Figs 428C & D)

Petiole wing

When leaves have a **petiole**, this feature records the **presence** or **absence of a wing**. The petiole is regarded as winged when there is a thin flange of tissue along the length (or at least in part) of the petiole. This feature has one of the following values:

not winged (Fig. 428E)
winged (Fig. 428F)

Petiole attachment to lamina

When the **petiole** is **present**, this feature describes how the petiole is attached to the leaf lamina (blade). The petiole is either:

> **attached to surface of leaf lamina**, hence, lamina is peltate (Fig. 428D)
> **attached to base of leaf lamina** (hence, not peltate) (Fig. 428C). Note: this is the most common form of petiole attachment to the leaf lamina (blade)

Petiole swollen at either end

When the **petiole** is **present**, this feature describes the **presence** or **absence of a swelling** at the base and/or apex of the petiole. The petiole is either:

> **not swollen** – more or less the same diameter/width throughout
> **swollen** – at tip, or base, or both. The 'tip' of the petiole refers to the point of attachment with the lamina, whereas the 'base' refers to the point where the petiole is attached to the branchlet (twig).

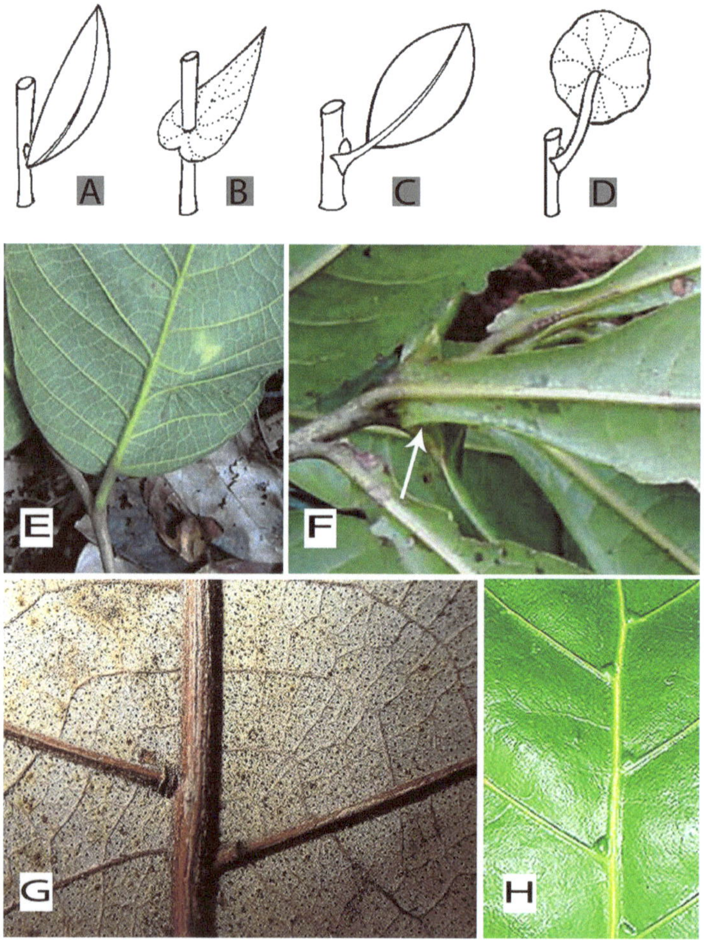

Fig. 428. Petiole features, glands and domatia on leaves (diagrams © Royal Botanic Gardens Sydney)

Leaves lower surface colour

The colour of the **lower** (abaxial) **surface of the leaves** is recorded as:

blue-green, pale green, green, yellow, brown, red, grey. Qualifiers such as glossy or dull are also included.

Leaves upper surface colour

The colour of the **upper** (adaxial) **surface of the leaves** is recorded using the same categories as that used for lower leaf surface. Qualifiers such as glossy or dull is also recorded.

Leaves indumentum (hairs) presence

The **presence** or **absence of hairs** on mature (simple) leaves or leaflets (of compound leaves) is recorded. The value of this feature is either **present** or **absent**.

Leaves indumentum (hairs) density

When indumentum (hairs) is present on mature leaves, this feature records the density of this indumentum. The indumentum is recorded as either **dense** or **sparse**.

Note: This feature is often best observed through a 10X hand lens, as for "**Mature twig indumentum (hairs) density**"

Leaves gland-dotted

This character records the **presence** or **absence of glands** in mature leaves. These glands often appear as numerous semi-transparent dots distributed across the lamina (Fig. 428G). This feature is recorded as **absent** or **present**.

Leaves domatia presence

Domatia are parts of plants that have been modified into cavities that are used by other organisms (e.g., ants). Domatia can occur on leaves (Fig. 428H), stems and even roots.

This feature records the **absence** or **presence of domatia** on the leaf. It can have the values: **absent** or **present**

Leaves domatia distribution

If domatia are present, then this character describes their position on the leaf as either:

scattered along midrib (Fig. 428H)
scattered across lamina

Simple Leaves

Leaves lamina shape

This feature describes the shape of the leaf lamina (blade) based on the position of its widest part. The values include:

broadest above middle – equivalent to oblanceolate, obovate, spathulate, and other similar shapes that are broadest towards the apex of the leaf (Fig. 429A)
broadest at or near middle – equivalent to elliptic, oval, and other similar shapes (Fig. 429B)
broadest below middle – equivalent to lanceolate, ovate, triangular and other similar shapes that are broadest towards the base of the lamina (Fig. 429C)
equally broad throughout much of length – equivalent to oblong and often strap-like (Fig. 429D)

Leaves (lamina length, in cm)

The length of the leaf lamina (blade) (in cm) is measured from the base (at point of attachment of the petiole, when petiole attached to base of leaf blade) to the leaf apex, or the longest axis of peltate leaves

Leaves (lamina width, in cm)

This feature records the width of the leaf lamina (blade) (in cm) at its widest part. This measurement is taken at right angles to the mid-vein or the medial (central) axis of the lamina when the mid-vein is absent or not visible

Leaves symmetry at base

This feature describes the **symmetry of the base of the leaf lamina** (blade) on either side of the central vein/axis as being either:

very asymmetric (Fig. 429E)
symmetric (Fig. 429F)

Note: Leaf bases that are only slightly asymmetric are scored as 'symmetric'.

Leaves with margin toothing

The margin of the leaf lamina (blade) may have teeth present. This feature describes the **presence** or **absence of teeth** and the margin is described as:

entire – lacking teeth, usually smooth (Fig. 429G)
crenate – teeth shallow/small and rounded (Fig. 429H)
serrate to dentate (toothed) – more or less strongly to distinctly and sharply toothed (Fig. 429I)

Note: this feature should not be confused with whether the leaves are dissected or lobed, or whether the leaf margin is undulate.

Leaves dissected or lobed

The **presence** or **absence of lobes** on the margin of the leaf lamina (blade) is described as:

dissected or lobed (Figs 429J & K)
not dissected or lobed (Fig. 429G)

Note: No distinction is made between dissected and lobed leaves. Also, this feature should not be confused with whether the margin of the leaf lamina (blade) is entire or variously toothed, or whether the leaf margin is undulate

Leaves dissection type

When the leaf lamina (blade) is dissected or lobed, the dissection or lobing is described as either:

pinnately lobed (Fig. 429J)
palmately lobed (Fig. 429K)

Leaves shape of apex

The shape of the apex of the leaf lamina (blade) is described as:

emarginate or retuse – having a notch at the apex or ending in a rounded apex with a rounded sinus (cavity) at the centre (Fig. 429L)
rounded – apex rounded like an arc of a circle (Fig. 429M)
obtuse – apex gradually ending in a rounded blunt point (Fig. 429N)
acute – should be sharp to touch like the point of a needle, apex with two almost straight sides (Fig. 429O)
mucronate – lamina ending abruptly by a hard, short point (Fig. 429P)
long-tapering – apex gradually ending in a long reducing point. This definition includes acuminate (Fig. 429Q)

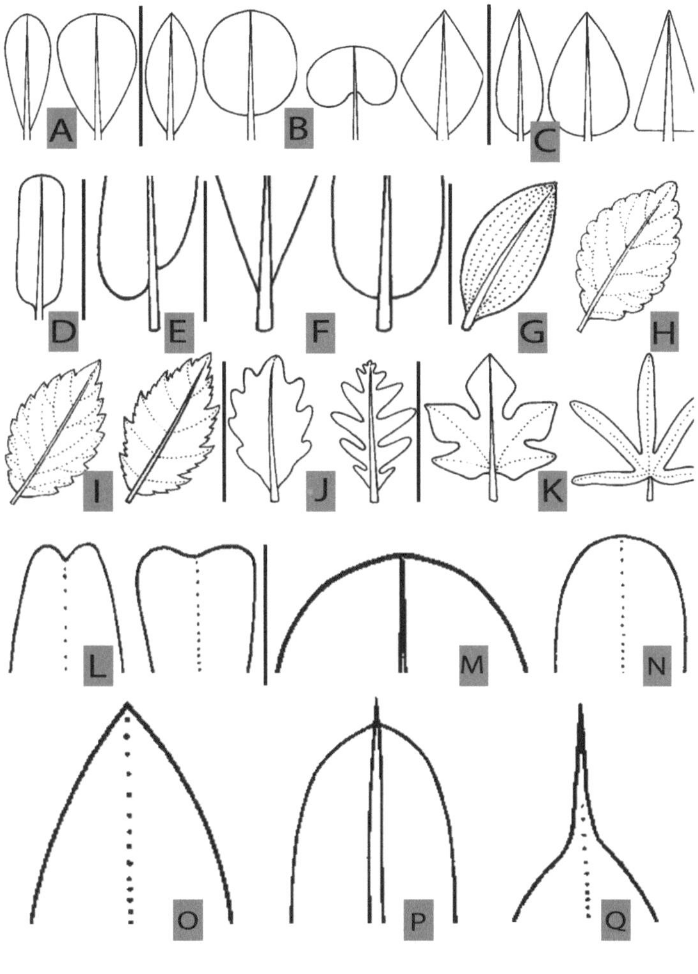

Fig. 429. Leaf lamina features: shape, base, margin and apex (diagrams © Royal Botanic Gardens Sydney)

Compound Leaves

Leaves when compound, leaf form

When the plant has compound leaves, the types of leaves are recorded as:

with one leaflet (unifoliate) – a compound leaf reduced to a single leaflet. Compound leaves that consist of a single leaflet are often difficult to distinguish from simple leaves. They are usually recognised by the articulated or jointed 'petiole', which is a petiole plus a petiolule (see definition below) (Fig. 430A)
with two leaflets (bifoliate) – these compound leaves are referred to as bifoliate (Fig. 430B)
with three leaflets (trifoliate) – these compound leaves are referred to as trifoliate (Fig. 430C)
pinnate – more than three leaflets and the leaflets are arranged along an unbranched rachis (axis of the leaf) (Figs 430D & E)
bipinnate – more than three leaflets. This is like pinnate, except the rachis (main axis) is branched once (Fig. 430F)
multiple compound – this type of compound leaf has a rachis with more than two orders of branching before leaflets are formed (Fig. 430G)
palmate – this type of compound leaf has more than three leaflets attached at one point to the petiole (Fig. 430H)

Petiolule of leaflet, swollen or not

The petiolule is the stalk of a leaflet in compound leaves. This feature records the **presence** or **absence of a swelling** at either end of the petiolule. The petiolule is recorded as either:

not swollen (about the same diameter or width throughout length of petiolule)
swollen at tip, or base, or both

Rachis presence

The rachis is here used to describe the **presence** or **absence of a stalk-like axis** of a compound leaf. It is either **absent** or **present** (Figs 430I & J)

Note: the rachis is regarded as **absent** for compound leaves with only one, two or three leaflets, and for palmate compound leaves that have more than three leaflets attached at one point

Rachis wings

When the rachis is present, this feature records the **presence** or **absence of a wing** along the axis of the rachis. The rachis is scored as either:

wing **absent** (such that **rachis not winged**)
wing **present** (hence, **rachis winged**).

Rachis swelling

When the rachis is **present**, this feature records the **presence** or **absence of a swelling** at either end of the rachis. The rachis has either:

swellings **absent** (hence, **rachis not swollen**, more or less the same diameter/width throughout),
swellings **present** (hence, with rachis swollen at either end (Fig. 430J)

Leaves when compound, paripinnate or imparipinnate

When the tree has **pinnate compound leaves**, this feature describes the **presence** or **absence of a terminal leaflet**. The values for this feature are either:

without a terminal leaflet (paripinnate) – there is an even number of leaflets, such that the compound leaves are paripinnate (Fig. 430D)
with a terminal leaflet (imparipinnate) – there is an odd number of leaflets with one leaflet inserted at the apex; compound leaves imparipinnate (Fig. 430E)

Leaves when compound, leaflet lamina shape type

This feature describes the **shape of the leaflet lamina** (blade) based on the position of its widest part. The values include:

broadest above middle – equivalent to oblanceolate, obovate, spathulate, and other similar shapes (Fig. 429A)
broadest at or near middle – equivalent to elliptic, oval, and other similar shapes (Fig. 429B)
broadest below middle – equivalent to lanceolate, ovate, and other similar shapes (Fig. 429C)
equally broad throughout much of length – equivalent to oblong and strap-like (Fig. 429D)

Leaves when compound, leaflet lamina length (cm)

This feature records the **length of the leaflet lamina** (blade) (in cm) from the **base** (at point of attachment of the petiolule) to the **leaflet apex**.

Leaves when compound, leaflet lamina width (cm)

This feature records the **width of the leaflet lamina** (blade) (in cm) at its **widest part**. This measurement is taken at right angles to the mid-vein or the medial (central) axis of the lamina when the mid-vein is absent or not visible.

Leaves when compound, leaflets arrangement

This feature describes how the **leaflets are inserted on to the rachis**. The feature records the arrangement as either:

leaflets opposite – leaflets arranged in pairs, opposite one another on the rachis (Figs 430D & E)
leaflets alternate – leaflets occurring singly along the rachis and alternating from one side of the axis to the other
leaflets inserted at one point of the leaf axis –leaflets in palmatifid arrangement or appearing whorl-like (Fig. 430H)

Leaves when compound, leaflet symmetry, at base

This feature describes the **symmetry of the base** of the leaflet lamina (blade) on either side of the central vein/axis as being either:

asymmetric (Fig. 429E)
symmetric (Fig. 429F)

Leaves when compound and imparipinnate, terminal leaflet buds

When the compound leaves are terminated by a single leaflet (that is, imparipinnate), then the apex of the compound leaf has the following values:

terminal developing leaflet buds **curled back on itself**
terminal developing leaflet buds **straight**
terminal developing leaflet buds **absent**

Note: There is a problem with *Kingiodendron novoguineense* Verdc. This species is paripinnate, but it can have only 1-leaflet. Therefore, this species has also been recorded as **'terminal developing leaflet buds absent'** and **'terminal developing leaflet buds straight'** (by misinterpretation)

Fig. 430. Compound leaflet arrangement, rachis and venation types (diagrams © Royal Botanic Gardens Sydney)

Venation

Venation, layout of secondary veins on leaf/leaflet

This feature describes the arrangement of the secondary veins on the leaves or leaflets (for compound leaves). The values recorded include:

single-veined – the leaf or leaflet with only one vein (Fig. 430K)
pinnate – secondary veins arising from the midrib along its length. The venation of *Calophyllum* species is scored as pinnate (Fig. 430L)
trinerved – three large veins arising from the base (Fig. 430M)

palmate – more than three large veins arising from the base (Fig. 430N)
parallel-veined – numerous small veins running in parallel from base, not arising from a midrib. The venation of *Araucaria hunsteinii* is parallel-veined (Fig. 430O)

Secondary veins (open or closed)

This feature describes the closeness of the secondary veins as either:

open – spaced far apart to easily see tertiary veins (Figs 431A & B)
closed – spaced so close together that tertiary veins cannot be easily seen between them. For example, the close secondary veins in *Calophyllum* species (Figs 431C & D)

Secondary veins prominence

This feature describes the **distinctiveness/visibility of the secondary veins** as:

prominent
not prominent, but visible
not visible

Intramarginal veins presence

This feature records the **presence** or **absence of an intramarginal vein** and is recorded as either:

present (Fig. 431E)
absent (Fig. 431F)

Stipulaes

Stipules presence

This feature records the **presence** or **absence of stipules** at the base of the leaf. Since the **stipules may not be persistent,** their **presence** may be indicated by the **presence of stipular scars**. This feature is recorded as either **absent** or **present**

Stipules freedom

When present, the stipules are either:

free from one another (Figs 431G & N)
joined to each other (Figs 431H–L)

Stipules position

The **position of the stipules** is recorded as either:

joined across twigs and so growing between opposite leaves and leaving a scar between them when they fall; hence, interpetiolar (Fig. 431K)
laterally placed whether free from each other or joined together (Fig. 431G)

Stipules encircling twig

When stipules are present, they may be either:

> **encircling the twig** (amplexicaul) (Fig. 431L)
> **not encircling the twig** (Figs 431G & N)

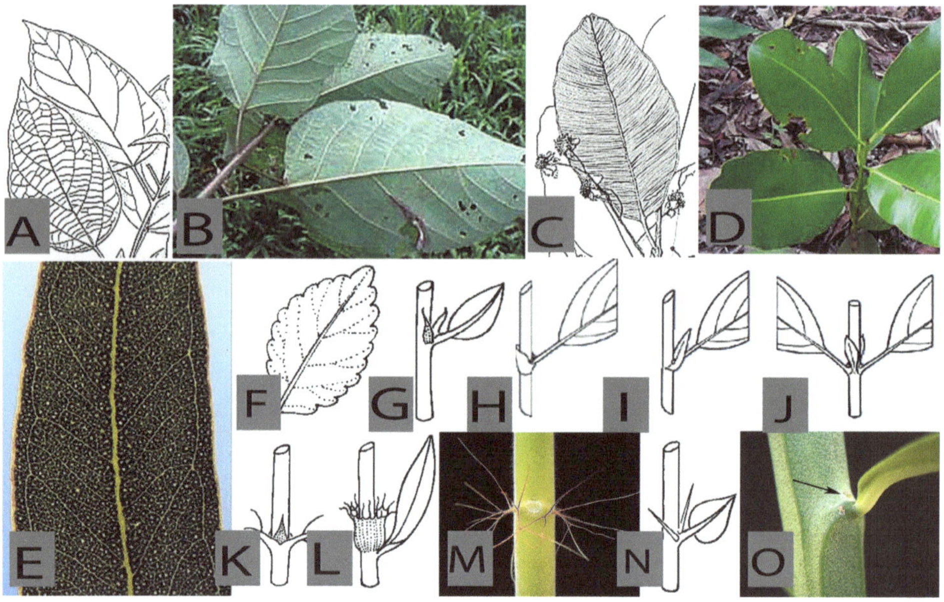

Fig. 431. Secondary venation and stipules (diagrams © Royal Botanic Gardens Sydney)

Stipules form

When stipules are present, several different **shapes (form) of stipules** may be present. The shapes include:

> **scale-like** – often more or less translucent, usually significantly reduced in size and frequently more or less triangular. Two scaly stipules occur on the two lateral sides of leaf bases enclosing the leaf bud. When the leaves unfold, these scaly stipules fall off. Scaly stipules are present in species of, for example: *Ficus*, *Artocarpus* and *Magnolia*
> **collar-like** stipules are distally truncate such that no clear apex is recognisable, often the stipules are more or less encircling the twig (Fig. 431L)
> **hair-like** stipules are greatly reduced and usually linear (Fig. 431M)
> **leafy** stipules are more or less similar in shape to a leaf, usually green (Fig. 431G)
> **spiny** stipules reduced to a more or less sharp, linear point (spine) (Fig. 431N)
> **represented by glands** stipules modified and glandular (Fig. 431O)

Stipules margin

The presence of hairs on the margin of stipules is recorded as either:

> **fringed** – (fimbriate), hence, hairs present
> **not fringed** – hence, hairs absent

Stipules size

The **size of the stipules** is classified as either:

large – easily visible (without magnification)
small – not easily visible (often sufficiently small that careful examination is required to view these stipules)

Stipules persistence

The stipules may remain on the twigs and hence are **persistent**, or they fall off, hence do not persist and are scored as **non-persistent** (caducous).

4. FLOWER AND FRUIT FEATURES

The definitions of the technical terms used for the flower and fruit features are organised into the following seven sections

- **General Flower Features**
- **Perianth** (calyx and corolla)
- **Stamens** (male reproductive structures)
- **Gynoecium** (female reproductive structures – ovary, style, stigma)
- **Fruits**
- **Cones**
- **Seeds**

General Flower Features

Arrangement of flowers

This feature refers to the **position of the inflorescence** (arrangement of flowers) on the vegetative axis. It is recorded as either:

terminal at end of branchlets (axes) (Fig. 432A)
axillary arising from between a leaf and a branchlet (axis) (Fig. 432B)
leaf-opposed arising opposite a leaf, not between a leaf and a branchlet (axis), this character state includes inflorescences that are laterally inserted on branches behind (below) a leaf (Fig. 432C)
on the trunk or branches (cauliflorous or ramiflorous), no distinction is made between cauliflorous and ramiflorous because species which have flowers arising directly from the trunk (cauliflorous) often also have at least some flowers arising directly from the branches (ramiflorous) (Fig. 432D)

Arrangement of flowers, axis structure

The **absence** or **presence of an inflorescence** (flowering) **axis** is recorded by this character. The inflorescence is described as consisting of either:

Flowers arising from a single point

Recorded as either as:

flowers single (solitary), only one flower present in each inflorescence (Fig. 432E)
more than one flower present in each inflorescence which arises from either the branch, stem or trunk of the tree (Figs 432B–D, F–H)

Flowers arranged along an axis

Either as:

flowers on an unbranched axis (Fig. 432G)
flowers on a branched axis (Figs 432B, C, F & G)

Flowering cones/strobili presence

The flowers of Conifers are arranged in flowering strobili (strobilus, singular) often generally referred to as 'flowering cones'. This character generally records the **absence** (dicotyledonous plants) or **presence** (Conifers) of strobili, However, the Podocarpaceae (as illustrated in Fig. 432I) are dicotyledonous plants that have female flowers arranged in strobili. This feature is recorded, as either:

absent or **present** (Fig. 432I)

Fig. 432. Arrangement of flowers and flowering cones (strobili)

Flowers sexuality

The flowers are either described as:

unisexual with flowers either male or female (Fig. 433A)
bisexual with androecium (stamens) and gynoecium (ovary, with or without style, with stigma) (Fig. 433B)

Flowers unisexual position

When the flowers are **unisexual**, the flowers either occur on the same plant (hence, plant monoecious) or male flowers occur on one plant and female flowers on a separate plant (hence, plant dioecious).

Therefore, the plants are recorded as either:

with male and female flowers on the same plant (monoecious)
with male and female flowers on different plants (dioecious) (Fig. 433H)

Flowers stalked

The flowers are directly attached to the axis of the inflorescence or they occur on a short to long stalk. The flowers are recorded as either:

not stalked (sessile) (Fig. 433C)
stalked (pedicellate) (Figs 433D–H)

Flowers symmetry

The shape of flowers varies considerably between species and this variation is often reflected in the number of planes of symmetry within the flower. Architecturally, they may be regular, with many planes of symmetry to very irregular.

The symmetry of flowers is described as:

with many planes of symmetry (actinomorphic) (Fig. 433E)
slightly asymmetric with one plane of symmetry (zygomorphic) (Fig. 433F)
completely asymmetric – Currently, no species with irregular flowers are known for Papua New Guinea

Flowers length (mm)

The **length of the flower** is measured in **millimetres (mm)** from the base of the perianth (from the distal end of the pedicel (stalk) if flower pedicellate) to the end of the perianth (sepals and/or petals).

Note: often the style and stigma are distinctly exerted far beyond the perianth. These features are not included in this measurement.

Flowers diameter (mm)

The **diameter of the flower** is classified according to:

small (< or =10 mm diam.)
large (>10 mm diam.)

Fig. 433. Flower sexuality, symmetry, perianth, stamens, gynoecium and general fruit features (diagrams © Royal Botanic Gardens Sydney)

Perianth

Perianth presence

The absence or presence of a perianth in the flowers is recorded as either:

absent or **present**

Note: this feature is not concerned about the number of distinct whorls of perianth. There may be both sepals and petals present or just one of these whorls.

Perianth type

The perianth of the flowers is recorded as:

with distinct sepals and petals (Fig. 433G)

whorls integrating from sepals to petals (e.g., as for *Nymphaea*)
with all sepals and/or petals (hence tepals) **similar**

Perianth colour

The colour of the perianth which is closest to the stamens and/or ovary, usually regarded as the corolla (petals), or if only one perianth whorl, then this character refers to the colour of that whorl, which is recorded as: **white**, **yellow**, **orange**, **pink**, **red**, **blue**, **purple**, **mauve**, **green**, **brown**, **grey**, **cream-coloured**

Note: often several colours are present. The inner perianth may consist of more than one colour and these colours should be recorded. However, the various hues/shades of colour are not recorded, but rather only the basic colour types (listed above) should be used.

Inner perianth parts

The number of parts of the inner perianth, whether free (not joined) or variously joined to each other. In the *PNGtrees* database, the value '100' is arbitrarily assigned when there are so many perianth parts that it is difficult to count them.

Inner perianth parts, extent of fusion

The **extent of fusion** (joining) of the parts of the inner perianth (usually the corolla or petals) or the only perianth whorl. This is recorded as:

free – when all the parts of the perianth are not united to each other (Fig. 433G)
some or partly joined – when at least some parts of the perianth are joined together (Fig. 433F)
all joined – all the parts of the perianth are joined together such that there is a corolla tube with corolla lobes absent or greatly reduced and so not obvious

Stamens

Stamens number

The number of stamens, whether free (not joined) or variously joined to each other. In the *PNGtrees* database, the value '100' is arbitrarily assigned when there are many stamens (Fig. 433H)

Stamens filaments

This feature records the **absence** or **presence** of **staminal filaments**.

The staminal filaments are either:

absent (hence anthers sessile)
present (Fig. 433I)

Stamens freedom

The **extent of fusion** (joining) **of each of the stamens together**.

This is recorded as either:

free from each other (Fig. 433J)
joined (connate), at least in part (Fig. 433K)

Stamens joined to perianth

The **extent of fusion** (joining) **of each stamen to the perianth** (adnation), either to the petals (epipetalous) or to the sepals (episepalous).

The stamens are either:

free of the perianth – stamens not joined to the perianth
joined to the perianth – (epipetalous/episepalous)

Gynoecium

Ovary (gynoecium) position

This feature records the position of the ovary with respect to the point of insertion of the petals and/or sepals.

The ovary is recorded as:

superior – ovary seated above the base of the petals and sepals (hypogenous) (Fig. 433L)
partly inferior (perigenous) (Fig. 433M)
inferior – ovary seated below base of the petals and sepals (epigenous) (Fig. 433N)

Carpels (gynoecium) constitution

The gynoecium consists of one or more carpels which are variously fused (joined) or not united together.

This character records the **presence of one carpel**:

solitary (monomerous) – the ovary consisting of a single carpel (Fig. 433O)

or,

the **extent of fusion** when there is **more than one carpel** as:

separate (when more than one), each carpel completely free from the other carpels. The flower is regarded as apocarpous
joined (when more than one carpel – syncarpous), all carpels completely joined together (Fig. 433P)
partially joined, by base – the distal parts of the carpels are free from each other, not united, and the styles are also separate
partially joined by styles - the basal parts of the carpels are free from each other, not united, but are joined together by their styles

Locules number

This feature records the **number of locules** (chambers that contain the ovules) of the gynoecium. (Fig. 433P illustrates 1, 2 and 3 locules)

Styles presence

The gynoecium consists of an ovary and one or more stigmas. The stigma(s) are inserted on the end of a style or the style is absent. This feature records the **absence** or **presence of one or more styles**.

The style is recorded as:

absent,
solitary (including joined together), as illustrated here (Figs 433B, L–N, Q)

or

free – (two or more styles that are entirely free from each other)

Styles number

This character records the **number of styles**

Fruits

Arrangement of axis of fruits

The **absence** or **presence of an infructescence** (fruiting) **axis** is recorded by this character.

The infructescence is described as consisting of either:

fruits arising from a single point, either as:

fruits single – (solitary), only one fruit present in each infructescence (Fig. 433R)
fruits arising from a single point – but with more than one fruit present in each infructescence, which arises from either the branch, stem or trunk of the tree (Figs 433S & T)

fruits arranged along an axis, either as:

fruits on an unbranched axis (Fig. 433U)
fruits on a branched axis (Fig. 433V)

Fruit length (mm)

The **length of the fruit**, in dicotyledonous plants, measured in **millimetres (mm)** along the longest axis

Fruit colour

When the plant is a dicotyledon, the **colour of the mature fruit** is recorded as: **white**, **cream-coloured**, **yellow**, **green**, **blue**, **purple**, **orange**, **red**, **brown**, **black**, **grey**

Fruit spiny

This feature records the **absence** or **presence of spines** on the **surface of the fruit** (in dicotyledons) as either:

not spiny or **spiny** (Figs 433W & X)

Fruit fleshy

The mature fruits of dicotyledons are either:

non-fleshy (Figs 433W & X)
fleshy (Fig. 433Y)

Fruit structure

The mature fruits of dicotyledons are:

simple – a fruit which is derived from a **single** flower –a flower that has a **single carpel** or **several fused carpels** (Figs 433R & Z)
aggregrate – a fruit that has developed from several separate carpels of one flower (Fig. 433Aa)
multiple (excluding figs) – a fruit which consists of the carpels from **several flowers** in an inflorescence forming a multiple fruit (infrutescence) (Fig. 433Ab)
syconium (fig) – the '**fig**' is a specific example of a **multiple fruit** where the individual achenes (dry, one-seeded, indehiscent fruits) are borne on the inside of a hollowed-out receptacle or peduncle (Fig. 433Ac)

Fruit dehiscent or indehiscent

The mature fruits of dicotyledons **open in a set way** (dehiscent) to release their seeds or they **do not open** on maturity (indehiscent).

The fruits are recorded as:

indehiscent (Fig. 434A)
dehiscent (Fig. 433X)

Fruit dehiscence type

When the fruits of dicotyledons are dehiscent, the fruit is described as:

capsule – a simple, dry fruit that opens in a definite way, consisting of two or more carpels (Figs 433X & 434B)
follicle – a simple, dry, dehiscent fruit with one carpel that opens along one side of the fruit (Fig. 434C)
legume – a simple, dry, dehiscent fruit with one carpel that opens along two sides of the fruit (Figs 433Z & 434D)
loment – a special type of legume that separates transversely between seed sections Fig. 434E)

Fruit indehiscence type

When the **fruits** of dicotyledons are **indehiscent**, the fruit is described as:

achene – a simple, dry, 1-seeded, indehiscent fruit that has developed from a flower with a superior ovary (Fig. 434F)
berry – a simple, indehiscent, more or less juicy/fleshy, few- to many-seeded fruit, with a fleshy fruit wall (pericarp) (Fig. 433Y)
drupe – a simple, indehiscent, more or less fleshy fruit that is derived from a single carpel, usually one-seeded,

in which the exocarp (outer-most part of pericarp) is thin, the mesocarp (middle layer of pericarp) is fleshy, and the endocarp (inner-most layer of pericarp) is stony (Fig. 434A)

hesperidium – a special type of **berry** that has a thick skin, is septate, and with the bulk of the fruit derived from glandular hairs (characteristic of the Rutaceae, e.g., oranges, lemons, grapefruit) (Fig. 434G)

nut – a simple, dry, indehiscent, 1-seeded fruit with a hard fruit wall (pericarp), usually derived from a 1-loculate ovary, as in the Fagaceae (Fig. 434H)

pepo – a special type of **berry** that has a leathery, non-septate rind (pericarp) derived from a flower with an inferior ovary (Cucurbitaceae, e.g., watermelon, pumpkin, cucumber) (Fig. 434I)

pome – a simple, indehiscent, fleshy fruit, the outer part of which is formed by the floral parts that surround the ovary. This special type of simple fruit is often referred to as an accessory fruit (Rosaceae, Fig. 434J)

samara – a simple, dry, indehiscent, 1- or 2-seeded fruit with the pericarp bearing a wing-like outgrowth (e.g., Ulmaceae, Combretaceae – Combretum, Fig. 434K)

schizocarp – a fruit with two or more united carpels that split apart at maturity (a feature of fruit in the Lamiaceae)

syconium - sometimes the **'fig'** is incorrectly referred to as if it were a simple fruit rather than a special type of **multiple fruit**. The individual fruits within the fig are achenes. Refer to definition of achene above (Fig. 434L)

Fig. 434. Fruit types and seeds (diagrams © Royal Botanic Gardens Sydney)

Cones

Cones presence

The seeds of Conifers are usually arranged in **woody fruiting strobili** (strobilus, singular), referred to a **cone** or **fruiting cone**.

Cones are either:

absent (dicotyledonous plants)
present (conifers – strobili) (Fig. 434M)

Cones length (mm)

The **length of cone**, in Conifers, measured in **millimetres (mm)** along the longest axis

Cones diameter (mm)

When the plant is a conifer, the diameter at the widest part of the mature cone, measured in **millimetres (mm)**

Cones colour

When the plant is a conifer, the **colour of the mature cone** is either: **green** or **brown**

Seeds

Seeds number per fruit

The **number of seeds** produced by each fruit is recorded. In the *PNGtrees* database, the value **'100'** is arbitrarily assigned when there are too many seeds to count

Seeds size length (mm)

The **size of seeds**, in **millimetres (mm)**, is measured along the longest axis

Seeds wings

This feature records the **presence** or **absence of one or more wing** appendage on the surface of the seed. The seed is recorded as:

not winged (Fig. 434N)
winged (Fig. 434K)

Seed shape

The **shape of the seed**, at least in cross-section, is recorded as:

Irregular – none recorded so far
broad (as wide as long) (Fig. 434O)
narrow (longer than wide) (Fig. 434N)

Seed size diameter/width (mm)

This feature records the maximum diameter or width of the flattened seeds, in **millimetres (mm)**. When one or more wings are present, these are excluded from the measurement of the seed.

The seed size is categorised as:

< 1 mm diam. – less than 1 mm diameter
1-10 mm diam.
>10 mm diam. – greater than 10 mm diameter

Note: the range of values for the diameter (mm) of seeds for some species has also been provided when known.

Standard system of orthography to be used in recording of vernacular names

Reproduced from

J.S. Womersley (1969). 'Plant collecting for Anthropologists, Geographers and Ecologists in New Guinea' *Botany Bulletin* Vol. 2: 1–70 (Department of Forests, Port Moresby, Papua New Guinea)

Use Symbol	for sound	Use Symbol	for sound
a	**ah** – as 'a' in father	**ğ**	– as in Scottish 'loch'
ȧ	– as 'a' in mat (seldom occurs)	**h**	– as in how
e	**eh** – as 'a' in fate	**j**	soft **j** – as in jug
ė	– as 'e' in ten (seldom occurs)	**k**	hard **c** – as 'k' in kettle
i	**ee** – as 'i' in marine	**kh**	**kh** – as in Asian Khan (guttural)
o	**oh** – as 'o' in note	**gh**	**gh** – as in Turkish Ghazi (guttural)
ŏ	– as 'aw' in law	**kw**	**qu** – as in quick
u	**oo** – as 'u' in flute	**c, m, n, p**	– as in English
ai	– as 'ai' in aisle	**ng**	**soft g** – as in Singer
au	– as 'ow' in how	**ńğ**	**hard g** – as in Finger
ao	– as above, but slightly separated, e.g., Maca-o	**ph**	– only when separate as in 'loophole' (symbol 'f' used in other cases)
ei	– as 'ei' in eight	**th, r s, sh,**	– as in English
b	– as in English	**x**	– as in English
ch	– as 'ch' in church (never used for hard **ch** as in Scottish 'loch' – refer **ğ**)	**y**	– as in Yard (not used as terminal letter, then use 'i')
d, f	– as in English	**z**	– as in English
g	hard **g** – as in 'gay' (for soft use 'j')	**zh**	– as **s** in treasure

Note: Only when there is a decided emphatic stress on a certain sound of a word should the acute accent mark be made. For example, Tongátabu, Saráwak

Additional reading: for a comprehensive overview of various aspects of linguistics, as applied in the field, refer to Thieberger N (ed.) (2012) 'The Oxford Handbook of Linguistic Fieldwork' 545 pp. (Oxford University Press, Oxford).

PNGtrees – Datasheet

Barry Conn (NSW) & *Kipiro Damas* (LAE)

Contact email: kdamas@fri.pngfa.gov.au

Data are grouped and ordered according to the following topics or features:

Literature[4] – Habit – Field Characters – Habit – Indumentum – Leaves – Flowers – Fruits –– Distribution – Administration – Notes

Taxon name:

12. **Family name:**

13. **Group** 1. Conifer 2. Dicotyledon

14. **Timber tree** <yes/no> ❑ 1. yes ❑ 2. no

15. **Timber groups** <hardwoods, or not> ❑ 1. major exportable hardwoods ❑ 2. commercial hardwoods ❑ 3. minor hardwoods ❑ 4. softwoods ❑ 5. plantation species ❑ 6. occasional timber

16. **Tradename** <forestry/timber name>:

17a. **Other Vernacular (Common) name:**

17b. **Language Group <name of language>:**

17c. **Name of informant:**

Habit

18. **Habit** ❑ 1. emergent trees ❑ 2. large trees (those making up the canopy of the forest) ❑ 3. small trees (sub-canopy sized trees)

18a. tree m high

19. Trunk <**bole shape in section**> ❑ 1. cylindrical ❑ 2. markedly fluted

19a. dbh cm

20. Trunk <**bole shape straight, or not**> ❑ 1. crooked ❑ 2. straight

20a. bole m long

21 **Buttresses** <present/absent> ❑ 1. present ❑ 2. absent ❑ U. unknown

21a. if present, buttress m high

[4] There are several database fields that record the primary and secondary scientific references related to each of the tree records. Since these data are added after the plant collection, they are not included here.

22. **Spines** <present/absent> ❑ 1. present ❑ 2. absent

23. **Spines** <location> ❑ 1. on trunk ❑ 2. on branches

> If Spines **absent**
> → '24. Aerial roots'

24. **Aerial roots** <present/absent> ❑ 1. present ❑ 2. absent

25. **Stilt roots** <present/absent> ❑ 1. present ❑ 2. absent

Field Characters

26. **Bark outer colour** < use only for trees greater than 50 cm dbh>
❑ 1. White ❑ 2. cream-coloured ❑ 3. yellow ❑ 4. green ❑ 5. orange ❑ 6. red ❑ 7. grey ❑ 8. brown ❑ 9. Black ❑ 10. purplish

27. Bark <**continuity**-rough or smooth> ❑ 1. rough ❑ 2. smooth

28. Bark <**texture**>
❑ 1. scaly or flaky ❑ 2. fissured ❑ 3. peeling ❑ 4. cracked ❑ 5. furrowed cork ❑ 6. pustular ❑ 7. tessellated ❑ 8. pitted

29. Bark **lenticels** (pustules) <shape> ❑ 1. elongated laterally ❑ 2. elongated vertically ❑ 3. rounded/swelling ❑ 4. irregular

30. Bark **subrhytidome** <under-bark> <colour> ❑ 1. white ❑ 2. yellow ❑ 3. orange ❑ 4. green ❑ 5. pink ❑ 6. red ❑ 7. brown ❑ 8. black ❑ 9. purple ❑ 10. mottled ❑ 11. grey

31. Bark <**thickness** measurement (mm)>

Min:	Lower range:	Mean:	Upper range:	Max:

> Use 'Min' and 'Max' cells for measurements when bark is 'rarely as thin as … mm'
> or 'rarely as thick as … mm'
> If only one measurement put value in 'Mean' cell

32. Bark blaze <**layering**> ❑ 1. one layer ❑ 2. two layers <inner & outer>

33. Bark blaze <**aromatic or not** - use only for trees greater than 50 cm dbh> ❑ 1. faintly to non-aromatic ❑ 2. strongly aromatic

34. Bark blaze <**aromatic type**> ❑ 1. unpleasant ❑ 2. onion-like ❑ 3. cinnamon-like ❑ 4. resinous/liniment-like ❑ 5. spice-like ❑ 6. pleasant ❑ 7. pine-like ❑ 8. almond-like

35. Bark outer blaze <**colour**> ❑ 1. white ❑ 2. yellow ❑ 3. orange ❑ 4. pink ❑ 5. red ❑ 6. Brown ❑ 7. black ❑ 8. green ❑ 9. mixed colours ❑ 10. grey ❑ 11. purple

36. Bark outer blaze <**markings** or not>
❑ 1. markings absent ❑ 2. speckled ❑ 3. with stripes

37. Bark outer blaze <**texture**> ❑ 1. smooth ❑ 2. fibrous
❑ 3. granular with splinters ❑ 4. granular without splinters ❑ 5. corky

38. Bark inner blaze <**colour**>
❑ 1. white ❑ 2. yellow ❑ 3. orange
❑ 4. pink ❑ 5. red ❑ 6. brown
❑ 7. green ❑ 8. mixed colours ❑ 9. grey ❑ 10. purple

> Only score Bark inner blaze (characters 38-40) when character 32. Bark blaze <layering> = 1. one layer

39. Bark inner blaze <**markings** or not>
❑ 1. markings absent ❑ 2. speckled ❑ 3. with stripes

40. Bark inner blaze <**texture**> ❑ 1. smooth ❑ 2. fibrous
❑ 3. granular with splinters ❑ 4. granular without splinters ❑ 5. corky

41. Bark **exudate** (sap) <present or absent> ❑ 1. present ❑ 2. absent

42. Bark exudate (sap) <**colour**> ❑ 1. white/milky ❑ 2. yellow ❑ 3. red ❑ 4. brown ❑ 5. colourless ❑ 6. green
❑ 7. blue ❑ 8. orange

43. Bark exudate (sap) <**abundant or not**>
❑ 1. flowing ❑ 2. not readily flowing (spotty)

44. Bark exudate (sap) <**changing colour** on exposure to air, or not>
❑ 1. colour changing on exposure to air ❑ 2. colour not changing on exposure to air

45. Bark exudate (sap) colour <when changed after exposure to air>
❑ 1. grey ❑ 2. orange ❑ 3. brown ❑ 4. black ❑ 5. golden-coloured ❑ 6. red ❑ 7. green ❑ 8. purple ❑ 9. yellow

46. Bark exudate (sap) <**sticky or not**> ❑ 1. not sticky ❑ 2. sticky

47. **Terminal buds** <enclosed by leaves or not>
❑ 1. enclosed by leaves ❑ 2. not enclosed by leaves

Indumentum

48. Complex hairs <need 10X lens - present or absent>
❑ 1. present ❑ 2. absent

> If Complex hairs absent
> ➞ '50. Stinging hairs'

49. Complex hairs <need 10X lens - type>
❑ 1. disk-shaped (peltate) ❑ 2. star-like (stellate) ❑ 3. T-shaped
❑ 4. club-shaped (clavate) ❑ 5. head-like (capitate) ❑ 6. awl-like

50. Stinging hairs <urticating hairs> ❑ 1. present ❑ 2. absent

51. Mature twig indumentum (hairs) <present or absent>
❑ 1. present ❑ 2. absent

> If hairs absent
> ➞ '53. Leaves <position on branchlet>'

52. Mature twig indumentum (hairs) <density>
❑ 1. dense ❑ 2. sparse ❑ U. unknown

Leaves

53. Leaves <**position on branchlet**> ❑ 1. clustered at end of branches <internodes indistinct> ❑ 2. spaced along branches <internodes readily visible>

54. Leaves <**insertion/arrangement**>
❑ 1. opposite (in pairs, opposite one another on the branchlet)
❑ 2. whorled (with more than two leaves at one node of a branchlet)
❑ 3. spiral (leaves occurring singly at a node and arranged spirally up the branchlet)

55. Leaves <per whorl>

Min:	Lower range:	Mean:	Upper range:	Max:

Refer character 31 on when to use 'Min', 'Max' and 'Mean' cells

56. Leaves <**simple or compound**>
❑ 1. simple (a leaf composed of a single blade)
❑ 2. compound (a leaf made up from two or more leaflets)

57. **Petiole <present or absent>** ❑ 1. absent ❑ 2. present

If petiole present:
57a. mm long

58. Petiole <**winged or not**> ❑ 1. not winged ❑ 2. winged

59. Petiole <**attachment to blade**>
❑ 1. attached to surface of leaf lamina (blade) <peltate>
❑ 2. attached to base of leaf lamina (blade) <not peltate>

60. Petiole <**swollen at either end, or not**>
❑ 1. not swollen ❑ 2. swollen <at tip, or base, or both>

61. Leaves <**lamina shape type**>
❑ 1. broadest above middle ❑ 2. broadest at or near middle
❑ 3. broadest below middle ❑ 4. equally broad throughout much of length
❑ 5. rounded

If 56 = compound do not score 61, go to 69

For characters 62 & 63: refer character 31 on when to use 'Min', 'Max' and 'Mean' cells

62. Leaves <**lamina length (cm)**>

Min:	Lower range:	Mean:	Upper range:	Max:	Unit:
					cm

63. Leaves <**lamina width (cm)**>

Min:	Lower range:	Mean:	Upper range:	Max:	Unit:
					cm

64. Leaves <**symmetry at base**> ❑ 1. very asymmetric ❑ 2. symmetric

65. Leaves <**margin toothed, or not**>
❑ 1. entire ❑ 2. crenate ❑ 3. serrate to dentate (toothed)

66. Leaves <**dissected/lobed, or not**>
❑ 1. dissected or lobed ❑ 2. not dissected or lobed

67. Leaves <**dissection type**> ❑ 1. pinnately lobed ❑ 2. palmately lobed

68. Leaves <**shape of apex**> ❑ 1. emarginate or retuse ❑ 2. rounded ❑ 3. obtuse ❑ 4. acute ❑ 5. mucronate
❑ 6. acuminate
❑ 7. long-tapering

From character 56

69. Leaves <**compound leaf form**>
❑ 1. with one leaflet ❑ 2. with two leaflets ❑ 3. with three leaflets (trifoliate)
❑ 4. pinnate (unbranched with more than three leaflets)
❑ 5. bipinnate (with the rachis branched once)
❑ 6. multiply compound (a compound leaf with more than two orders of branching before leaflets are formed)
❑ 7. palmate (with more than three leaflets attached at one point to the stalk)

70. **Petiolule <of leaflet, swollen or not at either end>**
❑ 1. not swollen ❑ 2. swollen <at tip, or base, or both>

71. **Rachis <present/absent>** ❑ 1. absent ❑ 2. present

72. Rachis <**winged or not**> ❑ 1. absent ❑ 2. present

73. Rachis <**swollen at either end, or not**> ❑ 1. absent ❑ 2. present

74. Leaves <**when compound - paripinnate or imparipinnate**>
❑ 1. without a terminal leaflet (the number of leaflets even-paripinnate) ❑ 2. with a terminal leaflet (the number of leaflets odd-imparipinnate)

75. Leaves <**when compound - leaflet lamina shape type**>
❑ 1. broadest above middle ❑ 2. broadest at or near middle
❑ 3. broadest below middle ❑ 4. equally broad throughout much of length

76. Leaves <**when compound - leaflet lamina length (cm)**>

Min:	Lower range:	Mean:	Upper range:	Max:	Unit:
					cm

77. Leaves <**when compound - leaflet lamina width (cm)**>

Min:	Lower range:	Mean:	Upper range:	Max:	Unit:
					cm

For characters 76 & 77: refer character 31 on when to use 'Min', 'Max' and 'Mean' cells

78. Leaves <**when compound - leaflets opposite or alternate**>
❑ 1. leaflets opposite
❑ 2. leaflets alternate
❑ 3. leaflets arranged from one

79. Leaves **<when compound - leaflet symmetry, at base>**
❑ 1. asymmetric ❑ 2. symmetric

80. Leaves **<when compound - imparipinnate, terminal leaflet buds>**
❑ 1. terminal developing leaflet buds curled back on itself
❑ 2. terminal developing leaflet buds straight
❑ 3. terminal developing leaflet buds absent

81. **Venation** <layout of secondary veins on leaf/leaflet>
❑ 1. single-veined <the leaf or leaflet with only one vein>
❑ 2. pinnate <secondary veins arising from the midrib along its length>
❑ 3. trinerved <three large veins arising from the base>
❑ 4. palmate <more than three large veins arising from the base>
❑ 5. parallel-veined <numerous small veins running in parallel from base, not arising from a midrib>
❑ U. unknown

82. **Secondary veins <closed or open>**
❑ 1. open <spaced far apart to easily see tertiary veins>
❑ 2. closed <spaced so close together that tertiary veins cannot be easily seen between them>
❑ U. unknown

83. Secondary veins **<prominence>**
❑ 1. prominent ❑ 2. not prominent, but visible ❑ 3. not visible

84. **Intramarginal veins <present/absent>** ❑ 1. absent ❑ 2. present

85. Leaves **lower surface <colour>**
❑ 1. blue-green ❑ 2. pale green ❑ 3. green ❑ 4. dark green ❑ 5. yellow ❑ 6. brown ❑ 7. red ❑ 8. grey ❑ 9. white
❑ 10. golden

86. Leaves **upper surface <colour>**
❑ 1. blue-green ❑ 2. pale green ❑ 3. green ❑ 4. dark green ❑ 5. yellow ❑ 6. brown ❑ 7. red ❑ 8. grey

87. Leaves **indumentum (hairs) <present/absent** - on mature leaf or leaflet> ❑ 1. absent ❑ 2. present

88. Leaves indumentum (hairs) **<indumentum density** - on mature leaf or leaflet> ❑ 1. dense ❑ 2. sparse

89. Leaves **<gland-dotted or not**, often pellucid, apparent as numerous semi-transparent dots distributed across the leaf> ❑ 1. absent ❑ 2. present

90. **Domatia <present/absent>** ❑ 1. absent ❑ 2. present

91. Domatia **<distribution>** ❑ 1. scattered along midrib ❑ 2. scattered across lamina

92. **Stipules** <or stipular scars **present or absent**> ❑ 1. absent ❑ 2. present

If 92 = absent, go to 100

93. Stipules **<freedom>** ❑ 1. free <from one another> ❑ 2. joined

94. Stipules <**type – interpetiolar or lateral**>
❑ 1. joined across twigs <growing between opposite leaves and leaving a scar between them when they fall; interpetiolar>
❑ 2. laterally placed <whether free or joined>

95. Stipules <**encircling the twig, or not**>
❑ 1. encircling the twig <amplexicaul> ❑ 2. not encircling the twig

96. Stipules <**form**> ❑ 1. scale-like ❑ 2. collar-like ❑ 3. hair-like ❑ 4. leafy ❑ 5. spiny ❑ 6. represented by glands

97. Stipules <**margin with fine hairs/fringed, or not**>
❑ 1. fringed <fimbriate> ❑ 2. not fringed

98. Stipules <**size**>
❑ 1. large <easily visible to the eye> ❑ 2. small <not easily visible to the eye>

99. Stipules <**persistence**> ❑ 1. not persistent ❑ 2. persistent

Flowers

100. **Arrangement of flowers** <position>
❑ 1. terminal <at branch ends>
❑ 2. axillary <from between a leaf and branch>
❑ 3. leaf-opposed <arising opposite a leaf, not between a leaf and a branch> ❑ 4. on the trunk or branches <cauliflorous-ramiflorous>

101. Arrangement of flowers <**axis absent, unbranched or branched?**> ❑ 1. flowers single <solitary>
❑ 2. flowers arising from a single point ❑ 3. flowers on an unbranched axis ❑ 4. flowers on a branched axis

102. Arrangement of flowers <**cones/strobili present, or not**>
❑ 1. absent ❑ 2. present

103. Flower sexuality <**bisexual or unisexual**>
❑ 1. unisexual ❑ 2. bisexual ❑ U. unknown

If 103 = bisexual, go to 105

104. Flowers unisexual <**male and female flowers - on same or different plants**> ❑ 1. with male and female flowers on the same plant <monoecious>
❑ 2. with male and female flowers on different plants <dioecious> ❑ U. unknown

105. Flowers <**stalked or not**>
❑ 1. not stalked <sessile> ❑ 2. stalked <pedicellate>

If stalked, then pedicel   mm long

106. Flowers <**symmetry**>
❑ 1. with many planes of symmetry <actinomorphic>
❑ 2. slightly asymmetric
❑ 3. with one plane of symmetry <zygomorphic>
❑ 4. completely asymmetric
❑ U. unknown

For characters 107, 108a & 108b: refer character 31 on when to use 'Min', 'Max'and 'Mean' cells

107. Flowers <**size length (mm)**> ❑ U. unknown

Min:	Lower range:	Mean:	Upper range:	Max:	Unit:
					mm

108a. Flowers <**size diameter (mm)**>
❑ 1. small (< or =10 mm diam.) ❑ 2. large (>10 mm diam.) ❑ U. unknown

108b. Flowers <**size diameter (mm) – actual measurement**>

Min:	Lower range:	Mean:	Upper range:	Max:	Unit:
					mm

109. Perianth <**present or absent**>
❑ 1. absent ❑ 2. present ❑ U. unknown

110. Perianth <**type**>
❑ 1. with distinct sepals and petals whorls
❑ 2. intergrading from sepals to petals
❑ 3. with all sepals and/or petals (hence tepals) similar
❑ 4. petals absent
❑ U. unknown

111. Perianth <**colour**, always inner most parts - next to stamens & ovary> ❑ 1. white ❑ 2. yellow ❑ 3. orange ❑ 4. pink ❑ 5. red ❑ 6. blue ❑ 7. purple ❑ 8. mauve ❑ 9. green ❑ 10. brown ❑ 11. grey ❑ 12. cream-coloured ❑ U. unknown

112. Inner perianth parts <**number visible, whether free or joined - if many then score as "100"**> ❑ U. unknown

Min:	Lower range:	Mean:	Upper range:	Max:

For characters 112 & 114: refer character 31 on when to use 'Min', 'Max' and 'Mean' cells

113. Inner perianth parts <**extent of joining**>
❑ 1. free ❑ 2. some or partly joined ❑ 3. all joined ❑ U. unknown

114. Stamens <**number if there are a lot, enter "100"**> ❑ U. unknown

Min:	Lower range:	Mean:	Upper range:	Max:

115. Stamens <**filaments present or absent**>
❑ 1. absent ❑ 2. present ❑ U. unknown

116. Stamens <**whether at least some are joined to each other or not**> ❑ 1. free of each other ❑ 2. joined <connate> ❑ U. unknown

117. Stamens <**adnate to perianth, or not**>
❑ 1. free of the perianth
❑ 2. joined to the perianth <epipetalous/episepalous>
❑ U. unknown

118. Ovary <**gynoecium, position**>
❑ 1. superior <seated above petals and sepals; hypogenous>
❑ 2. partly inferior <perigenous>
❑ 3. inferior <seated below the petals and sepals; epigenous>

119. Carpels <**gynoecium, constitution**>
❑ 1. solitary <monomerous>
❑ 2. separate (when more than one) <apocarpous>
❑ 3. joined (when more than one) <syncarpous>
❑ 4. partially joined, by base
❑ 5. partially joined, by styles

For characters 120 & 122: refer character 31 on when to use 'Min', 'Max' and 'Mean' cells

120. Locules <**number**>

Min:	Lower range:	Mean:	Upper range:	Max:

121. Styles <**absent, single, or many and free**>
❑ 1. absent ❑ 2. solitary <including joined together>
❑ 3. free <more than one style, entirely free from each other> ❑ U. unknown

122. Styles <**number of styles** - if there are more than one> ❑ U. unknown

Min:	Lower range:	Mean:	Upper range:	Max:

Fruits

123. **Arrangement of fruits** <axis absent, unbranched or branched?>
❑ 1. fruits single <solitary> ❑ 2. fruits arising from single point
❑ 3. fruits arranged on unbranched axis ❑ 4. fruits arranged on branched axis

If Cone present → '127. Cone <size length (mm)>'

124. Arrangement of fruits < **cones present, or not**>
❑ 1. absent ❑ 2. present

For characters 125–128: refer character 31 on when to use 'Min', 'Max' and 'Mean' cells

125. Fruit <**size length (mm)**> ❑ U. unknown

Min:	Lower range:	Mean:	Upper range:	Max:	Unit:
					mm

126. Fruit <**size diameter (mm)**> ❑ U. unknown

Min:	Lower range:	Mean:	Upper range:	Max:	Unit:
					mm

If Fruit present → '130. Fruit <colour>'

127. Cone <**size length (mm)**>

Min:	Lower range:	Mean:	Upper range:	Max:	Unit:
					mm

128. Cone <**size diameter (mm)**>

Min:	Lower range:	Mean:	Upper range:	Max:	Unit:
					mm

129. **Cone** <**colour**> ❑ 1. green ❑ 2. brown ❑ 3. red ❑ 4. orange ❑ 5. black ❑ 6. blue

130. **Fruit** <**colour**> ❑ 1. white ❑ 2. cream-coloured ❑ 3. yellow ❑ 4. green ❑ 5. blue ❑ 6. orange ❑ 7. red ❑ 8. brown ❑ 9. grey ❑ 10. black ❑ 11. purple ❑ U. unknown

131. Fruit <**surface spiny or not**> ❑ 1. not spiny ❑ 2. spiny

132. Fruit <**fleshy or not**> ❑ 1. non-fleshy ❑ 2. fleshy

133. Fruit <**simple, aggregate or multiple**>
❑ 1. simple ❑ 2. aggregate ❑ 3. multiple <excluding figs> ❑ 4. syconium (fig) <specific example of multiple>

134. Fruit <**dehiscent or indehiscent**>
❑ 1. indehiscent ❑ 2. dehiscent

If indehiscent → '136. Fruit indehiscence <type>'.
If dehiscent → '135. Fruit dehiscence <type>.

135. Fruit dehiscence <type>
❑ 1. capsule ❑ 2. follicle ❑ 3. legume ❑ 4. loment

136. Fruit indehiscence <type> ❑ 1. achene ❑ 2. berry ❑ 3. drupe ❑ 4. hesperidium ❑ 5. nut ❑ 6. pepo ❑ 7. pome ❑ 8. samara ❑ 9. schizocarp ❑ 10. syconium (fig) ❑ 11. naked seed only

137. **Seeds** <**number per fruit. If many, then "100"**> ❑ U. unknown

Min:	Lower range:	Mean:	Upper range:	Max:

For characters 137: refer character 31 on when to use 'Min', 'Max' and 'Mean' cells

138. Seeds <**size length (mm)**>
❑ 1. barely visible (to 1 mm long) ❑ 2. to about 5 mm long
❑ 3. about 10 mm long ❑ 4. much more than 10 mm long
❑ 5. 100 mm long or much longer ❑ U. unknown

mm long

139. Seeds < **winged or not**> ❑ 1. not winged ❑ 2. winged

If winged: wing mm long

140. Seed <**shape, at least in section**>
❑ 1. irregular ❑ 2. broad (as wide as long) ❑ 3. narrow (longer than wide)

141. Seed <**size diameter/width (mm)**>
❑ 1. < 1 mm diam. ❑ 2. 1-10 mm diam. ❑ 3. >10 mm diam. ❑ U. unknown

mm diameter

Distribution

143. Distribution <Province>
❑ 1. West Sepik ❑ 2. East Sepik ❑ 3. Madang ❑ 4. Morobe
❑ 5. Western Highlands ❑ 6. Eastern Highlands ❑ 7. Southern Highlands
❑ 8. Western ❑ 9. Gulf ❑ 10. Central ❑ 11. Northern
❑ 12. Milne Bay ❑ 13. Papuan Islands ❑ 14. New Britain
❑ 15. New Ireland ❑ 16. Manus ❑ 17. Bougainville

Administration

144. Reference collections <**vouchers for *PNGtrees* project**>:

Collector(s) name:

Collection number:

Date of collection:

Locality of collection:

Include Province, nearest named place, geocodes (latitude, longitude, elevation)

145. Images <**present, or not**>
❑ 1. bark ❑ 2. blaze ❑ 3. fruit ❑ 4. illustration ❑ 5. leaves ❑ 6. no images ❑ 7. flowers
❑ 8. specimen

Notes

147. Notes

Add any additional comments here and other features of the plant, forest, soils that have not recorded above

Please enter your name:

Email address:

Acknowledgements

We gratefully acknowledge the generous support that many people have provided throughout this project. The documentation of the trees of Papua New Guinea began in March 2003, with supplementary support from *The Australia & Pacific Biological Foundation* (APBF). This initial phase of the project concentrated on preparing an interactive identification tool for the commercial trees of the Morobe Province of Papua New Guinea. It was a three-year project to evaluate the feasibility of preparing a complete account of the trees occurring in the entire country. Other areas that were surveyed outside the Morobe Province included: APBF funded surveys of the lowland forests of Wanang (Madang Province) and upper montane forests of Mount Wilhelm (Eastern Highlands); the three year *African-Caribbean-Pacific Forest Research Network* (ACP FORENET) project, funded by the European Commission and the Secretariat of the African-Caribbean-Pacific countries, generously supported coastal and near-coastal ultra-mafic forests of Kamiali (Morobe Province); *National Science Foundation*, in collaboration with the Bernice P. Bishop Museum (Honolulu, U.S.A.), supported a preliminary survey of the montane forests of Teptep (Madang Province); and *Mundango Abroad* funded a preliminary survey of savannah woodlands of the National Capital Territory and surrounding lowland vegetation (Central Province), as well as lowland and montane forests of the Kiunga–Tabubil area (Western Province). *Ok Tedi Mining Limited* (OTML) generously provided logistical support and access to OTML lease areas. They also assisted by introducing us to community representatives of the Bianglopmik (Lake Vivian) region (North Fly District, Western Province). OTML generously provided field equipment and helicopter and fixed-wing support so that we could survey the flora of this region.

The publication of this guide to the *Trees of Papua New Guinea* was generously funded by the ACP FORENET project, the Royal Botanic Gardens Sydney, with additional support provided by the Menai District membership of the *Australian Plants Society New South Wales.*

The development of the descriptive data set was based on the work of several previous initiatives; namely, the *Australian tropical rain forest trees*, *The tree and shrub genera of Borneo*, *The flowering plants of Australia* and *FloraBase.* The authors of these publications enthusiastically supported the *PNGTrees* project, making available their descriptive data structure and providing helpful advice. Paul I. Forster (BRI) and Pieter C. van Welzen (L) provided advice on nomenclature of Euphorbiaceae. The late Lyn A. Craven (then CANB) provided current identifications for the genus *Syzygium* (Myrtaceae). Peter G. Wilson (NSW) provided advice on the Myrtaceae and nomenclatural issues. Laurie W. Jessup (BRI), Toby D. Pennington (E) and Peter Wilkie (E) assisted with nomenclature of the genera within the Sapotaceae and relevant references. Mark Coode (then K) kindly assisted with several taxonomic issues in the Elaeocarpaceae and Combretaceae. Bruce Webber (CSIRO, Perth) assisted with identity of species of *Ryparosa* (Achariaceae). Tim Utteridge (K) assisted with scientific literature for *Sterculia.* Billy Bau (previously LAE) provided information on *Eucalyptopsis papuana* from the Western Province and Bega Inaho (Goroka) provided additional information for *Casuarina oligodon* in the Eastern Highlands.

Gerhard Rambold (BMBF) provided prompt advice on technical issues relating to the implementation of *NaviKey.* Gregor Hagedorn (BBA) provided considerable expert advice on the use of *DeltaAccess* and *DiversityDescriptions* software. We gratefully acknowledge Murray Henwood (SYD) for assisting with the development of the interactive identification key. We warmly thank the staff of the Papua New Guinea National Herbarium (LAE), together with the Papua New Guinea Forest Research Institute, for supporting all aspects of this project. In particular, we thank the late Roy Banka, Robert Kiapranis, Forova Oavika, Nalish Sam, Simon Saulei, and Terry Wara for providing resources and logistical support within Papua New Guinea. The success of the project depended on this support. Expert field support was provided by Roy Banka and Tory Kuria (both then LAE), Dubi Damas, Kaigube Fazang, Peter Homot, Michael Lovave, Silva Masbong, Oliver Paul, Simon Sennart and Bernard Sule, (all from LAE). Field assistance was also provided by Darren Crayn (then NSW, July 2003); Elizabeth Brown (then NSW, November 2004); Julisasi Tri Hadiah (Kebun Raya Bogor, December 2007); Kathi Downs and Louisa Murray (both NSW, May 2008), Shelley James (then BISH, September – October 2010) and on several occasions Allen Allison (BISH).

The botanical illustrations incorporated into the three volumes of the *Trees of Papua New Guinea* were expertly drawn by: Jill Curtis, Bore Doviong, Semeri Hitingnuc, Taikika Iwagu, Terry Nolan, Faye Owner, Damaris Pearce (all previously LAE), Armstrong Bellamy (Bulolo University College), Anita Podwyszynski (then MEL). Botanical diagrams included in the *Data Dictionary* were drafted by un-named illustrators (at NSW) and were originally published in Harden (1990–1993). We sincerely thank the Directors and Managers of the National Herbarium of Victoria (MEL), National Herbarium of New South Wales (NSW) and the Papua New Guinea National Herbarium (LAE) for kindly allowing us to use these illustrations. The Royal Botanic Gardens Kew kindly granted permission for us to publish an image of an herbarium collection of *Cryptocarya pulchella*. W.R. (Bill) Barker (Adelaide, South Australia) provided images of *Goniothalamus grandiflorus* and *Ternstroemia merrilliana* for inclusion in this publication. The Australian Tropical Herbarium (CNS) kindly granted permission for us to publish an image of an herbarium collection of *Heritiera littoralis*.

The *PNGplants* database has been extensively used throughout this project to check the plant collector's notes for details of morphological features and to verify the distribution of the species within Papua New Guinea. We are extremely grateful to the Australian herbaria that generously made their herbarium data available to the *PNGplants* project. We gratefully acknowledge Linn Linn Lee (then NSW) who was the developer of the *PNGplants* database. Her excellent computer programming has enabled LAE to start data processing their important collections. Jessie Waibauru (PNG Forest Research Institute) provided computer support for the LAE data processing staff. Gary Chapple (then NSW) provided database management assistance throughout the project, resolving many difficult issues to ensure that the database was fully functional. More recently, Wayne Cherry (NSW) has generously continued to provide IT support for this long-term project and assistance with the production of the plant distribution maps. Alan Wallace (Yarrawonga, Victoria) expertly produced the general map of Papua New Guinea (used in the Introduction, Volume 1) and provided expert image manipulation assistance and advice. Dubi Damas (LAE), as well as Balpina Tiki and Brenda Paul (then LAE) have specifically data processed many herbarium records from Papua New Guinea so that these records are available for the *PNGtrees* project. We thank Billy Bau (then LAE) for co-ordinating the data processing project.

We sincerely thank Tim Entwisle and Frank Howarth (both then NSW), as well as David Mabberley (then NSW), Marco Duretto (NSW) and Brett Summerell (NSW) for their on-going support for this project. Their commitment to the *PNGtrees* project as a research priority for the Royal Botanic Gardens and Domain Trust (Sydney, Australia) has enabled one of us (BJC) to continue working in Papua New Guinea. The generous supplementary financial support provided by all funding agencies involved with this long-term project is gratefully acknowledged. Without their support, this collaborative project would not have been possible.

Susan Hanfling (then The University of Sydney), Ross Coleman, Murray Henwood and Susan Murray-Smith (The University of Sydney) provided considerable guidance and encouragement during the preparation of this project for publication. We thank them for their continuing support.

We also acknowledge and thank the people of the following regions: Vanimo (West Sepik, Sandaun Province); Teptep and Wanang (Madang Province); Bulolo, Cromwell Ranges, Indagen, Gumi, Hobu, Kamiali, Oomsis, Wagau and Yalu areas (Morobe Province); Goroka, Mount Gahavisuka and Mount Wilhelm (Eastern Highlands); Bianglopmik (Lake Vivian), Kiunga–Tabubil and Morehead areas (Western Province); Purari (Gulf); Central Province and National Capital Territory; Oba Bay and Galehi Island group (Milne Bay); and Asengseng, Biala and Kimbe (West New Britain), for welcoming us onto their land so that we could gather data on the tree species included in this project. These people generously shared with us their extensive knowledge about these trees, they provided invaluable field assistance and friendship. Vojtech Novotny and staff, *Binatang Research Centre* (Nagada, Madang) willingly supporting our work at Wanang (Madang).

Finally, we acknowledge the enormous contribution made by the many plant collectors who have accessed all parts of New Guinea. They often coped with the extreme physical difficulties of under-taking field work here, often suffering injury and diseases. While compiling the bibliography for this book, a summary of the many scientific references studied, the contributions made by previous plant systematists is immense. We dedicate this publication to the memory of past collectors and researchers, and acknowledge the ongoing contributions made by current collectors and researchers. Our publication has been 'built' upon the work of those who have gone before us.

REFERENCES (Volume 3)

Airy Shaw HK (1972) *Gonystyloideae*,Thymelaeaceae – Addenda, corrigenda et emendanda. In Steenis CGGJ, van (ed.). 'Flora Malesiana, Series I. Vol. 6.' pp. 976–982 (P. Noordhoff Ltd.: Leiden)

Anonymous (without date-a) '*Barringtonia calyptrata*.' In Hyland BPM, Whiffin T, Zich FA (eds).'Australian Tropical Rainforest Plants'. (Australian Tropical Herbarium; CSIRO Plant Industry; and Centre for Australian National Biodiversity Research) http://keys.trin.org.au/key-server/data/0e0f0504-0103-430d-8004-060d07080d04/media/Html/taxon/Barringtonia_calyptrata.htm (accessed March 2018)

Anonymous (without date-b) '*Gmelina dalrympleana*.' In Hyland BPM, Whiffin T, Zich FA (eds).'Au*stralian Tropical Rainforest Plants*'. (Australian Tropical Herbarium; CSIRO Plant Industry; and Centre for Australian National Biodiversity Research) http://keys.trin.org.au/key-server/data/0e0f0504-0103-430d-8004-060d07080d04/media/Html/taxon/Gmelina_dalrympleana.htm (accessed February 2018)

APG (2003) An update of the angiosperm phylogeny group classification for the orders and families of flowering plants: APG II. *Botanical Journal of the Linnean Society* 141: 399–436 http://dx.doi.org/10.1046/j.1095-8339.2003.t01-1-00158.x

Armstrong K (2011) Systematics and biogeography of the pantropical genus *Manilkara* Adans. (Sapotaceae). . A thesis submitted for the degree of Doctor of Philosophy Thesis, University of Edinburgh & Royal Botanic Garden Edinburgh,

Armstrong K (2013) A revision of the Asian-Pacific species of *Manilkara* (Sapotaceae). *Edinburgh Journal of Botany* 70: 7–56 http://dx.doi.org/https://doi.org/10.1017/S0960428612000327

Ashton PS (1982) Dipterocarpaceae. In Steenis CGGJ, van (ed.). 'Flora Malesiana, Series I. Vol. 9.' pp. 237–552 (Martinus Nijhoff/Dr W. Junk Publishers: The Hague)

Backer CA, Bakhuizen van den Brink RCJ (1963) *Saurauia*. 'Flora of Java. Vol. I.' pp. 324–326 (N.V.P. Noordhoff: Groningen, The Netherlands)

Bailey IW (1956) The relationship between *Sphenostemon* of New Caledonia and *Nouhuysia* of New Guinea. *Journal of the Arnold Arboretum* 37: 360–365

Bakker K, Steenis CGGJ, van (1957) Pittosporaceae. In Steenis CGGJ, van (ed.). 'Flora Malesiana, Series I. Vol. 5.' pp. 345–362

Bank M, Van der, Fay MF, Chase MW (2002) Molecular Phylogenetics of Thymelaeaceae with Particular Reference to African and Australian Genera. *Taxon* 51: 329–339 http://dx.doi.org/10.2307/1554930

Barker RM (1986) A taxonomic revision of Australian Acanthaceae. *Journal of the Adelaide Botanic Gardens* 9: 1–292

Barker WR (1980) Taxonomic revisions in Theaceae in Papuasia. I. *Gordonia*, *Ternstroemia*, *Adinandra* and *Archboldiodendron*. *Brunonia* 3: 1–60

Barker WR (1982) Theaceae. In Royen P, van (ed.). 'The Alpine flora of New Guinea. Vol. 3.' pp. 1397–1454 (J. Cramer: FL-9490 Vaduz)

Bartish IV, Swenson U, Munzinger J, Anderberg AA (2005) Phylogenetic relationships among New Caledonian Sapotaceae (Ericales): molecular evidence for generic polyphyly and repeated dispersal. *American Journal of Botany* 92: 667–673 http://www.jstor.org/stable/4126197

Bayer C, Fay MF, Bruijn AY, de, Savolainen V, Morton CM, Kubitzki K, Alverson WS, Chase MW (1999) Support for an expanded family concept of Malvaceae within a recircumscribed order Malvales: a combined analysis of plastid atpB and rbcL DNA sequences. *Botanical Journal of the Linnean Society* 129: 267–381

Bayer C, Kubitzki K (2003) Malvaceae. In Kubitzki K (ed.). 'The families and genera of vascular plants. Vol. 5.' pp. 225–311 (Springer-Verlag: Berlin)

Bentvelzen PAJ (1962) Primulaceae. In Steenis CGGJ, van (ed.). 'Flora Malesiana, Series I. Vol. 6.' pp. 173–192 (P. Noordhoff Ptd.: Leiden)

Bernardi L (1964) La position systematique du genre *Sphenostemon* Baillon sensu van Steenis. *Candollea* 19: 199–205

Borssum Walker J, van (1966) Malesian Malvaceae revised. *Blumea* 14: 1–213

Bremekamp CEB (1953) The delimitation of the Acanthaceae. *Proceedings de Koninkliike Nederlandse Akademie van Wetenschappen, Series C* 56: 533–546

Bremekamp CEB (1955a) The Acantheae of the Malesian area. *Proceedings de Koninkliike Nederlandse Akademie van Wetenschappen, Series C* 58: 162–171, 295–306

Bremekamp CEB (1955b) The *Thunbergia* species of the Malesian area. *Verhandelingen der Koninklijke Nederlandsche Akademie van Wetenschappen. Afdeeling Natuurkunde, Sectie 2* 50: 1–390

Bremekamp CEB (1957) New Scrophulariaceae and Acanthaceae from New Guinea. *Nova Guinea, New Series* 8: 129–155

Bremekamp CEB, Nannenga-Bremekamp NE (1948) A preliminary survey of the Ruelliinae (Acanthaceae) of the Malay Archipelago and New Guinea. *Verhandelingen der Koninklijke Nederlandsche Akademie van Wetenschappen. Afdeeling Natuurkunde, Sectie 2* 45: 1–339

Bremer B (2009) A review of polecular Phylogenetic studies of Rubiaceae. *Annals of the Missouri Botanical Garden* 96: 4–26 http://dx.doi.org/10.2307/40390045

Bremer B, Andreasen K, Olsson D (1995) Subfamilial and Tribal relationships in the Rubiaceae based on rbcL sequence data. *Annals of the Missouri Botanical Garden* 82: 383–397 http://dx.doi.org/10.2307/2399889

Bremer B, Eriksson T (2009) Time tree of Rubiaceae: Phylogeny and dating the family, subfamilies, and tribes. *International Journal of Plant Sciences* 170: 766–793 http://dx.doi.org/10.1086/599077

Bremer K (1994) 'Asteraceae, cladistics and classification.' (Timber Press: Portland, Oregon) 752 pp.

Buwalda P (1949) Apiaceae. In Steenis CGGJ, van (ed.). 'Flora Malesiana, Series I. Vol. 4.' pp. 113–140 (Leyden)

Buwalda P (1951) Notes on New Guinea Umbelliferae. *Journal of the Arnold Arboretum* 32: 59–66

Cerceau-Larrival M-T (1964) Mise au point taxonomique concernant *Cyclospermum leptophyllum* (Pers.) Sprague. *Bulletin de la Société Botanique de France* 3: 93–96

Conn BJ (1979a) 'Botany.' (Office of Forests: Waigani, Papua New Guinea) 390 pp.

Conn BJ (1979b) Notes of *Neuburgia*. *Brunonia* 2: 99–105

Conn BJ (1995) Loganiaceae. In Conn BJ (ed.). 'Handbooks of the Flora of Papua New Guinea. Vol. 3.' pp. 132–188 (Melbourne University Press: Carlton)

Conn BJ (2018) Transfer of *Rapanea brassii* P.Royen to *Myrsine* (Primulaceae) *Telopea* 21: 157–159 http://dx.doi.org/10.7751/telopea12696

Conn BJ, Brown EA (1993) Review of *Fagraea gracilipes* Complex (Loganiaceae). *Telopea* 5: 363–374 http://dx.doi.org/dx.doi.org/10.7751/telopea19934980

Conn BJ, Damas KQ (2013) A new species of *Saurauia* (Actinidiaceae) from Papua New Guinea. *Telopea* 15: 9–12 http://dx.doi.org/10.7751/telopea2013003

Conn BJ, Frodin DG (1995) *Osmoxylon* in the Solomon Islands. In Conn BJ (ed.). 'Handbooks of the flora of Papua New Guinea. Vol. 3.' pp. 271–285 (Melbourne University Press: Carlton)

Croft JR (1981) Bombacacae. In Henty EE (ed.). 'Handbooks flora of Papua New Guinea. Vol. 2.' pp. 4–18 (Melbourne University Press: Carlton)

Cuénoud P, Del Pero Martinez MA, Loizeau P-A, Spichiger R, Andrews S, Manen J-F (2000) Molecular Phylogeny and Biogeography of the Genus *Ilex* L. (Aquifoliaceae). *Annals of Botany* 85: 111–122 http://dx.doi.org/10.1006/anbo.1999.1003

Danser BH (1940) On some genera of Santalaceae *Osyrideae* from the Malay archipelago, mainly from New Guinea. *Nova Guinea New Series* 4: 33–149

Danser BH (1955) Supplementary notes on the Santalaceous genera *Dendromyza* and *Cladomyza*. *Nova Guinea New Series* 6: 261–277

Davies FG (1981) *Gynura* in Malesia and Australia (Asteraceae). *Kew Bulletin* 35: 711–734

Davis AP, Govaerts R, Bridson DM, Ruhsam M, Moat J, Brummitt NA (2009) A global assessment of distribution, diversity, endemism, and taxonomic effort in the Rubiaceae. *Annals of the Missouri Botanical Garden* 96: 68–78 http://dx.doi.org/10.2307/40390048

Der JP, Nickrent DL (2008) A molecular phylogeny of Santalaceae (Santales). *Systematic Botany* 33: 107–116 http://dx.doi.org/10.1600/036364408783887438

Ding Hou (1960) Thymelaeaceae. In Steenis CGGJ, van (ed.). 'Flora Malesiana, Series I. Vol. 6.' pp. 1–48 (P. Noordhoff Ltd.: Leiden)

Duke NC (1990) Morphological variation in the mangrove genus *Avicennia* in Australasia: Systematic and ecological considerations. *Australian Systematic Botany* 3: 221–239 http://dx.doi.org/10.1071/SB9900221

Duke NC (1991) A systematic revision of the mangrove genus *Avicennia* (Avicenniaceae) in Australasia. *Australian Systematic Botany* 4: 299–324 http://dx.doi.org/10.1071/SB9910299

Endress ME, Bruyns PV (2000) A revised classification of the Apocynaceae s.l. *The Botanical Review* 66: 1–56

FloraBase (2003) 'FloraBase – the Western Australian Flora. Version 2.' In. (Western Australian Herbarium: Perth) http://florabase.dec.wa.gov.au (accessed September 2005)

Forster PI (1992a) Circumscription of *Tabernaemontana pandacaqui* (Apocynaceae) in Australia. *Australian Systematic Botany* 5: 521–531 http://dx.doi.org/10.1071/SB9920521

Forster PI (1992b) A taxonomic revision of *Alstonia* (Apocynaceae) in Australia. *Australian Systematic Botany* 5: 745–760 http://dx.doi.org/10.1071/SB9920745

Forster PI (1992c) A taxonomic revision of *Alyxia* (Apocynaceae) in Australia. *Australian Systematic Botany* 5: 547–580 http://dx.doi.org/10.1071/SB9920547

Forster PI (1992d) A taxonomic revision of *Carissa* (Apocynaceae) in Australia. *Australian Systematic Botany* 5: 581–591 http://dx.doi.org/10.1071/SB9920581

Forster PI (1992e) A taxonomic revision of *Ichnocarpus* (Apocynaceae) in Australia and Papuasia. *Australian Systematic Botany* 5: 533–545 http://dx.doi.org/10.1071/SB9920533

Forster PI (1992f) A Taxonomic Revision of *Melodinus* (Apocynaceae) in Australia. *Australian Systematic Botany* 5: 387–400 http://dx.doi.org/10.1071/SB9920387

Fosberg FR, Sachet M-H (1972) *Thespesia populnea* (L.) Solander ex Correa and *Thespesia populneoides* (Roxburgh) Kosteletsky (Malvaceae). *Smithsonian Contributions to Botany* 7: 1–13

Francis WD (1970) 'Australian rain-forest trees.' (Australian Government Publishing Service: Canberra) 468 pp.

Frodin DG (1975) *Schefflera*. *Journal of the Arnold Arboretum* 56: 427–448

Green PS (1994) Oleaceae. In Wilson AJG (ed.). 'Flora of Australia. Vol. 49, Oceanic Islands 1.' pp. 327–334 (Australian Government Publishing Service: Canberra)

Green PS (2004) Oleaceae. In Kadereit JW (ed.). 'The Families and Genera of Vascular Plants. Vol. VII, Flowering Plants - Dicotyledons - Lamiales (except Acanthaceae including Avicenniaceae).' pp. 296–306 (Springer-Verlag: Berlin, Heidelberg, New York)

Harden GJ (1990–1993) 'Flora of New South Wales Volumes 1–4.' (New South Wales University Press/NSWU Press: Kensington, NSW, Australia)

Heel WA, van (1972) Taxonomic position of *Papuodendron*. *Reinwardtia* 8: 319–321

Henwood MJ, Hart HM (2001) Towards an understanding of the phylogenetic relationships of Australian Hydrocotyloideae (Apiaceae). *Edinburgh Journal of Botany* 58: 269–289

Herrmann-Erlee MPM, Lam HJ (1957) Revision of the Sapotaceae of the Malaysian area in a wider sense VIII. *Blumea* 8: 448–451

Herrmann-Erlee MPM, Royen P, van (1957) Revision of the Sapotaceae of Malaysian area in a wider sense IX. *Blumea* 8: 452–509

Hua P, Howard RA (2008) Icacinaceae. In 'Flora of China Vol. 11', 505–514 (http://www.efloras.org/florataxon_aspx?flora_id=2&taxon_id=10447)

Hwang S-m, Grimes JW (1996) Styraceae. In 'Flora of China Vol. 15', 253–271 (http://www.efloras.org/florataxon_aspx?flora_id=2&taxon_id=10861)

Hyland BPM, Whiffin T, Christophel DC (1993) 'Australian tropical rain forest trees.' (CSIRO Publishing: East Melbourne)

Jarvie JK, Ermayanti (1995–1996) The tree and shrub genera of Borneo. http://www.phylodiversity.net/borneo/delta (accessed September 2005)

Jessup LW (2001) New combinations and a new name in Australian Sapotaceae. *Austrobaileya* 6: 161–163 http://www.jstor.org/stable/41738971

Keng H (1969) Labiatae. *Garden's Bulletin Singapore* 24: 13–180

Keng H (1978) Labiatae. In Steenis CGGJ, van (ed.). 'Flora Malesiana, Series I. Vol. 8.' pp. 301–394 (Sijthoff & Noordhoff International Publishers: Alphen aan den Rijn, The Netherlands)

Kiew R (1998) Name changes for Malesian species of *Chionanthus* (Oleaceae). *Blumea* 43: 471–477

Koster JT (1966) The Compositae of New Guinea I – Eupatorieae. *Nova Guinea Botany* 24: 497–614

Koster JT (1970) The Compositae of New Guinea II – *Dichrocephala* and Senecioneae. *Blumea* 18: 137–145

Koster JT (1972) The Compositae of New Guinea III – Inuleae, Helenieae. *Blumea* 20: 193–226

Koster JT (1975) The Compositae of New Guinea IV – additions and corrections to I, II, and III. *Blumea* 22: 207–217

Koster JT (1976) The Compositae of New Guinea V – aditions to part I, Cichorieae. *Blumea* 23: 163–175

Koster JT (1979) The Compositae of New Guinea VI – additions to previous articles, Heliantheae. *Blumea* 25: 249–282

Koster JT (1980) The Compositae of New Guinea VII – additions to previous articles, Senecioneae. *Blumea* 26: 233–243

Kostermans AJGH (1950) Notes on *Pterocymbium* R.Br. (Sterculiaceae). *Reinwardtia* 1: 41–49

Kostermans AJGH (1957) Lauraceae. *Reinwardtia* 4: 193–256

Kostermans AJGH (1959) A monograph of the genus *Heritiera* Aiton (Stercul.). *Reinwardtia* 4: 465–583

Kostermans AJGH (1960) Micellaneous botanical notes 1. *Reinwardtia* 5: 233–254

Kostermans AJGH (1977) New species of *Diospyros* (Ebenaceae). *Blumea* 23: 449–474

Kostermans AJGH (1982) The genus *Mastixia* Bl. (Cornaceae) in Ceylon. *Reinwardtia* 10: 81–92

Lam HJ, Royen P, van (1952) Revision of the Sapotaceae of the Malaysian area in a wider sense II – *Burckella* Pierre. *Blumea* 6: 580–593

Lam HJ, Royen P, van (1957) Revision of the Sapotaceae of the Malaysian area in a wider sense IIa. *Blumea* 8: 201–203

Leenhouts PW (1962) Loganiaceae. In Steenis CGGJ, van (ed.). 'Flora Malesiana, Series I. Vol. 6.' pp. 293–387 (P. Noordhof Ltd.: Leiden)

Lindau G (1905) Familie Acanthaceae. In Schumann KM, Lauterback KAG (eds). 'Nachträge zur flora der deutschen Schutzgebiete in der Südsee.' pp. 385–390 (Gebrûder Borntraeger: Leipzig)

Lindau G (1913) Neue Acanthaceae Papuasiens – Allgemeine Bemerkungen über das Vorkommen der Acanthaceae in Papuasien. *Botanische Jahrbücher für Systematik, Pflanzengeschichte und Pflanzengeographie* 50: 165–170

Lindau G (1918) Neue Acanthaceae Papuasiens. II. *Botanische Jahrbücher für Systematik, Pflanzengeschichte und Pflanzengeographie* 55: 135 & 136

Lowry PP (1986) A systematic study of *Delarbrea* Viell. (Araliaceae) *Allertonia* 4: 169–201

Markgraf F (1921) Apocynaceae. *Botanische Jahrbücher für Systematik, Pflanzengeschichte und Pflanzengeographie* 61: 164–222

Markgraf F (1972) Florae Malesianae Praecursores LIII. Apocynaceae II. 6. Urnularia, 7. Willughbeia, 8. Kopsia. *Blumea* 23: 377–414

Markgraf F (1974) Florae Malesianae Praecursores LIV. Apocynaceae IV. *Alyxia*. *Blumea* 23: 377–414

Markgraf F (1979) Florae Malesianae Praecursores LIX. Apocynaceae V. *Ochrosia*, *Neisoperma Blumea* 25: 233–247

Mathias ME, Constance L (1955) *Oreomyrrhis* revision with key to New Guinea species. *University of California Publications. Botany* 27: 347–416

Mathias ME, Constance L (1977) A new species of *Oreomyrrhis* (Umbelliferae, Apiaceae) from New Guinea. *Journal of the Arnold Arboretum* 58: 190–192

Matthews KM (1976) A revision of the genus *Maxtixia* (Cornaceae). *Blumea* 23: 51–93

Munir AA (1982) A taxonomic revision of the genus *Callicarpa* L. (Verbenaceae) in Australia. *Journal of the Adelaide Botanic Gardens* 6: 5–39

Munir AA (1984a) A taxonomic revision of the genus *Gmelina L.* (Verbenaceae) in Australia. *Journal of the Adelaide Botanic Gardens* 7: 91–116

Munir AA (1984b) A taxonomic revision of the genus *Premna* L. (Verbenaceae) in Australia. *Journal of the Adelaide Botanic Gardens* 7: 1–44

Munir AA (1985) A taxonomic revision of the genus *Viticipremna* H.J. Lam (Verbenaceae). *Journal of the Adelaide Botanic Gardens* 7: 181–200

Munir AA (1987a) A taxonomic revision of the genus *Faradaya* F. Muell. (Verbenaceae) in Australia. *Journal of the Adelaide Botanic Gardens* 10: 165–177

Munir AA (1987b) A taxonomic revision of the genus *Vitex* L. (Verbenaceae) in Australia. *Journal of the Adelaide Botanic Gardens* 10: 31–79

Munir AA (1989) A taxonomic revision of the genus *Clerodendrum* (Verbenaceae) in Australia. *Journal of the Adelaide Botanic Gardens* 11: 101–173

Nooteboom HP (1977) Symplocaceae. In Steenis CGGJ, van (ed.). 'Flora Malesiana, Series I. Vol. 8.' pp. 205–274 (Noordhoff International Publishing: Leyden)

Payen JPDW (1967) A monograph of the genus *Barringtonia* (Lecythidaceae). *Blumea* 15: 157–262

Pennington TD (1991) 'The Genera of Sapotaceae ' (Royal Botanic Gardens Kew & New York Botanical Garden: Kew, New York) 295 pp.

Percival M, Womersley JS (1975) 'Floristics and ecology of the mangrove vegetation of Papua New Guinea.' (Division of Botany, Department of Forests: Lae) 96 pp.

Philipson WR (1980) Araliaceae. In Steenis CGGJ, van (ed.). 'Flora Malesiana, Series I. Vol. 9.' pp. 1–105 (P. Noordhoff Ltd: Leiden)

Radford AE, Dickison WC, Massey JR, Bell CR (1998) 'Vascular plant systematics.' In Massey JR, Murphy JC (eds). (Harper and Row: New York, U.S.A.) http://www.ibiblio.org/botnet/glossary/

Randeria AJ (1960) Inuleae (Asteraceae). *Blumea* 10: 176–317

Reeder JR (1946) Notes on Papuasian Saxifragaceae. *Journal of the Arnold Arboretum* 27: 275–288

Robbrecht E (1988) Tropical woody Rubiaceae. *Opera Botanica Belgica* 1: 1–272

Royen P, van (1952) Revision of the Sapotaceae of the Malaysian area in a wider sense III – *Minusops* L. *Blumea* 6: 594–595

Royen P, van (1953a) Revision of the Sapotaceae of the Malaysian area in a wider sense IV *Blumea* 7: 364–400

Royen P, van (1953b) Revision of the Sapotaceae of the Malaysian area in a wider sense V. *Blumea* 7: 400–412

Royen P, van (1957) Revision of the Sapotaceae of the Malaysian area in a wider sense VII. *Blumea* 8: 235–445

Royen P, van (1960a) Revision of the Sapotaceae of the Malaysian area in a wider sense XX. *Blumea* 10: 1–117

Royen P, van (1960b) Revision of the Sapotaceae of the Malaysian area in a wider sense XXIII. *Blumea* 10: 432–606

Royen P, van (1964) Sterculiaceae. In 'Manual of the forest trees of Papua and New Guinea. Vol. 3'. (Eds Womersley JS, White KJ, Colwell SJ) pp. 1–39 (Division of Botany, Department of Forests: Lae)

Royen P, van (1975) Sertulum Papuanum 20. The Botaginaceae of the alpine regions of New Guinea. *Pacific Science* 29: 79–98

Royen P, van (1982a) Myrsinaceae. In Royen P, van (ed.). 'The alpine flora of New Guinea. Vol. 3.' pp. 1949–1990 (J. Cramer: FL-9490 Vaduz)

Royen P, van (1982b) *Saurauia*. In Royen P, van (ed.). 'The alpine flora of New Guinea. Vol. 3.' (J. Cramer: FL-9490 Vaduz)

Royen P, van (1982c) Theaceae. In Royen P, van (ed.). 'The alpine flora of New Guinea. Vol. 3.' pp. 1397–1454 (J. Cramer: FL-9490 Vaduz)

Royen P, van, Lloyd D (1975) Anthemideae (Asteraceae). *Blumea* 22: 197–206

Schodde R (1972) A review of the family Pittosporaceae in Papuasia. *Australian Journal of Botany. Supplement* 3: 1–60

Shan RH, Constance L (1951) *Saniculus* revision (no New Guinea material recorded). *University of California Publications. Botany* 25: 78

Sleumer H (1942) Icacinaceae. In: Engler HGA and Prantl KAE, with Harms H and Mattfeld J (eds). *Die Natürlichen Pflanzenfamilien* Vol. 20b.' pp. 322–396

Sleumer H (1969). Materials toward the knowledge of the Icacinaceae of Asia, Malesia, and adjacent areas. *Blumea* 17(1):181–264.

Sleumer HO (1972a) Cardiopteridaceae. In Steenis CGGJ, van (ed.). 'Flora Malesiana, Series I. Vol. 7.' pp. 93–96 (Noordhoff International Publishing: Leyden, The Netherlands)

Sleumer HO (1972b) Icacinaceae. In Steenis CGGJ, van (ed.). 'Flora Malesiana, Series I. Vol. 7.' pp. 1–87 (Noordhoff International Publishing: Leyden, The Netherlands)

Sleumer HO (1987) A revision of the genus *Maesa* Forsk. (Myrsinaceae) in New Guinea, the Moluccas and the Solomon Islands. *Blumea* 32: 39–65

Sleumer HO (1988) The genera *Discocalyx* Mez, *Fittingia* Mez, *Loheria* Merr., and *Tapeinosperma* Hook.f. (Myrsinaceae) in New Guinea. *Blumea* 33: 81–107

Smith AC (1973a) Myrsinaceae of the Pacific region. *Journal of the Arnold Arboretum* 51: 1–41

Smith AC (1973b) Studies of Pacific Island plants, XXV. The Myrsinaceae of the Fijian region. *Journal of the Arnold Arboretum* 54: 1–41

Stearn WT (1976) Union of *Chionanthus* and *Linociera* (Oleaceae). *Annals of Missouri Botanical Gardens* 63: 355–357

Steenis CGGJ, van (1972a) Pittosporaceae – Addenda, corrigenda et emendanda. In Steenis CGGJ, van (ed.). 'Flora Malesiana, Series I. Vol. 6.' pp. 960–963

Steenis CGGJ, van (1972b) Primulaceae – Addenda, corrigenda et emendanda. In Steenis CGGJ, van (ed.). 'Flora Malesiana, Series I. Vol. 6.' p. 964 & 965 (P. Noordhoff Ltd.: Leiden)

Steenis CGGJ, van (1972c) Umbelliferae – Addenda, corrigenda et emendanda. In Steenis CGGJ, van (ed.). 'Flora Malesiana, Series I. Vol. 6.' p. 983 & 984

Steenis CGGJ, van (1976) Addenda, corrigenda et emendanda – Pittosporaceae. In Steenis CGGJ, van (ed.). 'Flora Malesiana, Series I. Vol. 7.' p. 829 & 830

Steenis CGGJ, van (1977) Bignoniaceae. In Steenis CGGJ, van (ed.). 'Flora Malesiana, Series I. Vol. 8.' pp. 114–186 (Sijthoff & Noordhoff Internal Publishers: Alphen aan den Rijn, The Netherlands)

Stevens PF (1974) Three new species of *Phaleria* (Thymelaeaceae) from Papuasia. *Journal of the Arnold Arboretum* 55: 264–268

Sugumaran M, Wong KM (2012) Studies in Malesian Gentianaceae I: *Fagraea* sensu lato—complex genus or several genera? A molecular phylogenetic study. *Gardens' Bulletin Singapore* 64: 301–332

Sugumaran M, Wong KM (2014) Studies in Malesian Gentianaceae, VI. A revision of *Utania* in the Malay Peninsula with two new species. *Plant Ecology and Evolution* 147: 213–223 http://dx.doi.org/10.5091/plecevo.2014.971

Takeuchi W (2007) Additions to the flora of the Kaijende Highlands, Papua New Guinea: occurrence records, synonymies, and descriptions of new taxa. *Edinburgh Journal of Botany* 64: 159–172 http://dx.doi.org/10.1017/S0960428607000893

Takeuchi W (2008) *Saurauia taylorii* (Actinidaceae), a distinctive new species from the Kaijende Highlands of Papua New Guinea. *Blumea* 53: 335–340

Takeuchi W (2010) A new addition to the endemic genus *Fittingia* (Myrsinaceae) of New Guinea: *F. headsiana* from the southern limestone, with a synoptical key to the species. *Harvard Papers in Botany* 15: 37–40 http://dx.doi.org/10.3100/025.015.0117

Tantra IGM (1976) *Revision of the genus Sterculia L. in Malesia. Lembaga Penelitian Hutan* 102: 1–194

Thiele KR, Adams LG (1999) 'The families of flowering plants of Australia.' (CSIRO Publishing: Collingwood)

Tipot L (1995) *Anacolosa* Blume. In Soepadmo E, Wong KM (eds) 'Tree flora of Sabah and Sarawak' Vol. 1, pp. 274–275

Utteridge TMA (2007a). Icacinaceae. In Heywood VH, Brummitt RK, Culham A, Seberg O (eds). 'Flowering Plant Families of the World', p. 173 (Royal Botanic Gardens, Kew)

Utteridge TMA (2007b). Stemonuraceae. In Heywood VH, Brummitt RK, Culham A, Seberg O (eds). 'Flowering Plant Families of the World', pp. 310–311 (Royal Botanic Gardens, Kew)

Vink W (1958) Revision of the Sapotaceae in the Malaysian area in a wider sense XIII. *Blumea* 9: 21–74

Watson L, Dallwitz MJ (1992 onwards) 'Oleaceae.' In.'The families of flowering plants: descriptions, illustrations, identification, and information retrieval. Version: 9th January 2018'. delta-intkey.com/angio

Webb C, Jarvie JK, Schori M, Rachman I, Mayar U (2005) Trees of Borneo. http://www.phylodiversity.net/borneo/ (accessed November 2005)

Webb C, Jarvie JK, Schori M, Rachman I, Mayar U (2008+) 'Tree of Borneo - a JavaScript by Cam Webb.' In. http://phylodiversity.net/borneo/ (accessed May 2018)

Wilkie P, Clark A, Pennington RT, Cheek M, Bayer C, Wilcock CC (2006) Phylogenetic relationships within the subfamily Sterculioideae (Malvaceae/Sterculiaceae-Sterculieae) using the chloroplast gene *ndhF. Systematic Botany* 31: 160–170 http://dx.doi.org/10.1600/036364406775971714

Womersley JS (ed.) (1978) 'Handbooks of the flora of Papua New Guinea.' Vol. 1 (Melbourne University Press: Carlton) 278 pp.

Wong KM (2012) Studies in Malesian Gentianaceae IV: A revision of *Picrophloeus*. *Gardens' Bulletin Singapore* 64: 511–522

Wong KM, Sugumaran M (2012a) Studies in Malesian Gentianaceae II: A taxonomic framework for the *Fagraea* complex, including the new genus *Limahlania*. *Gardens' Bulletin Singapore* 64: 481–495

Wong KM, Sugumaran M (2012b) Studies in Malesian Gentianaceae III: *Cyrtophyllum* reapplied to the *Fagraea fragrans* alliance *Gardens' Bulletin Singapore* 64: 497–510

Yaoli L, Hua Z, Junbo Y (2002) Systematic position of the genus *Mastixia*: evidence from rbcL gene sequences. *Acta Botanica Yunnanica* 24: 352–358

INDEX (Volumes 1–3)

Family names treated in all volumes of *Trees of Papua New Guinea* are given in bold, upper case, whereas other family names are given in roman with only first letter in upper case. Pages where descriptions of families, genera and species are in bold; pages with illustrations or photographic images are listed in bold and underlined. Page numbers in roman (not bold) refer to minor references. Each page number is prefixed by "1." (for pages in Volume 1), "2." (Volume 2) and "3." (Volume 3).

Ximeniaceae 3.50
Xylocarpus 2.313
Xanthophyllum papuanum Whitmore ex Meijden 1.28, **1.386**, **1.387**
Xanthophytum 3.136, 3.137
Xanthostemon 1.25, 1.27, 2.140, 2.141, 2.143
Xanthostemon crenulatus C.T.White **2.233**
Xerochrysum 3.230
Xerochrysum bracteolatum (Vent.) Tzveley 3.235
Xerospermum 2.283
Ximenia 3.50
Ximenia americana L. 3.50

Erratum Volume 2

Basisperma lanceolata C.T.White has been incorrectly referred to as *Basisperma lanceolatum* C.T.White (Volume 2, p. 140 and in Index (p. 391).

Printed in the USA
CPSIA information can be obtained
at www.ICGtesting.com
LVHW071712041124
795688LV00026B/762
9781984505101